TEXTBOOK OF HUMAN DEVELOPMENT

A LIFESPAN DEVELOPMENTAL APPROACH

Textbook of Human Development

A Lifespan Developmental Approach

Dr. Sushila Srivastava
M.A. (Human Development & Family Relations)
M.Sc. (Psychology)
M.Sc. (Counselling & Psychotherapy) and Ph.D.
Formerly Professor and Head
Department of P.G. Studies and Research in Home Science
JBAS Women's College
University of Madras, Chennai
Consulting Neuropsychologist and Family Therapist
Apollo Hospitals, Chennai

Dr. K. Sudha Rani
M.Sc., B.Ed., M.Phil., Ph.D.
Associate Professor
Department of Home Science
Anna Adarsh College for Women
University of Madras, Chennai

S Chand And Company Limited
(ISO 9001 Certified Company)

S Chand And Company Limited

(ISO 9001 Certified Company)

Head Office: D-92, Sector–2, Noida – 201301, U.P. (India), Ph. 91-120-4682700

Registered Office: A-27, 2nd Floor, Mohan Co-operative Industrial Estate, New Delhi – 110 044, Phone: 011-49731800

www.**schandpublishing.com;** e-mail: **info@schandpublishing.com**

Marketing Offices:

Chennai : Ph: 23632120; chennai@schandpublishing.com

Guwahati : Ph: 2738811, 2735640; guwahati@schandpublishing.com

Hyderabad : Ph: 40186018; hyderabad@schandpublishing.com

Jalandhar : Ph: 4645630; jalandhar@schandpublishing.com

Kolkata : Ph: 23357458, 23353914; kolkata@schandpublishing.com

Lucknow : Ph: 4003633; lucknow@schandpublishing.com

Mumbai : Ph: 25000297; mumbai@schandpublishing.com

Patna : Ph: 2260011; patna@schandpublishing.com

First Edition 2014
Reprints 2018, 2020, 2022 (Twice)

Reprint 2024

ISBN: 978-93-837-4679-8 **Product Code:** H5HUD41PSYH10ENAA14O

PRINTED IN INDIA

By Vikas Publishing House Private Limited, Plot 20/4, Site-IV, Industrial Area Sahibabad, Ghaziabad – 201 010 and Published by S Chand And Company Limited, A-27, 2nd Floor, Mohan Co-operative Industrial Estate, New Delhi – 110 044.

PREFACE

Human Development is a scientific study of the multiple changes — physical, motor, cognitive, language, emotional, and social, that an individual undergoes from the time of conception to late adulthood and various influences that have shaped our identities. In addition to describing these changes, it also explains the reasons for these changes and predicts those changes that may occur. Hence, Human Development is an exciting portrayal of life processes that take place in our bodies, personalities, thinking, feeling, behavior, relationships and in the roles that we play during different periods of our life. This scientific study equips us to understand ourselves and provides insight for our future, by which, we can adjust our own life course so that our development proceeds in new directions.

This book entitled *Textbook on Human Development* is based on the latest syllabi prescribed by the Indian Universities for the undergraduate and postgraduate courses dealing with Human Development. The contents of the syllabi are such that students and staff have to refer to a number of books on different topics, for meaningful coverage of the topics in the syllabi. The authors have taken great interest to include in this book all the information relevant to syllabi by referring several standard books written by eminent authors. The subject matter is explained in a simple and lucid language with a number of illustrative diagrams. The authors have used '3-Cs'—Clear, Complete and Concise—while preparing the chapters. For the benefit of the readers, cross-references are given at the appropriate places. They have adopted chronological approach of Human Development, which presents all aspects of development during each stage of life. All the chapters in the book are arranged in a proper sequence that permits each topic to build upon earlier studies. This book is tailor-made to suit the latest syllabi, based on undergraduate and postgraduate level courses in Human Development.

The book will be very useful not only to the students but also to the subject teachers. The students have to omit nothing and possibly have to cover nothing more. Keeping in view the awareness of the present day students, most of the questions have been selected and have been given at the end of every chapter.

KEY FEATURES

The key features of the book are as follows :

- Text is written in a simple language and presented in a clear and concise manner.
- Contents are supported by interesting facts, figures and pictures, suitable to the recent trend.
- Sufficient examples have been provided within the chapters to elaborate the concepts.
- Points to remember are highlighted and various types of questions are given at the end of each chapter with the objective that students should acquire knowledge thoroughly.
- Approach of the book resembles classroom teaching.

Divided into 8 units, the text consists of 13 chapters. In Chapter 1, introduction to human development is given. Chapter 2 discusses the techniques for studying human development. Chapters 3, 4 and 5 describe prenatal development, child birth and neonate or newborn, respectively.

Chapter 6 deals with infancy and babyhood Chapters 7 and 8 explain early childhood and nursery school education. Chapters 9 and 10 concentrate on the late childhood and adolescence. Chapters 11 and 12 describe adulthood and middle adulthood. The last Chapter 13 deals with old age.

The text is supported by a number of questions for practice. It also provides bibliography at the end of the book for further reading.

We wish to express our profound thanks to M/s S. Chand & Company Pvt. Ltd., New Delhi, Publishers, who appreciated our reference work and agreed to publish this book at national level. We also wish to thank Professor (Mrs.) Rekha Swamy and Mr. M.T. Yuvanesan and all those who had become part of this project knowingly or unknowingly.

We are quite sure that this book will meet the requirements of degree students in full measure. Students are advised to retain this book with them as this book contains very valuable information, which will be of great use later in their life, irrespective of their specialization.

Any suggestions for the improvement of the book will be acknowledged, appreciated and incorporated in the next edition.

Dr. Sushila Srivastava
Dr. K. Sudha Rani

CONTENTS

UNIT-I

UNIT-II

UNIT-III

UNIT-IV

UNIT-VII

UNIT-VIII

UNIT — I

CHAPTER 1

INTRODUCTION TO HUMAN DEVELOPMENT

OBJECTIVES

To enlighten students about:

- Human Development-its definition, content, goals, need and importance of studying human development
- Basic concepts in human development-Meaning and Importance of Growth, Development, Maturation and Learning- Domains of Development, and Developmental Stages
- Principles of human development and growth
- Developmental Tasks of different stages.
- Determinants of human development and growth.

1.1. INTRODUCTION

Biologically, life begins at the time of conception, when the female germ cell (ovum) fuses with the male germ cell (sperm) to form a single cellular zygote. Birth is merely a break in the path of growth and development that has been going on for about nine months after conception. In order to develop into a complete human being, this single cellular zygote undergoes a series of developmental processes. Human beings constantly change both physically and psychologically, by undergoing multiple processes of development from the moment of conception until death. We start small, grow up and grow old.

1.1.1. What is Human Development?

All the human beings undergo dramatic changes as they pass from the embryonic and fetal stages through infancy, childhood, adolescence, adulthood and old age. The Field of Human Development is the scientific study of the "processes" of development, and about how these depend on inherited traits, past experiences and present circumstances. It focuses on long-term sequences and pattern of changes in human behavior as well as in the characteristics that remain stable. It strives to trace the ways people develop and change across the life span .Human development studies about the changes that take place in our lives, in our bodies, our personalities, our ways of thinking, our feelings, our behavior, our relationships and in the roles that we play during different periods of our lives. These changes are due to the interplay of biological, cognitive, and socio-emotional processes that produces a "pattern of changes". This pattern of change makes a young child obviously different from an infant; and an adolescent to differ clearly from an adult.

The study of Human Development emphasizes two types of changes in human beings over time-quantitative and qualitative.

(*i*) Quantitative Change refers to the easily measurable and sometimes obvious features of human development, including physical growth (changes in height and weight).

(*ii*) Qualitative Change refers to the alterations in human functioning through the life span.

1.1.2. Content of Human Development

Life is characterized by continuous changes. In order to maintain the constancy of life, these changes are stringed together. Both constancy and changes are fused together in the course of development. Human development is a field devoted to understanding constancy and change from conception through old age, to describe and identify those factors that influence these consistencies and changes. The ultimate goal of human development is to help people live meaningful and productive lives.

Human Development encompasses the growth and maturation of individual organism; its cognitive and emotional components, personality structure; factors that promote or retard any aspects of development, types of interaction between human beings and environmental factors. Human development is based on the significant findings of biological and behavioral research. Its major emphasis has been to:

1. Understand and control the basic processes and dynamics underlying human behavior at various stages of life, and the process that account for these changes. For example, what are the common and characteristic age changes in appearance, behavior, or goals, from one development period to another; such as from infancy to babyhood or childhood to adolescence. Its main concern is the individual's direction of growth.
2. Find out whether the changes in any particular trait, ability or behavior are continuous (increasing gradually and steadily over time) or discontinuous (occurring in sudden spurts or stages); when these changes occur, what causes them; and whether they are individual or universal.
3. Explore whether the rate and pattern of development are the same for everyone.
4. Study the changes in behavioral capacities and processes occurring as a function of time. Human development specialists also seek to recognize what different behaviors mean at different ages. Though the changes are predictable in terms of the order in which they will appear, what is not predictable is the exact age at which the child will exhibit a particular stage of understanding.
5. Focus on the effects of environmental influences upon individual patterns of development-factors that promote or retard any aspects of development, types of interaction between human organisms and environmental factors.
6. To throw light on the ways in which people change throughout life, as well as in characteristics that remain fairly stable. These changes are rapid and pronounced in the early years that signify the fact - the human being is "growing up". However, these changes do not cease, but continue at a slower rate, until deterioration, which is characteristic of old age.

As human beings are complex, the study of life-span development is "inter-disciplinary". Human development as a specialized field integrates the finding of other disciplines (biological and behavioral research), to focus on the understanding of the growing child and organizes different findings into a coherent body of knowledge and makes it available to a variety of fields for application. It draws on many fields or disciplines such as psychology, psychiatry, sociology, anthropology, biology, genetics, family science, education, history, philosophy and medicine. It is largely based on developmental psychology.

1.2. FOUR GOALS OF THE SCIENTIFIC STUDY OF HUMAN DEVELOPMENT

The four goals of the scientific study of Human development which work together are as follows:

1. Description: The first goal is to describe, as completely and precisely as possible human beings' (i) psychological functions at different ages and (ii) the characteristics of changes in those functions at different ages. In pursuing this goal, human developmentalists carefully observe the behavior of people of different ages, seeking to specify how human beings change over time. For this, they observe large groups of children, and establish norms, or averages, for behavior at various ages. They attempt to describe both normal development and individual differences in development. For example, in language development, they attempt to "describe" when normal children say their first word or the size of their vocabulary at different ages.

2. Explanation: The second more recently developed goal is to "explain age changes" in behavior- to discover the process underlying these changes. In pursuing this goal of explanation, Human developmentalists hope to understand why humans show universal patterns of development and why some individuals turn out so differently than others do. They are interested in explaining both the typical changes within the individual and differences in development between individuals. The answers to questions about the how's and why's of age changes and of individual differences are enormously complex. Both maturational processes and learning experiences must be considered. Obviously, it is easier to describe development than to explain it.

Investigations of individual differences may contribute to an understanding of the determinants (such as heredity or environment), of general age changes in various developments. Age trend data are important for several reasons. Such information may be useful in formulating general principles of development; and to provide averages or norms of various aspects of development that can be used in evaluating the status of individual children. (For example, is this particular child below or above average in height? Is his vocabulary large, small, or average for his age?) Standards or norms derived from age trend research may also be useful in diagnosing problems of physical or psychological development.

3. Optimization: Finally, the optimization of human development is the most practical goal of the science of development. How can human beings be helped to develop in positive directions? How can their capacities be enhanced, and how can any developmental problems they suffer be overcome? The goal of optimizing development often cannot be achieved, however, until researchers are able to describe development and explain how it comes about.

4. Prediction: This knowledge may make it possible to "predict" what language ability at a given age can tell about later behavior.

Modification: Finally, awareness of how language develops may be used to "modify" behavior.

1.3. NEED AND IMPORTANCE OF STUDYING HUMAN DEVELOPMENT

The study of human development is intriguing and informative about human beings. It is a lively and important field of research and study. It gives answers to questions that are intellectually challenging, practical and useful. Human development, as a scientific field, has contributed significantly to our understanding of human beings and in a general way, to our knowledge of how they develop. By understanding this subject, developmentalists know what to expect to, during different developmental stages and they learn the parameters of human growth and development.

- Since development consists of orderly sequence of differentiation in growth and behavior, Human Development specialists attempt to predict the direction that a person will take on the developmental journey. They use comprehensive testing, (both biochemical examinations and psychological testing) in predicting further causes of growth and maturation, learning and adjustment. With the help of laboratory and psycho-diagnostic assessment methods, they can specify the individual's position in his peer/age group and the rate at which he/she is likely to move.

- Knowledge of the developmental patterns for different age groups, enables people, especially parents, and teachers to know what to expect of a human being at every age and to know, in a general way, at what age different forms of behavior will emerge into more mature forms. Otherwise, there would be a tendency to expect too much or too little of the child at a given age. Both of these are bad. In the former case, the child is likely to develop feelings of inadequacy because he does not measure up to the standards his parents and teachers have set for him. Expecting too little gives him too little incentive, with the result that he does not do as much as he is capable of doing.
- Each human being is unique. There are striking and minute differences in all aspects of appearance, growth and behavior, which increase with age. A study of Human development enables to develop competency and recognize individuality. This implies the ability to recognize the uniqueness of each human being's traits and views of life.
- Another advantage of knowing how development occurs is that it gives the adult, information as to when to stimulate and when not to stimulate growth in the child, in order to guide his development into desired channels. It gives a basis for planning the environmental encouragement that must be offered and the correct timing for this encouragement. When the child is beginning to walk, for example, he must be given opportunities to practice walking and the necessary motivation. Absence of either one may delay the onset of walking beyond the time when it would normally occur.
- Knowledge of what the normal developmental pattern is, makes it possible for parents, teachers, and others who work with children to prepare the child ahead of time for the changes that will take place in his body, his interests, or his behavior. While this psychological preparation will not eliminate all the tensions that normally accompany adjustment, it will go a long way toward minimizing them. The child who is prepared for what will be expected of him when he enters school, for example, makes better adjustments to school and is happier there than is the child who had no foreknowledge of what to expect.
- Research findings in Human development have a direct and practical application to child rearing, education, health and social policy. For example, if parents are enlightened about the factors that increase the risks of antisocial behavior among their offspring and the ways to prevent it, they may use this knowledge.
- An understanding of adult development, too, has practical implications. It can help people deal with life's transitions: a woman returning to work after maternity leave, person changing his career or about to retire, a widow or widower dealing with loss, someone coping with a terminal illness.
- The pattern of development is approximately the same for all human beings. Many aspects of life unfold in a predictable way. For example, children sit before they walk and walk before they run. This predictability permits the scientific study of developmental change. Knowing what to expect at a particular age group helps us in setting up standards, or "measuring rods" such as height/weight scales, age-weight scales, scales for mental age, and social/emotional development. These scales help us to judge each child in terms of the norms/standards for that child's age. In case there are irregularities or undue delays, it is a signal that the child must be medically examined for impairment.

1.4. BASIC CONCEPTS IN HUMAN DEVELOPMENT

Growth, Development, Maturation and Learning: Human growth and development relate to physiological, psychological and environmental processes of continuous and orderly change through time. They start from the time of conception and continue until the close of our lifetime. They bring about changes in the physical, mental, emotional, social and moral components of being. A human being does not change or grow as fast as other animals. The growth and development of the human being takes long years. Some changes are predictable and sequential. In other words, they take place in a fixed order. For example, infants are expected to roll over before they sit, sit before they stand, stand before they walk and walk before they run. When the child has passed through each successive stage of development, he reaches the end of this process, which is called maturity. The concepts of growth, development, maturation and learning are important to our understanding of Human Development.

1.4.1. Growth

Biologists typically define growth as the physical changes that occur from conception to maturity . Growth refers to organic changes and is basically quantitative in nature. It refers to changes in body size, structure, bodily dimensions and increase in magnitude, muscular strength and in its different organs. Growth, therefore involves changes in body parts as well as in overall structure and weight, which can be readily measurable in terms of standardized quantitative units, such as weight in pounds, and height in inches. It is an integrated unitary process.

One of the most noticeable features of early development is the increase in size that occurs with age. During infancy and childhood, the body steadily becomes larger, taller and heavier. The rate of growth in the various parts of the body, however, is not the same in either an absolute or a relative sense. It is largely due to multiplicity of cells and increase in intracellular substances, that growth implies a net increase in the size of mass tissues. Hypertrophy or increased cell size contribute to growth to a lesser extent.

1.4.2. Development

Development refers to systematic changes and continuities in the individual that occur between conception and death, or from "womb to tomb". By describing changes as "systematic", we imply that they are orderly, patterned, and relatively enduring; and by "continuities" in development, we remain the same or continue to reflect our past .

"Development means a progressive series of changes in an orderly, coherent pattern toward the goal of maturity. It is a process in which the internal physiological changes and the psychological processes stimulated by them are integrated (or responded to) in a way, which enables the individual to master further, its new environment".

Development is the total process whereby an individual adapts to his environment. Obviously since growth, maturation and learning are processes that account for adaptive changes, they are all aspects of development. The term developmental processes refer to structural and/or behavioral changes, which occur within individuals as a function of time- i.e. changes in physical characteristics (such as height, weight or skeletal structures); intellectual functions (for e.g. Performance on tests of intelligence or creativity); social characteristics (for e.g. aggressiveness or independence) and effective processes. Development is a complex process of integrating many structures and functions. From the dependency of infancy, the person moves to the maturity and responsibility of adult life.

Development consists of a transition from lower to higher stages of activity or function on the part of a child. The changes, which occur in the development, may be change in size, change in proportion, disappearance of old features and acquisition of new features etc. Development of physical and mental traits of the individual comes partly from an intrinsic maturity of those traits and partly from exercises and experiences that he undergoes.

Maturation, Learning and Motivation: All the characteristics and abilities a person acquires and all developmental changes result from two basic, though complex processes—learning and maturation. Since the two processes almost always interact, it is difficult to separate their effects from each other or to specify the relative contribution of each to human development. Clearly, growth in height is not learned but depends on maturation, a biological process. But improvements in motor activities, such as walking, depend on maturation and learning, and the interaction between them. The process of normal development is always forward and is propelled by maturation and learning.

There are two essentially antagonistic processes in development which take place simultaneously throughout life-"growth or evolution" and "atrophy or involution". Both begin at conception and end at death. In the early years, growth predominates; even though atrophic changes occur as early as embryonic life. In the later part of life, atrophy predominates, though growth continues as is shown in the growth of hair and in cellular replacements. With aging, some parts of the body and mind change more than others. Thus, the individual is not of the same biological age all over.

1.4.3. Maturation

By maturation is meant the development or unfolding of traits potentially present in the individual resulting from his hereditary endowments. It is an individual's unique genetic plan. 'Maturation' is development of the organism as a function of time or age; it refers to neurophysiologic-biochemical changes from conception to death. All definitions of maturation stress that it is relatively independent of external environmental conditions, experiences, or practice.

Just as seeds systematically unfold to become mature plants (assuming that they receive the necessary nourishment from their environment), human beings "unfold" within the womb. Their genetic "program" then calls for them to walk and utter their first words at about one year of age, to achieve sexual maturity at about age 12-14, and even to undergo the aging process and die on a roughly similar schedule. Thus, one reason human beings are so similar in many important respects is that genetically programmed maturational processes guide all of us through many of the same developmental changes at about the same points in our lives.

Maturation largely explains such things as the time a child's teeth erupt, the child's developing ability to grasp objects and to walk, and the time at which an adolescent girl first menstruates. The maturational process depends most strongly on the individual's genetic master plan, which functions as a timetable of sorts, largely (but not entirely), determines when certain events will occur. The genetic master plan may limit progress as well. For example, before a baby can walk, he or she must have the necessary strength and balance, prerequisites that are determined largely by maturation. The child is ready to walk only when these prerequisites are met. The appearance of a trait through maturation is frequently characterized by a striking suddenness. For example, in the case of walking, each successive stage makes a sudden appearance.

1.4.4. Learning and Experience

The second critical developmental process is "learning", or the process through which experience brings about relatively permanent change in thoughts, feelings or behavior. Any relatively permanent changes in behavior, caused by interaction with the environment are due to learning. These changes are not due to maturation. When a child recites the alphabet, imitates a brother's fear of cockroaches, sings along with his mummy, learning has occurred A child's understanding of sex roles, morality, and problem-solving are dependent on learning. Yet we cannot see learning; we can only infer it from behavioral change. A certain degree of physical maturation is clearly necessary before a child can run. However, careful instruction and long, hard hours of practice are just as clearly required.

In contrast to maturation, learning is extremely dependent on the environment. Children learn what they see and experience. Many of our abilities and habits do not just "mature," as part of nature's ground plan. Parents, teachers, other important people, and a host of other environmental factors show us how to behave in new ways and we change by the events we experience during our lives. There is some evidence that environmental enrichment can optimize development. The developmental changes are generally the product of both the aspects- "nature" (genetic endowment and maturation) and "nurture" (environmental influences and learning).

The Link between Maturation and Learning: Learning and maturation cannot be isolated from each other. Some events, such as physical growth, are more clearly due to maturation. In other events, such as acquiring a vocabulary, learning seems more important. Yet a complete understanding of human behavior must deal with both. Development is best understood as the result of the interaction of maturation and learning. The interactions between maturation and learning processes are particularly clear in motor development-especially postural responses, locomotion, and manipulation. In summary, development is a multifaceted and complex process, involving gains and losses, growth and aging, and more, brought about by both maturation and learning.

1.5. DOMAINS OF DEVELOPMENT

To make the vast, inter-disciplinary study of human development more orderly and convenient, the field of Human Development is divided into three separate domains -: Physical, cognitive, and psychosocial. All these domains are intertwined. Each domain affects the other and each domain is important throughout life.

Physical development includes the growth of the body and its organs during childhood, the appearance of physical signs of aging during adulthood, and the gains and losses in motor abilities that occur over the years. This may influence other domains of development. For e.g., dramatic physical and hormonal changes affect the developing sense of self. In some aged people, physical changes in the brain may lead to intellectual and personality deterioration .

Cognitive development involves changes and stability in mental processes, such as perception, language use, learning, attention, memory, thinking, reasoning and creativity. Cognitive advances are closely related to physical and emotional growth. The ability to speak depends on the physical development of the mouth and brain.

Psychosocial Development: Psychosocial development refers to change and stability in personal and interpersonal phenomena such as motives and emotions, personality traits, interpersonal skills and relationships, and roles played within the family and in the larger society. This can affect cognitive and physical functioning for e.g., anxiety about taking a test can impair performance.

Though these domains are dealt separately, these domains of development are not really distinct. People are whole beings, and their behavior is not sharply divided into three neat categories. Instead, they combine in an integrated holistic fashion. Each domain influences and is influenced by the other periods of development. Development is a unified process and involves inter-connected changes across all domains.

1.6. GENERAL PRINCIPLES OF HUMAN DEVELOPMENT

The study of human behavior and development is not only a search for "facts" but also finding a "pattern" in the facts .There are certain features, which are characteristic of human development, and which influence greatly the form it takes. The developmental principles set forth are largely descriptive and generally accepted. They enable us to understand the development, which has taken place and what is still to come .The most important principles are discussed here.

- **Development follows a pattern-growth and development are orderly and sequential:** Every species (whether animal or human) follows a regular pattern of development peculiar to that species. The rate and limits of development are similar for all members of that particular species. A child's maturation is predictable and follows a generally universal schedule. Certain characteristics that are common to the human species include rapid growth during the first year, slow growth during middle and late childhood, and appearance of secondary sex characters during early adolescence. The onset, length and effect of each phase vary with each child but the basic development sequence is the same for all children. The milestones of development appear in an orderly sequence. No child for example, learns to walk without having first learned to stand, nor does any child speak clearly, before he has passed thoroughly the babbling stage. These patterns or stages of learning follow each other in a fairly fixed sequence, and appear at certain ages consistently.

The first pair of principles has to do with the directional flow of physical growth and development. In higher animals, growth invariably proceeds in two related directions - the Cephalocaudal and the Proximodistal.

(*i*) **The Cephalo-Caudal Growth Principle ("head to toe" sequence):** According to this principle of developmental direction, all the parts of the body do not grow symmetrically but are subject to polarity and gradients of growth. It refers to the fact that in both the prenatal and postnatal life, the development proceeds from the upper portions of the body toward the lower portions, referred to as "head to toe" sequence. This means that improvements in the structure and function in a child's body come first in the head region, then in the trunk and last in the leg region. The baby's head becomes functional before his hands and feet. He uses mouth, eyes and ears before he grasps with his hands or walks with his feet. This growth pattern helps to explain why children sit before they can stand and crawl before they can walk.

(*ii*) **The proximo-distal Growth Principle ("near to far" sequence):** It states that growth proceeds outward, from the central axis of the body towards periphery or peripheral segments of the body. In other words, development proceeds from the centre line of the body towards the distant or peripheral parts. Hence, in a fetus, the head and the trunk are fairly well developed before the rudimentary limb buds appear. This growth pattern explains for instance why children in the early years are more adept at controlling larger muscles than the finer. Motor control gradually advances from the larger fundamental muscles to smaller muscles, which execute refined movements. This trend is exhibited in the development of postures, grasping, and locomotion.

The cephalocaudal and the proximodistal trends overlap and correlate.

- **Every Individual Normally Passes Through Each Major Stage of Development:** Every child has unique pattern of growth. Although no two individuals are exactly alike, all normal children tend to follow a general sequence of growth characteristic of the species and its cultural group based on a genetic sequence. All children pass through the same fundamental form at approximately the same time. Not only does total development follows a pattern, but the specific phases of development such as motor, social and play also follow a pattern. Each stage of development is the outcome of the one preceding it and the prerequisite of the one following it. Each stage has certain characteristics some of which stand out more conspicuously than others. Since there are individual differences in the rate of growth, age limits for different stages can be regarded as merely approximate and suggestive.
- **Development Proceeds from General to Specific Response:** Development proceeds from the simple to the complex, from the homogenous to the heterogeneous, and from

the general to the specific. From a single celled zygote, there develops by differentiation, multitude of cells of highly varied in structure and function. The first cells formed by division of the zygote are all of the same kind, differing only in their position with respect to each other. As differentiation proceeds, the cells change in character, forming different kinds of tissues with specialized functions: nerves, skin, bone, blood, muscle, and so on. In all phases of development, whether motor or mental, the child's responses are of a general nature before they become specific. In both prenatal and postnatal developments, general activity precedes specific ones. For example, the newborn infant moves his whole body at one time, instead of moving any one part of it. The earliest emotional response of the new born is generally diffused excitement and this slowly gives way to specific emotional patterns of anger, joy, fear etc.

- **Development is a Lifelong and an Orderly Process:** In the past, it was assumed that most aspects of development (physical, cognitive, emotional and social) reached their zenith in late adolescence and somehow magically stopped after that point. Today's human developmentalists reject the traditional (and incorrect) notions that development occurs only from conception to adolescence. On the contrary, they firmly believe that the process of development is continuous and occurs throughout the life span. It has no discontinuity. Although some aspects of physical growth stop, development in terms of change and adaptation continues throughout life.

  Changes in the body and behavior patterns take place continuously. No traits, whether physical or mental develop suddenly. On the contrary, they are all product of a growth, which started before birth. One will grow because of a strong impulse to grow which is inherent in the organism-the product of his heredity and experience. As growth is continuous, what happens at one stage carries over into and influences the next and ensuing stages. The milestones of development appear in an orderly sequence. As the life span increases, it becomes more important that adults continue learning for years to prepare themselves for new and changing challenges.

- **Development Reflects Both Continuity and Discontinuity:** While some human development specialists emphasize that development is a gradual, continuous process of growth and change, others describe it as a series of distinct stages, each preceded by abrupt changes that occur from one phase to another. For example, physical growth and language development, show smooth and incremental changes. Those who emphasize continuous development tend to emphasize the importance of environmental influences and social learning in the growth process. On the contrary, those who emphasize discontinuous development, tend to stress the role of heredity (nature) and maturation in the growth sequence. Both are extreme points of view and hence many do not agree with either. The current trend is to recognize that some aspects of development are continuous, whereas others show stage-like characteristics. Environment continuously affects people, but because people grow and develop from within, in stages, they can in turn influence their environment.

- **Development reflects both Stability and Change:** The question arises: "Are there elements of personality that remain stable? If a person manifests certain personality characteristics during childhood, will these persist into adolescence or adulthood?" There is evidence for personality stability in some people, and change of personality in others. Sometimes external events of a traumatic nature completely change the course of a person's life. For this reason, developmental trends are not always predictable .One of the reasons for these inconsistencies is the fact that early childhood experiences have declining effects as people get older. For example, family disruption, mental conflicts and disengaged child relations increase antisocial behavior in childhood. However, these effects do not generally persist into early adulthood .

- **Development is Cumulative:** We all recognize that our lives today are affected by what has happened before. Psychoanalysts especially emphasize the influence of early childhood experiences on later adjustment. However, a traumatic incident or abusive childhood may have serious consequences, but neither is 100% predictive of later adjustment. Countless people have emerged from dysfunctional family backgrounds and found nurturing environment that enable them to lead productive and meaningful lives.

  Even the seemingly sudden spurts in tempo of development lead into and grow out of quieter, less dramatic periods. It may be possible that in the quieter periods the child is mobilizing his forces for subsequent spurts. For example, the first step in walking cannot be taken until a long chain of learning in bodily control has preceded. This is true of speech also; it gradually evolves from the coos, gurgles and babbling sounds made by the baby from the time of birth. Each of them is a milestone that marks progress in a long process.

- **Development always involves both gain and losses at every age.** Development at every age involves both growth and decline. Indeed, for every gain there may be a corresponding loss.

- **Development is related to environment:** Family, peers and community are important factors creating the social and emotional climate for the child. Family and community settings vary considerably and as a result so their rules and regulations, institutions, economics, values, expectations and resources. As the children grow and interact with others they are socialized as members of their environment groups. When environment differs, learned behavior also differs. What is true and correct behavior for one group may not be so for another. For example, in most western cultures, competitiveness is recognized as positive virtue but the same competitive behavior is viewed negatively in some eastern societies.

- **Development is Variable;The Tempo of Development is not even:** The sequence of development does not move at a steady pace. The rate of development changes at different periods. Not all dimensions of the person grow at the same rate. A child may be exceptionally bright, but lags in physical growth and development. There are periods of accelerated growth and periods of decelerated growth. Development is very rapid in early infancy and the early preschool years. During the later preschool and school years, the rate of growth slackens. However, this does not mean that significant changes are not taking place. Before puberty, certain phases of growth become accelerated before they taper off to the adult level.

- **Development is sometimes Cyclical and Repetetive:** There may be some repetition during anyone's life. A person may face an identity crisis during adolescence and another at middle age. Likewise, vocational adjustments are necessary when one enters or retires from employment. In addition to repetition in an individual's life, there may be a repetition of similar phases occurring at different times in the life cycle of other individuals. Different persons may experience similar stages of life, but with individual and cultural differences. One may marry, and another may remain single.

- **Each Child Grows in His Own Unique Way:** Majority of the people fall in the "normal range", when they are assessed on almost every trait measured by any scale. Being in the "normal range" is desirable while the extremes (such as negative or positive) may or may not be desirable. Each child grows in his own unique way. While all children pass through the sequence of each developmental stage, some may omit some of the intermediate steps. For example, some children may start walking upright, without creeping or crawling even though most children crawl, creep and walk in sequence. A sequence may be disturbed because of a structural defect.

- **Development Reflects Gender Differences:** There are definite differences between boys and girls. Within each gender, there is considerable difference in the ages at which children arrive at maturity. Physical differences between boys and girls are most evident. There seems to be very little difference between boys and girls in general intellectual capacity, but there are certain definite differences in interests and behavior. Whether these differences in interests and behavior are due to inherited genetic differences or a product of the way children are reared is not clear, but much depends upon which interest or which trait is under discussion. Research studies of the gender differences reflect the fact that parents often raise boys and girls differently. Many differences that were formerly thought to be a result of inheritance and of gender have been found to be a result of the differential treatment that boys and girls receive
- **Development reflects Cultural and Class Differences:** Cultural and class differences exert a profound influence on human development because both culture and socio-economic status influence parental beliefs regarding desirable and undesirable long-term socialization goals and child behavior. Comparisons of Asian cultures with Western cultures indicate differences in values. Asian cultures often emphasize the group over the individual and cooperation over compensation and dominance. Western cultures place greater emphasis on attending to the self. Cross-cultural differences exist also in social time clocks. Each society prescribes an ideal time for assuming various responsibilities and for the bestowal of privileges, but these ages differ from one culture to another. Cultural variations are more determinative than chronological age.
- **Developmental Influences are Reciprocal:** Rather than being passive recipients of care, infants and children are active, influential partners in their interactions with the people around them. A quite, pleasant, easy-to-care child may have a very positive influence on parents, encouraging them to act in a friendly, warm and loving manner. On the contrary, an overactive, hard-to-care for child who is easily upset may stimulate parents to be short-tempered and rejecting. From this point of view, children though involuntarily, are partly responsible for creating their own environment. Moreover, due to individual differences, different people, at diverse developmental stages, interpret and act on their environments in differing ways that create various experiences for each person.
- **Heredity and Environment Influence Development:** Development is influenced by both nature and nurture. Human development is the product of ongoing interactions between a changing person and his or her changing world; a wide range of factors, both inside and outside the person, affect development. The critical question is not which factor-heredity or environment is responsible for our behavior, but how these two factors interact and how they may be controlled, so that optimum development takes place.
- **Development is Multidimensional and Interdisciplinary:** Human development is a complex process that may be divided into four basic dimensions-Physical, Cognitive, Emotional and Social developments. Though each dimension emphasizes a particular aspect of development, there is considerable inter-dependency among these areas. In describing all four of these areas, life-span development has become a multidisciplinary science, borrowing from biology, sociology and anthropology. The most up to date knowledge available is taken from each of these disciplines and used in the study of human development .

- **Development reflects Individual Differences:** Whereas there is some repetition of developmental sequences from one person to another, there is also a wide range of individual differences. Many of these differences are present at birth. Individuals differ in timing and rates of development; in such factors as height, weight, body build, physical abilities and health; in cognitive characteristics, emotional reactions and personality characteristics. They differ in social abilities, leisure-time preferences, and relationships with friends, vocational interests; job competence, marriage and family situations and life styles. Human developmentalists measure consistencies or homogeneity across individuals and also heterogeneity or inconsistencies within individuals .

1.7. DEVELOPMENTAL STAGES

What is a Developmental Stage? A stage is a period during which certain changes occur. "Developmental stage" refers to a period of life during which much of behavior is dominated by a particular quality of thinking or a particular mode of social relationship. A single stage is one-step in the process of development.

Scientific studies of human beings have shown that the human life span may be divided roughly into certain distinct or major periods, each characterized by certain specific developmental features, traits and characteristic patterns of behavior, which overshadows in importance the rest of the development occurring at that age. No precise ages mark the beginning or end of each period, but approximate age ranges are associated with each. There are no sharp dividing lines between the so-called developmental stages. Very often, the child is in one stage in one part of her development and in another stage in another part. For example, a girl may have begun to menstruate before she has outgrown many of her childish feelings and thoughts. As the child emerges from one developmental period to another, there is a gradual shift in emphasis on the dominant form of development taking place at that time.

The developmental stages begin from the moment of conception and go on until the child reaches maturity. Every child is expected to go through the same stages in the same order although not exactly the same age. This is because each stage depends on the previous one or is somehow preordained biologically. There are of course individual differences, as individual development is a result of genetic, maturational and environmental factors. The objective of this developmental-level organization is an understanding of the whole person with his or her various abilities and achievements, dynamics and motives, needs and problems as they appear in each phase of life. For the purpose of systematic presentation, the life-span is divided into eight stages.

Prenatal Period (conception to birth): This 9-month period is the most rapid time of change, during which a child is transformed into a human baby with remarkable capacities for adjusting to life in the surrounding world.

Fertilization: Unification of ovum and sperm

Zygote: Cell division and implantation of fertilized ovum

Embryo: Emergence of major body structures and organs

Fetal: Refinement of physiological structures and assumption of biological functions, including reflexive motility gains in viability

Infancy and Toddlerhood (birth to age 2)

This period brings dramatic changes in the body and brain that support the emergence of wide array of motor, perceptual, and intellectual capacities; the beginnings of language; and first intimate ties to others. Infancy spans the first year; toddlerhood spans the second, during which children take their first few independent steps, marking a shift to greater autonomy.

Infancy - Birth: Transition to extra uterine environment effected by labor

Neonate: Adaptation to demands of extra uterine life; gains in bodily equilibrium

Middle: Enlarging experiential world through perception and motility

Late: Acquiring verbal communication and becoming conscious of others and oneself .

Early Childhood (2 to 6 Years)

The body becomes longer and leaner, motor skills are refined and children become more self-sufficient. Make-believe play blossoms and supports all aspects of psychological development. Thought and language expand at an astounding pace, sense of morality becomes evident, and children establish ties with peers. Forming, modifying and refining traits and attitudes, gains in communication skills and autonomy, formation of self-concept are some of the features of this stage.

Middle Childhood (6 to 12 years): Children learn about wider world and master new responsibilities that increasingly resemble those they perform as adults. Improved athletic abilities, participation in organized games with rules, more logical thought processes, and mastery of basic literacy skills and advances in self-understanding, morality, and friendship are hallmarks of this period. Interacting with those outside the home, school attendance, role playing, development of sex identity and firm peer relationships and group-mindedness are some features of this stage.

Adolescence (12 to about 20 Years): This period initiates the transition to adulthood. Puberty leads to an adult-size body and sexual maturity. Thought becomes abstract and idealistic, and schooling becomes increasingly directed toward preparation for higher education and the world of work. Young people begin to establish autonomy from the family and define personal values and goals.

Puberty: Increased self-awareness; bodily and sexual maturation; personality reorganization

Middle: Developing intense peer relations; experiencing many ambiguities and conflicts

Late: Preparing for role of adult life; assuming greater responsibilities (social, economic, etc.)

Young Adulthood (20 to 40 Years) Physical condition peaks, and then declines slightly. Lifestyle choice influence health. Cognitive abilities and moral judgments assume more complexity. Educational and career choices are made. Personality traits and styles become relatively stable, but changes in personality may be influenced by life stages and events. Decisions are made about intimate relationships and personal lifestyles. Most people marry, and most become parents. Formation of adult pattern of life, acceptance into adult society, marriage and family responsibilities, achieving maximum global capacity are some features of this stage.

Middle Adulthood (40 to 60 Years): Full participation in adult society; 'family development' concerns about family and vocational advance. Some deterioration of sensory abilities, health, stamina, and prowess may take place. Women experience menopause. Most basic mental abilities peak; expertise and practical problem solving skills are high. Creative output may decline but improve in quality. For some, career success and earning powers peak; for others, burnout or career change may occur. Sense of identity continues to develop; midlife transition and double responsibilities of caring for children and elderly parents may cause stress. Launching of children leaves empty nest. Gradual decline in physical abilities, relinquishment of some responsibilities, modification of family structure (children reaching maturity and leaving home), efforts for maintenance of adult fitness are some features of this stage.

Late Adulthood (60 years and above): Most people are healthy and active, although health and physical abilities decline somewhat. Slowing of reaction time affects some aspects of functioning. Most people are mentally alert. Although intelligence and memory may deteriorate in some areas, most people find ways to compensate. Retirements from workforce may offer new options for use of time. People need to cope with personal losses and impending death. Relationships with family and close friends can provide important support. Search for meaning in life assumes central importance.

Increased decline of physical and cognitive powers, restriction of social interaction, frequently increased dependence upon others, and terminal decline are some features of this stage.

Death: Loss of life-sustaining functions are some features of this stage.

1.8. DEVELOPMENTAL TASKS OF DIFFERENT STAGES

In any culture, young people growing up from the stage of infancy through the other stages of life are confronted with the need to master certain skills and to learn certain behavior patterns that are essential to personal and social adjustment at those ages. At each period of his growth and development, the child faces a somewhat different set of demands that must be mastered if the individual is to have a normal schedule of development towards maturity. Indeed some of the tasks that he must learn are pertinent to his very survival, especially in the earlier years. Every society is age-graded and has a set of social expectations regarding age-appropriate behavior during the life span. Children soon realize the approval and disapproval of their behavior based on the societal expectations. These societal expectations determine the pattern of their learning.

One generally accepted definition of developmental tasks has been developed by Robert Havighurst (1953). He has defined the developmental tasks as follows: "A developmental task is a task which arrives at or about a certain period in the life of the individual, successful achievement of which leads to his happiness and to success with later tasks, while failure leads to unhappiness in the individual, disapproval of the society and difficulty with later tasks". The developmental task concept helps the student of human development what to look for and how to understand the individual's behavior.

The tasks listed by him based on psychological, biological and cultural factors is crucial to the individual's subsequent development. On the other hand, if these developmental tasks are not mastered at the appropriate age, the individual suffers from immaturities, incompetencies and is at a disadvantage in accomplishing other tasks at a later developmental period. For example, learning to walk and talk are major tasks of infancy. If the child failed to master these two skills during infancy, he will have a serious problem when he enters a nursery school. This may interfere with the acquisition of not only other motor skills but could adversely affect the development of the child's overall development and personality.

Sources of Developmental Tasks: A developmental task involves the following three forces, namely,

Physical Maturation of the Organism: The physiological maturity of an individual sets general limits for the individual's responses. For example, a child cannot walk much before 10 or 12 months of age due to lack of adequate strength and motor development. Therefore, a specific developmental task becomes a necessary learning only when the individual has the physiological ability to learn it.

Cultural Pressures: Each culture specifies the periods of learning and development that are expected of its members at successive maturity levels. Certain expected developmental learning in weaning, toilet training, learning to talk, relating to others is a part of nearly every culture; but different in the timing and in the manner whereby each is to be learned. This, in turn, makes each of these developmental tasks a unique learning in every culture. Member of different socio-economic and social-groups face somewhat different developmental tasks. Although each culture expects the members of that culture to master certain developmental tasks, cultural values change. Some of the old developmental tasks may be eliminated and replaced by new ones, or their relative importance may be lessened.

Personal Values, Needs and Aspirations: Developmental tasks may arise from the personal values, needs and aspirations. For example, if a child does not see the task of relating to his peer group as an important step in his development, he probably will not work at this task even though he has the physiological maturity for it and even though the culture expects it to be learned. If on the other hand, he perceives this task as important, he will work at it and probably master it to some extent thereby progressing a step further in his development of self.

Havighurst has prescribed developmental tasks for the following stages of development – Infancy and early childhood, middle childhood, adolescence, early adulthood, middle adulthood and later maturity.

Infancy and Early Childhood (Birth to 6 years)

The developmental tasks of these periods are enumerated in terms of the following broad units.

- Learning to walk
- Learning to take solid foods
- Learning to talk
- Learning to control elimination of body wastes
- Learning sex differences and sexual modesty
- Achieving physiological homeostasis
- Forming simple concepts of social and physical reality
- Learning to relate oneself emotionally to parents, siblings and others, and
- Learning to distinguish right from wrong and developing a conscience

Middle Childhood (6 to 12 Years)

During the years of middle childhood, as the child meets the world, he is moved by what Havighurst means three outward pushes.

(*a*) The social thrust from the home to the peer group environment

(*b*) The physical thrust into a world of games and of work demanding neuromuscular skills for e.g. handwriting, and

(*c*) The intellectual thrust into the world of adult ideas, symbolism and communication.

Out of these pushes, emerged the developmental tasks of middle childhood, which are

- Learning physical skills necessary for ordinary games
- Building wholesome attitudes toward oneself as a growing organism
- Learning to get along with age- mates
- Learning an appropriate masculine or feminine role
- Developing the basic skills of reading, writing and arithmetic
- Developing concepts necessary for daily living as tools of thought
- Developing conscience, a sense of morality and of values
- Achieving personal independence
- Developing attitudes towards social groups and institutions

Adolescence (12 to 20 Years)

Havighurst classifies the tasks of adolescence in terms of peer influence, movement towards independence and autonomy and the attainment of an ethical code and system of positive value. The first two tasks are associated with peer relationships, the next six, with the thrust towards independence and self-responsibility and the last two, towards achieving the traits that characterize the good man and the good citizen. The important developmental tasks in adolescence are

- Achieving new and more matured relations with age mates of both sexes
- Accepting and achieving masculine or feminine social goal
- Accepting one's physique and using the body effectively
- Achieving emotional independence
- Achieving assurance of economic independence through actual work experience or through educational planning for such independence
- Selecting and preparing for an occupation
- Preparing for marriage and family life
- Developing skills necessary for civic competence
- Acquiring a set of values and an ethical system as basis of behavior; desiring, and achieving socially responsible behavior.

Early Adulthood (20 to 40 Years)

Developmental tasks of early adulthood includes

- Selecting a mate
- Learning to live with a marriage partner
- Starting a family
- Rearing children
- Managing a home
- Getting started in an occupation
- Assuming civic responsibilities
- Finding a congenial social group

Middle Adulthood (40 to 60 Years)

As life progresses, middle-aged people find themselves fulfilling different roles and functions. In family life, the developmental tasks become reciprocal, the members interacting with one other in achieving them. The tasks include:

- Achieving civic and social responsibilities as natural leaders and members in a civic life of the community
- Establishing and maintaining an economic standard of living
- Assisting teen age children as the latter move towards independence to become responsible and happy adults by serving as models
- Developing adult leisure time activities
- Relating to one's spouse as a person, as the children grow and require less time and attention
- Accepting and adjusting to the physiological changes of middle age
- Adjusting to ageing parents; making old age satisfactory to them and at the same time promoting self - satisfaction.

Later Maturity (60 years and above)

According to Havinghurst, man learns his way through life and hence he continues to learn his tasks in old age also. As opposed to the pushing and looking forward to types of earlier age, the developmental tasks of later maturity are of a defensive or holding nature. These learnings, which confront the individual in later maturity are:

- Adjusting to decreasing physical health and strength
- Adjusting to retirement and reduced income
- Adjusting to the loss of spouse by death
- Establishing affiliation with one's old age group
- Meeting social and civic obligations
- Establishing satisfactory living arrangements

These six developmental tasks categorized by Havighurst have many educational implications that make an individual aware of many problems which confront children and youth in their advance towards maturity.

Factors Responsible for the Failure to Master Development Tasks

1. Retardation in developmental level: In the case of over protected children, they will not be able to take decisions.
2. Lack of opportunity: The child, if denied of an opportunity to show the talents, will lag behind in the development.
3. Lack of motivation
4. Poor health
5. Physical defect
6. Low intellectual level

1.9. THE DETERMINANTS OF HUMAN DEVELOPMENT

Human developmentalists are interested in the study of:

(*i*) Universal processes as well as the individual differences among human beings

(*ii*) Both the influences on development and their outcomes.

All of us know that people differ in gender, height, weight, and body build, physical characteristics such as hair, skin color, height, weight, eye color and shape; in constitutional factors such as health and energy levels; in intelligence, and in personality characteristics and emotional reactions. Their environment also differ in terms of their life styles, homes, communities and societies they live in, the relationships they have, the kind of schools they attend and also how they spend their free time.

Human development and human behavior are not a result of a single cause; rather numerous causes are involved, each related to the other and interdependent. Some play a more important role than others do. Individual differences are mainly due to differences in characteristics, influences on development and/or developmental outcomes and the factors that affect it cannot always be measured precisely or even discovered.

The factors, which influence development, can be broadly divided into two groups: **biological or genetic factors and environmental or contextual factors.** Both work together in the development of the human being. In fact, the biological determinants of development, the social contexts of development, and the interaction between the two represent the essential aspects of an ecological or systems perspective to human development.

The interactive relationship between heredity and environment is a reciprocal or bidirectional one. This means that the environment or contexts of life act on the individual's characteristics (e.g., child's temperament or disposition, child maturational processes) and the individual acts on his/her environment (e.g., parents, siblings, peers, or teachers). Thus, the individual plays an active role in contributing to his or her development .

Heredity ⟶ Environment
⟵

The influences are classified into the following two categories:

Internal and External influences: Internal influences are the inborn genetic endowments that people receive from their parents-the influence of heredity. External influences or environmental influences come from the people's experience with the environments. These two sources of influences are not independent of each other. Inborn qualities affect the treatment one receives from the other people around them and the environment opportunities or other people's approach to a child may either enhance or suppress the inborn potentials. Thus, both heredity and environment interact and influence the developing child.

I. Biological Determinants: Each and every human being has inherited a general biological code from his or her parents. The biochemical agents that carry this code are genes and chromosomes. There are two primary types of inheritance:

1. *General inheritance,* or those attributes that make any species, including the human species, like other members of the same species. For example, all normal human beings have a brain, two lungs, and two hands, which have four fingers and one thumb.
2. *Specific inheritance* or those attributes that are transmitted from our family ancestors and that distinguish us from other people. This type of inheritance may lead to similarities along family lines such as facial resemblance.

Hereditary factors operate from the moment of conception in determining some features of human growth and development. Many human physical traits are inherited. The effects of genetic factors are obvious in connection with the human being's physical development, his skin color, body build, height, other bodily characteristics, susceptibility to some diseases (e.g. diabetes and some types of cancer) and the level of intelligence and personality development. The physical resemblance of members of the same family provides some support for this view. However, we do not yet fully understand the scientific mechanisms of the interaction of genetic and environmental factors in controlling human growth and development. The relationship of this nature-nurture interaction to human behavior is even less clear. This is particularly true for our understanding of human intelligence and human personality.

Nature of heredity

Heredity operates in the following way:

1. In general, like produces like. Nature sees to it that each species or genes breed true to its type; somewhere there are laws governing occasional deviations.
2. Only certain traits are inheritable. The laws of heredity do not cover all human traits, but a fraction of human behavior.
3. The child's maternal and paternal lines each contribute fifty percent of his total inheritance. More specifically, one-half comes from his parents, one-fourth from his grandparents, and one-eighth from his great grandparents and so on for all the other more remote ancestors.
4. Within the limits of potential traits transmissible by heredity, chance plays an important role, making absolute predictions, almost impossible.
5. Some traits are dominant over others, causing apparent exceptions to the principle of 'like produces like'.

Hereditary Endowment: The part played by heredity can be summarized as follows:

(*i*) Every man and every woman at conception receives 23 chromosomes from each parent or 46 in all.

(*ii*) In mating, each passes one-half of his or her chromosomes to every child.

(*iii*) The father's role is that of passing one half of his chromosomes by way of sperm.

(*iv*) The mother although she acts as an incubator and nourishes the egg, contributes no more to the child's heredity than does the father.

(*v*) These 46 chromosomes compromise everything that determines the heredity of the child

Any differences in ability, interest, emotional adjustment and the like among the siblings in the same home must be the result of heredity, since the environment is the same.

II. Environment or "Contexts" of Development

A person's environment consists of the sum total of the stimulation, which he receives from conception until his death. The environment is everything that affects the individual except his genes. The environment or "contexts" of life play a large role in the development of human beings throughout the life span. It is a potent factor in causing human beings to differ in abilities, emotional characteristics, interests and other psychological characteristics and personality. Environment causes "learning" of new forms of behavior. It influences physical development- a good or poor diet may produce differences in physical stature. In the intellectual sphere, children obviously need an environment that stimulates the use of their minds in order to realize their intellectual potentialities.

Environmental Influences can be divided under two broad categories as

Category I

The individual continually responds to and acts on contexts, which include a person's biological makeup, physical environment, and cognitive processes, as well as historical, social, and cultural contexts. Social and cultural contexts have received the most attention in research on life-span development. These contexts are the environmental settings in which people live. They range from families to peer groups to schools to neighborhoods to entire cultures.

- *Immediate Environments* are those that the human being interacts with directly (e.g., the infant interacts with the family, and the adult interacts with the work setting), and
- *Larger environments* are those that the human being interacts with indirectly, usually through the medium of an immediate environment. For example, the child may interact with the values of his or her culture through the medium of the family or the school, or the adult may interact with cultural expectations of job performance in the work setting. In other words, the culture of a society is a significant context that the individual experiences indirectly through the medium of other direct contexts.

A social role is a pattern of behavior that is expected of fellow members by the members of the social group. Socializations thus, impose the attitudes, appreciations, social roles, and skills of a culture on an individual. Thus, socialization is limited by individual characteristics, and this in turn, may affect the development of an individual. Culture is constantly changing, often through contact with other cultures .

Category II

- *Prenatal environment:* Factors affecting development from conception to birth such as good maternal health, proper nourishment, diet, medicines taken by the mother during pregnancy, radiation, maternal infection & illnesses, X-ray exposure and injuries suffered during pregnancy are included under prenatal environment.
- *Post-natal Environment:* includes a wide variety of physical, psychological and social influences on the individual after it is born. They include climate, atmosphere,

temperature, cleanliness, availability of food and other physical aspects. Similarly the child is influenced by the mother, father, family members, teachers and other persons in its social environment. Later, he is influenced by other social factors like tradition, customs, values, rituals, culture, religion, nationality, caste etc. Social environment refers to all forces and influences that in general form environment. It includes all types of activities-social, cultural, spiritual and economic which affect development.

Normative and Non-Normative Influences: Contexts, like individuals, change. Thus, individuals are changing beings in a changing world. To understand similarities and differences in development, we must look at influences that occur in a similar way for majority of people in a given group, and also at those that touch only certain individuals. We should also consider influences of time and place. Because of these changes, three types of influences are exerted by contexts (1) normative age-graded influences, (2) normative history graded influences, and (3) non-normative life events.

Normative age-graded influences: are highly similar for individuals in a particular age group. These influences may be biological or environmental, as they affect the people in a particular age group in a highly similar way. For example, biological events like onset of puberty, menopause or deterioration in old age exert more or less same influences across various socio-cultural groups. The timing of these biological events is fairly predictable within a normal range. For example, people do not experience onset of puberty at age 35 or menopause at 12. On the contrary, the timing of social events (such as entry into the school, marriage, parenthood and retirement) is more flexible and varies in different times and places.

Normative history-graded influences: are common to people of a particular "cohort"- a group of people, who are of the same age at same place, time, and generation and who have common biological and environmental influences. Examples include economic changes (such as the Great Depression in the 1930s), war (such as World War II in the 1940s), the changing role of women, the current technology revolution, political upheaval (such as the decrease in hard-line communism in the 1990s), and the 9/11/2001 terrorist attacks and the changes they have produced.

Non-normative influences: include the unusual life events or occurrences that have a major impact on the individual's life. They are either typical events, that happen at a typical time of life (such as marriage in childhood, pregnancy in early adolescence, or the death of a parent when a child is young) or atypical events (such as a fire that destroys a home, winning the lottery, or getting an unexpected career opportunity with special privileges, having a birth defect or being exposed to terrorist attacks).

Four Different Levels of Environmental Influences

Urie Bronfenbrenner identifies four different levels of environmental influences, which may be normative or non-normative:

- *Microsystem* level is the most intimate environment. The immediate surrounding includes home, school, day care centre, with significant people like parents, teachers, caregivers and peers at the school and siblings.
- *Mesosystem* is the interlocking of various systems a person is involved with. The linkage between home and school, home and work, work and community, for instance. Here, the influence of one setting with the relationships in another setting is considered. For example, how does home-environment affect the child's adjustment at school, or how the working conditions of parents affect the parent child relationships, influencing the child's development in turn.
- *Exosystem* refers to the larger environment of institutions like school, church, media and government agencies. Influences of media on a persons' aspirations or attitudes, or influences of democratic government etc. that occur at this level of environment.

- *Macro system* is the widest environment including cultural patterns of religion, government, education and economy. These are the most global influences, which affect a majority or people in the society. For example, the importance of education or attitudes towards corruption may be an outcome of the socio-cultural patterns at large.

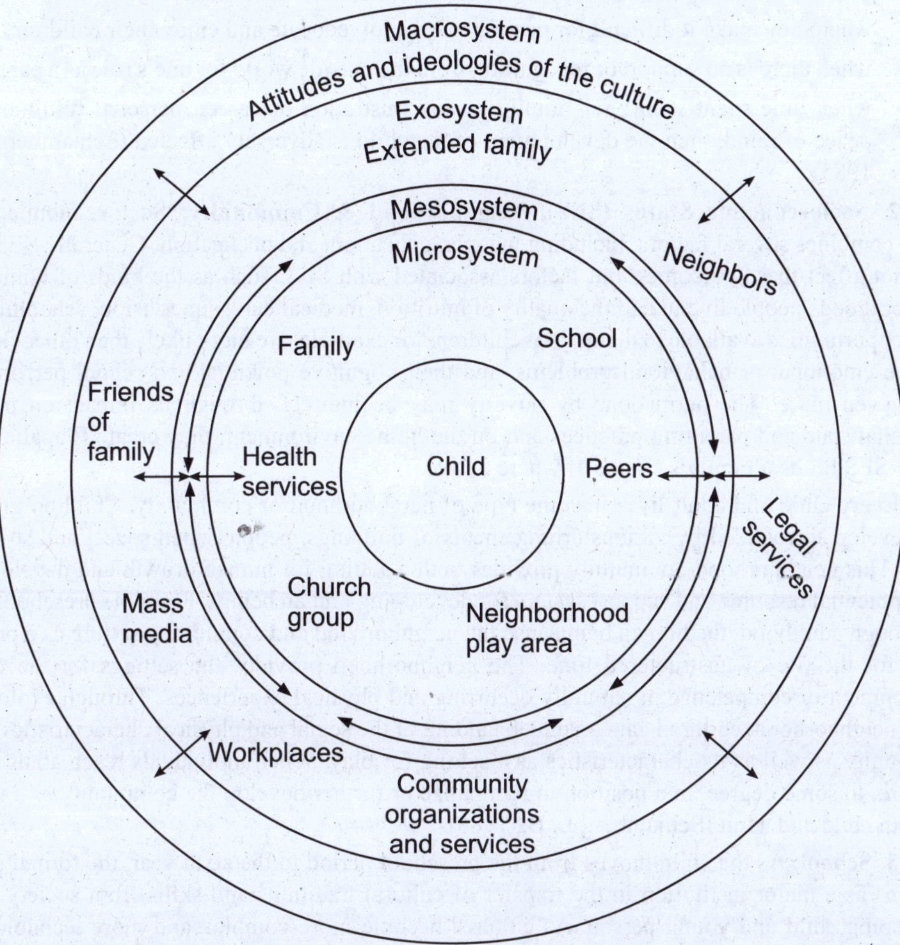

Fig. Bronfenbrenner's ecological model for understanding social influences.

Immediate Contexts: The individual continually responds to and acts on contexts, which include a person's biological makeup, physical environment, and cognitive processes, as well as historical, social, and cultural contexts. Social and cultural contexts have received the most attention in research on life-span development. These contexts are the environmental settings in which people live. They range from families to peer groups to schools to neighborhoods to entire cultures.

1. The Family: The vast majority of children grow up in a family context. This context usually includes a father and/or a mother and, in many instances, brothers and sisters. The family provides the conditions for a child's exchange of substances (breathing, feeding, and excretion). Family provides a continuing pattern a stimulation or a psychological environment, in which the child develops. The parent-child relationship is another factor that has great influence on the development of the child. (Kaluger and Kaluger, 1974, Wallace P.M. and goldstein J.H., 1994). The family has been shown to have an impact on important processes, including the development of self-concept, sex roles, language, intellectual abilities, and interpersonal skills.

Urie Bronfenbrenner (1979) has indicated that many of the problems that are facing both families and children come from the circumstances in which the family finds itself, (and the way of life resulting from the circumstances). When these circumstances and the way of life they generate.

- undermine relationships of trust and emotional security between family members;
- when they make it difficult for parents to care for, educate and enjoy their children;
- when there is no support or recognition from the outside world for one's role as a parent and
- when time spent with one's family means frustration or career, personal fulfilment and peace of mind, then the development of the child is adversely affected (Schiamberg L.B., 1985)

2. Socioeconomic Status (SES), Neighborhood & Community: Socioeconomic status (SES) combines several factors, including income, education, and occupation. Generally SES itself does not affect these outcomes, but factors associated with SES, such as the kinds of homes and neighborhoods people live in and the quality of nutrition, medical care, supervision, schooling, and other opportunities available to them. Poor children, for example, are more likely than other children to have emotional or behavioral problems, and their cognitive potential and school performance suffer even more. The harm done by poverty may be indirect, through its impact on parents' emotional state and parenting practices and on the home environment, they create (Papalia *et al.*, 2004). SES limits a family's choice of where to live.

Every child and adult lives in some type of neighborhood or community, Children grow up and develop surrounded by various arrangements of buildings, people, open space, and streets or roads. This neighborhood-community provides both a setting for human growth and development and a potential resource and support system for developing human beings. From the preschool years on through adulthood, the human beings use the neighborhood and community setting as a primary arena for the use of unstructured time. The neighborhood provides the settings for the child's development of competence in naturally occurring and physical experiences. Through exploration of the neighborhood, children gain an understanding of the social and physical characteristics of the community as well as its characteristics as a setting for play. When individuals reach adult status, they are, to some degree, in a position to reorganize or further develop the community as a setting for both child and adult (Schiamberg L. B., 1985).

3. School: As the child moves from the preschool period to the sixth year, the formal school emerges as a major institution in the transfer of cultural traditions and skills from society to the developing child and young person. As cultures become more complex and more technological, they produce a more sophisticated, elaborate, and abundant collection of skills, knowledge, and information. These must be transmitted to the developing individual (as well as to adult education programs) as necessary prerequisites for effective participation in the culture. Historically the role of the school in the industrialized and technological societies has been to serve this function of cultural transfer and transmission.

In serving this function, the formal school provides an environment for the growing child, which is made up of four major features:

(*i*) The *curriculum*, or what is taught;

(*ii*) The *physical setting*, or the design of space (e.g., the arrangement of classroom, and play areas);

(*iii*) The *methods of instruction*; and

(*iv*) *The characteristics of the classroom group* (the size of the group, the patterns of interactions, and the teacher's style of leadership).

***The relationship of the school and the family*:** Both the school and the family are systems in their own right that interact in the process of educating the child and the adolescent. The school and the family are interdependent. Schools depend on parents to support the school, its activities, and its programs and to encourage the child to participate. Families depend on the school to teach their children not only how to read, write, and work with numbers but how to develop their physical skills, their communication skills, their social skills, and so on. The ability of the child to take full advantage of the school program is, in part, a function of family encouragement and support of the child and the school.

***The relationship of the school and the world of work*:** One of the problems that adolescents in our society face is the need to make some commitment to a vocation or a career in the face of little or no direct experience in the world of work or knowledge about occupations. It has been suggested that the young are systematically excluded from the working world of adults as a function of the inherent age segregation in our society and of the school in particular. Systematic attempts have been made to overcome this problem by reorganizing and rethinking the relationship between the school and the world of work. Such efforts include programs designed to inform high-school and grade-school students about occupations and types of jobs (Schiambcrg L.B., 1985).

4. The World of Work: One of the first things that people want to know on first meeting an individual, is the nature of his or her occupation, which generally defines his or her lifestyle, interpersonal relationships, and to some extent, future potential for development. The world of work may become the central life focus for many people because it represents the primary basis for scheduling human activities on a daily, weekly, or yearly basis over the lifespan. Because of its economic and social significance, the world of work defines the material resources for behavior, for family life, and for development itself.

Work and the family system: If the opportunity to work is absent, or if the nature of the work is not sufficiently rewarding, severe repercussions are likely to be experienced by the individual worker and his or her family. The evidence is overwhelming that unemployment and underemployment among breadwinners is the primary factor leading to continued marital instability among the poor. The absence of work or having work that fails to fulfill the function of economic security, self-esteem, identity, and a sense of mastery over the chaos of one's environment prevents one from finding the stable basis required to build a lasting familiar relationship (Schiamberg L.B., 1985).

5. Peer Group and Friends: The peer group consists of individuals who are approximately of the same age and of the same social class. Peer group and friendship relationships influence development throughout the life span. From the preschool years through the years of adulthood, peer groups serve as a source of information for the individual about social expectations and behavioral roles as well as a source of mutual support. The peer group projects a pattern of conformity. The concept of interpersonal authority is introduced to the child through the peer group. Through his peers, the child comes in contact with various attitudes toward himself, toward adults, and toward those things that are to be valued or disregarded. The child learns concepts of cooperation, sharing and participation from the peer group. The child's peer group enables the child to become independent of his parents and other authorities. Thus, even at early age the peer group influences a child's development. (Kaluger & Kaluger-1974).

During the preschool and early school years, the peer group offers an environment that helps the child to move out of the family. The peer group has its own values and expectations of behavior. Peer relations during these early years are marked by informality and the absence or roles in-group membership. Participation in preschool peer groups is largely the result of the physical closeness of the other children. In other words, children play together because they happen to live near one another or to be in the same class (preschool class, swim class, and so on).

Peer relations during middle childhood are characterized by same-gender groups. Children learn such things as appropriate behaviors and the roles they may be expected to play in later life-what is expected of males and females in society. Peer groups also provide the opportunity for the child to learn about competition and cooperation. Peer relations during adolescence provide several critical experiences:

- The individual develops a greater sensitivity to the needs of the "best friend". These early intimate relationships provide a valuable training ground to later interpersonal relationships.
- The peer group further develops and supports appropriate sex-role behaviors and expectations.
- Interpersonal relationships with the opposite sex often occur through support of the peer group.
- The peer group helps the adolescent to break away from the home.

The peer group helps the adolescent to develop an identity by providing an arena for testing ideas and behaviors.

During the adult years, peers and friends provide a dynamic source of information for social behavior in work, school, or community settings. Many adults who retire from jobs report missing the supportive influence of coworkers more than they miss the work itself. In late adulthood, peers and friends are a potential resource and support network for negotiating the experiences or aging (Schiamberg L. B. 1985).

6. A Larger Context: Culture and Race/Ethnicity: The "immediate" environments that we bave just described do not exist in a vacuum. Rather, they occur in a larger context: the culture. Culture refers to a society's or groups' total way of life, including customs, traditions, beliefs, values, language and physical products-from tools to artworks- all of the learned behavior passed on from parents to children. The *culture* or a society is the collection or principles, beliefs, norms, rules, and expected behaviors that govern the organization of that society. Culture shapes our behavior, how we dress, what we cat, how we solve problems, what we value as important, and how our institutions (government, work and business, schools, and families) are organized. Our cultural patterns for organizing social institutions such as work and family exert a considerable influence on the conditions of human development (Schiamberg L. B., 1985).

Some Cultures have variant *subcultures*, associated with certain groups, usually ethnic groups, within a society. An ethnic group consists of people united by ancestry, religion, language, and/or national origins, which contribute to a sense of shared identity and shared attitudes, beliefs, and values. Most ethnic groups trace their roots to a country of origin, where they or their forebears had a common culture that continues to influence their way of life. The term race, historically viewed as a biological category is now considered a social one, similar to ethnicity (Papalia *et al*., 2004).

A child is born in a specific culture and is thus subjected to the socializing forces found in that culture. During the brief period of childhood, the whole process of socialization must occur. Each new generation acquire the patterns of living inherent in their culture. A social role is a pattern of behavior that is expected of fellow members by the members of the social group. Socialization imposes the attitudes, appreciations, social roles, and skills of a culture on an individual. Thus, socialization is limited by individual characteristics, and this in turn may affect the development of an individual (Kaluger and Kaluger-1974). Culture is constantly changing, often through contact with other cultures.

7. The Historical Context: At one time, developmental scientists paid little attention to the historical context-the time in which people grow up. Then, as the early longitudinal studies of childhood extended into the adult years, investigators began to focus on how particular experiences, tied to time and place, affect the course of people's lives (Papalia *et al.*, 2004).

QUESTIONS

SECTION "A"

Short Answer Type:

1. What is Human Development? Give any two definitions.
2. How does heredity influence as a determinant of human development?
3. List the principles of human growth and development.
4. What are the four goals of human development?
5. Define maturation and growth.
6. What is a developmental stage?
7. Give the significance of studying human development.
8. Differentiate between growth and development.
9. What is developmental task?
10. Write a note on heredity endowment in human development.

SECTION "B"

One Page Answer Type:

1. Bring out the differences between maturation and learning.
2. Write about the domains of development.
3. List out the major developmental stages, explaining any two.
4. Describe the content of human development.
5. Mention in detail about the determinants of development.
6. Write about the developmental tasks of any two different stages in life span.

SECTION "C"

Essay Answer Type:

1. Discuss the factors influencing growth and development.
2. Write about the principles of human growth and development.
3. Explain the need and importance of the study of human development.
4. Write about the major developmental stages.

CHAPTER

2

TECHNIQUES FOR STUDYING HUMAN DEVELOPMENT

OBJECTIVES

To enlighten students about:

- Dimensions of Developmental Research
- Various Research Methods

2.1. INTRODUCTION

As people began to appreciate and value children, they realized that a better understanding of childhood would contribute to

- The development of theories of human behavior that could be used both to interpret and to predict behaviors, and
- Research, which is a controlled, objective, systematic and patient study of some phenomena in some field that is carried out to learn more about a subject.

It is believed that this knowledge could contribute in a practical way to improve the quality of life both at the individual and societal levels. The earliest research efforts were directed toward describing and differentiating age-related behavior to develop theories and establish norms. Norms are the behavior, skills and parameters considered descriptive or normal for a defined age group based on observation or assessment of large populations. Norms can serve as guidelines for assessing developmental progress and for identifying variations and deviations. Norms can provide guidance for anticipating and facilitating the emergence of skills and behaviors.

As more refined measurement techniques and analysis procedures become available, more relationships between antecedent and consequences are being identified that have implications both for theory building and for clinical application.

2.2. DIMENSIONS OF DEVELOPMENTAL RESEARCH

All scientific developmental research relies on systematic and objective methods of observing, recording and describing events. The following is an outline of the six **dimensions of developmental research.**

1. Descriptive vs Explanatory

Descriptive research describes only what has occurred, while explanatory research attempts to explain how something has occurred; that is, what caused it. Descriptive research is often a good way to begin, as it is generally less subject to error but they can be inaccurate. The more objective they are, however, the more accurate they are likely to be; for example, the people standing in a given room can be objectively counted. The description is open to personal interpretation and is more likely to be inaccurate. For this reason, developmental researchers often begin with objective descriptions and then, through careful experimental research, begin to examine cause-and-effect relationships in the hope that they may eventually be able to explain how and why the events they have described are occurring.

2. Naturalistic vs. Manipulative

When conducting naturalistic research, researchers refrain from interacting with the subjects of their observations in order to examine behavior in a natural setting. Careful, detailed records of the observations are kept. Naturalistic research can be conducted in an informal or structured manner. Parents who simply watch their children are engaged in informal naturalistic observation. In a more structured naturalistic observation, the behaviors observed are clearly defined beforehand, and careful reports are kept. During manipulative research, experimenters purposely expose their subjects to different situations and observe the effects caused by this exposure. This kind of research often can be carefully controlled in a laboratory setting, allowing close and careful observations of each studied behavior.

3. Historical vs. Ahistorical

If research is fundamentally dependent on past events, it is considered historical research; if not, it is called ahistorical.

4. Theoretical vs. Serendipitous

Research designed to investigate a particular theory is called theoretical research, while research designed simply to investigate phenomena without regard to theoretical speculations is called serendipitous or atheoretical.

5. Basic vs. Applied

Basic research is the foundation on which applied research can be built. Basic research advances knowledge, while applied research advances already developed technology. Once the basic knowledge has been gathered, applied research is concerned with assembling it for a particular purpose. The space program is a good example of applied research, as most of the basic knowledge about rockets, aerodynamic, and space had been gathered beforehand.

6. Single Subject vs. Group

In the single-subject, the behavior and behavior changes of only one person at a time are of interest, while in group research the researcher looks at group averages, ignoring whether those averages accurately reflect the behavior patterns of any given individual within the group.

2.3. RESEARCH METHODS

Research is a controlled, objective, systematic and patient study of some phenomena in some field that is carried out to learn more about a subject. Researchers in human development work within two methodological traditions: ***quantitative and qualitative.***

Quantitative research deals with "hard", objectively measurable data; for example, how much fear or anxiety patients feel before surgery, as measured by standardized tests, physiological changes, or statistical analysis. Behaviorists generally use quantitative research.

Qualitative research deals with "soft" data about the nature or quality of participants' subjective experiences, feelings, or beliefs-for instance, how patients describe their emotions before surgery.

Quantitative research is based on the **scientific method.** One important way scientific enquiry differs from ordinary inquiring is that scientific enquiry specifies a systematic and formal process for gathering facts and searching for a logical explanation of them. This process is called the scientific method. Scientific method involves careful observation and recording of data, testing of alternative hypotheses and interpretation of data and drawing conclusions.

Developmental research essentially involves scientific methods. It is a series of steps that allow us to be clear about what we studied, how we studied it and what our conclusions were. Sufficient details must be given to allow others to replicate our research and verify our conclusions. Careful use of the scientific method enables researchers to come to sound conclusions about human development. Two key issues at the outset of a scientific investigation are how the participants will be chosen and how the data will be collected. These decisions often depend on what questions the researcher wants to answer. All these issues play a part in a research design, or plan. The following steps of the scientific method provide a framework for objective enquiry. They are:

- *Identifingy a problem* to be studied, often on the basis of a theory or of previous research
- *Formulating hypotheses* – a tentative proposition to be tested by research
- *Collecting data*
- *Analyzing the data* to determine whether or not they support the hypothesis
- *Drawing conclusions* about the hypothesis
- *Disseminating findings* of the study available to scientific community so that other observers can check, learn from, analyze, repeat, and build on the results.

Qualitative research takes a more open-ended, exploratory route. Instead of generating hypotheses from previous research, qualitative researchers gather data and then examine it to see what hypotheses or theories may emerge. Qualitative research is highly interpretive; it cannot yield general conclusions, but it can be a rich source of insights into individuals' attitudes and behavior.

The selection of quantitative or qualitative methods depends on a number of factors: the topic for study, how much is already known about it, the researcher's expertise and theoretical orientation, and the setting. Quantitative research is often done in laboratory settings, where controlled conditions can produce replicable (repeatable) results. Qualitative research is most appropriate in everyday social settings, for investigating topics about which little is currently known. Qualitative research can be extremely time-consuming and expensive. Investigators may combine the two methods. Often qualitative research yields findings that point the way to quantitative research.

It is important that a student understands some of the basic methods of research. The research method – the way a researcher obtains the information, largely determines the legitimacy of the study's conclusions. Some of the reported research findings will be quite reliable and worthy of trust while others will be contrived or based on faulty logic. Therefore, the researcher should be able to make an intelligent estimate of how reliable the results are, based on the research methodologies used.

2.3.1. Normative approach

The developing child is not only learning from an adaptation to his environment but is also changing physically and neurologically as an organism. It is always difficult to determine whether a certain behavior is generated principally by maturation process or by adaptation to environmental impacts. Some of the issues related to nature-nurture have stimulated the collection of normative data-to answer the question of behavior which can be normally expected to appear in children of various chronological ages. Normative data in child psychology provides basis for practical implications in education and training as well as supplying a background or frame of reference for the study and interpretation of children's behavior and psychological development.

Most research in human development concerns changes that occur as people develop. Two basic designs have been relied on extensively to achieve the goal of describing development: the cross-sectional design and the longitudinal design. A third design, the sequential study has come into use in an attempt to overcome the limitations of the other two techniques. Each of these designs attempts to capture the significance of developmental changes of individuals .

Cross-sectional design

In a cross-sectional design, people who differ in age are compared at the same point in time. By comparing the responses of participants in the different age groups, investigators can often identify age-related changes in whatever aspect of development they happen to be studying. A researcher interested in the development of vocabulary might gather samples of speech from a number of 2-,3-, and 4-year-olds; calculate the mean (or average) number of distinct words used per child for each age group; and compare these means to describe how the vocabulary sizes of children of ages 2;3, and 4 differ. A cross-sectional research design compares measurements or observations of some particular trait or behavior on different age groups at approximately the same time. For example, intelligence scores of 5 to 65 year-olds can be compared.

Advantages

- This approach is reasonably easy and efficient in terms of the time taken to conduct one's research.
- Cross-sectional design are likely to yield valid conclusions when there is little reason to believe that the cohorts being studied have had widely different experiences while growing up.(A cohort can be defined as a group of people of the same age who are exposed to similar cultural environments and historical events as they are growing up.)
- The cross sectional study provides information about age differences by seeing how different age groups differ, and we can attempt to draw conclusions about how performance changes with age.
- Different groups can be compared with respect to a variety of dependent variables, such as, intelligence, memory, peer relations, attachment to parents and so on. All of this can be accomplished in a short time.

Longitudinal design

A study that makes repeated measurements or observations of the same individuals over a period of time is called a **longitudinal design**. **Longitudinal** approach is a research strategy in which the same individuals are studied over a period of time, usually several years or more. Data are obtained by studying the same children over a long period of years in their different stages of development. The time period may be relatively brief-six months to a year-or it may be very long, spanning a lifetime.

In a longitudinal design, the performance of one group of individuals is assessed repeatedly over time. The language development study would be longitudinal rather than cross-sectional. If we identify a group of 2-year-olds, measured their vocabulary sizes, waited a year until they were age 3 and measured their vocabularies again, and did the same thing a year later when they were of age 4, so that we can compare mean scores at the three ages. In any longitudinal study, whether it covers only a few months in infancy, 20, or 50 years, the same individuals are studied as they develop. Thus, the longitudinal design provides information about age changes rather than age differences .

By repeatedly testing the same participants, investigators can assess the stability of various attributes and the patterns of developmental trends for each person in the sample. They can also identify general developmental trends and processes by looking for commonalities, such as the points at which most children undergo various changes and the experiences, if any, those children seem to share prior to reaching these milestones. Finally, the tracking of several participants over time will help investigators to understand individual differences in development, particularly if they are able to establish that different kinds of earlier experiences lead to very different outcomes.

Advantages

- The unique quality of the longitudinal method is its ability to allow a researcher to answer questions about the evolution of behavior within an individual, and to examine the stability of behavior for an individual as he or she grows older.
- Longitudinal studies provide a wealth of information about such important issues as stability and change in development, to examine the impact of early events in a child's life on subsequent behavior patterns.
- A longitudinal design is the only way of answering whether individuals' IQ test scores are stable over time, whether difficult babies become difficult children or law-breaking adults, whether underweight newborns are still small for their age years later-because the same people are studied at different ages.

Disadvantages

- Longitudinal projects can be very expensive and time-consuming.
- This method is more difficult to employ because the experimenter has to wait for several years of development of the childhood to elapse and during this time, children may leave the community where the research is being conducted. They move away, get sick, or become bored with repeated testing, and they occasionally have parents who, for one reason or another, will not allow them to continue in the study.
- The focus of the research in human development is constantly changing, and longitudinal questions that seem very exciting at the beginning of a long-term project may seem rather trivial by the time the project ends.
- Another shortcoming of longitudinal research is the cross-generational problem. Children growing up in one era may be exposed to very different kinds of experiences than children from another era. As a consequence, the patterns of development that characterize one generation of children may not always apply to other generations. In other words, cross-generational changes in the environment may limit the conclusions of a longitudinal project to those children who were growing up while the study was in progress.

Sequential Designs

Sequential designs combine the cross-sectional and longitudinal approaches in a single study. Sequential designs combine the best features of the cross sectional and the longitudinal approaches by selecting participants of different ages and then studying each of these cohorts over time. Hence, they improve on both. Sequential designs can begin to untangle the effects of age, cohort, and time of measurement and to indicate which age trends are truly developmental in nature. Sequential designs provide a way to examine various combinations of the three basic developmental effects, and these designs provide the most complete view of human development. However, this completeness comes at a price.

Advantages

- Sequential designs help address most of the limitations described earlier concerning single cross-sectional and longitudinal studies. For example, sequential designs help isolate cohort effects, and they help determine whether age-related changes are due to participant dropout or to some other cause.

- They are time saving – in only 2 years, we have learnt about the long-term effects of the program on those children who are still between the target ages of 6 and 10. A standard longitudinal approach would require 4 years to provide similar information.
- Third, the sequential design actually yields more information about long-term effects than the longitudinal approach does. If we had chosen the longitudinal design, we would have data on the long-term effects of a program administered only to 6 year-olds. However, sequential approach allows us to perform a second cross-sectional comparison to determine whether the program has comparable long-term effects, when administered to 6-8 and 10 year olds. Clearly, this combination of the cross-sectional and longitudinal designs is a rather versatile alternative to either of those approaches.

Disadvantages

- Sequential designs are extremely complex, and not always able to provide definitive answers.
- These designs are very expensive to conduct. Consequently, few sequential studies exist.

2.3.2. Observation Technique

An observation in science is the gathering of research data from the real world by recognizing and noting facts or behaviors as they occur. It is a basic tool and method of gathering information for most scientists. It is used not only to gather information but also to generalize about individuals. Researchers observe large numbers of children and record information about their growth and development at various ages to derive averages for the appearance of various skills, behaviors or growth measures.

Systematic Observation: Systematic observation involves watching people carefully and recording what they do or say. Scientific observation requires an important set of skills. For observation to be effective, they have to be systematic. We need to have some idea of what we are looking for, to know whom we are observing, when and where we will observe, how the observations will be made and in what form they will be recorded. Now such technological devices as portable videotape recorders and computers enable researchers to analyze moment-by-moment changes in behavior-for example, the interaction between spouses, making naturalistic observation more accurate and objective than it would otherwise be. Electronic recording devices (audiovisual equipment , special effects generators, videotapes, sound spectrograms) make it possible to record behavior as it occurs and then to analyze segments of the behavior carefully and repeatedly at a later date. Newer techniques are continually being developed that make the analysis of naturally occurring behaviors even easier.

Observers must be careful not to disturb or affect the events under investigation. Observation method produces more detailed and greater depth of insight than the social survey method but it is effective only for a smaller range of samples. For e.g. naturalistic observation has been used extensively to observe young children's interactions in a nursery school or preschool settings, but it would be much harder to use this method to study adults at work. We can make our observations in two places- A laboratory, a controlled setting with many of the complex factors in the "real world" removed, and the everyday world.

Systematic observation can take two forms: ***Naturalistic observation and Structured observations***

Naturalistic Observation: Naturalistic observation means observing people's behavior in their common everyday surroundings or real-life settings such as homes, schools, neighborhood, playgrounds, work settings, shopping malls, beaches, and other natural places where people's behavior happens spontaneously. On-going behavior is intensively watched as it occurs in these places. The researchers may choose to focus on naturally occurring spontaneous behavior as subjects work or play freely at home, at school, or at work . A naturalistic observation method for conducting research on human development usually occurs in the "real" world where behavior happens spontaneously. There may be no attempt to control the environment of the individuals being studied and observed.

The researchers do not try to influence, manipulate or alter behavior of the subjects they are studying or the environment; they watch behavior as it occurs, and simply record what they see by means of notepad, videotape or other methods. However, the researchers must decide beforehand what variable to record, as they cannot keep track of everything that someone does. For example, researchers who wish to study friendships might decide to observe children at the start of the first year in a middle school (chosen because many children will be making new friends at this time). They could decide to record when children sit in the lunchroom and who talks to whom.

Naturalistic studies result in "normative" (typical) information about people and their surroundings. For example, we could use naturalistic studies to examine the motor development of a child or of children. Naturalistic observations are recording of the behavior of relatively large number of people. The purposes of naturalistic observations include the following:

- To record information about development at various ages
- To suggest average ages for the appearance of skills, behavior, and growth measurements

Some observations can be done without the subjects' knowledge and without any intrusion into their activities. Arnold Gesell introduced the one-way window, through which the observer can see without being seen, as a means for observers to watch without interfering with people's activities.

To keep to a minimum the stress that being observed inevitably creates; observers try to put their subjects at ease before the observation begins. They may spend some hours or days in the setting to let the subjects get used to their presence. Naturalistic observation has been used more often to study child development than adult development, largely because infants and young children often cannot be studied through self-report techniques that demand verbal skills. The greatest advantage of naturalistic observation is that it is the only technique that can tell us what children or adults actually do in everyday life. Modern audio-video equipment allows for the recording of naturalistic observations. Behavior can thus be repeated through replays, allowing a very high degree of confidence in the accuracy of the observations.

Advantages

- A unique advantage of natural observation is that only natural observations can tell us about peoples' "real lives," "typical activities", and "normal encounters."
- Naturalistic observation provides insights that we sometimes cannot achieve in the laboratory.
- An advantage of naturalistic observation is that it is independent of the participants' ability or willingness to report on given matters.

Disadvantages

- Naturalistic observation provides information about what is happening, but not why or how it is happening or how the behavior might change under a different set of circumstances. Because observers make no effort to influence what is happening, they are limited to recording what they see.
- The mere presence of an observer can sometimes make people behave differently than they otherwise would, and they may act more stiffly, shyly, self-consciously, politely and positively. Even so, it is unlikely that they can or will disguise completely their usual

ways of behaving just to put on a good show for the observer. After the first few visits from an observer, a person usually begins to act in his or her customary ways.

- Some behaviors (for example, heroic efforts to help other people) occur too infrequently and unexpectedly to be observed in this manner.
- Many events are usually happening at the same time in a natural setting, and any of them may be affecting people's behavior. This makes it difficult to pinpoint the cause of the behavior or of any developmental trends in the behavior.
- Naturalistic observation can provide a rich source of ideas for more extensive future study. But it is not a particularly strong technique for testing hypotheses.
- The researcher lacks control over the behavior of the individuals being observed. The observer might be biased, have certain expectations, and look for those behaviors to record.

An alternative to observations by unfamiliar people is for parents, teachers, babysitters, and other familiar people to record children's activities.

Structured observations or laboratory observation: Structured observations differ from naturalistic observations in that the researcher creates a setting that is particularly likely to elicit the behavior of interest. In laboratory observation, researchers observe and record behavior in a controlled situation, such as a laboratory. Making observations in a laboratory allows us to control certain factors that influence behavior but are not the focus of our inquiry. By observing all participants under the same conditions, investigators can more clearly identify differences in behavior not attributable to the environment.

Structured observations can be more efficient than naturalistic observation for producing particular kinds of data. For instance, there is no need to wait in the schoolyard to observe adolescents' cooperation and competition, when the researcher can structure games, races, and problems that will elicit these kinds of behavior in a half-hour session. Structured situations let researchers focus effectively on just the behavior they are interested in. Structured observations are particularly useful for studying behaviors that are difficult to observe naturally. However, investigators using this approach must be careful that the settings they create do not disturb the behavior of interest.

Advantages

- Most structured observations have the advantages of giving researchers more control over the situation and of giving them a chance to look at how different people behave in a single, standard situation.

Disadvantages

- First, it is almost impossible to conduct research without the participants' knowing they are being studied.
- Second, the laboratory setting is unnatural and therefore can cause the participants to behave unnaturally.
- Third, people who are willing and able to come to a university laboratory may not fairly represent the population we are interested in studying. Those who are unfamiliar with university settings, and with the idea of "helping science" may be intimidated by the setting.
- Finally, some aspects of life-span development are difficult if not impossible to examine in the laboratory.
- Like naturalistic observations, structured observations raise concerns about the intrusiveness of observers and their equipment. Although behavior in structured

observations is more constrained than in naturalistic observations, the researcher still want subjects to feel comfortable and not to act as if they are under a lens. Researchers must try to make the setting itself comfortable and unthreatening.

2.3.3. Clinical Investigations

Clinical Investigations are usually studies done in facilities where people come to receive advice or treatment for problems. Consequently, they often deal with maladjustment of some kind. They may, however, also be used to study healthy people. Clinical investigations may involve in-depth laboratory tests, physical examinations, radiological scans, interviews or surveys, as well as observations by professional specialties depending on the nature of the study. Sharing information by an inter- disciplinary team allow each participant to have a better picture of the individual under study.

Case Studies A researcher following the progress of a subject over an extended period of time is conducting a case study. Its aim is the same that of other longitudinal approaches of the accumulation of developmental information. When a researcher wishes to go into considerable detail in order to gain information about a developmental process, the case study is an appropriate choice.

An early form of the case study method was the **"baby biography".** Case study was developed from psychoanalytic theory. "Case study" consists of the results of intensive investigation of the past history and/or current influences on the subject. Case study or the clinical method, as it is sometimes called, is an in-depth look at a single individual or intensive investigation of a particular case by bringing together a wide range of information on one child or individual, including interviews, observation, opinions about the individual, test scores, and sometimes-psychological measures.

Case study approach provides a specialized longitudinal investigation of the behavior, emotions, beliefs, or life history of a single individual in more depth than is generally done with groups of subjects. Hence, emphasis is placed on accumulating developmental data of the same individual over a span of years. It takes into account all the pertinent factors of the case or situation. It strives to obtain a complete picture of a child or individual's psychological functioning and the experiences that led up to it.

The case history is typically prepared for the children who are having trouble in adjusting to the stress of the environment in which he lives. It involves an attempt to update all the relevant facts about the child namely parents, neighbors, relatives, teachers, physicians, and any other persons who may shed some light on the child's problem and his environment so that these facts may be seen in perspective. It aims at studying everything about that case rather than something about everything. The unit of study is an individual rather than a group of subjects. Hence, a large quantity of personal data from several sources is usually assembled for a single case study, which is not at all possible in a longitudinal group. The purpose of the study is to shed light on some problems of adjustment for which diagnosis, therapy and prognosis are desired. Proper insights may be obtained as to how the child may be helped to lead a happier and protective life.

Case studies are performed mainly by mental health professionals when, for either practical or ethical reasons, the unique aspects of an individual's life cannot be duplicated and tested in other individuals. A case study provides information about one person's fear, hopes, fantasies, traumatic experiences, upbringing, family relationships, healthy or anything that helps the psychologist understand the person's behavior.

Advantages

- The case study or clinical method offers useful, in depth information giving a rich description of an individual that offer valuable insights into the many factors that affect development.

- Case studies can provide us with a wealth of new information. Some case studies are done by lay persons in the form of autobiographies, biographies, diaries, collection of letters, record books, baby books, and the like. Many insights have been discovered or rediscovered, in such sources.
- Case studies have also had a prominent place in the clinical treatment of maladjusted and emotionally disturbed individuals. Case studies are often used by researchers who study individuals who exhibit behavior that is an exception from the normal, such as a child genius or a serial murderer.

Limitations

- Case studies do not yield information about causes and effects or offer explanation. They provide only description of developmental changes.
- Information is collected unsystematically and subjectively, permitting too much flexibility for researcher's theoretical preferences to bias their observation and interpretations.
- The case study method is used only occasionally by researchers because of the great investment in time and funds required. When such studies are performed because of these requirements, only a small number of individuals are included in the project.
- The data are recorded on only one individual and it is difficult to generalize from one case to the whole population. The information gained from only one person being generalized to a large number of other individuals indicates its **questionable validity.** Therefore, it is necessary to do many case studies in order to demonstrate a common behavior pattern.
- Another problem is the extended interaction between the observer or experimenter and the subject under study. Because case studies normally involve frequent contacts between researchers and the subjects over a long period of time, researchers and the subjects become familiar with each other, and the objectivity of the results may be in question. The experimenter might even become a part of the subject's treatment and the same results would not necessarily be found by a different researcher
- The subject of a case study is unique, with a genetic makeup and personal history that no one else shares. In addition, case studies involve judgments of unknown reliability.

2.3.4. Anecdotal record

The data obtained by this approach have been typically based on incidental observation. From this observation certain concepts and generalization about child behavior has been developed. This method frequently provides chances to formulate hypothesis that stimulates further study and research.

2.3.5. Biographical method

An early form of the case study method was the "baby biography". Over the past two centuries, a small number of parents have kept detailed observational diaries of their children's behavior. Charles Darwin in 1601 was the first to keep a record of developmental changes observed in his son. He wrote a biographical account of his infant son's development. The biographer often is the mother who observes and records the behavior of the infant and young children as development occurs. The mother's baby diary illustrates a simple version of biography. In the babies' record, the observer, usually the infant's mother, records such elementary data as 'the day on which the baby sat alone for the first time', 'when he spoke his first word' or so forth.

Disadvantages

- It involves an inordinate amount of time, which the experimenter must devote for observational recording.

- It seems doubtful that many parents can record the behavior of the children from an old objective point of view, since common observations demonstrates them to be more prone to anticipate the first word, or social smile of their infants than an impersonal outsider.
- The biographers' views are usually based on economic status, educational background and many other factors that are positively related to children's psychological development.
- There is possibility for the biographer's biased observations based on their interest.

2.3.6. Rating scale method

It is the measuring instrument that requires a rater or observer to assign the related subjects to categories (on continuum) or numerals. These scales are easy to construct and more quick to use. This method consists of relatively crude scaling procedure that has been proved useful when more precise test for measurement is not available. In this method, descriptions of different degrees of quality are arranged along a line from high to low or otherwise, and this line forms the scale. Therefore, it can also be referred to as 'rating scale procedure'.

Disadvantages

- In this procedure the observer indicates where he believes a child stands on a continuum with respect to some characteristics or type of behavior.
- Possibility for the raters' prejudice and bias on the ratings is probable.

2.3.7. Self-report Measures: Interviews, Questionnaires and Tests

Self-reports: Although the experimental methods are often preferred by researchers, they are not the only ways of obtaining information about changes through the lifespan. When direct observation is impossible, researcher must sometimes rely on **survey** techniques, such as conducting interviews or administering questionnaires.

Self-report methods rely on information that is provided by the subject himself rather than being inferred from observation or measurement of behavior and performance. In this way, they constitute a major departure from observation techniques, psychometric tests and experimental situation. Self-report methods frequently constitute the only "direct" approach to the investigation of the subjective life of the human beings, their attitudes, values, motives, beliefs, perceptions etc. Use of self-report presumes that the subject is sufficiently mature in a cognitive sense to supply the desired kind of information. Hence, they are inapplicable to infants and can only be employed in a very limited sense in the preschool children.

Self-reports actually represent a special case of using tasks to measure people's behavior. Self-reports are simply people's answers to questions about the topic of interest. When questions are posed in written form, the self-report is a questionnaire; when questions are posed orally, the self-report is an interview. In either format, questions are created that probe different aspects of the topic of interest.

Interviews, written questionnaires, and tests and scales designed to measure abilities or personality traits all involve asking people questions. These self-report measures are often standardized, meaning that they ask the same questions in precisely the same order for everyone so that the responses of different individuals can be directly compared. Self-reports are useful because they can lead directly to information on the topic of interest. They are also relatively convenient, particularly when they can be administered to groups of participants.

Interview: Collecting information through an **interview** involves orally asking people questions about some aspect of their lives, attitudes or behaviors; participants respond orally to the investigator's queries. Interview is a face-to-face interpersonal role situation in which a person, the interviewer asks a person who is being interviewed, the respondent (interviewee) questions designed to obtain answers pertaining with the research problem.

People's ideas, motives, opinions, or reactions to stressful life events or reactions to some positive events, like achieving a position or winning awards, can be traced through an interview. Data from interviews and questionnaires come in the form of words rather than observed actions.

This tool permits the researcher to ask specific, predetermined questions to all participants and to formulate others in response to answers given by the individuals involved in the research project. The investigator has the opportunity to clarify or repeat questions and can provide deeper interpretations of issues not readily accomplished with other methods and also avoid misunderstandings. Interviewers have to work sensitively and skillfully, especially with children, with very simple, short, and specific questions in order to get true indications of their subjects' abilities, without misinterpreting or distorting the responses they give. In these cases, a less structured interview is called for. With older children and adults, researchers can often use paper and pencil questionnaires, which subjects fill out themselves. Compared to in-person interviews, this method has both advantages and disadvantages. In developmental psychology, interviewing parents, children, peers and teachers or caregivers helps getting relevant information.

Advantage

- As "interviews" are conducted face-to-face, much detailed and personal information can be obtained with probing follow-up questions to clarify responses. Interviewers review feelings, emotions and attitudes, all of which are sometimes more important than factual information.
- Its advantage lies in its standardization of responses, and its protection of subjects' anonymity.
- Another advantage is that it is a flexible method so that a broad range of subjects may be explored, depending on the needs of the interviewers. Questions may be predetermined and the same ones asked for everyone to be certain to obtain information on the same topic from each person.

Disadvantages

- Interviews are expensive, and usually involve only a limited number of subjects. It involves transportation and secretarial transcribing costs that may be prohibitive for its use as a common tool of research.
- Second, it is time-consuming in that it may be difficult to schedule interviews conveniently for both researcher and subjects. Travel to and from subjects' homes; for example, requires much advance planning and coordination.
- The person acting as interviewer may unconsciously influence or bias the subjects. Negative or positive facial expressions may act to elicit responses from subjects that the researcher wishes to hear. Much skill is required to conduct an interview properly and the unskilled or inexperienced interviewer may not obtain accurate or valid information from individuals.
- The success of the interview depends on the ability of the interviewer to establish a rapport with the subject and to encourage self-disclosure. Not all interviewers are so skillful or patient. They run the risk of asking leading questions, not probing responses deeply enough, not establishing rapport with their young subjects, and not interviewing all subjects in the same way. Such data supplied by the subjects, present serious difficulties with respect to sincerity and authenticity of the data.
- Some subjects are less verbal than others, making it difficult for the interviewers to obtain

information. Sometimes subjects give false data simply because they do not remember accurately. Interviewers need training in how to be both objective and professional. Because of biases, an interviewer might distort or misunderstand a subject's responses.

- Prepared and practiced interviews have been used many times to probe into people's attitudes and knowledge. Countless interviews and questionnaires given to adults, parents, teachers, and children have been used to collect data about development.

In a ***survey method*** of interview, researchers ask a large number of people questions about their own behavior or that of their children, and the answers are tabulated and reported. Most of us are familiar with attitude surveys. Their results give public officials some idea of how people are thinking and may affect public policy. Psychologists frequently use such instruments to collect data.

Questionnaires,Schedules and Checklists

According to Goode and Hatt (1952), a questionnaire refers to a device used for securing answers to the questions using a form, which the respondent has to fill. Collecting data via a questionnaire involves putting one's questions on paper and asking the respondents to write their responses on them. They may be used to obtain relevant information from older children and adolescents. It is the most flexible of tools, which possesses some unique advantages over other kinds of tools in collecting both quantitative and qualitative information. Careful preparation of a good questionnaire calls for a great deal of time, personal care and work. This is also widely used as an instrument to elicit the attitude and opinion of the children.

i. Standardized: The questions asked, their content, sequence and wordings are fixed.

ii. Unstandardized: These are more flexible and open; the questions asked, their content, sequence and wordings are in the hands of the researcher. The questions could be open-ended or closed-ended.

Advantage

- Its advantage lies in the economy of administration (an entire group can fill out a carefully constructed questionnaire at one time under supervision)
- Large numbers of people may be surveyed fairly easily throughout the mail or in large groups, with a minimum expense.
- Data are standardized and easy to summarize.
- As questionnaires are given anonymously, people usually respond honestly

Disadvantage

- Questions can be misunderstood, and wrong answers can be obtained.
- If the researchers omit significant questions, they may not receive some important information.

Schedule/Checklists: At certain times an interviewer asks questions verbally, and then records the responses. Checklists provide a short form of questionnaires that obtain data easily and quickly. A schedule is critically a set of questions that are asked and filled in by an interviewer in a face to face situation with another person. It is different from a questionnaire in that the schedule is administrated personally to a respondent or a group of respondents, while a questionnaire is usually mailed. The advantages of the schedule over the questionnaire are that it provides opportunity to establish rapport, to explain the purpose of and to make the meaning of the items clear. It also economizes on expenditure of time and money and provides both complete and usable returns. The handicap that the schedule presents, is the inability of the researcher to contact personally all the respondents required, either individually or in a group.

Psychological Tests: They are standardized in the sense that they are administrated under controlled situations and that it is usually known how a representative body of children respond to the test. Standardized tests are tests that have been determined to a great many people representing the population for whom they were designed in order to determine statistical norms (standards) for that population. The purpose of this standardized or structured format is to treat each person alike so that responses of different participants can be compared.

A "psychological test" poses questions or presents tasks designed to measure a person's attitudes, aptitudes or personality traits. Subjects used in the process of standardization should reflect all the characteristics (e.g., age, sex, culture, occupational background) of the population on which the test will be used. These are instruments designed to describe and measure a sample in relation to certain aspects of human behavior or inner qualities, later knowledge about the response norms for evaluating the child's performance with respect to the general population of the child of his age, gender and so on.

Psychological tests are of various types depending on the phenomena or traits they are devised to describe and measure. Chief among those are :

(*a*) Achievement test

(*b*) Intelligence test

(*c*) Aptitude test

(*d*) Interest inventories

(*e*) Personality measures

Among the many ways of classifying psychological tests, some of them are distinguished below:

(1) Performance test and paper and pencil test

(2) Individual test and group test

(3) Power test and speed test

(4) Standardized test and non-standardized test /teacher made test

Some specific examples are:

Tests of intelligence — *Terman & Merrill performance test, Stanford Binet test, Weschler's Intelligence scale for children and adults (WISC)*

Performance Test — *Koh's Block design test, Raven's progressive matrices test*

Personality measures — *Personality inventory by Singh & Singh.*

When choosing a test, the researcher must be concerned with whether it is valid. Validity is the indication of how accurately a test measures what it is supposed to measure. The measurement of psychological traits and abilities is more elusive. If a standardized test yields the same or similar results each time it is taken, we say it has good test-retest reliability.

Advantages

- A benefit of standardized tests is that they allow rapid and cost-efficient assessment of the abilities of many persons.
- Self-reports are useful because they can lead directly to information on the topic of interest.
- They are also relatively convenient, particularly when they can be administered to groups of participants.

Disadvantages

- Self reports are not always valid measures of people's behavior because answers are sometimes inaccurate.
- When asked about past events, people may not remember them accurately.
- Sometimes people answer incorrectly due to response bias.
- Answers to interviews and questionnaires may be misleading if respondents try to present themselves in a positive or socially desirable light. For example, many people would be reluctant to admit that they have no friends at all.
- Despite scientific rigor in the standardization of norms, they may discriminate against some normal persons, who, for various reasons, score distant from these norms.
- Self-reports cannot be used with infants, very young children, or other individuals who cannot read or understand speech very well.
- Because individuals of different ages may not understand and interpret questions in the same way, the trend in age differences in responses may reflect age differences in comprehension or interpretation rather than differences in the quality of interest to the researcher.

As long as investigators keep these weaknesses in mind, self report is a valuable tool for human development research.

2.3.8. Projective techniques

Projective techniques have been developed by psychologists to use projection of respondents for inferring about underlying motives, urges or intentions that are such that the respondent either resists revealing them or is unable to figure out himself. In projective techniques, the respondent is supplying information, tends unconsciously to project his own attitudes or feelings on the subject under study. Projective techniques play an important role in researches or in attitude surveys. The use of these techniques requires intensive specialized training. The stimulus may be a photograph, a picture, an inkblot and so on. Responses to their stimuli are interpreted as indicating the individual's own view of his personality structure, needs, tension, etc. in the context of pre-established psychological conceptualization of what the individuals' responses to the stimulus mean. We may now briefly deal with the important projective techniques.

Word Association tests: These tests are used to extract information regarding such words, which have maximum association. In this sort of test, the respondent is asked to mention the first word that comes to mind, ostensibly without thinking, as the interviewer reads out each word from a list. If the interviewer says 'cold', the respondent may say 'hot' and the like ones. The general technique is to use a list of as many as 50 to 100 words. Analysis of the matching words supplied by the respondent indicates whether the given word should be used for the contemplated purpose. This technique is frequently used in advertising research.

Sentence Completion tests: These tests happen to be an extension of the technique of word association test (i.e.) the informant may be asked to complete the sentence (such as persons who wear khadi are ------) to find association of khadi clothes with certain personality characteristics. Several sentences of this type might be put to the informant on the same subject. Analysis of replies from the same informant reveals his attitude towards this subjects and combination of these attitudes of all the sample members is then taken to reflect the use of the population. This technique permits use of not only the words but ideas as well and thus helps in developing hypothesis and in the construction of questionnaire. This technique is also quick and easy to use but it often leads to analytical problems, particularly, when the response happens to be multi-dimensional.

Story Completion tests: Such tests are a step further wherein the researchers may contrive stories instead of sentences and ask the informants to complete them. The respondent is given just enough of the story to focus his attention on a given subject and he is asked to supply a conclusion to the story.

Pictorial techniques: There are several pictorial techniques. The important ones are as follows:

Thematic apperception test (TAT): The TAT consists of a set of pictures (some of the pictures deal with the ordinary day-to-day events while others may be ambiguous pictures of unusual situations) that are shown to respondents who are asked to describe what the picture represents. The replies of the respondent constitute the basis for the investigator to draw inferences about their personality structure, attitudes, etc.

Rorschach test: This test consists of 10 cards having prints of inkblots. The design happens to be symmetrical but meaningless. The respondents are asked to describe what they perceive in such symmetrical inkblots and the responses are interpreted on the basis of some predetermined psychological framework. This test is frequently used, but the problem of validity still remains a major setback in this test.

Holtzmann's inkblot test (HIT): This test from W.H.Holtzmann is a modification of the Rorschach's test explained above. This test consists of 45 inkblot cards which are based on color, movement, shading and other factors drawn in from the subject and the responses from the subject are interpreted at 3 levels of form appropriate test. Form responses are interpreted for knowing the accuracy(F) or inaccuracy(F-) of respondent's percepts, shading and color for ascertaining his affection and devotional needs and movement responses for assessing the dynamic aspects of his life.

Holtzmann inkblot test has several special features or advantages. For example, it elicits relatively constant number of responses per respondent. Secondly, it facilitates studying the responses of a respondent to different cards, in the light of norms of each card instead of dumping them together. Thirdly, it elicits much more information from the respondent that is possible with merely 10 cards as in Rorschach test; the 45 cards used in this test provide a variety of stimuli to the respondent and the information elicited by the test are comparatively wider.

There are some limitations of this test as well. One difficulty that remains in using this test is that most of the researchers have to interpret the protocol of the subject and understand his personality (or attitude) through them knowing the determinant of each of his response as a must. This fact emphasizes that the test must be conducted individually and a host of test inquiry must as well be conducted for knowing the nature and sources of responses, and this limits the scope of HIT as a group test for personality. Not only this, the usefulness of HIT for purposes of personal selection, vocational guidance, etc. is still to be established.

Play techniques: Under this, subjects are asked to improvise or act out to the situation in which they have been assigned various roles. The researcher may observe such traits as hostility, dominance, sympathy, prejudice or the attitude of younger ones through manipulation of dolls. Dolls representing different racial groups are usually given to children who are allowed to play with them freely. The manner in which children organize dolls would indicate their attitude towards the class of persons represented by dolls. This is also known as doll- play test and is used frequently in studies pertaining to sociology. The choice of color, form, words, sense of orderliness and other reactions may provide opportunities to infer deep - seated feelings.

Conclusion: These, then, are the most commonly used techniques of collecting data about human development- Normative approach, self-report measures (interviews, questionnaires, and tests) and techniques of behavioral observation (both naturalistic and structured). Since each method has its limitations, our knowledge is advanced the most when multiple methods are used to study the same aspects of human development and these different methods lead to similar conclusions.

QUESTIONS

SECTION "A"

Short Answer Type:

1. List the techniques of studying human development.
2. Explain rating scale.
3. What is case study?
4. How anecdotal method is considered a method of child study?
5. Enumerate any six methods of child study.

SECTION "B"

One Page Answer Type:

1. Describe the questionnaire method.
2. Enumerate the different methods adopted for child study and explain any one method.
3. Describe schedule and its advantage in collecting data for child study.
4. Briefly explain case study as a method of child study.
5. Brief on checklist as a method of child study.
6. Explain the importance of studying child development.
7. Discuss about any two methods of studying human development.
8. Explain the observational methods of human development.
9. Bring out the differences between longitudinal and cross sectional methods of normative approach.
10. Compare quantitative and qualitative research, and give an example of each.

SECTION "C"

Essay Answer Type:

1. Discuss in detail any six techniques used in human development.
2. Compare the advantages and disadvantages of various forms of data collection.
3. List the advantages and disadvantages of longitudinal, cross-sectional and sequential research.

UNIT — II

CHAPTER

3

PRENATAL DEVELOPMENT

OBJECTIVES

To enlighten students about:

- Conception, Signs and Symptoms of Pregnancy, Sex Determination of the Child
- Prenatal Diagnostic Tests
- Stages of Prenatal development- period of the Ovum, Period of Embryo and Period of the Fetus; Hazards During Pregnancy
- Factors affecting Prenatal Development; Complications During Pregnancy
- Genetic Counseling
- Care of the Pregnant Women.

3.1. INTRODUCTION

Both parents contribute equally to the beginning of a new life and that this new being grows from single cells, one male and one female in origin. In the past, sexual intercourse was the only way for the egg and sperm to unite and begin the development that results in human being. But now artificial/ assisted means of reproduction have been successfully utilized. Whether by artificial means or by natural means, fertilization begins with the period of the zygote, the technical term for the fertilized egg.

Two events precede fertilization or conception. They are :

(*i*) **Ovulation:** A female newborn has about 400,000 immature eggs (ova) in her ovaries each one encased in its own sac, called a "follicle". The ovum is the largest cell in the human body. However, the size of it is only one-fourth size of a "dot" and can be seen without a microscope sometimes. After the attainment of sexual maturity, a female ovulates about once in every 28 days, usually midway in her menstrual cycle. Ovulation is the process by which one mature follicle in one of the two ovaries rupture, expelling a ripened ovum (sometimes two or more ova) which travels toward the uterus (the womb) by way of the fallopian tube. The mature ovum is one of the most massive and probably the most complex of all living cells. The process of fertilization normally occurs during the ovum's journey along the fallopian tube.

(*ii*) **Ejaculation of semen:** The second event is the ejaculation of semen fluid of high sperm density and vitality into the vagina, near the neck of the uterus, within about 2 to 3 days before and up to about one day after ovulation. The tadpole-like spermatozoon, at 1/600 inch from top of its head to the tip of its tail is one of the smaller cells in the body. However, it is much more active than the ovum. Spermatozoa are produced in the testicles (testes) of a mature healthy male at a rate of about several hundred million a day and ejected in his semen at sexual intercourse. The average ejaculation carries about 500 million sperm cells. The sperm enter the vagina and attempt to swim through the cervix, the opening to the uterus, and into the fallopian tubes, where only one sperm can fertilize the egg, to create new human being.

3.2 CONCEPTION OR FERTILIZATION

Once in every 28 days (usually around the middle of the woman's menstrual cycle) an ovum ripens in one of the two ovaries and is discharged into the corresponding fallopian tube or oviduct and it slowly moves towards the uterus. This ovum is propelled by small hair like cilia that lines the tube, toward the uterus. It takes about 3-7 days for the ovum to reach the uterus. During sexual intercourse, a man ejaculates millions of sperm, or spermatozoa, his reproductive cells. These sperm are produced in the testes, then mixed with seminal fluid and ejaculated. Out of the millions of sperm that are ejaculated into the woman's vagina and that swim through the cervix and into the uterus, only one will merge with the mature ovum in the fallopian tube, which is called as conception. Conception typically takes place within one of the **fallopian tubes,** which are part of the female reproductive system.

Fallopian tubes are the pair of slender ducts that connect the uterus to the region of each of the ovaries in female reproductive system. The instance that sperm penetrates the ovum, a special reaction occurs that immediately makes the ovum impervious to other sperms. Fertilization normally occurs during the brief time while the ovum passes through the fallopian tube, and it is most likely if intercourse occurs on the day of ovulation or during the five days before. If fertilization does not occur, the ovum and any sperm cell in the women's body will die. The sperms are absorbed by the woman's white blood cells and the ovum passes through the uterus and exits through the vagina.

The chances that a woman will become pregnant following intercourse vary from couple to couple depending on the fertility of the woman and the sperm production of the man. If we assume that both partners are healthy, the one variable that seems the most influential is the woman's age.

As the sperm enters the ovum, the protoplasm within the ovum begins to move and nuclear material (a pronucleus) with 23 chromosomes migrates to the center to meet the pronucleus and the 23 chromosomes of the sperm. Over the next 24 hours, the genetic material of two individuals "fuses" and is translated into a new living entity called "Zygote". The fertilized ovum, **the Zygote,** now has 46 chromosomes and will soon begin the process of division called **mitosis**. Fertilization or conception marks the beginning of pregnancy. Human development, therefore, begins with the impregnation of an ovum by a sperm.

3.3 SEX DETERMINATION OF THE CHILD

At the moment of conception, the 23 chromosomes from the sperm and the 23 from the mother's ovum form 23 pairs. Twenty-two pairs are autosomes- chromosomes-that are not related to sexual expression. The twenty-third pair are sex chromosomes-one from the father and one from the mother-that govern the baby's sex. Sex chromosomes are either X chromosomes or Y chromosomes. The sex chromosomes of every ovum is an X chromosome, but sperm may contain either an X or a Y chromosome. The Y chromosome contains the gene for maleness, called the SRY gene. When as ovum (X) is fertilized by an X-carrying sperm, the zygote formed is XX, a female. When an ovum (X) is fertilized by a Y-carrying sperm, the resulting zygote is XY, a male.

3.4 DETERMINING PREGNANCY

Premarital examinations of both men and women contemplating marriage and also thorough preconceptual physical examination of both partners are mandatory. Every married woman should be aware of the probable signs of pregnancy so that she gets to know when she becomes pregnant or when she can suspect pregnancy; she should consult a physician for confirmation. The early detection and official diagnosis of pregnancy is very important in safeguarding the health and well-being of both mother and child. Medical personnel use three distinct categories of pregnancy criteria.

(1) **Presumptive Symptoms of Pregnancy:** These symptoms include that a pregnancy has been initiated but also may reveal the existence of other conditions. They are,

- *Failure to experience the anticipated menstrual period:* If the married woman who has previously menstruated regularly does not menstruate for more than 10 days beyond the expected date, she has good reason to suspect that she is pregnant, although this is by no means a positive proof that she is pregnant.
- *Morning sickness:* Some women, usually about two weeks after the first missed menstrual period, may have nausea without vomiting for a few hours in the morning and some may even actually vomit. This is commonly known as morning sickness. However, this sign, unless it is accompanied by other symptoms may be of no diagnostic value.
- *Abnormal fatigue and need for great amounts of sleep:* Extreme fatigue is sometimes another symptom of early pregnancy.
- *Frequent urination and/ or bladder irritability:* Due to the stretching of the base of the bladder by the growing uterus, there may be an increased frequency in the desire to urinate. This causes a sensation like that of a full bladder. However, frequent urination is also a sign of some nervous tension, it cannot by itself be considered a sign of pregnancy. It is the first additional evidence.
- *Alteration of skin pigment around the nipples of the breast:* About the second month there is an increase in the size and firmness of her breasts and the greater prominence of the veins of the breast. The nipple becomes darker and more prominent, and the areolas (the dark circles around the nipples) increase in size and also become darker.
- *Softening of the cervix*
- *Tingling sensation or pain in the breasts:* There is often a pricking or tingling sensation in the breasts even before they increase in size. Sometimes they become very tender soon after conception and may remain so for some time. Change is more pronounced in women who are pregnant for the first time than in women who have had previous pregnancies.
- *Pattern of Basal Temperature:* This can serve as a possible sign of pregnancy. A level of 98.8 to 99.9 degree Fahrenheit, sustained for more than 16 days after ovulation is highly suggestive of pregnancy. Such a diagnosis is correct in at least 97% of cases.
- *Fluttering sensation in the lower abdomen (caused by movement of the fetus)*
- *Constipation*
- *Weight gain*

(2) **Probable Symptoms of pregnancy:** These indicate a greater-than-average chance of conception although they also could result from other conditions having similar symptoms. Such symptoms include

- Positive results of a laboratory test for pregnancy
- Abdominal enlargement: By the end of the 3rd month the women may be aware of the enlargement of the abdomen and feel softness just above the pubic bone.
- Uterine changes/enlargement:
- Uterine contraction (painless or with a sensation of tightening and pressure).

(3) **Positive Signs of pregnancy:** These indicate the definite existence of a growing fetus and are not usually present until the 4th month after conception. These symptoms include:

- *Fetal Heart Sounds*: Detection of the fetal heart beat is an absolute sign of pregnancy. The sound can be detected by the doctor with his stethoscope, or sometime by placing his ear against the abdomen around mid of 5th month.
- *Fetal movements within the uterus:* This constitutes a positive sign of pregnancy and may be felt fairly early in the 5th month.
- *Presence of a fetal skeleton as shown by X-ray:* Occasionally, X-ray is used in diagnosing pregnancy. However, since the skeleton of the fetus rarely shows up before the middle of the 4th month, this test is usually not necessary and is rarely used. Legally, any one of these three is acceptable as a positive sign of pregnancy.

Since none of the above symptoms is a definite proof of pregnancy, the woman must see her physician for his expert opinion.

Pelvic Examination: The physician will conduct a simple painless pelvic examination. He will inspect the mucous membrane of the vagina, which is ordinarily pink in color like mucous membrane elsewhere in the body, but will take on a bluish cast in the first pregnancy. He will palpate the uterus to determine its size, shape and consistency.

Laboratory Diagnostic Tests: Laboratory diagnosis is used extensively to assist medical personnel in early detection of pregnancy. Most tests analyze for the presence of specific level of a hormone called "chorionic gonadotropin" which is found abundantly in the uterus of pregnant women. The tests are about 95% accurate. They are quickly and efficiently performed while being relatively economical in cost.

3.5 PRENATAL DIAGNOSTIC TESTS

It has become an accepted practice abroad to obtain medical tests to determine the normal development of a fetus. But people strongly disagree or object to abortion if the tests suggest that the fetus is likely to be born with a birth defect.

Amniocentesis: It is the most widely used prenatal medical procedure. It involves inserting a hollow needle into the abdomen to obtain a sample of "amniotic fluid" containing fetal cells. The fluid is withdrawn by syringe and tested to discover if the fetus is suffering from any chromosomal or metabolic disorders. Amniocentesis is performed between the 12th and 16th weeks of pregnancy. The earlier it is performed, the more useful it is in deciding whether a pregnancy should be terminated. One to more weeks are required for test results.

This procedure has some disadvantages. Firstly, it can be performed only in the second trimester of pregnancy, after the fetus is fairly well developed. Secondly, it results in fetal loss during the process of amniocenteses. Some of these fetuses are normal and would have survived if the test has not been done.

Ultrasound sonography: It is a prenatal medical procedure in which high-frequency sound waves are beamed at the uterus; their reflection is translated into a picture on a video screen that reveals the size, shape, structure and placement of the fetus. This procedure permits assessment of fetal age, whether growth is normal, detection of multiple pregnancies, and identification of gross physical defects indicated by an elevation of a feto-protein in the amniotic fluid. This technique can reveal disorders such as microcephaly, a form of mental retardation involving an abnormally small brain. Ultrasound sonography is often used to guide amniocentesis, chorionic villus sampling, and fetoscopy. When ultrasound sonography is used 5 or more times, the risk of low birth weight may be increased.

Chorionic villus sampling (CVS): Chorionic villus sampling is another test to detect the condition early in pregnancy. The test involves inserting a thin catheter into the uterus through the vagina , or a hollow needle is inserted through the abdominal wall. A small plug of tissue is removed from the end of one or more chorionic villi, the hair like projections on the membrane surrounding the developing organism. Cells are examined for genetic defects. It can be performed by the ninth week after conception, and results are available within 24 hours. Chorionic villi sampling helps one to decide whether abortion should be done near the end of the first trimester of pregnancy, a point when abortion is safer and less traumatic than after amniocentesis in the second trimester. Safer and simpler methods can be used to treat the fetus or the mother, if required. If no abnormality is detected, the couple's anxiety can be relieved earlier in the pregnancy.

The Maternal Blood test (alpha-fetoprotein-AFP): By the second month of pregnancy, some of developing organism's cells enter the maternal blood stream. The maternal blood test (AFP) is a prenatal diagnosis technique that is used to assess blood alpha-fetoprotein level. An elevated level of alpha-fetoprotein may indicate kidney disease, abnormal closure of the esophagus, or neural tube defects, such as anencephaly (absence of most of the brain) and spinal bifida (bulging of the spinal cord from the spinal column). Isolated cells can be examined for genetic defect, such as Down syndrome. This test is administered to women at 14 to 16 weeks into pregnancy, only when they are at risk of bearing a child with defects in the formation of the brain and spinal cord.

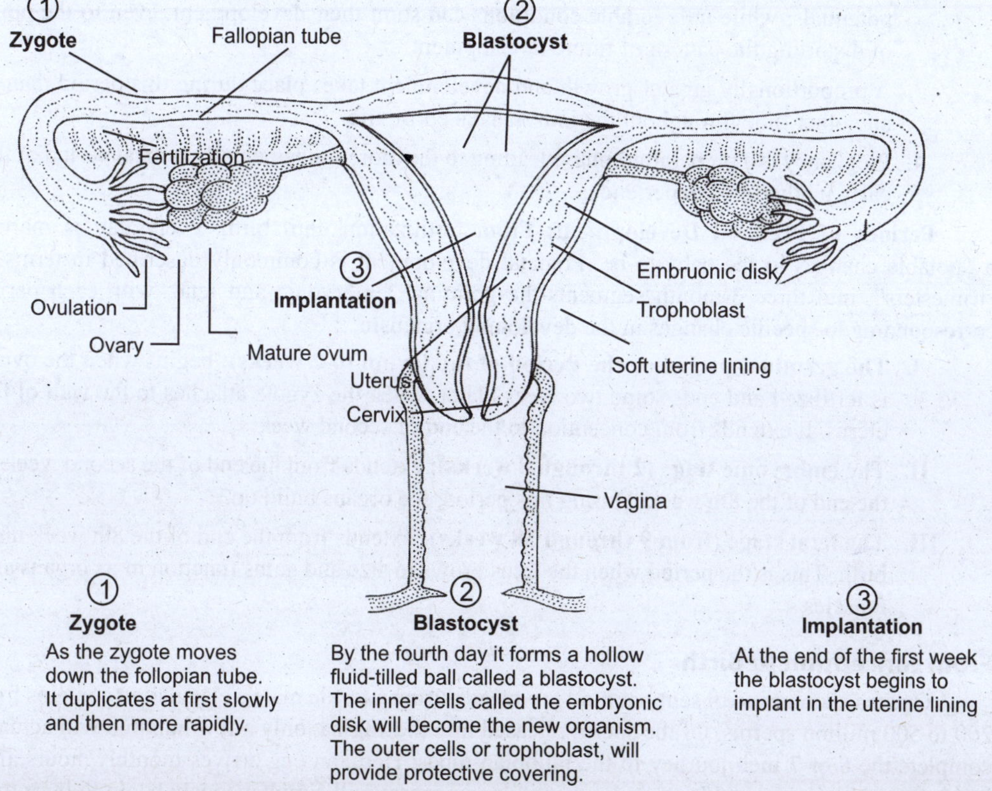

Fig. 3.1: Female reproductive organs, showing fertilization, early cell duplication, and implantation. (Adapted from K.L. Moore and T.V.N. Persaud, 2003, Before We Are Born, 6th ed., Philadelphia, Saunders, P. 36: Reprinted by permission of the publisher and authors.)

Fetoscopy: A small tube with a light source at one end is inserted into the uterus to inspect the fetus for defects of the limbs and face. It also allows a sample of fetal blood to be obtained, permitting diagnosis of such disorders as hemophilia and sickle cell anemia, or neural defects. It is usually performed between 15 and 18 weeks after conception, but can be done as early as five weeks. Entails some risk of miscarriage.

Preimplantation Genetic Diagnosis: After in vitro fertilization and duplication of the zygote into a cluster of about eight cells, one cell is removed and examined for hereditary defects. Only if that cell is free of detectable genetic disorders, is the fertilized ovum implanted in the woman's uterus. This permits parents at high risk of bearing offspring with a genetic disorder and women of advanced childbearing age to avoid implantation of the most abnormal embryos.

3.6 PRENATAL DEVELOPMENT

Every living organism begins life as a single cell. The first major and the shortest developmental stage in the life span of human being is the prenatal period, which is the period between conception and birth. The many changes that transform the fertilized egg into a newborn human are known as Prenatal Development. This period normally extends to about 266 days or 280 days from the pregnant woman's last menstrual period or to nine calendar or 10 lunar months (of 28 days each).

The prenatal period is important for four reasons:

1. The hereditary endowment which serves as the foundation for later development is determined once and for all, at this time
2. Favorable conditions in the mother's body can foster the development of hereditary potentials, while unfavorable conditions can stunt their development, even to the point of distorting the pattern of future development.
3. A proportionally greater growth and development takes place during this period than at any other time throughout the individual's entire life
4. Pregnancy is a preparatory phase leading to the more fundamentally critical period of the early motherhood experience.

Periods of Prenatal Development: From fertilization until birth, every day is marked by notable changes in the baby-to-be. Prenatal development is commonly described in terms of "trimesters", into three 3-month segments-the germinal, embryonic and fetal, with each period corresponding to specific changes in the developing organism.

I. **The germinal period or the Period of the Ovum (0-2 weeks):** begins when the ovum is fertilized and ends some two weeks later, when the zygote attaches to the wall of the uterus. It extends from conception to the end of second week.

II. **The embryonic stage (2 through 8 weeks):** extends from the end of the second week to the end of the 8th week. During this period, the organs build up.

III. **The fetal stage (from 9 through 38 weeks):** extends from the end of the 8th week until birth. This is the period when the fetus grows in size and gains function in its organs and muscles.

From conception to Birth

One tea spoon or so of seminal fluid produced during a fertile male's ejaculation contains from 200 to 500 million sperms. Of the sperm released into the vagina, only a few hundred will actually complete the 6 or 7 inch journey to the fallopian tubes. Here, an egg arrives monthly, hours after it is released by an ovary. If an egg is present, many sperm will simultaneously begin to bury their way through the cluster of nurturing cells that surround the egg. When one sperm finally penetrates the cellular wall of the egg, chemical changes occur in the wall immediately, blocking out all other sperms. Then the nuclei of the egg and sperm fuse and the two independent sets of 23 chromosomes are interchanged. The development of a new human being is under way.

I . The Period of the Ovum: The period of ovum is characterized by the (i) growth of the zygote after fertilization, and (ii) establishment of a linkage between the zygote and the mother's support system. It is a critical period for the developing fetus.

During the entire two weeks of this period, the zygote remains practically unchanged in size because it receives little or no nourishment from outside. It has been kept alive by the nourishment it received from the yolk of the ovum. By the time it reaches the uterus, the size of the zygote is about that of a pinhead. After fertilization, the zygote begins a 3-to-4 day journey down the fallopian tube toward the uterus by the action of the cilia and the active concentration of the walls of the oviduct. Cell division by mitosis begins within 36 hours after fertilization and continues even more rapidly. In mitosis, the zygote divides, forming 2 daughter cells called "blastomeres", which are identical in make-up to the original cell and then doubles to 4, 8, 16 and 32 in a geometrical progression. The early mitotic cell divisions in the development are called "cleavage". The first cleavage takes about 24 hours; each subsequent cleavage takes 10 to 12 hours. Since the daughter cells of the zygote are smaller than the original parent cell, the entire organism does not increase in size. Sixty hours after fertilization, a mulberry shaped 12-16-cell structure called "Morula" begins floating in the mother's fallopian tube, (Latin word meaning mulberry). In the Morula, the nucleus of each cell will contain the full complement of 23 pairs of chromosomes. These chromosome pairs are always identical to those formed at fertilization.

Types of twins

Sometimes the two cells that result from the first division of the zygote separate entirely, and instead of remaining in a single cluster, they may begin to form two separate zygotes which are called as. ***Identical twins*** *and their heredity is the same. The production of identical twins is unusual.*

The more common type of twins come from two separate eggs that have been fertilized by two separate sperms and. is called ***"fraternal or dizygotic"*** *twins; they are no more alike in hereditary characteristics than any other pair of brothers or sisters.*

Morula still has not changed in total size. No differentiation in cell appears at this point. The cells have merely decreased in size with each cleavage. Every time the cells divide they become smaller, allowing the total mass, called **"blastula"** to pass through the fallopian tubes. Until now, each cell is "totipotent" which means that, any cell, separated from others, can develop into a whole human infant. However, by the time, the morula has formed, the cells are no longer totipotent. Those on the inside of the berry are large while those on the outside are small. Specialization has begun. Floating slowly through the fallopian tube, the morula gently descends, to rest on the uterine wall about 4 days after fertilization.

Cell division soon converts the zygote into a hollow fluid-filled ball of cells termed as a **blastocyst,** a more thoroughly specialized and organized sphere of cells. This stage of development lasts for about a week after conception, until the sphere is implanted in the uterine wall. During the blastocyst period, cells begin to differentiate. As the blastocyst passes into the uterine cavity, fluid seeps in between the cells causing them to separate into 2 parts:

(1) an outer layer called "trophoblast" which will eventually form into the accessory tissues which protect and nourish the individual during prenatal development, and

(2) an inner cell mass or "embryonic disk" which will turn into the embryo and later the fetus.

The blasotocyst should continue to develop and travel into the uterus. The blastocyst may float unattached in the uterus for approximately 48 hours. When a blastocyst remains trapped in the fallopian tube, the pregnancy is ectopic or tubal. An **"ectopic pregnancy"** is dangerous and will cause the mother, a great deal of pain. The blastocyst will have to be surgically removed or the fallopian tube will burst, causing hemorrhage.

While the fertilized ovum is completing its journey down the fallopian tube, the lining of the uterus is completing its preparation to receive the ovum. This preparation consists of an increase in the blood vessel and glandular systems of the wall so that it will be a soft, thick, cushion like structure in which the ovum can be embedded and receive nourishment.

This type of preparation occurs during each menstrual cycle and is brought about by the secretion of two hormones, **estrogen**, and **progesterone**.

Implantation

Once the zygote enters the uterus, it attaches itself to the uterine wall, and a series of complex connections between the zygote and the mother's body begin to form. The **trophoblast,** which is the external cellular layer of the blastocyst, produces fine spindle like structures that penetrate the uterine lining of the uterus or epithelium, and begins to develop nurturing connections with the mother's body. By about 10-12 days after conception, the trophoblast sends out tiny tendrils called chorionic villi that draw oxygen, nourishment and productive antibodies from the mother. Implantation usually occurs about ten days after fertilization. The implanting blastocyst releases an enzyme that literally makes a hole in the soft sponge tissue of the endometrium until it completely burrows itself in the uterine wall. At this time, the period of ovum comes to an end and the new individual ceases to be an independent free-floating organism and begins to establish a dependent relationship with the mother.

Period of the Embryo: This is the second stage of prenatal development wherein rapid changes occur from two to 8 weeks after conception. Period of the embryo begins from the time of the zygote's attachment to the uterine wall and forms additional layers of cells. All the essential features of the body, both external and internal are established at this time. During this period of the embryo, the cellular division continues and specialization occurs at a very rapid rate and life-support systems and organs appear. This specialization of cells becomes apparent as skin, hair, sensory organs, a cartilage skeleton, a nervous system, a digestive system, a circulatory system, and other internal organs.

Development proceeds according to two fundamental principles-both before and after birth; the "Cephalocaudal" principle dictates that development proceeds from the head, then trunk and then the lower extremities and the "Proximo-distal" principle, dictates that development proceeds from parts near the center of the body to outer ones- from mid-line of the body-spine, heart, and face-outward to shoulders, arms, legs, hands and feet. After the period of the embryo, the changes that occur are in actual or relative size to the functioning of the parts of the body already formed, rather than in the appearance of new features.

Two weeks after conception, the embryonic disk folds and forms the distinct layers of cells called an embryo. Its inner cell mass that will become a recognizable embryo begins to differentiate itself into three distinct layers:

- the ectoderm (outer layer), from which will develop the epidermis or outer layer of the skin, the hair, the nails, parts of the teeth, skin glands, sensory cells and the nervous system (brain, spinal cord nerves, sense organs and skin).
- the mesoderm (middle layer), from which will develop the dermis or inner skin layer, the muscles, skeleton, and the circulatory and excretory organs.
- the endoderm (inner layer), from which will develop the lining of the entire gastrointestinal

tract, the Eustachian tubes, trachea, bronchia, lungs, liver, pancreas, salivary glands, thyroid glands, and thymus.

Accessory Apparatus: While the inner cell mass is being differentiated into a recognizable embryo, the outer layers of cells that separated from the inner layer shortly after implantation now develops into the accessory apparatus, the embryo's life-support system which will protect and nourish the embryo until the time of birth. These consist of the placenta, umbilical cord and amniotic sac. Both the umbilical cord and placenta maintain the connection with the mother's body through which the embryo obtains nutrients and expels wastes.

Placenta: The placenta develops where the zygote has embedded itself in the uterine wall at the time of implantation. It is a pie-shaped multipurpose organ, connected to the embryo through the pulsating umbilical cord, which eventually grows to be about an inch thick and 8 to 10 inches in diameter. It has a vein that carries oxygen, sugars, fats, rudimentary proteins and minerals to the embryo while two arteries carry waste products, carbon dioxide and urea from the embryo, eventually to be disposed by the mother's lungs and kidneys. The embryo receives oxygen, water, immunities to some disease (e.g., measles, polio and hepatitis) and nutrients (e.g., measles sugars, fats and proteins) from the mother across membranes in the placenta. The placenta also helps to combat internal infections against various diseases. It produces the hormones that support pregnancy, prepare the mother's breasts for lactation and eventually stimulate the uterine contractions that will expel the embryo from the mother's body .

Through the placenta, the blood vessels of both the mother and embryo are brought into close contact and they do not actually mix, but oxygen, nutrients and waste pass between them through the thin capillary walls of the embryo. The placenta screens out some harmful substances including most bacteria, but viruses, gases and many drugs pass through the placenta from the mother to the embryo.

The Umbilical Cord: The umbilical cord is developed from the placenta and is attached, at the other end, to the abdominal wall of the embryo. It is a rope like structure containing blood vessels but no nerves; the umbilical cord eventually becomes the thickness of a man's finger and measures 10 – 20 inches in length. The umbilical cord consists of major blood vessels that pass through the placenta en route to and from the mother's body. The placenta consists of a number of semi permeable membranes that allow only molecules of relatively small size to pass. For this reason, the red blood cells of the mother and those of the unborn infant never mix prior to birth. This separation of blood is essential because the mother's blood type may be different from – and incompatible with – that of the embryo. Moreover, as the nutrients and wastes can pass through the placental barrier, a shared bloodstream is unnecessary.

The Amniotic Sac: The third form of accessory apparatus to develop during the period of embryo is the amniotic sac, made up of four membranes and attached to the placenta. Placenta expands to form a balloon like sac, the amniotic sac, inside which the embryo grows. The sac is filled with a watery fluid, the amniotic fluid, in which the embryo develops. It encases the developing baby, serves as a shock absorber for the floating embryo and keeps the walls of the uterus from restricting continued development. It also keeps the temperature of the prenatal environment constant and serves to prevent adhesions between the embryo and the amniotic membrane. The outer layer of this protective "bag of waters" is called the chorion; the inner membrane, the amnion. These two membranes, together with a third membrane derived from the uterine wall of the mother (the deciduas capsularis), extend from the wall of the uterus and enclose the developing embryo.

There are no direct neural connections between the maternal and embryonic nervous systems; only chemicals can cross the placental barriers. However, a mother's emotional state may indirectly influence the physiological function of her baby.

In the 3rd and 4th weeks after conception, the cells of the pea-sized embryo multiply rapidly and organize themselves into functional units. A neural groove is formed, from which the brain, the spinal cord, and the nerves will eventually develop. At about 22 days, the muscular system also forms, and the nerves and muscle cells then form the heart. The heart develops into a tube and then into a chambered pump. A system for digesting food and kidney-like structures begin to form. All these developments take place according to a master plan.

In the 5th week, the buds that will become arms and legs appear. Growth of the brain is faster than that of all of the other body parts. By the 6th week, the head is bent over the abdominal bulge. The heart and circulatory system, lungs and respiratory system, liver, pancreas, kidneys, genitals, nervous system, mouth, stomach, and intestines will undergo very rapid development. A hand with webbed fingers appears. By the 7th week, the fingers are all clearly visible and toes appear. The head becomes more rounded and is supported by a neck area. The abdominal bulge and the umbilical cord become smaller. Development progresses during the second month, the head elevates, the neck emerges, and rudiments of the nose, eyes, mouth and tongue appear.

At the end of the first month, the embryo is about one-fifth of an inch long. At the end of the second month, many more changes have taken place. The length of the embryo has increased to about $1\frac{1}{2}$ inches from head to buttocks and it weighs about $1\frac{1}{3}$ ounce. By the end of the embryonic period, the embryo has developed arms, legs, fingers, toes, face, and a heart that beats, a brain, lungs and all of the major organ systems. At this point, it is called a fetus rather than an embryo. Since all the organ systems have been started in the second month, the individuals have achieved a degree of completeness that marks the "fetal stage". The fetus appears to be clearly human in appearance, although the head area is so large that it makes up about half of length of the fetus. By the end of the eighth week, the organism definitely resembles a human being. The fetus now builds on this basic form.

The embryonic stage is a critical period as all the organs and the body structures develop. If organs like the heart, eyes, lungs, arms and legs do not form now, then they will never develop. The embryonic cells are particularly susceptible to their environment during this stage of development, which poses both serious risk and great biological advantage. The risk is that the embryo is vulnerable to abnormal development if it is exposed to radiation, toxins or infections during this critical period. The advantage is that the embryo is also very responsive to chemical message from genes and other cells that organize the sequence of specialized cell development.

Period of the Fetus (from 9 through 38 weeks)

The final and longest phase of prenatal development, the "Period of the fetus", begins at the end of the 8th week or second month of gestation and ends with birth. Fetus is a French term for "pregnant" or "fruitful". Technically an embryo is called a fetus when the first bone cell appears. Since the differentiation of tissue into various bodily organs and systems occur during the embryonic phase of development, the fetal period is largely one of structural refinement and proper organ positioning for most body systems. Few new structures appear. Cartilage formed in the late phase of the embryo is now in part converted into the bone mass.

During the early fetal period, growth is accomplished chiefly through a continuous process of mitosis, but in the later fetal months it results primarily from increase in size of the individual cells rather than from formation of new cells. Structures such as the nervous system, glands, skeleton, muscles and sense organs reach a much higher degree of development by the time of normal birth. The fetus is less susceptible than the embryo to internal and external injuries to its organs, since the vital organs have usually passed their critical period.

Fetus at 12 weeks (3rd month)

About fifteen weeks after conception, the pituitary gland begins secretion of somatotrophin- the growth hormone regulating many differentiation processes in the body. Significant hormones regulating metabolic and growth patterns begin. During the fetal stage (after the eighth week), the body begins to lengthen rapidly. At the end of the 3rd month, the fetus is about three inches long and weighs about three ounces. During this stage, the fetus is capable of breathing movements, sucking movements, and head turning. As the fetus is very small, the mother does not feel fetal kicking and head turning.

One of the most interesting events that occur during the second and early part of the third month is sex differentiation. During this period, the external genitals develop. Up to about 5 weeks, the fetus has undifferentiated sex gonads. Toward the end of the 8th week, the reproductive system begins to develop. The gonads (the ovaries and the testes) initially appear as a pair of blocks of tissues in both sexes. In the case of the male, genetic action on the Y male sex chromosome causes the fetal gonads to produce the male sex hormone androgen. As a result, the previously undifferentiated sex gonads become male testes. In the case of the female, as there is no Y chromosome (females are XX), there is no production of androgen by the undifferentiated sex gonads. At about the tenth week, the gonads become ovaries.

Until about $8\frac{1}{2}$ weeks, the fetus has led a relatively passive existence, floating quietly in the amniotic fluid. Muscles become well-developed and spontaneous movements of the arms and legs may be observed. The nervous system is still very incomplete. However, at this time, the fetus becomes capable of responding to tactile (touch) stimulation. The trunk flexes, the head extends. From this point on, motor functions become increasingly more differentiated and complex.

In the third month after conception, the fetus's eyelids form and are sealed shut. The roof of the mouth closes. The fetus digests amniotic fluid, excretes urine from functioning kidneys and breathes fluid in and out of its lungs. A male fetus develops a penis, nerves connect to muscles, and the fetus begins to make reflexive kicking, darting and dodging movements. Toes now curl, thumb opposes to fingers, head turns, mouth opens and closes and swallows and the fetus can suck his or her thumb. Earlier, the fetus which has responded to stimulation with the whole body now can move and respond with specific parts.

By the end of the first trimester (one- third of length of pregnancy or 12.7 weeks), most major organs are present, a large head and face are well formed, and a heart beat can be detected with a stethoscope. During the third month, the arms and legs lengthen and nails grow on the finger and toes. Feet, vocal cords and ear have appeared. The external sex organs can be easily differentiated; the head is extremely large in proportion to the remainder of the body

Fetus at 16th week (4th month)

By the end of the 4th month, the fetus has grown to 6 inches in length and from $3\frac{1}{2}$ to 4 to 7 ounces. At this time, a growth spurt occurs in the body's lower parts. Prenatal reflexes are stronger. It grows faster than in any other month. Now the mother can sense "quickening", the first perceptible movements of the stronger, larger fetus kicking against her abdomen.

At this time, we find the continued development of movements, including sucking, head turning, and a variety of limb, foot and hand movements. The skin of the fetus is covered with a fine hair, usually shed before birth. By the fourth month, the head is erect on the neck, the external ears are formed and stand out from the head and the legs are well developed. Stronger neck muscles and a bonier skeleton helps support the fetus with even more human-looking head. Finger and footprints have formed on the tiny touch pads of palms and soles. A female fetus develops inner and outer genitals-uterus, vagina and associated structures.

Meanwhile the placenta has begun to produce most of the hormones that prepare the mother's body for producing milk and the infection-fighting substances to protect the fetus. The mouth becomes capable of protrusion and closing, a precursor of later sucking movements. Blinking of the eyes occurs, although the lids are still tightly closed. The hands become capable of gripping in addition to closing.

By the end of the fourth month, eyebrows and eyelashes start appearing. It now opens and closes its fists, moves its thumb independently and even sucks its thumb. Only this specific area will respond to touch stimulation and facial expression will change when cheeks are touched. The heart is now pumping 25 quarts of blood/day. The placenta has begun to produce enough progesterone to maintain pregnancy. Antibodies of the mother reach the fetus through placenta. These antibodies will protect the new born against certain diseases during the first month of life. Later additional protection will be gained from mother's milk.

Fetus at 20 Weeks (5th Month)

The 5th month is the midpoint of the pregnancy. The baby has grown considerably, weighs from one half to one pound, and is about one foot in length. Blood cell formation in the fetus bone marrow commences. The skin is fully developed. Hair and nails appear and sweat glands are developed. By the fifth month, fetus occupies the entire uterine cavity. The expanding uterus pushes the mother's other internal organs. Therefore, she needs to urinate more often and is able to eat less food at one time. The mother typically begins to "show" her pregnancy during this month as the abdominal walls expand outward to accommodate the developing baby.

The fetus bounds and turns in the fluid-filled uterus. The mother feels periods of quietness as the fetus sleeps or rests-between periods of wakeup activity. The fetus sheds old cells and develops new ones. These dead skin cells mix with fat from the oil glands and covers the body with a protective cheesy substance called "vernix". Vernix will cover and protect the skin, keeps the fetuses skin supple as it floats in mineral-rich amniotic fluid, a very "hard water". The internal organs have assumed positions. The fetus has period of sleep and wakefulness and may even hiccup.

Fetus at 24 Weeks (6th month)

Now the fetuses' eyes are completely formed and taste buds appear on the tongue. Intestine descends into the abdomen. Cartilage continues to turn into bone. Development of six layers of cells in cerebral cortex-the part of the brain responsible in adults for complex conscious thought-is completed. The fetus can reflexively grasp, breathe, swallow, hiccup and taste. The fetus needs to be kept warm as it lacks fat under the sensitive skin. During the sixth month, several interesting changes occur. The fetus may now weigh 2 pounds and is about 14 inches long. Vigorous and frequent fetus movements make the mother well aware of the life within her. The fetus can make irregular breathing movement; and it has a fairly well developed grasping reflex.

At the end of the 6th month, eyes, eyelids and eyelashes form. The fetus opens and closes the eyelids for the first time (previously the eyelids had been fused shut) and moves its eyes around. The fetuses eyes are light sensitive and he or she can hear uterine sounds and respond to vibrations and acoustical stimulation. The body is lean but strikingly human in proportions, and the skin is wrinkled. The fetus now is still a vulnerable creature barely equipped to survive outside the womb. Also at 24 weeks, a healthy fetus reaches the "age of viability", meaning it now has about 50% chance of servival outside the uterus if given high- quality intensive care; although currently over half of the surviving fetuses born at 24 weeks have serious anomalies, by 22 to 28 weeks, most systems function well. By this age, the fetus has a distinctly baby-like look, but babies born this early have trouble breathing because their lungs are not yet mature.

In the next three months, rapid development continues and the bones begin to form. The first bone to form is the breastbone. As the bones form, they soon contain enough calcium for X-rays to reveal a skeleton consisting of 222 bones. Because of the rapid rate of bone growth, mothers need more than the ordinary amounts of calcium. During the last 3 months of pregnancy, the brain grows at a particularly rapid rate. Though pregnancy in general requires solid nutrition, fetal brain development in particular requires proper nourishment.

Fetus at 28 Weeks (7th month)

By this time, the child's nervous, circulatory and other bodily systems are sufficiently well structured to function adequately in the extra-uterine life, although special care is required. Sensitivity of the fetus develops later than mobility. Cutaneous reactivity and especially the pain reaction are slow to unfold during the prenatal period. The temperature senses are well developed. There is a stronger reaction to stimuli that are warmer than to colder stimuli. The gustatory sense is well developed, and the taste buds are more widely distributed in the fetus than in an adult, being found not only on the tongue but also on the hard palate, the tonsils, and parts of the esophagus. Basic odors and tastes such as sweet, salt, sour and bitter can be differentiated by the fetus. The olfactory sense is well developed before birth and functions immediately after birth. Both full-term and prematurely born infants react differently to sweet and salt and to sour and bitter. Although the senses of sight and hearing are less developed before birth than most other senses, pupillary reflexes such as reactions to a beam of light, occur in the prematurely born. In the seventh month, the fetus's eye can distinguish light from dark. Reactions to changes in temperatures approximate those of the full-term infant. Occasionally a fetus born around the 26th to 29th week can survive. However, the mortality rate is high because the respiratory system is not yet adequately developed to support life outside the uterus.

Many reflexes, including sucking and grasping, are established. During the seventh month, the testes of most male fetuses begin to descend into the scrotum from the abdominal cavity, where, protected from the body's internal temperature, the sperm produced after puberty will be able to survive. The ova of the female fetus are already formed in the ovaries . At this time the fetus has proportion much like those of the average new born. By the end of this month it may weigh 3 pounds and 16 inches.

Fetus at 32 weeks (8th month)

In the eighth month of prenatal development, the fetus's body prepares for life outside the uterus. The head and body of the fetus become more proportionate during the third trimester.. By now, most of the organs are functioning. Therefore the fetus gains up to about 8 ounces per week. At eight months, it weighs 4 to 5 pounds and is 17 to 18 inches long. For fetuses weighing 3 pounds or more, the chances of survival outside the uterus increase to 85 percent. The lungs are still immature, the alveoli, or tiny air sacs in them, not prepared to turn oxygen into carbon dioxide. The fetus's digestive and immune systems are also immature. However, under the skin, a vital layer of insulating fat is deposited around the body; the fetus gains an additional 2 pounds. This fat increases the fetus's chances of survival outside the womb.

In the eighth month, its neuromuscular activity increases. At this point, the nerve cells begin to function. As a result, the fetus begins to lurch, roll, startle, or lift his or her head in response to a loud or sharp noise. The fetus can be soothed by the mother's heartbeat and rhythmic walk and aroused into vigorous kicking by the sounds of television etc. Apparently, the fetus at this age can also learn. Research studies suggest that fetuses can hear voices while they are in the uterus.

The mother must adjust her posture to compensate for her abdominal burden. The fetus acquires most of its antibody from the mother during the last couple of months. It can now perform many of the activities that it will perform as a newborn. Some liquid passes through the digestive tract and the fetus urinates a little each day. It continues to move through late in pregnancy, and it is usually too cramped to turn completely around. It is usually resting in an upside-down position in the uterus, and this seems to be the best position for delivery. Nevertheless, it can really wallop the mother's abdominal wall with feet, head and elbows. In general, the fetus' movements are limited because of the increased size. Its growth rate also slows down in the last few weeks before birth and there are changes in placenta. The fetus is nearly ready to be born.

Fetus at 36-40 weeks (9th month)

During the end of eighth and ninth months of pregnancy, "the finishing touches" are added to the unborn child. The wrinkled skin of the fetus that makes it look like an elderly person begins to fill out with fat. At nine months, the dull redness of the skin fades into pink, and it becomes smoother and is covered with a protective waxy substance called vericaseosa; the limbs become rounded, and the fingernails and toenails are well formed. By the end of the ninth month, the nails have grown to the ends of the fingers and toes.

During this period, the movements of the fetus are active and sustained, muscle tone good, brief and erratic following of objects with eyes, in prone position attempts to lift head, definite periods of alertness felt, cries well when hungry and disturbed, hands held as fists, good grasp, and strong sucking reflex are found. At full term (40 weeks) the body is plump, the skin has lost most of its lanugo hair, although the body is still covered with vernix; and all the organs necessary to carry an independent life are functioning. By 40 weeks, the fetus is ready to be born, and a new phase of development begins. At full-term of birth, the infant is about 20 inches or 50 centimeters long and on an average weighs 7 pounds 4 ounces, or about 3,300 grams.

In the last two months of gestation the fetus rapidly accumulate fat deposits. The fatty tissues give the fetus a plump smooth look. The fetus is usually expelled from the uterus about 38weeks (nine months or 266days) after conception The baby gains about one-half pound per week from this time until birth. The brain of a full-term infant is one-fourth of the adult human brain, which still makes it relatively large for the size of the infant when compared to the infant's other organs that are about 1/20 of the size and weight of adult organs. By the end of the ninth month all intrauterine development has been completed. The baby is now ready to enter the world.

3.7 HAZARDS DURING PRENATAL DEVELOPMENT

(i) Period of the Zygote

1. **Death of Zygote:** The zygote may die before it becomes lodged in the uterine wall, if it has too little yolk to keep it alive, or if it remains so long in the tube that the yolk is used up.
2. **Implantation may not take place:** When there is glandular imbalance, between the function of the mother's pituitary gland and the ovaries, the walls of the uterus do not prepare themselves to receive the zygote. Hence, the zygote disintegrates and is washed out of the body with the next menstrual flow.
3. **Wrong implantation:** The zygote may become implanted in the wrong place, such as a small fibroid tumor or the wall of the fallopian tube, where it cannot get nourishment and as a result, it will die.
4. **Ectopic Pregnancy:** It occurs when the fertilized ovum attaches and grows in an area other than within the uterus, such as fallopian tubes, ovary, abdomen or cervix. Such pregnancies have to be terminated by surgery. Studies indicate that the number of ectopic pregnancies are increasing due to the following probable causes: postponement of childbearing, which causes the fallopian tubes to age (2) previous abortion;(3) pelvic inflammatory disease (PID) (4) sexually transmitted diseases (STDs); (5) frequent douching with commercial preparations; and (6) previous surgery. Any condition that affects the fallopian tubes can impede transport of the fertilized ovum, thus contributing to an ectopic pregnancy.
5. **RH Incompatibility:** This involves an expectant mother with Rh-negative blood who carries a fetus with Rh-positive blood. Initial prenatal examination will reveal Rh incompatibility. The Rh factor is a protein found in the blood. Because some of the

baby's red blood cells cross the placenta and enter the mother's bloodstream during pregnancy and delivery, an Rh-negative mother will develop antibodies to the blood cells from Rh-positive baby. If she has another Rh-positive baby(next baby), the antibodies in her blood will pass through the placenta and destroy the (next) baby's red blood cells, possibly causing jaundice, anemia, mental retardation and even death.

(ii) Period of the Embryo

1. **Miscarriages:** Falls, emotional shocks, malnutrition, glandular disturbances, and other unknown causes may dislodge the embryo from its place in the uterine wall, thus resulting in a miscarriage or spontaneous abortion. Although it is true that a certain percentage of miscarriages come from the elimination of the unfit, most are the results of other causes. Other proved causes are amount of progesterone insufficiency, shortage of the thyroid hormone, insufficiency of Vitamin E, pronounced malnutrition or starvation and serious diseases such as pneumonia, smallpox, diphtheria, german measles and diabetes.

   For reasons yet unknown, female embryos have a better chance of survival than male. When miscarriage is due to a defective zygote, it usually occurs early in the prenatal period. If, on the other hand, it is due to some unfavorable condition in the prenatal environment, it generally comes between the tenth and eleventh weeks after conception.

2. **Spontaneous abortions:** Spontaneous abortions are most apt to occur either at implantation or during the embryonic period. They usually occur because there is faulty development in one of the critical organ systems. This can be viewed as nature's way of protecting the species from aberrations. The spontaneous abortion rate may be as high as 40% of all pregnancies. When the pregnancy is unwanted, or if the couple comes to know that the baby may be born deformed due to unfavorable prenatal environment, they may opt for voluntary abortion.

   Almost 90% of miscarriages occur primarily during the first trimester, by 12 or 13 weeks, and miscarriages beyond 20 weeks are rare. Early miscarriages are often caused by genetic defects that result in inadequate development of the placenta, the umbilical cord or the embryo itself, or by unsuccessful implantation. However, maternal age, health, and nutrition are also risk factors as are exposure to some toxic substances, such as X-ray radiation or disease that can be passed from mother to fetus. Fathers who have been exposed to chemicals, radiation or other potentially toxic effects may also contribute to the risk of miscarriage.

3. **Developmental irregularities:** Developmental irregularities of minor or major seriousness are most likely to occur during the period of the embryo when the different characteristics of the body are in the process of formation. Though tiny, the embryo's rapidly developing cells are highly susceptible to oxygen-deprivation, toxins, and viral agents. It is during the first trimester that almost all developmental defects-the cleft palates, missing limbs, blindness and monstrosities, which appear at birth, occur. It has been found out that structural abnormalities may be the result either of a good egg in a bad environment or a bad egg in a good environment. Cleft palate and harelip, which formerly were believed to be hereditary, have recently been demonstrated to be caused by glandular change in the maternal blood stream due to severe emotional stress on the part of the mother within the eighth and twelfth weeks of pregnancy, the period during which the upper jawbone of the human embryo forms.

When some foreign agent changes the rate of development, the course of growth in the different parts of the organism is altered and abnormalities result. If the mother develops a case of rubella during the first three or four months of pregnancy, such defects as blindness, deafness, anomalies in the structure of the heart, microcephaly or mental deficiency may result in her offspring. It is known that irradiation therapy by deep X ray or radium during pregnancy affects the developing embryo and causes deformities. Glandular deficiencies, as in the case of thyroid deficiency, which causes cretinism, deformities of physical structure, and mental deficiency, also play an important role in producing monsters. Harmful drugs when taken in the first trimester of pregnancy and serious malnutrition can affect the developing brain of the embryo unfavorably as can intense and prolonged maternal stress.

(iii) Period of the Fetus

1. **Miscarriages:** There is always the possibility of a miscarriage up to the fifth month of pregnancy, with the most vulnerable times when the woman's menstrual period would normally occur. With each passing week, voluntarily ending pregnancy by an abortion becomes increasingly difficult and dangerous as the fetus becomes more firmly attached to the uterine wall.
2. **Prematurity:** Normally, the fetus has reached a state of development by the end of the seventh lunar month, which makes survival possible, should birth occur at that time. This is known as the age of viability. By the end of the next month, the fetal body is completely formed though smaller in size than the body of the normal, full-term infant. The chances of survival, should birth occur then, are greatly increased. Sometimes, even those fetuses who weigh less than the borderline size (premature) between viability and nonviabilty -2 pounds 3 ounces-do survive, but their chances are less than those of heavier fetuses, and their chances of malformation are greater. Approximately 50 percent more male fetuses die if born prematurely than is true of female.
3. **Complications of Delivery:** The ease or difficulty of childbirth has been found to be influenced by prenatal conditions, especially those existing during the period of the fetus. Of these conditions, maternal attitudes are reported to be the most detrimental. Maternal anxiety during pregnancy tends to lead to birth complications by affecting uterine contractions. As a result, labor time is longer and the chances of complications greater because the fetus must often be delivered by instruments. Furthermore, anxiety often leads to weight gain in pregnancy which further complicates birth.

   Pregnant women whose attitudes toward sex and pregnancy are rated negatively, and whose marital adjustments are rated negatively have been reported to have the greatest complications, not only during childbirth but also during the entire pregnancy period. Theses unfavorable attitudes carry over and affect the fetus's adjustment to postnatal life.
4. **Developmental Irregularities:** Markedly unfavorable conditions in the prenatal environment will have their effect on the developing fetus. Unfavorable conditions in the prenatal environment will retard fetal development, as in the case of cretins, whose physical and mental developments are deformed because of thyroid and pituitary deficiencies. Since growth is most rapid during the period of the fetus, and if the mother suffers from grave malnutrition, serious damage may be done to the fetus in the form of general physical weakness, rickets, nervous instability, mental deficiency, or a host of other physical abnormalities. Deficiency of vitamins C, B-6 or B-12, D, K, and E in the mother's diet during pregnancy has been found to lead to rickets, scurvy, and stillbirths.

The Rh blood factor or any diseased condition of the mother which affects her general metabolism, such as syphilis, gonorrhea, tuberculosis, diabetes, or toxins in the bloodstream may produce physical defects, mental deficiency, prematurity of birth, or stillbirths.The use of drugs, especially barbiturates and other "pain killers" prior to delivery may affect the oxygen supply to the fetal brain and cause brain damage of major or minor importance. If X-ray is used for therapeutic purposes when greater strength is needed, it may cause damage to the fetal brain, which results in mental deficiency.

3.8 FACTORS INFLUENCING PRE-NATAL DEVELOPMENT

On considering the prenatal environment in the mother's body, virtually everything that impinges on her well-being, from her diet to her moods, may alter her unborn child's environment and affect its growth. The individual is exposed to a number of factors prior to birth that can influence the quality of prenatal development positively or adversely. From the time before fertilization to that of birth, the mother's conditions psychologically, physically, and socially serve as the total environment for the developing organism. If she is healthy, comfortable, and happy in all these areas and receives proper prenatal medical care, the chances are overwhelming that she will have a healthy baby. By discussing prenatal factors that may influence the embryo and the fetus detrimentally, we are trying to increase the chances for giving birth to a strong baby.

3.8.1. Maternal Factors

(i) Maternal Nutrition

Maternal nutrition and health of the pregnant women are important factors influencing the well-being of the fetus as well as that of the mother and also the course of subsequent pregnancies. The expectant mother who regularly eats the right foods before and during pregnancy is more likely to have a normal pregnancy and less likely to have complications during birth than one who does not. Minimal requirements of proper daily diet include the three different kinds of essential building materials; (i) proteins for the growth and repair of the body, (ii) minerals and vitamins for growth and keeping the body in good working condition, and (iii) fats and carbohydrates for energy.

Pregnant women typically need 300 to 500 additional çalories a day, including extra protein. Those who gain 26 pounds or more pounds are less likely to bear babies whose weight at birth is dangerously low. Low birth weight (under 5½ pounds) is often associated with death, brain and central nervous system damage, and mental retardation. However, desirable weight gain depends on individual factors, such as weight and height before pregnancy.

Malnutrition during fetal growth may have long-range effects. Severe malnutrition of the mother increases infant mortality and results in small, underweight babies who tend to have fewer and smaller brain cells resulting in intellectual deficiencies. Dietary supplements, especially when combined with stimulating day care heal the damaging effect of prenatal malnutrition. If Vitamin-mineral supplementation is started early in pregnancy it can improve maternal health and prevent certain prenatal and birth complications.

When mothers do not consume adequate amounts of folic acid or foliate (a B vitamin), their babies are at risk for "spinabifida", a disorder in which the embryo's neural tube does not close properly during the first months of pregnancy resulting in permanent damage to the spinal cord and the nervous system. Many children with spinabifida need crutches, braces or wheel chairs. Women of childbearing age are urged to take foliate supplements and to include this vitamin in their diets by eating plenty of fresh fruits and vegetables even before becoming pregnant, since damage from folic acid deficiency can occur during the early weeks of gestation.

Other prenatal problems have also been traced to inadequate proteins, vitamins or minerals. However, certain vitamins (including A, B6, C, D, and K) can be harmful in excessive amounts. Iodine deficiency, unless corrected before the third trimester of pregnancy can cause cretinism, which may involve severe neurological abnormalities or thyroid problems. Malnourished women who take dietary supplements while pregnant tend to have bigger, healthier, more active and more visually-alert infants and women with low zinc levels who take daily zinc supplements are less likely to have babies with low birth weight and small head circumferences.

In summary, there is a direct and powerful connection between good nutrition before and during pregnancy and the unborn baby's life itself and its further physical and mental health. A woman generally does not need to increase her food intake considerably during pregnancy. Rather it is more important for her to eat a well-balanced, adequate diet of a variety of foods rather than increasing calories.

Nutritional Guidelines in Pregnancy

- Select foods from the Four Basic Food Groups
- 28-pound minimum weight gain
- Gradual, steady gain in weight
- 30 to 60 milligrams of elemental iron supplement daily
- 400 to 800 micrograms of elemental zinc supplement daily
- No weight-reduction diets
- No sodium restriction unless ordered by the physician
- No diuretics unless ordered by physician
- Iodized salt (if deserved)

[*Source: Corruccini C.G & Cruskie P.E,* 1975]

(ii) Exercise

In healthy physically fit women, regular moderate exercise such as walking, swimming, biking, or an aerobic workout is related to increased birth weight. Regular exercise prevents constipation and improves respiration, circulation, muscle tone and skin elasticity, all of which contribute to a more comfortable pregnancy and an easier safer delivery. However, pregnant women should avoid activities that could cause a high degree of abdominal trauma. However, every frequent vigorous exercise results in lower birth weight and long working hours also may be associated with a greater risk of premature birth.

(iii) Maternal Emotional State

Although most women are happy about conceiving a child, the fact remains that almost over half of the pregnancies are unplanned or unintentional. Even mothers who want babies are likely to experience at least some symptoms of anxiety and depression during their pregnancies. When a mother is emotionally aroused, her glands secrete powerful hormones such as adrenaline which may cross the placental barrier and enter the fetus's blood stream, which temporarily increases the fetuses' motor activity. However, a temporarily stressful experience such as falling will generally do not damage mother or fetus.

Stress refers to a person's physical and psychological response to threatening or challenging situations. Increased stress can harm prenatal development in several ways; First, when a pregnant woman experiences stress, her body secretes hormones that reduce the flow of oxygen to the fetus while increasing its heart rate and activity level. Second, stress can weaken a pregnant woman's immune system, making her more susceptible to illness, which in turn can damage fetal development. Third, pregnant women under stress are more likely to smoke or drink alcohol and are less likely to rest, exercise and eat properly. All these behaviors endanger prenatal development. Such mothers have to seek counseling. Severe emotional stress during pregnancy, such as anxiety, is associated with a high rate of miscarriage or spontaneous abortion, prematurity, prolonged and painful labor, premature delivery of low birth weight infant, respiratory illness, digestive disturbances, prenatal growth delays and certain physical defects, such as cleft palate and heart deformities in the fetus.

New born babies with records of high fetal activity as a result of severe and prolonged maternal tensions have a greater than normal rate of postnatal adjustment difficulties. Such infants tend to weigh less than the average baby, are more active, more finicky about eating, vomit more, are more diarrheic, cry more and squirm more. There is evidence of the possibility that wars and political crises may also be responsible for a variety of birth defects in new born.

(iv) Prescription and Non-Prescription Drugs Intake

Drugs taken by an expectant mother makes its way to the uterus and can enter the embryonic or fetal blood stream crossing the placenta, just as oxygen, carbon dioxide and water, causing harm. Vulnerability is greatest in the first few months of gestation, when development is most rapid. Surveys suggest that upto 60% of pregnant women take at least one prescription or more, over- the-counter drug during pregnancy, without consulting their doctors .

Today, nearly 30 drugs have been found to be teratogenic in clinically recommended doses. A teratogen is any disease, drug, or other environmental agent that can harm a developing fetus (for example, by causing deformities, blindness, brain damage or even death). Among them are the antibiotic tetracycline, certain barbiturates, opiates, and other central nervous system depressants, several hormones, certain anticancer drugs, and aspirin and other non-steroid anti-inflammatory drugs, which should be avoided during the third trimester.

A variety of agents have been linked to birth defects. Some cause death; some cause severe or mild disturbances, while others affect the weight of the infant or may injure the brain, which may not be discovered well into childhood. Effects of these agents may depend on such factors as the type of agent, dosage, time at which the fetus is exposed as well as on the genetic characteristic of the fetus. Certain antipsychotic drugs used for managing severe psychiatric disorders may have serious potential effects on the fetus, and withdrawal symptoms may occur at birth. It is advisable to taper off and then discontinue the use of such drugs as the delivery date approaches, or, if necessary, to prescribe the lowest dose possible.

(v) Caffeine

Coffee, tea, cola and cocoa, in limited quantities may not cause trouble for the fetus. On the other hand, heavy caffeine intake (more then 3-4 cups of coffee per day) is associated with low birth weight, miscarriage and newborn's withdrawal symptoms, such as irritability and vomiting. It may dramatically increase the risk of sudden death in infancy.

(vi) Nicotine (Tobacco)

The most well-known effect of smoking during pregnancy leads to low birth weight, prematurity, impaired heart rate and breathing during sleep, infant death and asthma and sometimes cancer. It also brings increased risks of prenatal growth retardation, miscarriage, infant death, and long-term cognitive and behavioral problems. Prenatally exposed youngsters have shorter attention span, poorer memories, lower mental test scores and more behavior problems in childhood and adolescence. Since women who smoke during pregnancy also tend to smoke after giving birth, it is hard to separate the effects of prenatal and postnatal exposure. Newborns whose mothers had smoked during pregnancy were shorter and lighter and had poorer respiratory functioning than babies of nonsmoking mothers. A mother's smoking during pregnancy also may increase her child's risk of cancer.

While examining the harmful effects of smoking on the fetus, it is revealed that nicotine, the addictive substance in tobacco, constricts blood vessels, lessens blood flow to the uterus, and causes the placenta to grow abnormally. This reduces the transfer of nutrients, so the fetus gains weight poorly. Also, nicotine raises the concentration of carbon monoxide in the blood stream of both mother and fetus. Carbon monoxide displaces oxygen from red blood cells, damaging the central nervous system and slowing down body growth in the fetuses of laboratory animals; "Passive smoking" (husbands, relatives, and co-workers use cigarettes) is also related to such problems.

(vii) Alcohol

Pregnant women who consume alcohol produce a cluster of symptoms dubbed "fetal alcohol syndrome" (FAS). Affected newborns have slow prenatal and postnatal growth, a small head, malformations of the heart, limbs, joints, body and face, disorders of the central nervous system and display excessive irritability, hyperactivity, seizures or tremors. Heavy drinkers, run a 30% or higher risk of having a child with FAS. Throughout childhood, slow information processing, short attention span, restlessness, irritability, hyperactivity, learning disabilities, retarded growth and motor impairments are common. As with heroin and cocaine, alcohol abuse is higher in poverty-stricken women. Therefore, no amount of alcohol is safe, and pregnant women should avoid it entirely.

(viii) Radiation

When mothers are exposed to radiation during pregnancy, additional harm can be caused to the embryo or fetus. Incidence of miscarriage, small head size (indicating an underdeveloped brain), physical deformities, and slow physical growth rise dramatically.

(ix) Maternal Infectious Diseases

Five percent of women catch an infectious disease while pregnant. Most of these illnesses, such as the common cold, seem to have no impact on the embryo or fetus. Several types of infectious diseases are transmitted by the mother, to the developing embryo through the placental membrane, and can infect the newborn during the birth process. The severity of influence of these various agents depends on when the disease is contracted by the mother. Among such illness are small pox, mumps, scarlet fever, chicken pox, as well as one of the major causes of severe birth defects, "rubella" or "German measles". The following table presents the common infections and their effects.

Table 3.1 Common infections and their effects.

S.No.	Infections	Effects
1.	Chicken pox	Physical malformations, mental retardation and low birth weight
2.	Hepatitis B	Abortion, neonatal hepatitis, increased incidence of abortion and premature labour.
3.	Influenza	Occasional association of congenital malformations, especially an encephaly.
4.	Malaria	Diminished growth, placental involvement.
5.	Mumps	Abortion, premature birth, or still birth which is uncommon.
6.	Rubella	Abortion, congenital malformation of heart, eye, ear, brain, dermato-glyphic abnormalities.
7.	Syphilis	Major cause of mid trimester, abortion, fetal death in uterus or premature labour and delivery, bone malformation
8.	Gonorrhea	Blindness in the newborn
9.	Tuberculosis	Small infants born to mothers with active disease congenital tuberculosis.
10.	AIDS	Weight loss, diarrhea and repeated respiratory illness, also brain damage

(x) Maternal Age

The safest time to bear a child appears to be from about age 17 or 18 to age 35. Women under 18 and over thirty-five have a higher probability of experiencing high-risk pregnancies. High-risk pregnancy is characterized by complications during the course of prenatal development and/or during birth in which the health and well-being of the child or mother are endangered.

One reason for increased rate of complications and fetal and infant mortality among teenage is that the reproductive system of the very young teen may not be physically mature enough to sustain a fetus and secondly, the teenagers do not receive prenatal care. However, if they receive appropriate prenatal care and medical treatment during the birth process, both teenage mothers and their babies usually are not at risk.

A variety of physical complications can be experienced in adolescent pregnancy. They are maternal toxemia and death; increase in the incidence of amnesia, postpartum infection and hemorrhage; prolonged and precipitate (too-quick) deliveries, and other complications. Social and psychological factors that place the single adolescent mother at risk during pregnancy and after delivery include interrupted education, lack of adequate prenatal care, reduced earning potential, improper nutrition, and interrupted physical and psychological development. The attributes to many of these psychological complications could be race, marital status, unsuspected infection, self-induced abortion attempts, endocrine disorders, reproductive-tract abnormalities, and disadvantageous psychological and socio-economic conditions.

The incidence of several complications increases however, as women grow older, especially beyond age 35. Women who delay conception due to getting advanced education and establishing careers face increased risk of infertility, miscarriage or still births, and babies born with chromosomal defects/abnormalities and may result in spontaneous abortion. The incidence of Down's syndrome increase significantly among women of this age group. However, poor health and environmental risks associated with poverty are the strongest predictors of pregnancy complications in both teenagers and older women.

3.8.2 Environmental Pollution

An astounding number of potentially dangerous chemicals are released into the environment in industrialized nations. Prenatal mercury exposure disrupts production and migration of neurons, causing wide spread brain damage. Another teratogen, lead, is present in paint flaking off the walls of old buildings and in certain materials used in industrial occupations. High levels of lead exposure are consistently related to prematurity, low birth weight, brain damage and a wide variety of physical defects. Even low levels do cause harm.

3.9. COMPLICATIONS OF PREGNANCY AND DELIVERY

Most pregnancies and deliveries occur with little difficulty to the mother or baby. Some however, are complicated by one or more conditions. The purpose of prenatal care is to monitor the progress of a pregnancy and delivery to ensure the health and well-being of both mother and child. Proper medical attention during the course of a pregnancy can help to detect problems if they arise, and treatment during pregnancy or delivery can minimize the effects of these complications.

3.9.1 Pathological Complications of Pregnancy

(i) Diabetes

Diabetes is a medical disease that is made worse by pregnancy and that increases the risks of pregnancy complications. When a diabetic woman becomes pregnant, the pancreas of her baby must adjust to an abnormally high sugar level and enlarges as it produces greater-than-usual amounts of its own insulin. Babies who mange to survive in this, usually are overweight and have a bloated appearance at birth. Their adjustment after birth is more difficult because of the diabetic condition of the mother during pregnancy.

On considering the effect of diabetes on pregnancy to the mother, there is an increased likelihood of preeclampsia and eclampsia, severe infection, a large infant which can present problems with delivery, such as shoulder dystocia, cesarean section delivery because of the macrosomia of the infant, hydramnios and postpartum hemorrhage. Similarly the effect of diabetes to the fetus may result in perinatal mortality, perinatal morbidity, perinatal hypoglycemia and hypocalcemia, congenital abnormalities, such as neural tube defects and diabetes in the offspring. Strict glucose control prior to and during early pregnancy is thought to reduce the risk of severe malformations.

(ii) Hypertensive Disease

Hypertensive disorders in pregnancy rank among the leading causes of maternal mortality and make a significant contribution to prenatal mortality.

- **Hypertension** is a blood pressure reading on two occasions of at least 30 mm systolic or 15 mm diastolic.
- **Pre-eclampsia** is hypertension with proteinuria, edema, or both, induced by pregnancy after the twentieth week unless it is a molar pregnancy. **Eclampsia** is the occurrence of convulsions in a woman who meets the criteria for pre-eclampsia.
- **Gestational hypertension** is hypertension that develops during the latter half of pregnancy or during the first 24 hours after delivery. Any other evidence of preeclampsia does not accompany this, and it disappears within 10 days following delivery.
- **Pregnancy-induced hypertension** involves hypertension along with preeclampsia, and eclampsia. It is rare prior to the twentieth week of pregnancy in the absence of a hydatidiform mole.

Clinical aspects of preeclampsia are blood pressure, weight gain, proteinuria, headache, epigastric pain (a sign of severe preeclamapsia) and visual disturbances such as slight blurring of vision to blindness.

The goals of treatment are termination of the pregnancy with the least possible trauma to the mother and fetus and the birth of an infant who ultimately thrives. Hospitalization is necessary when the patient has blood pressure of 140/90 or above with or without proteinuria.

(iii) Cardiac Complications

Maternal mortality associated with heart disease ranges between 1 and 5 %. The major cause of death being cardiac discommendation and heart failure. Most heart diseases found in pregnant women is the result of rheumatic fever.

(iv) Anemia

Both in early pregnancy and near term, the hemoglobin level of healthy women is usually 11.0 gms. per decilitre or higher. It is generally accepted that during pregnancy or the puerperium, women with hemoglobin levels less than 10.0 gms. per deciliter are considered anemic.

3.9.2 Other Complications of Pregnancy

Toxemia: Maternal toxemia is an acute hypertensive disease of pregnancy. It is typically characterized by high blood pressure, retention of body fluids, and presence of protein in the urine. It occurs most frequently among first-time mothers and can be expected after the sixth month of gestation of an otherwise uncomplicated pregnancy. The condition endangers the life of both the mother and the fetus. The condition can be treated successfully by administration of diuretics or drugs that reduce retention of fluids by causing frequent urination. A salt-restricted diet is also necessary to treat the condition.

Miscarriage: Another name for miscarriage is "spontaneous abortion". Most miscarriages result before the tenth week of gestation and result from a variety of causes including (1) abnormalities of a developing embryo frequently caused by chromosome errors, (2) acute infectious diseases, and (3) physical shocks and psychological stress.

Extra uterine Pregnancies: An "ectopic" or extra uterine pregnancy occurs when a pregnancy develops outside the uterus. Rather than traveling down the Fallopian tube to the uterus, the fertilized ovum implants in one of several places other than the uterus such as in the Fallopian tube, on the ovary itself, or on the lining of the intestinal area. These pregnancies usually are terminated by surgical removal of the area on which the blastocyst implants.

Habitual abortion: Among some women, spontaneous abortion occurs repeatedly and is known as habitual abortion. Habitual abortion usually threatens at the same stage of each pregnancy, and the measures needed to prevent a repetition of the miscarriage should be started as soon as the expectant mother knows she is pregnant. The cells that form the placenta and fetal membrane require large amounts of carbohydrate that can be assimilated easily.

Induced Abortion: The induced abortion is a deliberate interruption of the development of an embryo or fetus because of therapeutic or non-medical reasons. Such an abortion is usually performed in a hospital or clinic as it requires antiseptic conditions. Local anesthetics are used if needed. In the procedure called dilation and Curettage or D and C, the physician enlarges the opening of the uterus to permit entry of the surgical tools used to scrape the lining of the uterus. The tissues are removed from the lining with a curette, a scoop, with sharpened edges. Another method often used, called "Vacuum aspiration" employs suction to pull the embryonic tissue from inside the uterus. These techniques-the D & C and vacuum aspiration- can be used only during the first trimester of pregnancy.

Hemorrhage: Hemorrhage or excessive bleeding before or during delivery is a serious concern of pregnancy. The condition usually results from an improperly placed placenta that develops in the uterus. Frequently, in such instances, the placenta has developed over or near the cervical opening. Another frequent cause is premature separation of a normal placenta. While the cause of these problems is unknown, treatment has significantly lowered mortality rates among mothers but remains high for the fetus under these conditions.

Genetic Abnormalities/ Disorders: Some people have genetic disorders that disrupt the usual pattern of development. Genetics can derail development in two ways. First, some disorders are inherited, such as sickle cell disease, and second, sometimes the eggs or sperms do not include the usual 23 chromosomes but have more or fewer chromosomes instead.

Chromosomal Abnormalities: Genetic endowment can also influence human characteristics through chromosome abnormalities in which a child receives too many or too few chromosomes (or abnormal chromosomes) at conception. Most such abnormalities are due to errors in chromosome division during meiosis. Through an accident of nature, an ovum or sperm cell may be produced with more or fewer than the usual 23 chromosomes. In most cases, a zygote with the wrong number of chromosomes is spontaneously aborted but approximately one child in 200 is born with either more or very rarely, fewer chromosomes, than the normal 46. The sex cells, X and Y, seem to be especially prone to non disjunction. Those that survive gestation and contain extra or absence of sex chromosomes are characterized by chromosomal abnormalities. The greater the number of X chromosomes present, the greater the severity of mental retardation.

Nondisjunction of autosomal chromosomes usually result in products of conception that are spontaneously aborted. The exception to this principle is Down syndrome, caused by extra chromosomal material on the 21st autosomal chromosome pair.

There is a positive correlation between chromosomal problem and age of parents. Teenage mothers and older mothers (those past age 35) more frequently have babies with chromosomal disorders. Older fathers may also be implicated in faulty meiotic division of sperm resulting in inheritance of extra chromosomal materials.

Genetic Abnormalities: Most inherited diseases are caused by genes rather than chromosomal problems. Some genes that code messages for disease conditions are dominant in allelic gene relationships. Many of them create the diseased condition at different ages in varying degrees, and under different environmental conditions. Because of the high probability of passing a disease to offspring when even one parent is heterozygous for the disease, many couples with dominant gene diseases opt to remain childless, to adopt children, or to use noncoital reproductive techniques to produce children carrying only the genes of the disease-free parent. Examples of other dominant gene diseases are cortical cataracts, some form of deafness, muscular dystrophy, etc.

In order for biological parents to pass a disease carried on a recessive gene to any offspring, both parents must carry the recessive gene. Even when they are both heterozygous for the disease, the probability of passing the disease to an offspring is only 24%. Some examples of recessive gene disease are cystic fibrosis, glaucoma, phenylketonuria and Wilson's disease.

A small percent of the population, about 15% inherit red blood cells that lack major antigens called RH factor. Antigens are materials that stimulate the body to produce a rejection response. People lacking the factor (RH negative) will develop antibodies against the factor if red blood cells with the factor get into their blood. If an Rh-negative mother who has antibodies against the Rh factor becomes pregnant with a child who inherits the Rh factor, problems ensue. The antibodies will cross the placental barrier and destroy the red blood cells of the fetus, resulting in severe anemia (called erythroblastosis fetalis), and/or fetal death.

Another potential for antibody production exists between persons with type A, type B, and type O blood. If for example, a mother with type O blood has type A blood introduced into her blood stream, she may develop antibodies against type A. These antibodies may cross the placental barrier and attack type A blood cells of the fetus. ABO incompatibility disease is much milder than Rh incompatibility disease. It usually does not develop until after birth and can usually be treated successfully with phototherapy.

3.10. GENETIC COUNSELING

Is a service that offers relevant information to people who suspect that they or their unborn children are at risk for some genetically based problems. Families seek genetic counseling for a number of reasons, usually because of the birth of a child with anomalies, a family history of a genetic disorder or inferiority problems such as unexplained frequent abortions. Recent accomplishments in genetic counseling have helped to reduce infant mortality and morbidity. Refinements in chromosome studies and in biochemical and tissue culture methods have greatly improved our ability to diagnose, treat and advise families on genetic matters. From a sample of amniotic fluid, it is possible to detect all major chromosomal abnormalities and large number of inborn errors of metabolism. With this information, couples at risk can be better informed when they decide whether or not to have children. They may choose to conceive, have the amniotic fluid of the fetus tested for abnormalities and then choose whether to continue the pregnancy, depending on the results. This advance enables couples who in the past would not have chosen to have to go through the child bearing process.

3.11. CARE OF THE PREGNANT WOMEN

The joy and pride of expecting a baby is indeed great for the couple especially for the prospective mother. Every bride looks forward to it with joy, anticipation, excitement and fulfillment in a woman's life. However, pregnancy also has certain amount of fear and anxiety. Research had shown that the prenatal environment has marked influence on the subsequent pattern of the physical and psychological growth and development of the fetus. Hence, the antenatal care of the mother is extremely important. Women who start antenatal care can plan for a comfortable pregnancy and delivery of a healthy baby. The pregnant women should have good amount of exercise and periods of rest and sleep. Medications and alcohol should be avoided. The careful parent may take steps to avoid the various hazards, many of which are beyond the range of individual control and require efforts on national or even international scale.

Maternal Diet/Nutrition: The unborn child or fetus depends completely on the mother for its nourishment. As the mother is the developing child's sole source of nutrition, a balanced diet that includes foods from each of the five major food groups is vital. Majority of pregnant women need to increase their intake of calories by about 10 to 20% to meet the needs of both the expectant mother and the fetus (perhaps 300 calories a day beyond their maintenance level), but protein needs appear to go up much more markedly. The current recommendation is that a pregnant woman aged 19 or older needs to take in 1.3 grams of protein daily per kilogram (2.2 pounds) of her weight. For example, a woman weighing 125 pounds requires about 75grams of protein per day. Because they are still growing, the protein requirement for teenagers is still higher – perhaps 1.5 or 1.7 gram per day per kilogram of weight. Requirements for most vitamins and minerals also increase during pregnancy. For example, folic acid, one of the B vitamins is important for normal prenatal development. Calcium needs rise to 50 percent, from 800 mg to 1200 mg daily, and iron requirements also increase, to perhaps 75 mg daily.

A gain between 25 and 35 pounds during pregnancy is expected, assuming that her weight was normal before pregnancy. A woman, who was underweight before pregnancy, may gain as much as 40 pounds; while a woman who was overweight should gain at least 15 pounds (Institute of Medicine, 1990). Both quantity and quality of what a pregnant woman eats is very important. Hence, health care professionals typically recommend that pregnant women supplement their diet with additional proteins, vitamins and minerals. When a pregnant woman does not provide adequate nourishment, the infant is likely to be premature and have low birth-weight. Inadequate nourishment during the last few months of pregnancy can affect the nervous system because this is a rapid time of brain growth. Finally, babies who do not receive adequate nourishment are vulnerable to illness.

Medical Care: Throughout pregnancy regular medical care is important. It gives the doctor a chance to prevent later complication by diagnosing and treating any problems before they become serious. Vaccinations should be taken before conceiving. It is essential to see the doctor regularly during the nine months of pregnancy. The doctor will make a thorough check-up to ascertain the state of health.

The expectant mother should visit once in 4-8 weeks up to 20 weeks; once in 4 weeks between 20-30 weeks; once in two weeks between 30-36 weeks and once a week between 36-40 weeks. Blood pressure and hemoglobin are estimated, previous illness, heart and chest complaints, kidney trouble etc are noted. Tests for anemia, Rh factor, sugar and albumin are done. The mother is also immunized against tetanus in the last trimester, which produces antibodies in her blood. These antibodies reach the fetus and protect it from neonatal tetanus. The mother should not take any medicines without the consent of the doctor, especially during early pregnancy. Pregnant mothers also should avoid visiting sick people especially those with infectious diseases or going to congested, crowded areas during the first 3months of pregnancy.

Hygiene

Bathing: Daily bath in warm water is essential as it not only helps the body to be clean but also gives freshness. Daily bath is refreshing, relaxing and stimulating for the skin as perspiration is one of the problems during pregnancy. It also favors elimination. After the 7th month, sponge baths or shower baths instead of tub baths are advisable.

Care of The Breasts : During pregnancy, nature is preparing the mother for nursing her baby. A brassiere, which supports the breasts should be worn which gives relief from the discomfort of congestion. However, the breasts should not be compressed. A properly fitted brassiere also helps in maintaining good posture. If the colostrum which may begin to ooze from the nipples about the fourth month tends to be irritating, the nipples should be washed with warm water and soap and a little cold cream/ butter rubbed on. This helps to prepare or toughen the nipple for the baby's nursing. If the nipples are flat or inverted, such a condition makes nursing for the child almost impossible as it cannot grasp. Drawing out the nipples gently with the thumb and forefinger for a few minutes each day is helpful. Doctor's advice can be sought.

Bowels : If the bowels are kept active, the kidneys are relieved of some of their work during their pregnancy which throws little or no extra strain on the intestines.

Dental Care : During pregnancy, the mouth may be more acidic and extreme acidity may affect the teeth. If the mother has an infected tooth, it may release poisons into her system which may lead to serious consequences. Therefore, the teeth should be examined, X-rayed, cleaned and should be given immediate attention.

Sexual Relations : It should be avoided during the last two months of pregnancy.

Mental Hygiene : Anything which causes worry, anger and fear may be disturbing, and generally brings the autonomous nervous system into action, liberating the chemical substances like adrenalin into blood stream. These may be transmitted through the placenta, producing changes in the circulatory system of the fetus. Therefore, a pregnant woman should be thoroughly relaxed.

Clothing: The clothing should not constrict the veins of the lower extremities of the pregnant woman. As size increases, a properly fitting maternity dress may be worn, which supports the uterus without binding and can be adjusted to the changes in the figure.

Shoes: The pregnant woman should use properly fitting and comfortable shoes. She must avoid shoes with high heels.

Exercise: As pregnancy is a natural event, the expectant mother should carry on with her usual household work, walking, gardening without any alteration. However, she should not overdo exercise and feel exhausted . Enough exercise to the body is essential for strengthening the muscles for labor.

Two questions about exercise during pregnancy are relevant: Is it safe for the fetus, and does it make labor and delivery easier? The tentative answer to both questions seems to be "yes". Since blood oxygen levels appear to remain fairly constant in exercising pregnant women, the fetus does not appear likely to suffer from any oxygen deprivation.

The general rule of thumb now used by most physicians and midwives is that a woman can (or even should) maintain whatever level of exercise was typical for her before she became pregnant. Large increases in exercise level are not recommended. Furthermore, some kinds of complications of pregnancy may preclude exercise. So before embarking on or continuing with a vigorous program of exercise, a pregnant woman should be wise to consult her physician or midwife. Apart from maintaining physical fitness during pregnancy, the main argument for exercise is that it may shorten labor to some degree.

Rest and Sleep: Eight hours of sleep is a necessity. If she is unable to sleep, a glass of hot milk will induce good sleep. An afternoon nap is good.

Mother's work: Today, the majority of women of child bearing age hold jobs that are taken outside their homes. Many women work through their pregnancies, right up to the time of delivery. In a survey of 7700 pregnancies, it was found that women who continued working in their 3rd trimester bore infants who weighed from 5 to 14 ounces less than infants born to women who remained at home. The weight deficit was greatest when the mother herself was underweight or had high blood pressure. The women whose jobs required them to stand for long periods when they were in their 3rd trimester had fetuses, which were most severely underweight, probably because the blood supply to these mothers' uterus and placenta was poor. Many women work throughout their pregnancies without ill effects to their babies. The decision about how long to continue working has to be based on a variety of factors like the woman's health, the period of work she does, and the leave policy where she works.

Workplace Toxins: Working men and women with potential contact should go through training and follow exposure prevention guidelines: wash hands regularly, wear protective clothing, avoid skin contact, keep the work place clean, leave contaminated clothes and objects at work; and change into street clothes before leaving.

3.12. PREPARING FOR THE BABY

Most parents begin to get ready for the arrival of a baby as soon as the doctor confirms the woman's pregnancy. The earlier the preparation begins, the better chance a family will have to learn to accept, love and understand its new member. The preparation should include three important areas. They are physical well being, psychological health, and financial security.

Physical Preparation : A physical check up and a talk with the doctor about regular health habits and medications is a wise precaution for people. Some other conditions in the woman that might lead to miscarriages can also be determined.

Psychological Preparation : Psychological preparation means developing attitudes. There are three factors that affect attitudes so often. They are- knowledge about a situation, experience in dealing with it and mental flexibility towards it. It is ideal for the couple to prepare themselves mentally .

Financial Preparation : Having a baby is an added family expense. Saving some money regularly from the family income in preparation for the baby is a wise policy for a couple to follow.

Immediate Areas of Preparation : The family doctor or gynecologist may be prepared to take care of the child birth. Seeing a doctor early can give a woman the assurance that all is well with her and the baby. Clothing is essential for a new baby. Clothing and essential equipment for a new baby should be kept ready. Arrangements for help during the mother's stay in the hospital and on her return home should be made as early as possible to ease mother—to be anxiety.

Family Adjustment: In every family, the pattern of life changes with the arrival of any new member. To make baby feel welcome, all adjustments must be made by the other family members. Babies are too immature physically and emotionally to adjust to any pattern of life. A father-to-be is told that he will have to take on added home duties as well as care for the new baby. Unless he has some practice doing the chore and helping with baby care before the baby's arrival, he may not be able to deal with the real situation. Sibling, if any, should also be counseled, to receive the new arrival with pleasure.

Infant health care, both for pre-mature and full-term babies has improved substantially in the past 2 decades, especially for those born in developed nations. New medical treatments such as neonatal intensive care have allowed many babies born pre-maturely not simply to survive, but to lead healthy lives. Better access to health care, environmental interventions, improved nutrition, higher educational levels, and improved standards of living also have contributed to infant health as well as to the drop in infant mortality rate in many parts of the world (Children's Defense Fund, 2004); National Center for Health Statistics, 2004 C).

Things can sometimes go wrong, of course, but prenatal development normally occurs within a highly controlled and safe environment-the uterus, and it follows an orderly, biologically programmed sequence. Thus in about nine months, the one-celled zygote normally has developed into perhaps 10 trillion cells organized into organs and systems.

QUESTIONS

SECTION "A"

Short Answer Type:

1. Explain the process of conception.
2. List the sign and symptoms of pregnancy.
3. Explain the factors that affect prenatal development.
4. List out some of the pathological complications of pregnancy.
5. Mention the prenatal developmental periods.
6. Justify the need for medical supervision during prenatal period?
7. Explain the period of zygote.
8. What are the symptoms of pregnancy?
9. What is puerperium.
10. Give the importance of placenta during prenatal period.

SECTION "B"

One Page Answer Type:

1. Describe the periods of prenatal development.
2. Describe the signs and symptoms of pregnancy.
3. Examine the factors affecting prenatal development.
4. Discuss a few complications of pregnancy.
5. Specify the diagnostic tests of pregnancy.
6. Write about developmental irregularities.
7. What are the common hazards of pregnancy during the period of fetus?
8. What is the significance of genetic counseling?

SECTION "C"

Essay Answer Type:

1. Explain the stages of the prenatal period in detail.
2. Discuss the factors affecting prenatal development.
3. What is prenatal care and explain its importance? Describe the care to be taken by pregnant women.

CHAPTER

4

CHILD BIRTH

OBJECTIVES

To enlighten students about:

- Mechanical factors affecting Labour
- Normal birth - Signs of True labour, Stages of labour
- Gynaecological Problems during Birth/Delivery
- The various types of birth, the puerperium
- In vitro fertilisation

4.1. INTRODUCTION

Parenthood is one of the great events of a lifetime both physically and emotionally. It is a deep human experience. Whether it is essentially good experience or a bad one depends not only on the physical course of reproduction but also on the social and emotional impact of child bearing.

Pregnancy and the birth process are neither static nor brief experiences; rather they are periods of lifespan, filled with growth, change and exciting enrichment. The birth process is both rewarding and challenging because at the end, there is literally a new life for both the parents and also for the child.

After thirty-eight weeks in the womb, the fetus is considered "full term," or ready for birth. By this point, it will weigh around seven-and-half pounds. The fetus measures about twenty inches or so at this stage - almost one-third of its final height as an adult. Approximately 266days after conception, the new human being is ready to emerge into the outside world.

Birth, Labor and Delivery

Birth: Birth is both a beginning and an end. It is the climax of all that has happened from the moment of fertilization. The terms "parturition" (a bringing forth) or "labor" are also used to indicate the process of "Childbirth". Birth is the process through which a fetus is expelled from the environment of the womb to that of the world outside. It is the actual expulsion of the infant down the vaginal canal and through the vaginal opening. It is a transition from a protected and dependent existence in the uterus to a life as a separate organism with independent functioning in the outside world. The infant is compelled to depend exclusively on its own biological system. Birth, then is a bridge between two stages of life.

At the termination of pregnancy in the human female, the irregular intermittent contractions of the uterus that began in the early months of pregnancy become more regular and increase in frequency and intensity. This assumption of a rhythmic character by the uterine contractions marks the beginning of the process by which the maternal organism separates and expels the mature products of conception.

Birth Process

For 10 lunar months, the infant has been cradled, protected, nurtured and nourished within the controlled environment of the mother's uterus. Stimuli have been limited and attenuated; nothing has been demanded of the fetus but to grow. Most fetuses experience no discomfort or pain, only a little cramping of space, yet even this seems to afford security.

Birth process can be divided into three periods: **labor, delivery,** and **after birth.** The first period is the **"labor stage,"** in which muscle contractions of the uterus move the fetus along the birth canal. The second period is known as **"delivery,"** in which the fetus passes through the birth canal and emerges as a newborn infant. The third period is one in which the placenta and membranes are expelled from the birth canal as an **"after birth"** process.

Most obstetricians give mothers-to-be an expected due date or EDC (expected day of confinement), figured from the last menstrual period by means of Niagde's rule. Seven days are added to the first day of the last menstrual period. Then 3 months are subtracted from this date, for e.g., if Mrs. K's last period began on October 13, adding 7 days would bring one to October 20, and subtracting 3 months would bring the one to July 20. Mrs. K's due date would then be given as July 20. Only very small fractions of women actually deliver on their due dates. Most deliver within 10 to 15 days before or after the estimated date.

Labor: Labor is also known as "childbirth" or "parturition". Labor is the process by which the fetus, placenta and membranes, when they have reached full-term or nearing it, are pushed from the uterus by the mother through the birth canal. The uterine contractions that expel the fetus and placenta are known as labor. The fetus is only an inert passenger.

Labor consists of the regular, rhythmic muscular contractions of the uterus to aid the infant in moving through the birth canal. This results in the birth of infant, and the delivery of the remaining products of conception. The primary purpose of labor is to permit the contractions of the uterus to open the cervix (the lower part of the uterus) wide enough (approximately 4 inches) to allow the widest part of the infant-the head-to pass through.

Labor may end spontaneously or may require external aid to be completed. The term "Labor" is used after the 28th week of gestation; before then, the process is called "Abortion". Spontaneous expulsion of the products of conception before the period of viability of the fetus is termed **abortion or miscarriage.** When a full term fetus presenting by the vertex is expelled by natural efforts, unaided, within a period of twenty-four hours, the term *normal or natural labor* is used to designate the condition. Labor is termed *premature* or pre-term, if it sets in before 37 weeks.

4.2 MECHANICAL FACTORS IN CHILD BIRTH

Three important components are needed for normal labor. These are the passages – the shape and size of the bony and soft tissues of the woman's pelvis with adequate dimensions, passenger – the size of the fetus and its presentation, and the powers – the quality and frequency of the uterine contractions.

1. Pelvis Dimensions

The hard bony pelvis is essentially bowl-shaped when seen from above. The pelvis comprises of three important parts: these are the inlet, the mid-cavity, and the outlet. The fetus must pass through the pelvic outlet for delivery to occur. The women's pelvic size and shape can be influenced by a number of things, such as gender, racial characteristics, general body build, nutritional status (especially conditions such as rickets during childhood), congenital defects and disease or injury of the spine, pelvic bones or lower extremities.

There are four main types of pelvic shapes, namely, Gynecoid (normal female pelvis), Anthropoid, Android and Platypelloid. The gynecoid pelvis is found in about half of the obstetric population. Since important diameters may be smaller in the other pelvic shapes, they may be the source of difficulty at the time of delivery. The maternal soft tissues which are involved in labor and delivery are the upper and lower uterine segments, the cervix, the vagina and the introitus, along with ligaments and the pelvic diaphragm. The pelvic soft tissues can obstruct descent of the fetus, especially in very young women or in elderly.

2. Fetal Dimension

Pregnancy, labor and delivery are all directed towards the safe delivery of a healthy passenger, the fetus, obviously followed by placenta and membranes. The largest diameter of any fetal part is found in the fetal head, but the diameter of the presenting part will vary with attitude of the fetal head. In normal pregnancy the fetal head is well flexed on the fetal body and the presenting diameter, will be 9.5 cm. Clearly this will easily pass through a normal pelvis.

The fetus is well prepared for labor during the last trimester. While the skull bones of some fetus are firmly ossified and capable of little change in shape, generally these bones remain relatively soft and are able to change their shape and dimensions in order to accommodate itself to the women's bony pelvis. This is possible not only because the bones are soft but also because they are not united, remaining separated by membranous spaces known as sutures.

3. Fetal Posture and Presentation

During the last week before delivery, the fetus assumes a characteristic posture, that is partially an attempt to accommodate himself to the space inside the uterus. Generally, the fetus tries to conform to the shape of the uterine cavity by folding his extremities and bending his back. (The head is sharply flexed , the chin almost resting upon the chest, the thighs are flexed over the abdomen, the legs are bent at the knee joints and the arms are folded across the chest or are straight down at the sides).This is known as fetal attitude or fetal habitus.

Fetal Lie: The fetus also assumes a lie, which can be either transverse or longitudinal or breech.

Fetal Presentation

- **Longitudinal (Cephalic Presentation):** Whenever a portion of the infant is in the birth canal and is felt on vaginal examination, it is referred to as the presenting part; this determines the presentation of the fetus. Cephalic presentations are classified according to the relation of the head of the fetus to the body.
    - When the head is sharply flexed so that the chin rests on the thorax, the occipital area of the skull (vertex) is felt on the vaginal examination- **vertex presentation.**
    - Less commonly, the head may be sharply extended, with the occipital area in contact with the back; in this instance, the face is felt on vaginal examination- **face presentation.**
    - When the head is partially flexed, the large fontanel is felt on vaginal examination- **sincipital presentation.**
    - When the head is partially extended, the brow can be felt upon examination- **brow presentation.**
- **Breech Presentation:** Breech Presentations are classified according to the relation of the buttocks or back lower portion of the trunk of the body of the fetus.

- Full or complete breech-thighs flexed on abdomen and legs flexed on thighs.
- Single breech- with legs extended over anterior surface of the body.
- Incomplete breech- double footling posture

4. **Uterine Contractions:** Uterine contractions are essential for labor and subsequently, delivery. Uterine contractions begin at the uterine fundus, and then spread around and down the uterus, thereby propelling the baby downwards through the cervix. Uterine muscle is unusual in that it possesses the property of both contractibility and retractibility. As each fiber contracts and then reflexes, it does not return to its original resting length but becomes slightly shorter, thereby pushing the baby downwards through the lower part of the uterus, through the cervix.

   The contractions are involuntary and are usually associated with some degree of discomfort. During the contractions of labor, the actively contracting upper portions of the uterus become thicker, while the lower uterine segment (isthmus and cervix) become very thin and relaxed/ stretched. These changes divide the uterus into 2 distinct segment zones - the upper portion which is actively contracting and lower portion which is passively contracting.

   At the time of completion of a contraction of the upper uterine segment, the cells of the segment do not resume their original length but becomes fixed at a shorter length. While this occurs in the upper segment, the lower uterine segment becomes stretched with each contraction. Upon completion of the contraction, the cells in the lower segment remain stretched and fixed at a longer length; this is called receptive or postural relaxation. As the cells become stretched, this portion of the uterus and cervix becomes thinner (If the phenomenon did not occur fetus would not be pushed farther into the birth canal). The round ligaments also contracts with each uterine contraction, elevating the fundus and aligning the fetus more directly with the curve of the birth canal.

4.3. NORMAL LABOR

The mechanism of labor is the series of passive movements of the baby, particularly its presenting part, as it descends through the birth canal. These mechanical changes taking place during the process by which the fetus negotiates the passage from the pelvic brim to the exterior are the events of engagement, flexion, internal rotation, extension, external rotation and expulsion, which do not occur separately but rather overlap in time. Normal labor starts spontaneously between 38 and 42 weeks. Normal labor occurs when :

1. The fetus is born at full-term and presenting by the vertex.
2. The process is completed spontaneously by the natural efforts of the mother without any external aid to complete it.

The whole process is completed spontaneously within 24 hours and there are no complications in a normal labor. Nowadays, with modern management of labor, few women are in labor longer than 12-14 hours. No complications arise.

Causes of Labor: Approximately 266 days after conception, the new human being is ready to emerge into the outside world. Normally around 266 days of prenatal development, some factors, suspected to be hormonal signals -oxytocin from the pituitary gland to the blood, prompt uterine contractions and labor. "Parturition"- the process of *uterine, cervical and other changes* that brings in labor-typically begins about 2 weeks before delivery. In spite of a vast amount of research, so far it has not been possible to identify the exact cause of onset of labor in normal pregnancy. Probably, it may be due to :

- A disturbance in the balance between the uterine stimulating action of estrogen and uterine relaxing effect of progesterone level in the blood.
- Uterine distension that is, rapid increase in intrauterine pressure and the resultant tension enforced on uterine muscle fibers, which may initiate labor.

4.3.1 The Preparatory Stages or Signs of Labor

In the nine months of pregnancy, the tissues of the mother's cervix have helped to keep the fetus within the uterus. A series of events in the mother signal the preparation of her body for labor. Although there is no definite indication as to what makes labor begin, it appears that a group of events coincide to start the process.

Prelude to Labor:

- Lightening of the fetus occurs
- Braxton-Hicks contractions increase in frequency
- Fetus becomes less active
- Increased vaginal discharge

Early first stage of labor:

- Effacement of cervix completed; dilation begins.
- Contractions become stronger and occur more frequently

Onset of labor: Anyone or a combination of

- Regular contractions
- Appearance of "show"
- Membranes rupture

Transition

- Dilation completed
- Strong urge to bear down
- Fetus's head crowns at vaginal opening –(the stage of birth at which an infant's head passes through the vaginal opening)

Lightening: Towards the end of pregnancy, the fetus turns head down and comes to rest with his head in the lower part of the uterus, well down in the mother's pelvic basin. It is this change of position of the baby that gives relief from pressure to the mother which is called **lightening**. Lightening enables the mother to feel less pressure on the upper part of the abdomen and to breathe freely due to the relief of pressure exerted by the uterus, upon the diaphragm and therefore on the lungs, and heart. However, she may feel more discomfort in the pelvic region as the head of the fetus descends toward the birth canal. The lightening may come as early as four weeks before birth, or it may wait until the onset of **labor**, the process by which the baby is expelled from the mother's body. Lightening is a sign that **end** of pregnancy is approaching and birth can be expected within three weeks. At this time, frequency of micturition increases due to pressure of the fetal head and the bladder's limited capacity; it requires to be emptied more often and so results in frequent urination.

Braxton-Hicks contractions increase in frequency

Mild contractions called Braxton- Hicks Contractions occur throughout pregnancy, preparing the uterus for its eventual task of expelling the fetus and placenta. At about the same time of Lightening, the mother might begin experiencing mild "turning- up" contraction (Braxton Hicks Contractions), which are a prelude to the more vigorous contractions of labor. They are painless early in pregnancy but may be felt as "false labor" toward the end of the term. These are erratic contractions, which occur at irregular intervals, causing the uterus to contract and relax, whereas in true labor, the uterus contracts and retracts. These contractions do not cause dilation of the cervix. False or spurious labor pains occur more frequently in the first pregnancy than in later pregnancies. False pains are temporary, irregular and felt generally over the abdomen, instead of just above the pubis. False labor may also accompany the dropping of the baby's head into the brim of the pelvis. This is variously known as "lightening, settling or dropping"; with first babies, it may occur as much as two weeks before labor.

Taking up of the Cervix

Taking up of the cervix occurs because it is being drawn up and merged into the lower uterine segments. Softening of the cervix is usually looked for, when in the interest of mother or child, labor must be induced.

4.3.2 Signs of True Labor

True labor may start and progress rapidly, or the start may be slow, with contractions only occurring at long intervals, the so-called "sluggish uterus". The signs by which the onset of true labor is recognized must be clearly understood. They are:

- Slight uterine hemorrhage – the "Show"
- Formation of the "bag of waters"
- Painful uterine contractions
- Dilation and effacement
- Ruptured membranes

(i) Show

As labor progresses, the spiral muscles of the fundus of the uterus become more dominant, pulling and thinning the cervix and lower segment. As the cervix dilates in early labor, the mucous plug blocking the endocervical canal is dislodged. This together with some bleeding that occurs as the chorionic membrane "shears" off the lower segment, forms a blood stained "show". Until the start of labor, this mucus acts as a gelatinous plug in the cervix, sealing off the uterus. The mucus comes from the cervical mucosa, which secretes abundantly during labor; the slight hemorrhage comes from the lower uterine segment, where the beginning of dilatation causes a little separation of the membranes. It is almost invariably met with at the onset of labor. Real labor usually begins after the mucous plug is discharged and when the cervix begins dilating and effacing more rapidly.

(ii) Formation of the "Bag of Waters"

Another sign may be a gush of clear fluid from the vagina which follows what is called the "bursting of the bag of water", the rupturing of the amniotic sac that has enclosed the fetus, releasing the amniotic fluid.

When the cervix opens, the lower pole of the fetal membranes (chorion and amnion), which has been already detached by stretching of the lower uterine segment, being unsupported, tends to bulge into the cervical canal. It contains a little liquor amino, which has passed below the presenting part, and it has therefore received the name of "bag of waters". When the finger is passed into cervix during pain, this bag will be found to be convex and tense; as the pain passes off it becomes less tense and less distinct, and may even disappear altogether as the membranes come into contact again with the head. If intermittent pain and dilatation of the bag of waters is felt to grow tense during the pain, and to relax during the interval, the diagnosis of labor is more certain.

(iii) Painful Uterine Contractions

In the early months of pregnancy, a woman experiences irregular, intermittent contractions of the uterus. They become more regular and increase in frequency and intensity, toward the termination of pregnancy. These rhythmic uterine contractions which are "real", mark the beginning of the labor.

The pain of labor contractions is almost entirely cervical in origin and is associated with the resistance of the cervix to the dilating forces. During the early part of labor, pain is only felt during the terminal phase of the rise in intrauterine pressure. However, as labor progresses, pain is felt as soon as the intrauterine pressure rises above 20 mm Hg and does not disappear until pressure falls below 20 mm Hg. In well-established labor, a uterine contraction lasts for about 50-60 seconds and occurs every 2-4 minutes

The uterus and cervix is an active unit of muscular power providing the force by which the fetus (passenger) is pushed through the pelvis (passage).

Fig. 4.1 Birth of a baby showing rotation of the head and trunk through the mother's pelvis..

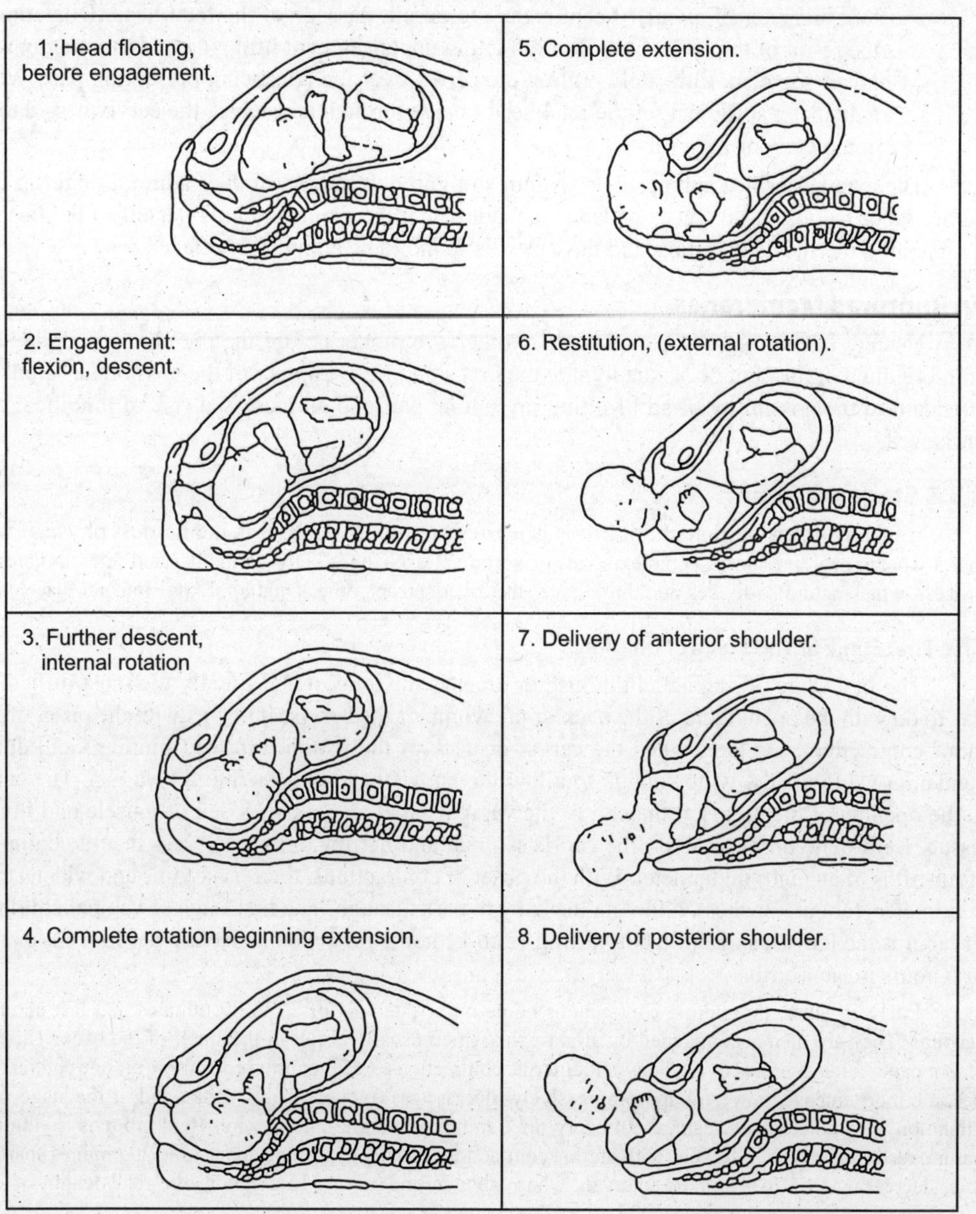

(iv) Dilatation and Effacement

As the baby's head presses down on the uterine floor, "dilation and effacement" occur. The pressure against the opening to the uterus (the cervix) causes it to dilate (enlarge) and efface (thin out).

- **Effacement** refers to incorporation of the cervical canal into the lower uterine segment. **Effacement of the Cervix** is the shortening of the cervical canal from a structure of approximately 2 centimeters in length to one in which the canal is replaced by a more circular orifice with almost paper-thin edges. The process proceeds downwards from above, that is from the internal to external orifice sphincter. It occurs as the muscle fibers near the internal orifice sphincter are pulled upward into the lower uterine segment. The process may occur late in pregnancy or be delayed until labor begins.
- **Dilation of the Cervix** involves the gradual widening of the cervical orifice sphincter to a diameter of about 10 centimeters to permit passage of the fetal head. Dilatation is the result of the contracting and retracting upper segment lifting up and thinning out the lower segment, ultimately pulling the cervix over the advancing presenting part. When a diameter sufficient for the fetal head to pass through is reached, the cervix is said to be completely or fully dilated.

The external orifice sphincter is seldom so tightly closed that it does admit a fingertip long before labor begins. A diagnosis of labor is made when the woman admits herself to the hospital with painful uterine contractions and the cervix is found to be completely effaced.

(v) Ruptured Membranes

Usually labor has been recognized by other symptoms before the membranes rupture and amniotic fluid drains, but occasionally it is the first sign. Early rupture of the membranes alerts the attendant to the possibility of an ill-fitting presenting part and an increased risk of umbilical cord prolapsed.

4.3.3 Stages of Labor

It is not surprising that childbirth is often referred to as labor. It is the hardest physical work that a woman may ever do. A complex series of hormonal exchanges between mother and fetus initiates the process, which naturally divides into three stages that overlap each other-Dilation, Expulsion and Placental.

The First Stage or The Stage of Dilation

The first stage of vaginal child birth or labor is the longest and usually the most difficult. It has to do with the opening up of the neck of the womb or the cervix. It begins with the onset of true labor contractions and ends when the cervix or neck of the womb effaces (thinning) and dilates (widening) sufficiently, wide enough to allow the baby's head to pass into the vagina. The cervix is the opening of the uterus at the end of the vaginal canal and is composed of muscle and fibrous tissue. Before the onset of labor, the cervix is thick and narrow, measuring less than 2 centimeter (four-fifths of an inch) in diameter. With the onset of contractions, the cervix thins and widens to 10 centimeters (about 4 inches), allowing the baby to pass through. The first stage of vaginal childbirth or labor is the longest stage of labor, lasting 12 to 14 hours for a woman having her first child and 4 to 6 hours in later births.

Early in labor, the uterine contractions come on at intervals of 20 to 30 minutes and last about 40 seconds. They are then accompanied by slight pain, which usually is felt in the small of the back. The term "labor pains" often are used as a synonym for uterine contractions. As labor progresses these uterine contractions become more intense, powerful and progressively increase in frequency until at the end of the stage when dilatation is complete, they recur about every three minutes and are quite severe. **Real labor** is rhythmic in nature, recurring at fixed intervals, with uterine contractions usually beginning about 15 to 20 minutes apart and then decreasing to 3 to 4 minute intervals when labor is under way. In addition, the total length of each contraction increases from less than $\frac{1}{2}$ minute to more than 1 minute. They cause the cervix or uterine opening to widen and thin to nothing, forming a clear channel from the uterus into the birth canal, or vagina.

Since the cervix of a young woman dilates more readily than does that of a woman who has her first child late in the fourth decade of life, the duration of the first stage of labor often is somewhat prolonged in women who become pregnant for the first time after they have passed the age of 35. A similar delay is to be anticipated if the cervix is extensively scarred because of previous labors, an amputation, deep catheterization or other operation on the cervix. Just as an abnormal position of the child and molding of the uterus may prevent the small descent of the child, an abnormally large child or an abnormally small pelvis may interfere with the descent of the child and prolong the first stage of labor.

The Second Stage or the Stage of Expulsion of the Baby

This stage begins when the cervix is sufficiently dilated to permit the passage of the child's head, (which begins to move through the cervix into the vaginal canal), and ends when the baby emerges completely from the mother's body. The second stage of labor is the expulsive stage during which the fetus is forced through the birth canal. The uterine contractions become more frequent, recurring at 2-5 minutes intervals and are stronger, lasting 60-90 seconds, the fetal head descends deeply into the pelvis. With each contraction, the fetal head becomes a little more visible, retreating a little between contractions but advancing slightly all the time.

Once the cervix is fully open, the baby is ready to be born. About the time that the cervix becomes fully dilated, the bag of waters breaks and the force of the strong, involuntary uterine contractions are augmented by voluntary bearing-down efforts of the mother. The mother also feels a natural urge to squeeze and push with her abdominal muscles. With each labor pain, she takes a deep breath and then contracts her abdominal muscles. The increased intra-abdominal pressure thus produced may equal or exceed the force of the uterine contractions. When it is properly used, these bearing-down efforts may double the effectiveness of the labor pains. As the child descends into and passes through the birth passage, the sensation of pain often is increased. This is especially true of the terminal phase of the stage of expulsion when the child's head distends and dilates the maternal soft parts as it is being born. At the end of this stage, the baby is born, but it is still attached to the placenta in the mother's body by the umbilical-cord, which must be cut and clamped.

This second stage is much shorter than the first, lasting about 50 minutes in a first birth and 20 minutes in later births. If this stage lasts longer than two hours, it signals that the baby needs more help. A doctor may grasp the baby's head with forceps or use vacuum extraction with a suction cry to pull it out of the mother's way. The manner in which the child passes through the birth canal in the second stage of labor depends upon the position in which it is lying and the type of the mother's pelvis.

The Third Stage or the Stage of Placental Expulsion

At this stage also known as the "afterbirth," - the expulsion of the placenta begins as soon as the baby has been completely born. It involves the "separation" and "expulsion" of the placenta (which is no longer needed to feed and give oxygen to the baby, that normally occurs when the uterus contracts and the muscle retracts following delivery of the fetus) and membranes and any remaining amniotic fluid from the uterus as well as the arrest of bleeding from the vessels in the uterus. It is the period of time that elapses between delivery of the fetus and delivery of the placenta.

With the expulsion of the child, the cavity of the uterus is greatly diminished. Consequently, the site of placental attachment becomes markedly reduced in size, with the result that the placenta (afterbirth) is separated in many places. Within a few minutes subsequent uterine contractions complete the separation and force the afterbirth into the vagina, from which it is expelled by a bearing-down effort. Even though the infant is safely delivered, all the products of conception must be expelled before the mother can begin the involution process, the return of the reproductive organs to their non- pregnant stage.

The third stage of labor is of short duration. It normally does not last longer than 20 minutes after the delivery, and may be complete within 5 minutes of delivery of the baby. This stage is virtually painless.

Occasionally, however, the separation may be delayed and accompanied by bleeding, in which case its artificial removal is necessary. The attendant always remains with the mother until the possibility of hemorrhage is eliminated by firm retraction of the uterus.

The immediate postpartum period i.e., the first post delivery hour, sometimes referred to as the fourth stage of labor, is a very critical period for the mother. It is the time that postpartum hemorrhage is most likely to occur because of uterine relaxation. After the baby and placenta are delivered, homeostasis is achieved at the placental site through vasoconstriction produced by the contractions of the myometrium.

Some factors affecting length of the process of child birth

The length of the child birth process is influenced by many factors. A small pelvis or an exceptionally large baby may slow it markedly. If the discrepancy is too great, the baby may not be able to traverse the pelvic passageway; in this situation, the baby can be safely delivered by cesarean section. Unusual position of the head or breech presentation also slows down the birth process. One of the factors that influence the length of the labor is number of previous vaginal deliveries experienced by the mother. It usually takes the first baby about 12 hours to traverse the birth passage. Subsequent babies experience substantially shorter labor; the second and third infants of a mother generally are born after about 4 to 8 hours of labor. Other factors known to increase the length of labor include maternal medication, poor maternal health, and a lapse of more than 7 years since the last pregnancy. The length of labor usually does not have a significant effect on the infant's health unless it is accompanied by a decrease in fetal oxygen level.

4.4. GYNAECOLOGICAL PROBLEMS DURING BIRTH/DELIVERY

Women who are healthy when they become pregnant usually have a normal pregnancy, labor and delivery. When women are not healthy or do not receive adequate prenatal care, problems can surface, during labor and delivery. A variety of circumstances can lead to complications in childbirth.

Possible Birth Difficulties: Precipitous (sudden or abrupt) deliveries can be dangerous to the fetus, as can prolonged labors and premature or low-birth weight deliveries.

- A **precipitous delivery** is dangerous to the fetus because the skull bones are compressed rapidly rather than molding gradually. This can cause tears in the membranous coverings of the brain. Another danger of precipitous labor is that the fetus may be born unattended. Such labors last less than 3 hours.
- With **prolonged labor** (over 24 hours), the fetus runs the risk of acquiring an infection, suffocating, or sustaining brain damage from insufficient oxygenation. Obstetricians may provide rest for the mother with weak contractions; in order to improve them, may stimulate contractions with drugs, or may perform a caesarean section to deliver the infant
- For a small minority of babies, the passage through the birth canal is a particularly harrowing journey causing **birth injury**. About two newborns in 1000 are injured in the process, either because of oxygen deprivation, diseases of infections, or mechanical injury.

Birth complications are hazardous not just for a newborn's health-they have long-term effects too. When babies experience many birth complications, they are at risk for becoming aggressive or violent and for developing schizophrenia. This is particularly true for newborns with birth complications that later experience family adversity, such as living in poverty. This highlights the importance of excellent health care through pregnancy and labor and the need for a supportive environment throughout childhood.

When complications arise or when the fetus is in distress, the childbirth team may resolve to remove the fetus from the mother's uterus surgically. Cesarean section is surgical procedure, used to remove the baby and placenta from the uterus by cutting through the abdominal wall. This procedure, which is called C-section, frequently is performed under regional anesthesia so that the mother is awake and aware.

Most pregnancies are uneventful, and most complications can be treated. The more common **birth complications** are listed below:

Anoxia and Brain Injury

Two of the most serious delivery complications are "anoxia" (oxygen deprivation to the brain) and "brain injury". A normal baby will establish respiration within one minute after birth. This often occurs spontaneously. Some fetuses, however, have difficulty initiating respiration, which leads quickly to anoxia. Brain tissue is especially sensitive to oxygen starvation and damage is irreversible. Common causes of respiratory distress involved in the pregnancy include maternal toxemia, hemorrhage, depression of the central nervous system due to medications, erythroblastosis fetalis, prolonged labor, trauma to the fetal head during birth, and placenta previa (premature separation of the placenta). Anoxia may result from prolapsed umbilical cord, placental insufficiency, premature labor, severe maternal bleeding, maternal hypertension, toxemia, neonatal pulmonary dysfunction, placental passage of maternal analgesics or anesthetics, or because of the malformation.

The result of anoxia may be permanent damage to the infants' brain cells or even death. The brain can also be injured during difficult deliveries, especially when forceps are used improperly during the procedure. A variety of problems can affect the baby depending on the degree of anoxia at birth. These include cerebral palsy, mild to severe mental retardation, hearing and speech impairments, and related behavioral problems. Milder cases of anoxia make some infants irritable at birth or delay their motor and cognitive development. However, the chances of anoxia are being reduced by the use of fetal monitoring procedures during labor and delivery.

Identifying High-Risk Newborns: Identifying high-risk newborns as early as possible is essential for their survival and well-being. These infants are in great danger at birth because of genetic defects, prenatal hazards or perinatal damage. The Apgar test is routinely used to provide a quick assessment of the newborn's heart rate, respiration, color, muscle tone and reflexes. The simple test yields scores of 0, 1 or 2 for each of the five factors. Infants scoring four or lower are at risk and they require medical intervention in intensive care units to survive.

Small-for-gestational-age (SGA) infants: Small-for-gestational-age (SGA) infants have weight inappropriate for gestational age, whether born before 37 weeks or at term. These variables, while given separate definitions, may occur in the same baby. These infants have respiratory problems, poor temperature control, and limited nutrient deposits, difficulties with sucking and swallowing, poor resistance to infection, fragile blood vessels that may hemorrhage, poor kidney function, and poor liver functioning.

Low Birth Weight and Prematurity: A low birth weight baby is one who weighs less than five and a half pounds (2500 grams) at birth and a premature baby (preterm infant) has a gestational age of less than thirty-seven weeks (eight and a half months). The low birth weight or premature baby has a higher incidence of problems and abnormalities. Lack of glycogen or fat stored in body tissues is a frequent problem. This increases the probability of hypoglycemia (lack of adequate glucose to tissue) which is especially threatening to brain cells and regulation of body temperature. Respiratory distress is also a major concern among these infants. The premature baby has underdeveloped lungs that handicap respiration efforts while the full-term low birth weight infant experiences the same problem owing to hypoglycemia. Feeding a premature infant also poses special problems because of underdeveloped sucking and swallowing mechanisms. Treatment for such infants is complex and costly but encouraging. These babies usually are placed in special incubators that carefully maintain proper warmth, air circulation, and humidity. Feeding with fluids is accomplished through nasal tubes that lead to the stomach.

Some of the causes of preterm labor are infection, having a problem with the placenta, having an excessively large uterus (due to multiple births), having too much amniotic fluid, having structural abnormalities of the uterus or cervix, such as cervical insufficiency. Having a cervix that is shorter than normal (less than 25 millimeters), that thins out (effaces) or opens (dilates) without contractions, is known as cervical insufficiency and it may be the result of having had cervical surgery, or it may be something the woman was born with, or the result of having abdominal surgery during pregnancy. Women who had a preterm delivery previously, or those with maternal age less than 17 or older than 35, African American, underweight women, those who had vaginal bleeding in the first or second trimester and those who did not have prenatal care are at high risk of this problem.

In addition to the problems the premature infants face in the first few weeks after birth, the later problem might be lower intelligence, learning difficulties, hearing and vision impairment, and physical awkwardness. Not all premature infants have eventual difficulties; in fact, the majority develops quite normally and is not discernibly different from their full-term peers.

Factors associated with low birth weight, preterm delivery and SGA include youthfulness or agedness of the mother, maternal prenatal infections, drug abuse, malnutrition, or emotional traumas during pregnancy. To prevent premature deliveries, one of the best ways is to promote good prenatal care. Expectant mothers who have access to good medical care are less likely to have a premature or under-weight baby. Another way is to use drugs that help to prolong pregnancy by relaxing the uterus and postponing labor.

Post maturity: Close to nine percent of pregnant women have not gone into labor 2 weeks after due date, or 42 weeks after the last menstrual period. At that point, a baby is considered "post mature". Post mature babies tend to be long and thin, because they have kept growing in the womb but have had an insufficient blood supply toward the end of gestation. Possibly, because the placenta has aged and become less efficient, it may provide less oxygen. The baby's greater size also complicates labor; the mother has to deliver a baby, the size of a normal one-month-old.

Since post-maturity fetuses are at risk of brain damage or even death, doctors sometimes induce labor with drugs or perform cesarean deliveries. However, if the due date has been miscalculated, a baby who is actually premature may be delivered. To help make the decision, doctors monitor the baby's status with ultrasound to see whether heart rate speeds up when the fetus moves; if not, the baby may be short of oxygen. Another test examines the volume of amniotic fluid; a low level may mean the baby is not getting enough food.

Box

- Babies born after pregnancies that last between 35 and 40 weeks after conception are full-term babies.
- Babies born earlier than this are called preterm babies.
- Babies born later than 40 weeks are called post-term babies.
- A low birth weight and premature baby is one who weighs less than five and a half pounds (2500 grams) at birth or has a gestational age of less than thirty-seven weeks (eight and a half months)

Stillbirth: A stillbirth occurs either because a child dies in the womb before birth, or because breathing is never established before death. The cause may be severe developmental abnormality or intrauterine infection, maternal illness, poor placental nutrition or oxygen supply or premature separation of the placenta. Sometimes no cause is found.

Abnormal Presentation

"Presentation" refers to the part of the baby that will appear first from the birth canal. In the weeks before the due date, the fetus usually drops lower in the uterus. Ideally, for labor, the baby is positioned head-down, facing the mother's back, with its chin tucked to its chest and the back of the head ready to enter the pelvis. That way, the smallest possible part of the baby's head leads the way through the cervix and into the birth canal. This normal presentation is called vertex (head down). Some babies present with their buttocks or feet pointed down toward the birth canal. This is called a breech presentation.

Other presentations which are abnormal are:

Frank breech, in which the baby's buttocks lead the way into the pelvis; the hips are flexed, and the knee extended.

Complete breech, in which both knees and hips are flexed, and the baby's buttocks or feet may enter the birth canal first.

Incomplete breech or footling breech, in which one or both feet lead the way.

Breech babies are at an increased risk of injury and a prolapsed umbilical cord, which cuts off its blood supply. Doctors estimate that about 90% of fetuses who are in a breech presentation before 28 weeks will have turned by 37 weeks, while over 90% of babies who are breech after 37 weeks will most likely stay that way.

Transverse lie, in which case, a few babies lie horizontally in the uterus, and this usually means that the baby's shoulder will lead the way into the birth canal rather than the head. A transverse lie is the most serious abnormal presentation, and it can lead to injury of the uterus as well as injury to the fetus.

In *cephalopelvic disproportion*, the baby's head is too large to fit through the mother's pelvis, either because of the size or because of the baby's poor positioning. Sometimes the baby is not facing the mother's back, but instead is turned toward her abdomen . This increases the chance of a lengthy, painful, childbirth, often called "back labor," or tearing of the birth canal.

In *malpresentation*, the baby is not "presenting" or positioned in the normal way. In malpresentation of the head, the baby's head is positioned wrong, with the forehead, top of the head, or face entering the birth canal, instead of the back of its head. Sometimes a placenta previa (when the placenta blocks the cervix) may cause an abnormal presentation. But many times the cause is not known. Abnormal presentations increase a woman's risk for uterine or birth canal injuries and abnormal labor.

Premature Rupture of Membranes (PROM)

Normally, the membranes surrounding the baby in the uterus break and release amniotic fluid (known as the "water breaking") either right before or during labor. Premature rupture of membranes means that these membranes have ruptured too early in pregnancy. This exposes the baby to a high risk of infection.

Umbilical Cord Prolapse

The umbilical cord is a baby's lifeline, as oxygen and other nutrients from the mother's body are passed to the baby through the umbilical cord and placenta. Sometimes, before or during labor, the umbilical cord can slip through the cervix after the water sac breaks, preceding the baby into the birth canal. The cord may even protrude from the vagina -- a dangerous situation because the blood flow through the umbilical cord can become blocked or stopped. One can probably feel the cord in the birth canal if it prolapses, and may see the cord if it protrudes from the vagina.

Umbilical Cord Compression

Because the fetus moves and kicks inside the uterus, the umbilical cord can wrap and unwrap itself around the baby many times throughout pregnancy. While there are "cord accidents" in which the cord gets twisted around and harms the baby, this is extremely rare and usually can't be prevented.

Sometimes the umbilical cord gets stretched and compressed during labor, leading to a brief decrease in blood flow to the fetus. This can cause sudden, short drops in fetal heart rate, called variable decelerations, which are usually picked up by monitors during labor. Cord compression happens in about one in 10 deliveries. In most cases, these heart rate changes are of no major concern, and the birth proceeds normally. But a C-section may be necessary if the baby's heart rate worsens or the baby shows other signs of distress.

Amniotic Fluid Embolism

This is one of the most serious complications of labor and delivery. Very rarely, a small amount of amniotic fluid – the fluid that surrounds the fetus in the uterus – enters the mother's bloodstream, usually during a particularly difficult labor or a C-section. The fluid travels to the woman's lungs and may cause the arteries in the lungs to constrict. For the mother, this constriction can result in a rapid heart rate, irregular heart rhythm, collapse, shock, or even cardiac arrest and death. Widespread blood clotting is a common complication, requiring emergency care.

Preeclampsia

Preeclampsia is a complication of pregnancy involving high blood pressure that develops after 20 weeks of pregnancy or shortly after delivery. Preeclampsia may lead to premature detachment of the placenta from the uterus, seziure, or stroke. As severe preeclampsia can affect many organs and cause serious or even life-threatening problems, women whose preeclampsia is getting worse need to deliver early.

Preeclampsia causes the blood vessels to constrict, resulting in high blood pressure and a reduced blood flow that can affect organs in the body, such as the liver, kidneys, and brain. When less blood flows to the uterus, it can mean problems for the baby, such as poor growth, too little amniotic fluid, and placental abruption (when the placenta separates from the uterine wall before delivery). In addition, the baby may suffer the effects of prematurity if the need arises to deliver early to protect the mother's health.

Eclampsia

Preeclampsia can lead to seizures, a condition called eclampsia. Eclampsia can have very serious consequences for both the mother and the baby.

Uterine Bleeding (Postpartum Hemorrhage)

After a baby is delivered, excessive bleeding from the uterus, cervix, or vagina, called postpartum hemorrhage, can be a major concern. Excessive bleeding may result when the contractions of the uterus after delivery are impaired, and the blood vessels that opened when the placenta detached from the wall of the uterus continue to bleed.

Oligohydramnios

The amniotic sac fills with fluid that protects and supports the developing baby. When there's too little fluid, it's called oligohydramnios. According to the March of Dimes, about 4 percent of pregnant women have low levels of amniotic fluid at some point, usually in their third trimester. If this happens near the end of pregnancy, labor will be induced. Some of the most common causes are leaky or ruptured membranes, placental problems, certain medical conditions, carrying twins or multiples and fetal abnormalities.

Ectopic pregnancy

When a fertilized egg implants outside the uterus, it's an ectopic pregnancy. One in 50 pregnancies is ectopic. Because the vast majority of ectopic pregnancies occur in a fallopian tube, they're often called "tubal" pregnancies. It's important to catch this type of pregnancy early because the growing embryo could rupture the fallopian tube and cause internal bleeding that can be fatal. Sine there's no way to transplant an ectopic pregnancy into the uterus, ending the pregnancy is the only option.

Placenta previa

In placenta previa, the placenta is lying unusually low in the uterus, next to or covering the cervix. It isn't usually a problem early in pregnancy. But if the placenta remains dangerously low as the pregnancy progresses, it can cause bleeding, which can lead to other complications and may require the woman to deliver early. Placenta previa is present in upto 1 in 200 deliveries. Women who have placenta previa when they give birth have to deliver by c-section.

Miscarriage

Miscarriage is the loss of a pregnancy in the first 20 weeks. About 10 to 20 percent of known pregnancies end in miscarriage, and more than 80 percent of miscarriages happen before 12 weeks. Most first-trimester miscarriages are believed to be caused by chromosomal abnormalities in the fertilized egg that keep the embryo from developing. An egg that doesn't implant properly in the uterus or an embryo with structural defects that prevent it from developing are also sometimes the causes. Vaginal spotting or bleeding is usually the first sign.

Age, a history of miscarriages, chronic diseases or disorders, uterine or cervical problems, history of birth defects or genetic problems, infection, smoking, drinking, and using drugs, medications, environmental toxins, paternal factors, obesity, diagnostic procedures, pregnant within three months after giving birth are some of the risk factors.

Gestational Diabetes

Gestational Diabetes develops during pregnancy, when a woman's body is not making enough insulin. It develops usually in second trimester. It cannot be treated by pills, most treatment is through diet or insulin.

Rh Negative Disease

Rh factor is determined by the presence of a protein surrounding red blood cells. Without the protein, a woman is considered Rh negative. If a mother is Rh negative, and her child is born Rh positive, she starts to build antibodies up against the next Rh positive baby.

During the beginning of the pregnancy, the mother is tested to see if she has been sensitized. RHOGAM is a medication given around 28 weeks to prevent the build-up of these antibodies. It is given again at birth, only if the baby is Rh positive.

Varicose veins

Varicose veins are veins that have become swollen. The veins in the legs are most commonly affected. You can also get varicose veins in the vulva (vaginal opening). They usually get better after the birth.

Placental abruption

Placental abruption (also known as abruptio placentae) is a complication of pregnancy, wherein the placental lining has separated from the uterus of the mother. It is the most common pathological cause of late pregnancy bleeding. In humans, it refers to the abnormal separation after 20 weeks of gestation and prior to birth. It occurs in 1% of pregnancies worldwide. Placental abruption has effects on both mother and fetus. The effects on the mother depend primarily on the severity of the abruption, while the effects on the fetus depend on both its severity and the gestational age at which it occurs. The heart rate of the fetus can be associated with the severity.

Perineal Trauma

Perineal trauma is any damage to the area between the vagina and the anus (back passage) during the birth of a baby. Tears can also occur inside the vagina and in the labia (lips of the vagina). This is not uncommon and as many as 85% of women will have some degree of perineal trauma and that 60 to 70% of these women will require suturing (stitches). Perineal trauma can occur during normal or assisted (ventouse or forceps) vaginal delivery, or is a deliberate incision (episiotomy) made by the midwife or doctor.

Polyhydramnios

Polyhydramnios means a pregnant woman has too much amniotic fluid in her uterus (womb). The amount of fluid around the baby gradually increases until there is about one litre (1.76 pints) surrounding him at 38 weeks. This amount decreases to about 800ml (1.4 pints) by 40 weeks. The baby will regularly swallow amniotic fluid, which then passes out of his body as urine. This is how he controls the volume of amniotic fluid around him. When this delicate balance is disturbed, the volume of amniotic fluid can increase rapidly. In severe cases of polyhydramnios, there may be as much as three litres (5.3 pints) of fluid, or three times the normal amount, around the baby.

Shoulder dystocia

Shoulder dystocia is a specific case of dystocia whereby after the delivery of the head, the anterior shoulder of the infant cannot pass below the pubic symphysis, or requires significant manipulation to pass below the pubic symphysis. It is diagnosed when the shoulders fail to deliver shortly after the fetal head. In shoulder dystocia, it is the chin that presses against the walls of the perineum.

Uterine fibroid

A uterine fibroid (benign (non-cancerous) tumor from smooth muscle tissue) originates from the smooth muscle layer (myometrium) of the uterus.

Fibroids are the most common benign tumors in females and typically found during the middle and later reproductive years. While most fibroids are asymptomatic, they can grow and cause heavy and painful menstruation, painful sexual intercourse, and urinary frequency and urgency. Symptoms caused by uterine fibroids are a very frequent indication for hysterectomy.

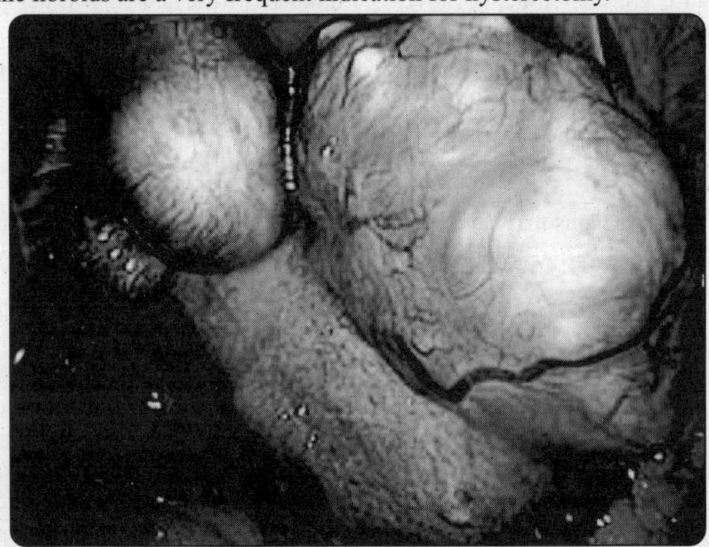

Fig. Cervical incompetence

Cervical incompetence is a medical condition in which dilation and effacement of the cervix may occur without pain or *uterine contractions*. In a normal pregnancy, dilation and effacement occurs in response to uterine contractions. Cervical incompetence occurs because of weakness of the cervix, which is made to open by the growing pressure in the uterus as pregnancy progresses. If the responses are not halted, rupture of the membranes and birth of a premature baby can result during the second and third trimesters.

The safety of the baby during labor

The fetus receives all the food he needs through the placenta from his mother's blood. One of the signs that the placenta is not working well is a fetus that is growing slowly-this slow growth may be found by feeling the size of the uterus or by ultrasound examination. From minute to minute, the fetus also needs a vital supply of oxygen from his mother. If he did not get that oxygen, he would soon die. Much of the care of the baby during the modern management of labor is devoted to a careful watch of his oxygen supply. Usually the baby's heart beats 120 to 140 times a minute, but it may get faster or slower if he runs short of oxygen. Midwives are therefore, trained to listen to the baby's heart rate frequently as labor progresses; if she hears a change, she will tell the doctor.

This is very satisfactory for the ordinary management of labor, but if the doctors feel there is a very high risk of the baby losing his oxygen supply, such as the baby who has stopped growing, a more sophisticated method of watching the baby is needed. These new methods mean that there is more machinery around the mother in the labor ward, but it enables those doctors to keep a close eye on the baby and deliver him quickly if necessary.

4.5. METHODS OF DELIVERY OR TYPES OF BIRTH

Attitudes toward the birth process have differed widely from era to era and from place to place. As safety has become more assured in most normal births in developed countries, health workers have focused on making childbirth experience more pleasant and on meeting emotional needs by bringing the father and other family members into the process. Many hospitals have established homelike birth centers, where labor and delivery take place under soft lights in the presence of father or other companions.

Physicians today know how to administer such drugs more carefully, and to monitor side effects that may arise from their use. At the same time, alternatives to medications have been developed that tend to enhance the experience and offer many benefits to the baby as well as to its parents.

i. Medicated Deliveries

There are numerous drug agents that are used in labor and delivery to minimize discomfort to the mothers. Such drugs include Analgesics, Amnestics, Sedatives, and Tranquilizers, which could be used alone or in combinations. Use of these agents allows the mother to be conscious but limits her participation in the birth. Such drugs also are known to cross the placenta and can have an adverse effect on the fetus. Like all other medications used in labor and delivery, these are used with caution and upon the recommendation of the physicians in accordance with the wishes of the mother.

ii. Home Birth

A small but growing percentage of women opt for the intimate, personal experience of home birth, which can involve the whole family. A home birth usually is attended by a trained nurse-midwife with the resources of medical science close at hand. Freestanding birth centers are another option. Studies suggest that both of these settings can be safe and much less expensive than hospital births in low-risk deliveries attended by skilled practioners.

iii. Natural Child birth or Spontaneous Birth

The usual method of childbirth is vaginal delivery. Spontaneous birth is usually regarded to as "natural" child birth because it occurs without outside aid and with a minimum of or no medication of the mothers. If the mother chooses to have no anesthetics during the labor or to take them only sparingly at the final most painful phase of delivery, the process is called "natural" child birth. In this type of birth, the position of the fetus in the mother's uterus and the size of the fetus make it possible for the fetus to emerge headfirst. After the head, one shoulder and then the other appear as the fetal body moves slowly in the birth canal. Next, the arms emerge, one at a time and finally the legs.

Natural childbirth methods are preferred by some women who want to participate as consciously as possible in the act of bringing a child into the world. Others, by contrast, want to go into the delivery room completely anesthetized. In natural childbirth, most women receive local anesthetics for the episiotomy inclusion, to make the vaginal area large enough for the passage of baby, drugs to relieve tension when requested, and oxytocin, a hormone naturally secreted by the pituitary gland to help the muscles of the uterus contract normally.

How natural should the childbirth a mother has, must be decided in terms of her individual temperament. Moreover, if natural childbirth is to include the father's presence in the delivery room, his temperament must be considered too. The infant who has been born spontaneously usually adjusts more quickly and more successfully to his postnatal environment than one whose birth has been difficult enough to require use of the instruments of caesarian section.

SOME VARIATIONS OF LABOR

iv. Induction Method

Induction means that the doctor begins labor artificially. It is very common and there are variety of reasons for it. Amongst the most common are high blood pressure or the fact that labor has not started two weeks after term. In both these situations, and in others, there would be an increased risk to the baby if pregnancy continued, so it is safer to start labor. The doctor usually ruptures the membranes, so that the amniotic fluid escapes, combining this with a drug which will make the uterus contract. The drug called Syntocinon, is given into a vein in a 'drip' or slow injection.

v. Cesarean birth

Cesarean delivery, sometimes called a "cesarean section", is a surgical procedure to remove the baby from the uterus by cutting through the abdomen without the necessity of going through labor. The operation is commonly performed when labor progresses too slowly, when the fetus seems to be in trouble, or when the mother is bleeding vaginally. The doctors may also use this method of labor, if they think that there will be some danger to the baby in the process of labor, or if they think that the bones of mother's pelvis are too small to let the baby through. It is also used during labor if the first stage becomes too long or if there is any worry about the baby's health, so that he must be born as soon as possible. Often a cesarean is needed when the fetus is in the breech position (feet first) or in the transverse position (lying crosswise in the uterus) or when its head is too big to pass through the mother's pelvis.

Surgical deliveries are more likely when the birth involves a first baby, a large baby or an older mother. It is a comparatively simple operation although it does take some time. The abdomen is opened, the lower part of the uterus opened cross wise, and the baby is then quickly delivered. After the placenta has been removed, the muscle wall is carefully sewn up, as is the wall of the abdomen, which is the most time consuming part of the operation. The operation is usually done under general anesthetic, with the woman asleep, but it is sometimes possible to do it with an epidural anesthetic- the woman is then able to see the baby immediately after birth and to hear his first cry. As this procedure is quick, very little of the anesthesia reaches the infant and the outcome for both mother and the infant is excellent in most cases.

Cesarean sections are safer than breech deliveries. However, Cesarean deliveries also bring risks. It is a major abdominal surgery that requires a longer recovery period than normal childbirth. They involve a higher infection rate than vaginal delivery, longer hospital stay, and the increased expense and stress that accompany any surgery. About four percent of cesarean results in serious complications such as bleeding and infections. Finally and perhaps most important, some mothers' psychological reactions to cesarean childbirth can be quite negative, especially if they had general instead of regional anesthesia and "missed the event".

vi. Breech Birth

Breech presentation delivery means that the baby is born bottom first, as opposed to a vertex delivery when he is born headfirst. When the baby is in a breech position, the doctors may try to turn him so that his head is down-this will be done if it would be safer for the baby to be born head first. A breech birth is always undertaken in hospital and a doctor usually does the delivery.

The condition in which the lower extremities or buttocks pass through the pelvis first is encountered about once in every 30 labors. Because the head in such cases is the last part of the child to be delivered and because this part of the delivery is the most difficult, the umbilical cord (navel string) may be compressed while the after coming head is being born, with the result that the child may be asphyxiated. Asphyxia or injuries to the child, which result from the attendant's effort to hasten the delivery and prevent its asphyxiation, are responsible for the loss of three times as many breech babies as head-on babies. As very small premature infants are particularly susceptible to the dangers of breech delivery, the mortality among them is very high when they are born breech first.

vii. Forceps delivery

When the fetus is too large to emerge spontaneously or when its position marks normal birth impossible, instruments must be used to aid in delivery. Obstetric forceps are simple metal instruments, which can hold and cradle the baby's head. They can be used to help in delivery when there is delay during the second stage-the second stage should never continue longer than one hour, it is often much shorter than that. The forceps will be used just to lift the baby's head out and speed things on; it is often a much simple and safer way of delivering a baby than allowing him to be pushed out with difficulty.

viii. Accelerated birth

The drug Syntocinon is often used to speed up labor, because a long labor is known to be more risky for the baby and is very tiring for the mother. Doctors have therefore, developed methods of shortening labor when necessary. This can be done by giving a very dilute solution of Syntocinon into the mother's vein as a drip or low injection. The number of contractions can be counted and the injection slowed or made faster to produce a contraction every two or three minutes. There are some machines, which will do this automatically by controlling the injection according to the number of contractions.

Planning for Birth or Preparing for Birth

No childbirth is completely free from pain; and analgesia, anesthesia and forceps have long been used to reduce labor pains. But in 1933 Grandly Dick Read, a British Obstetrician, suggested a method of almost drugless childbirth, with the father present in the delivery room to coach the mother during labor and birth. He concluded that fear was the main cause for the pain experienced at childbirth–a vicious circle with fear causing pain, which caused fear.

ix. Prepared Childbirth

Most doctors believe that delivery is easier and mother and child get off to a better start, when the parents involve themselves in preparing for childbirth. This involvement, they believe, can contribute much to making childbirth a happy experience. Many parents combat anxiety and fear by participating in one of the programs known as prepared childbirth. They read factual material on childbirth, attend lectures and discuss what they learn with other prospective parents.

Preparation for childbirth requires a woman with a number of valuable ways of dealing with pain, using knowledge, confidence and the techniques of rhythmic breathing when the husband becomes part of a team rather than a bystander. This creates a feeling of sharing and may make the transition to parenthood much easier for both parents. Prepared childbirth does not oppose the use of anesthesia or other drugs. The purpose of this is to reduce parental anxiety and to teach the mother to facilitate rather than hate labor and delivery.

Various methods used today emphasize the parents' preparation for childbirth. These involve:

(1) Training for the delivery through educational experiences and specific techniques of pain control

(2) Encouraging the wakefulness and participation of the mother as well as minimized use of drugs during labor and delivery, and

(3) Involvement of the husband in the labor and delivery.

Such approaches stress that women will be socialized to expect discomfort and pain during labor and delivery. The methods used in prepared childbirth techniques are an attempt to help mothers relax and redirect their conscious attention away from the discomforts of labor. They also practice breathing routines and exercises that prepare both parents for birth experience.

Prepared childbirth does not oppose the use of anesthesia or other drugs. The purpose of this is to reduce parental anxiety and to teach the mother to facilitate rather than insert labor and delivery. Preparation for childbirth requires a woman with a number of valuable ways of dealing with pain, using knowledge, confidence and the techniques of rhythmic breathing when the husband becomes part of a team rather there a bystander. This creates a feeling of sharing and may make the transition to parenthood much easier for both parents.

x. Recent approaches to child birth

The effort to reduce stress and control pain during labor has recently led to an increase in the use of some older and some newer non-medicated techniques. These include water birth, massage, acupuncture , hypnosis, and music therapy.

Waterbirth: Waterbirth involves giving birth in a tub of warm water. Some women go through labour in the water and get out for delivery, others remain in the water for delivery. The rationale for waterbirth is that the baby has been in amniotic sac for many months and that delivery in a similar environment is likely to be less stressful for the baby and the mother. Mothers get into the warm water when contractions become closer together and more intense. Getting into the water too soon can cause labor to slow or stop. Reviews of research have indicated mixed results for waterbirth.

Massage: Massage is increasingly used as a procedure prior to and during delivery . Reseachers have found that massage can reduce pain and anxiety during labor. A recent study revealed that massage therapy reduced pain in pregnant women and alleviated prenatal depression in both parents and improved their relationships.

Acupuncture: The ancient Chinese technique of acupuncture is another alternative to regular anesthesia during childbirth. Several long but thin needles are used in this form of anesthetic, stimulating the nerve connecting centers related to the painful area. Relaxation and numbness result in twirling needles or supplying them with a mild electric charge. The experimental use of acupuncture in childbirth involves the use of two or four needles in the ankle and another near the wrist to relax the abdominal area. Additionally a series of wired electrodes are often attached to the abdominal area. Increase of pains moderated by an increase in pulsating electric current applied the anesthetist or obstetrician. Light electric shocks are experienced by the mother. Self-regulation, of the current is a possibility, since only the mother knows the intensity of her contraction and how much pain she is willing to stand without diffusion. Deliveries through cesarean section using acupuncture as the only anesthetic have been reported since 1973. Patients report much less post-operative discomfort than from the use of other anesthetics. Only a limited number of experts are presently available for the professional use of either hypnosis or acupuncture.

Hypnosis: Hypnoses are sometimes used instead of drugs or anesthetics for childbirth. Occasionally "hypnoses" is used to facilitate the mother's relaxation and co-operation. In some cases with complications, such as heart weakness or a preceding spinal disease, that make the use of anesthetic or even analgesic drugs inadvisable because of side effects; hypnotic trance seems to be a proper non-detrimental substitute. To assume hypnotizability, one or two preparatory sessions are necessary for checking and raising the expectant mothers' susceptibility to a trance state. No detrimental side effects have been reported from hypnoses under professional guidance, and it is safe for the baby.

Music Therapy: Music Therapy during childbirth, which involves the use of music to reduce stress and mange pain, is increasingly used. More research is needed to determine its effectiveness.

4.6. THE 'PUERPERIUM'

This is the period from the birth of the baby until the mother's body has returned completely to normal. When labor has finished, a woman can find that her womb is still quite big. If her abdomen could be felt, she will feel the uterus almost up to the level of her navel, about the size it was at four months of pregnancy. It continues to contract from time to time, in order to remove the remains of the lining. She may feel some cramp-like 'after' pains during the first three or four days after delivery; they sometimes happen while she is breast-feeding, because a hormone is released into her blood at that time and it causes a contraction. There is no necessity to be worried about these pains, as they are helping the uterus to return to normal quickly.

We can notice a bloodstained discharge from the vagina, called the 'lochia'. At first, it will be almost pure blood but it will become progressively browner and finally disappear about two weeks after the delivery. If we ever observe a gush of blood or if bright blood should return, we must report this at once to the doctor. Very occasionally, a small amount of placenta is left in the womb and will cause some bleeding; the doctor will know whether anything needs to be done about it.

4.7. IN VITRO FERTILISATION

Introduction

- A Test tube baby is the colloquial term that refers to a child that is conceived outside the women's body. This process of artificial insemination is referred to *in vitro* fertilization.
- The term *in vitro* is used to any biological procedure that is performed outside the organism it would normally be occurring in, to distinguish it from an *in vitro* procedure, where the tissues remains inside the living organism within which it is normally found.
- However *in vitro* fertilization is usually performed in the shallower container called Petri dishes.

History

Test tube baby is the revolutionary treatment for those couples who can't have a baby on their own because of various types of infertility i.e., when the woman's fallopian tubes are damaged or the man's sperm count is low.

- It was first developed by Dr.Patrick C.Steptoe and Robert G.Edwards of Great Britain.
- The first "Test Tube Baby" , Louise Brown was born in the year 1978 .
- The second IVF baby was born in India, named "Durga" in Kolkata on October 3,1978.
- IVF is also used now to enable prospective parents with other reproductive problems (e.g. Inability to produce eggs, poor sperm quality, or endometriosis) to bear a child.

Indications

- Initially IVF was developed to overcome infertility due to problems of the fallopian tubes, but it turned out that it was successful in many other infertility situations as well.

Thus, for IVF to be successful it may be easier to say that it requires healthy ova, sperm that can fertilise, and a uterus that can maintain a pregnancy.

- This means that IVF can be used for females who have already gone through pregnancy.

Procedure

1. Ovarian stimulation

The treatment cycles are typically started on the third day of menstruation and consist of a regimen of fertility medications to stimulate the development of multiple follicles of the ovaries. In the most patients injectable gonadotropins are used under close monitoring. Such monitoring frequently checks the estradiol level and, by means of gynecologic ultrasonography, follicular growth. Typically, an approximate of 10 days of injection will be necessary. Endogenous ovulation is blocked by the use of GnRH agonists or GnRH antagonists.

2. Oocyte retrieval

Once the follicles are ready for the ovulation, Human Chorionic Gonadotropin (HCG) of 5,000 units is given. The eggs are retrieved 33-36hrs following the H. C. G. injection.

There are three methods, which clinics may use for egg retrieval.

(*i*) Ultrasound-guided aspiration: In this method the ultrasound probe is inserted through the vagina, which emits high-frequency sound waves, which are translated into the images of the pelvic organs and displayed on a monitor, so that the mature follicles can be seen as black bubbles on the screen. The doctor guides a needle through the vagina into each mature follicle. The follicular containing the egg is then sucked out through the needle into a test tube, and all the follicles are aspirated, one by one.

(*ii*) Laparoscopy: This is carried out under general anesthetic. The eggs are retrieved from their follicles using a very fine suction needle. However, this method is rarely used today, because the vaginal-ultrasound guided method is much quicker, easier and safer.

(*iii*) T.U.D.O.R.: This stands for Trans-vesical Ultrasound Directed Oocyte Recovery. This is an out patient procedure performed under a local anesthetic. In this method, a suction probed is guided by ultrasound control through the bladder. This technique also has the advantage of being able to retrieve eggs from an inaccessible ovary even if it is covered by adhesions.

The eggs are now incubated for 4-24 hours in a specially prepared culture medium in order to ensure that adequate maturation has occurred. 1,00,000 – 10,00,000 specially prepared progressively swimming sperms are then added to the incubated eggs. Fertilisation takes place in about 24 hours.

3. Fertilisation in Laboratory

In the laboratory, the identified eggs are stripped of surrounding cells and prepared for fertilization; in the mean time, semen provided by the male partner is prepared for fertilization by removing the inactive cells and seminal fluid. The sperm and the egg are incubated in the culture media for about 18 hrs. By this time, fertilization should have taken place and the fertilized egg would show two pronuclei.

In situations where the sperm count is low, a single sperm is injected directly into the egg using intra cytoplasmic sperm injection (ICSI). The fertilized egg is passed through a special growth medium and left for about 48 hrs until an egg has reached the 6-8 cells stage. The egg in 6-8 cell stages are transferred 3 days after retrieval. In many programs, however, embryos are placed into an extended culture system with a transfer done at the blastocyst stage, especially if many day-3 embryos are available. Blastocyst may give higher pregnancy rates if the embryo quality is in doubt.

4. Embryo Transfer

The embryos are judged to be the best, based on the number of cells, evenness of growth and degree of fragmentation. The number to be transferred depends on the number available, the age of the women and other health and diagnostic factors. They are transferred through a thin, plastic catheter, which goes through her vagina and cervix. This is a painless procedure and no anesthetic is required. Several embryos may be passed into the uterus to improve the chances of implantation and pregnancy.

5. Post Transfer

The patient has to wait two weeks before she returns to the clinic for the pregnancy test. During this time she may receive progesterone-a hormone that keeps a uterus lining thickened and suitable for implantation. Many IVF programs provide additional medications as part of their protocol.

Pregnancy

The chance of a successful pregnancy is approximately 20-30 % for each IVF cycle, although selected clinics are now able to quote rates upto 50% per cycle. There are many factors that determine success rates including the age of the person, quality of the eggs and sperm, the duration of the infertility, the health of the uterus and the medical expertise. It is a common practice for IVF programmes to boost the pregnancy rate by placing multiple embryos during embryo transfer. A flip slide of this practice is a higher risk of multiple pregnancies, itself associated with obstetric complications.

IVF programmes generally publish their pregnancy rates. However, comparisons between clinics are difficult as many variables determine outcome. Furthermore, these statistics depends strongly on the type of patients selected.

There are many reasons why pregnancy may not occur following IVF and embryo transfer, including

- The timing of ovulation may be misjudged, or ovulation may not be able to be predicted or may not occur.
- Attempts to obtain eggs that develop during the monitored cycle may be unsuccessful.
- The eggs obtained may be abnormal or may have been damaged during the retrieval process.
- A semen specimen may not be available to be provided.
- Fertilization of eggs to form embryos may not occur.
- Cleavage or cell division of the fertilized eggs may not take place.
- The embryo may not develop normally.
- Implantation may not occur.
- Equipment failure, infection and \ or human error or other unforeseen and uncontrollable factors, which may result in the loss of or damage to the eggs, the semen sample and \ or the embryos.

Complications

The major complication of IVF is the development of multiple births. This is directly related to the practice of placing multiple embryos at embryo transfer. Multiple births are related to increase pregnancy loss, obstetrical complications, prematurity, and neonatal morbidity with the potential for long term damage. Strict embryo transfer policies have been enacted to reduce this problem, but are not universally followed or accepted. Spontaneous splitting of embryos in the womb after transfer does occur, but is rare and would lead to identical twins. Recent evidence suggests that singleton offspring after IVF is at higher risk for lower birth weight for unknown reasons. Another major complication, related to the use of ovarian stimulation is the development of the ovarian hyper stimulation syndrome.If the underlying infertility is related to abnormalities in spermatogenesis, it is plausible, but too early to examine that male offspring is at higher risk for sperm abnormalities.

The issue of birth defect remains a controversial topic in IVF. Major birth defect includes chromosomal abnormalities, genetic imprinting defects, multiple organ abnormalities. Studies have found 30 – 40 % increased risk of birth defects associated with assisted reproductive technology when compared to children born after spontaneous conception. Possible explanation offered were the underlying cause of the infertility, factors associated with IVF/ICSI , culture conditions, and medications; however, the actual cause is not known.

Cryopreservation

1. Embryo Cryopreservation

If multiple embryos are generated, patients may choose to freeze embryos that are not transferred . Those embryos are placed in liquid nitrogen and can be preserved for a long time. There are currently 500,000 frozen embryos. The advantage is that the patients who failed to conceive may become pregnant using such embryos without having to go through a full IVF cycle, or, if pregnancy occurs, they could return for another pregnancy.

2. Oocyte Cryopreservation

Cryopreservation of unfertilized matured oocytes has been successfully accomplished, e.g. in women who are likely to lose their ovarian reserve due to undergoing chemotherapy.

3. Ovarian Tissue Cryopreservation

Cryopreservation of ovarian tissue is of interest to women who want to preserve their reproductive function beyond the natural limit, or whose reproductive potential is threatened by cancer therapy. Research is trying to address this issue.

Adjunctive interventions

There are several variations or improvements of IVF, such as ICSI, ZIFT, GIFT and PGD. An increasing number of fertility specialists and centers offer acupuncture as the part of these IVF protocol, or maintained a list of acupuncturists specializing infertility.

IntraCytoplasmic Sperm Injection: (ICSI) is a more recent development associated with IVF which allows the sperm to be directly injected into the egg using micromanipulation. This is used for sperm that have difficulty penetrating the egg and when sperm numbers are very low. ICSI results in success rates are equal to IVF fertilization.

Zygote Intrafallopian Transfer: (ZIFT) eggs are removed from the women, fertilized and then placed in the women's fallopian tubes rather then the uterus.

Gamete Intrafallopian Transfer: (GIFT) eggs are removed from the women and placed in one of the fallopian tube, along with the man's sperm. This allows fertilization to take place inside the women's body. Therefore, this variation is actually an in vivo fertilization, and not an in vitro fertilization.

Preimplantation Genetic Diagnosis: (PGD) can be performed on embryo transfer. A similar, but more general test has been developed called Preimplantation Genetic Haplotyping(PGH).

Acupuncture

Limited but supportive evidence from clinical trials and case series suggests that acupuncture may improve the success rate of IVF and the quality of life of patients undergoing IVF and that it is a safe adjunct therapy. However, this conclusion should be interpreted with caution because most studies reviewed had design limitations, and the acupuncture interventions employed often were not consistent with traditional Chinese medical principles.

Ethics & issues

Certain ethical issues have been raised from the beginning when IVF was introduced. These concerns include

- Bypassing the natural method of conception.
- Creating life in the laboratory.
- Fertilizing more embryos than will be needed.
- Discarding excess embryos.
- Unnatural environment for embryos.
- Using untested technology.
- Not affordable for many.
- Misallocation of medical resources.
- Creating embryos, freezing them, and keeping them "in limbo".
- Exposing embryos to unnatural substances.
- Destroying embryos in research.
- Potential to create embryos for medical purposes.
- Potential to protect embryos.
- Potential to modify embryos.
- Facilitates idea that embryos are commodities.
- Financial rewards for IVF doctors dissuade them from recommending other methods to the couples.
- Infertility is treated as a disease and not as a symptom of underlying medical problems.
- The long term effect on frozen embryos is unknown.

Pregnancy Past Menopause

While menopause has set a natural barrier to further conception, IVF has allowed women to be pregnant in their fifties and sixties. These are women whose uterus have been appropriately prepared to receive embryos that originated from an egg of an egg donor. Therefore, their children are not genetically linked to them. Even after menopause, the uterus is fully capable to carry out its function. Currently, the oldest woman to give birth is Adriana Iliescu, aged 66, from Romania.

Religious Objections

The Roman Catholic Church is opposed to in vitro fertilization in all instances and advocates that infertility is a call from God to adopt children. It "infringes[s] the child's right to be born of a father and mother known to him and bound to each other by marriage". Also, embryos are discarded in the process causing them to die. Some estimates of the number of embryos killed reach 6 million, and the Catholic faith sees embryos as human lives with the same rights as all others. Therefore, the faith views this procedure as always unacceptable. However, it allows the use of more natural techniques which seek to treat the underlying causes of infertility.

Regulatory Events

While in the United States IVF programmes operate under voluntary guidelines, programmes in many other countries are subject to regulations that control many aspects of IVF practice. In such settings regulations may dictate:

- The number of oocytes that can be fertilized.
- The number of embryos that can be transferred.
- The use of cryopreservation.
- The ability to perform tests or interventions on the embryo.

QUESTIONS

SECTION "A"

Short Answer Type:

1. What is normal puerperium?
2. What is tubal pregnancy?
3. What is breech birth?
4. Write a note on embryo transfer in IVF method.
5. List out a few types of birth.
6. What is precipitious birth?
7. Specify the stages involved in birth process
8. What is cryopreservation?
9. Explain birth process.
10. State the purpose of water birth.

SECTION "B"

One Page Answer Type:

1. What are the different types of birth?
2. Explain the stages of labour?
3. How does multiple pregnancies occur?
4. Specify the ethical issues in invitro fertilisation.
5. Mention about some premonitory signs of labour.

SECTION "C"

Essay Answer Type:

1. Briefly explain some of the gynaecological complications of pregnancy.
2. Discuss in detail about in vitro fertilisation.
3. Examine the different types of birth in detail.
4. Explain the mechanical factors affecting labour.

CHAPTER

5

NEONATE OR NEWBORN

OBJECTIVES

To enlighten students about:

- Medical Assessment of the Newborn.
- Adjustment of The New Born To Temperature, Breathing, Feeding And Elimination.
- Characteristic Functioning of the Major Systems.
- Physical Characteristics of Newborn or Neonate. The Neonates' Repertoires of Reflexes: Newborn States.
- Care of the Normal Newborn

Sleep, Oh my little ones, Sleep
Yours is the Golden tomorrow
Yours are the hands that will reap
Dreams that are sow, while you sleep
Fed with our hope and our sorrow
Rich with the tears that we weep

— Sarojini Naidu
The Bird of Time

5.1. INTRODUCTION

The term neonate literally means, "Newborn" and is applied to the first four weeks of a child's life – from the moment the umbilical cord is cut, about fifteen to thirty minutes after birth, until the dried stump of the cord falls off, about four weeks later. The term neonatorium refers to the first month of life. This neonatal period, is a time of transition from the uterus/ neonate's intrauterine life, when, as fetus, it was supported entirely by its mother, to an extra uterine existence or to an independent existence. Still enormously dependent on adults, the neonate is nevertheless embarked on its own unique existence.

Age Divisions: Age divisions show that there are two distinct divisions in the time between birth, and two years after birth. First is the period of neonate or newborn (0-2 weeks) and the next is the period of infancy (2weeks-2years). Hurlock (1981) postulates two divisions of this neo-natal stage, the first one being; the period of the partunate (from birth to 15-30 minutes after birth) and the next is the period of the neonate (from cutting and tying of the cord to approximately the end of the second week and postnatal life). The first period begins with the emergence of the fetus from the mother until the cord is cut, during which time the infant continues to be a parasite. In the next period, the infant is separate, independent and is no longer a parasite. He makes adjustments to the postnatal life outside the uterine walls of the mother, where he has lived for approximately 9 months.

5.2 CHARACTERISTICS OF NEONATE

Each period in the life span is characterized by certain developmental phenomena that distinguish it from the periods that precede or follow it. The characteristics of the neonate are listed as follows:

1. Neonatal period is a time of Radical Adjustments

At birth, the neonate is transferred from an internal to an external environment. Like all graduations, it requires adjustments on the individual's part. It may be easy for some infants to make these adjustments but so difficult for others that they will fail to do so.

2. Neonatal period is a Plateau in Development

The rapid growth and development that took place during the prenatal period suddenly came to a stop with birth. In fact, there is often a slight regression, such as loss of weight and tendency to be less strong and healthy than at birth, which normally lasts for several days to a week, after which the infant begins to improve. The halt in growth and development characteristic of this plateau is due to the necessity for making radical adjustment to the postnatal environment.

3. Neonatal period is a Crucial Time for Psychosocial Development

The foundations of psychosocial development are established in infancy, according to Erikson (1950) and others. Some researchers describe infancy as the most important stage in the life cycle in determining the future social and psychological well-being of the individual. It is not possible to predict with even reasonable accuracy what the individual's future development will be, based on the development apparent at birth. However, the newborn's development provides a clue as to what to expect later on. The significance of establishing a close, intimate attachment to a loving, nurturing caregiver is seen as having tantamount influence on the person as well as in learning to relate effectively with others as a social being.

4. Neonatal period is a Hazardous Period

Infancy is a hazardous period, both physically and psychologically. Physically, it is hazardous because of the difficulties the newborn infant faces while making necessary radical adjustments to the totally new and different environment. The high infant mortality rate is evidence of this. Psychologically, infancy is hazardous because it is the time when the attitudes of significant people towards the infant are crystallized. Many of these attitudes were established during the prenatal period and may change radically after the infant is born, but some remain relatively unchanged or are strengthened, depending on conditions at birth and on the ease or difficulty with which the infant and his parents adjust during the infancy period.

5.3 MEDICAL ASSESSMENT OF THE NEONATE

The Apgar Scale Assessment

The Apgar Scale which has a series of tests to measure the degree to which a newborn infant seemed capable of making the adjustments from intrauterine to extra uterine life, is used in virtually all hospitals. One minute after delivery, and then again five minutes after delivery, the scale's five subtests are administered to every infant. The Apgar score yields measures of Appearance (color), Pulse (heart rate), Grimace (reflex irritability), Activity (muscle tone), and Respiration (breathing) and **body skin color**.

Each of the five scales may be rated as zero, one or two; the maximum score is two for each of the five scales, for a total of 10 points. Score of 10 indicated infant in best possible condition. Generally, an infant with a score of 4 or less is in need of immediate medical assistance. The Apgar score is a good indicator of later neurological or muscular difficulties. It provides an immediate means of determining which infants need life-saving measures.

The Brazelton Neonatal Behavioral Assessment Scale

The Brazelton Neonatal Behavioral Assessment Scale is also a valuable and popular assessment device, used within 24 to 36 hours after birth. It assesses the newborn's neurological development, reflexes and reaction to people. The newborn is an active participant, and the score is based on the newborn's best performance. Sixteen reflexes, such as sneezing, blinking, and rooting are assessed along with reactions to circumstances, such as the infant's reaction to a rattle. The examiner makes detailed ratings of the newborn on each of the 27 items.

A very low Brazelton score can indicate brain damage or it can reflect stress to the brain that may heal in time. If an infant merely seems sluggish, parents are encouraged to give the infant attention and become more sensitive to the infant's needs .The Brazelton scale is more difficult and time consuming to administer than the Apgar, but it is especially valuable in assessing which infants may need special care and what kind of care they require.

Neonatal Intensive Care Unit Network Neurobehavioral Scale (NNNS)

Described as an offspring of the NBAS, the NNNS provides a more comprehensive analysis of the newborn's behavior, neurological and stress responses, and regulatory capacities. The NNNS was created to assess the at-risk infant, especially those who are preterm and/or substance-exposed, whereas the NBAS was developed to assess the behavior of normal, healthy, full term infants.

- The Transition of Fetus to Newborn: Birth process involves considerable stress for the baby. During each contraction, when the placenta and umbilical cord are compressed as the uterine muscles draw together, the supply of oxygen to the fetus is decreased. If the delivery takes too long, anoxia can develop . The baby has considerable capacity to withstand the stress of birth. Large quantities of the hormones-adrenaline and non-adrenaline are secreted, protecting the fetus in the event of raised oxygen deficiency. These hormones increase the heart's pumping, speed up heart rate, channel blood flow to the brain, and the blood-sugar level. Never again, in life will such large amounts of these hormones be secreted. This fact underscores both how stressful it is to be born and how adapted the fetus is for birth.

5.4 PHYSIOLOGICAL ADJUSTMENTS OF NEONATE TO RESPIRATION AND CIRCULATION, TEMPERATURE REGULATION, DIGESTION AND ELIMINATION

Physiological Adjustments: The mother's body maintains the homeostasis of the fetus before birth. Due to the undeveloped state of the autonomic nervous system at birth, the infant is unable to maintain homeostasis. However, once the autonomic nervous system matures, its homeostasis improves. Hence, the tendency to suffer illness especially respiratory and gastrointestinal decreases. The poor homeostasis of the infant's body immediately following birth is one of the causes for the high mortality rate at this time.

Childbirth is an exciting event in a family. Birth brings enormous changes in the life of the developing child. From the wider world outside, the forces that can affect his development increase markedly. Before this, only hereditary factors and limited intrauterine conditions could influence him. After birth, the number of environmental stimuli impinging on the infant and affecting his status is multiplied many times. With birth, the infant gets transferred from one kind of environment – the dim, warm, protected liquid of the uterus, where breathing and feeding are automatic into a radically different environment- the bright, noisy, cool and airy world , where for the first time, the infant must breathe and feed on his or her own.

Before birth, blood circulation, respiration, nourishment, elimination of waste, and temperature regulation were accomplished through the mother's body. The umbilical cord is cut immediately after birth and the baby is on its own. Before birth, oxygen came from the mother via the umbilical cord, but now the baby has to be self-sufficient and breathe on its own. Now 25 million little air sacs in the lungs must be filled with air. The first breaths may be the hardest ones at any point in life.

Adjustments of the newborn: Every newborn infant finds adjustment to postnatal life difficult at first. Some have trouble adjusting to temperature changes and develop colds, which may turn into pneumonia. Others find breathing difficult and must be given oxygen. Most choke when they attempt to suck and swallow, and many regurgitate more than they take in and get less nourishment than they need to grow or even to retain their birth weight. Few have any real trouble eliminating urine, but many have difficulties with feacal eliminations.

Infants must make 4 major adjustments before they can resume their developmental progress. While these adjustments are made, the infant remains on a plateau or may even regress to a lower stage of development. The adjustments are towards 1. breathing 2. temperature changes 3. sucking and swallowing and 4. elimination.

Breathing: Within moments of birth, each newborn must abandon one system of respiration- the placenta-and make functional another-the lungs. Until that sudden withdrawing of air into lungs occurs, the baby's life is in doubt. If the baby is live, it must begin breathing air within minutes after emerging from the birth canal. The first breath comes only after mucus and amniotic fluid have cleared from lungs. Some of the fluid is squeezed out through the infant's mouth and nose by pressure in the birth canal during birth itself. Some escape by gravity if the infant is held upside down. Once in the air, and even before the umbilical cord is clamped the newborn begins to snort and sneeze, trying to clear the air passages and to inflate the thousands of air sacs in the lungs.

During the prenatal period, the umbilical cord supplied oxygen to the fetus and carried back its carbon dioxide to the maternal system. During childbirth, oxygen transfer from the mother to the fetus is reduced slightly. On clamping the umbilical cord the oxygen tension in the arterial blood falls and the carbon dioxide tension rise. When the umbilical cord is cut, the newborns must begin to breathe on their own to obtain oxygen. Some find breathing difficult and must be given oxygen and warmth if it is to survive. Two processes are needed to supply oxygen, breathing to get oxygen into the lungs and circulation of blood to distribute the oxygen to the rest of the body. Almost immediately following upon its birth, the viable fetus starts the complex rhythmic contractions and relaxations of its chest muscles and diaphragm that are required for pulmonary respirations; and even when the fetus is born in a pre-viable state, that is, before the end of the 28th week, it frequently makes respiratory efforts.

The newborn consumes 6 ml. of oxygen per kilogram per minute, twice that of an adult. The normal infant takes his first breath, almost immediately after birth, and as he cries, the alveoli expand and lung capillaries fill with oxygen within few minutes and most infants will settle and fall asleep.

There are a number of factors which influence the ability of respiratory centers in the brain. The brain responds to various stimuli by initiating the first gasp and the first cry. Once breathing is established the pattern of respiration is primarily determined in the medulla.

Respiratory rate may range from 50 to 80 breaths per minute during the first 24 hours. After the first 24 hours, respiration average per minute may range from 30 to 60 per minute. Both respiratory rhythm and depth of breaths may be regular. Short rapid, shallow breaths are frequently followed by 5 to 10 seconds pause in breathing. Most babies start to breathe as soon as they hit the air; a few need a little slap; and one who is not breathing within 2 minutes after birth is in trouble.

If the stimulus of birth has not started respiration, clearing mucus from the nose and mouth using a suction tube may provoke the first gasp. If the delay in breathing is thought to be related to sedative drugs a stimulant injection may be given. If these measures are not rapidly effective, artificial ventilation is started. Mouth-to-mouth ventilation can be given, but passing a tube into the wind pipe (trachea) to administer oxygen is more efficient if a doctor skilled in the technique is available. In most cases natural breathing is established in a few minutes and the emergency is over.

Adjustments to temperature changes: Crying is a fairly efficient means of increasing the infant's body temperature by increasing the metabolic rate. The skin thermo-receptors of the newborn infant are highly sensitive, and a slight decrease in the average skin temperature provokes a prompt peripheral vasoconstriction. Similarly, a change in temperature in the opposite direction causes vasodilatation and some sweating. Newborns are usually wrapped in towels or receiving blankets. They are placed next to the mother's warm body or in an incubator.

Before birth, the child's temperature is likely to remain fairly stable since he is protected by the surrounding amniotic fluid. The baby, at birth, has the same temperature as the mother (98°-100° F or 36-38°C). The newborn emerges from the uterus warm and wet into a cooler environment where the processes of evaporation and radiation work to produce a rapid drop in body temperature. Having spent all of its days in a liquid environment of approximately 37°C (98.6°F), the newborn is suddenly thrust out into a delivery room temperature that is inevitably colder ranging from 15-28°. Once outside the uterus, his temperature is much more likely to vary in response to changes in the environment, and to changes in the weather. The temperature of the delivery room is usually 20◦ to 30◦F less than the maternal temperature; consequently, heat control becomes a critical factor. A drop of three to six degrees is not uncommon.

On the 3rd/4th day of life the body temperature may sometimes go up to 38-40°C, particularly if the infant is a heavy one. This condition is called **transitory fever** of the newborn, or **dehydrating fever**, and it is concomitant with the greatest physiological weight loss. The condition of the child hardly changes at all. The fever subsides quite soon after abundant liquid intake (water).

The full-term, healthy neonate can usually maintain normal body temperature in the face of a slight drop in room temperature. The premature baby, though, lacks this ability and is thus likely to succumb. In a protected environment, the temperature begins to rise spontaneously and returns to normal by 8 hours of age. Nevertheless, prevention of excessive heat loss, especially during the first 15 minutes of life, is extremely significant to the infants' ability to make a successful transition to extra uterine life.

In the newborn, the mechanisms of sweating and shivering are imperfectly developed. Three other mechanisms of great conservation and production are available to the normal full-term infant. They are constriction of blood vessels, positional changes and metabolism of brown fat.

The infant can easily lose heat, so care is taken by providing suitable clothing, a warm bedroom and minimal exposure at bath times. Temperature rise in infant can cause febrile convulsion. In order to avoid loss of body heat through evaporation, vigorous efforts to dry the infant are essential to prevent heat loss by evaporation. The preheating of blankets, towels, diapers, and cribs can help prevent massive heat loss by "conduction." It is very important not to overheat the baby by over wrapping him, laying him in a radiator, putting him in direct sunlight, or putting some external heat source to the cot along with him.

Sucking and Swallowing: During pre-natal period, nourishment to the fetus comes continuously from the nutrients in the maternal blood stream through the placenta and umbilical cord. After birth, nourishment must come from infant's own efforts by sucking and swallowing. Only after the reflexes of sucking become regular will the neonate be getting enough nourishment to regain his lost weight and resume the pattern of growth, which was interrupted at birth. These reflexes are imperfectly developed at birth and the infant often gets less nourishment than is needed and thus loses weight. Most choke, when they attempt to suck and swallow, or regurgitate. The fine co-ordination of these activities occurs late in intrauterine life and early in postnatal life. Sucking activities increases in rate with development. Not only must newborns breathe and warm themselves, but they must also begin drinking, digesting and excreting. Healthy newborns can suck and swallow, taking in an ounce or two of liquid every two hours or so during their first days.

Digestion and Elimination

Regurgitation: Regurgitation or splitting of milk is a frequent occurrence in young infants. Almost all babies gasp and vomit at least once during 36 hours because of mucus. Regurgitation frequently accompanies a burp or an air bubble released from the stomach. Even breast-fed babies swallow air while nursing and need to be "babbled" well during and after each nursing. The baby should be held in an upright position and patted or rubbed "gently" on the back to facilitate relaxation of the cardiac sphincter of the stomach, which allows escape of the swallowed air. Babies with weak cardiac sphincters tend to "spilt up" between as well as after feeding. Other common causes of regurgitation are over-feeding, too much physical activity after feeding or placement of the head lower than the stomach during or after feeding. The baby should be placed on the abdomen or right side after feeding to reduce the possibility of aspiration (inhalation) of the regurgitated milk. The infant who frequently vomits large amounts immediately after feeding should be medically evaluated even in the absence of other symptoms.

Difficulty in feeding may be the cause of under feeding. The infant may be incapable of taking feeds because of some forms of physical handicap such as nasal obstruction or cleft palate. Infants with cerebral dysfunction due to brain injury, congenital abnormality or infections are poor at sucking and swallowing. The preterm infant may not have the strength to feed from the breast or bottle. The major task of the newborn is to obtain enough food to keep warm and to grow. The infant must take in enormous quantities of milk. Because newborns sleep a great deal and because their stomachs hold only a small amount relative to their requirements, they naturally spend most of their waking hours eating. Because of evaporation of water from the tissues and the difficulty of setting the new process of independent digestion into efficient action, the newborn loses several ounces during the first 2 weeks. If everything goes well, however, he soon regains his birth weight, which within 6 months will be doubled and within the first year tripled.

Elimination: The infant's organs of elimination begin to work soon after birth; formerly, waste products were eliminated through the umbilical cord. Few have trouble in eliminating urine but many have difficulties in fecal elimination. Defecation occurs at an average of 4 to 7 times and urination at an average of 18 times. There are major alterations in patterns of elimination during the first year while there are individual differences. Bowel movements are generally frequent and sporadic during the first few weeks, but by the time the infant is 4 weeks old, the number generally falls to 3 or 4 evacuations daily. During the first few weeks of postnatal existence, the average infant urinates frequently, but gradually the number of micturition decreases and the volume increases. Their bowels first excrete a tarry waste left over from fluid and cells swallowed in the uterus. Soon their stomach and intestines begin to secrete the substances necessary for digesting nutrients.

Effect of Poor Adjustments of The Neonate

Loss of Weight: The small baby loses weight quickly and regains it more slowly because he can take only small feedings at first. It may take him several weeks to adjust to get back to birth weight. This delay doesn't handicap him. Eventually he will gain rapidly to make up for it. Some parents worry unnecessarily about the initial weight loss. The chance of dehydration or fever is small, and it can always be cured immediately by giving fluids. It's better for the mother to realize how natural the weight loss is and to resolve to leave the whole matter in the doctor's hands. This drop in weight in most babies for a few days after birth, is normally less than 10% of the weight at birth, and may be termed physiological weight loss.

Physiological Weight Loss or Gain: This is the result of loss of fluid by evaporation from the skin and is the cause of normal micturition, defecation and respiratory exchange. The artificially fed baby begins to gain weight about the 4th day of life and the breast fed and preterm baby between the 7th and 10th day of life. Infants vary greatly in the rate with which they gain weight. A weekly gain 175-240g is usual in normal healthy babies. Some infants increase in weight more rapidly. After the first week of life weekly weighing provides all necessary information.

Causes: Inadequate intake, underfeeding, difficulty in feeding, vomiting, intestinal obstruction, functional disturbance, diarrhea, excessive surface evaporation, excessive urine loss.

Disorganization of Behaviour: For the 1st day or 2 of the postnatal life, all infants show relatively disorganized behavior such as irregularities in breathing rate, frequent urinations and defecations, wheezing and regurgitation. This is due partly to pressure on the brain during birth, which results in stunned state and partly to the undeveloped state of the ANS, which controls homeostasis.

Gradually by the end of 1st week of post natal life, the infant normally achieves a more organized pattern of behavior. This disorganization of behavior is evident in irregularities in the rate of respiration and pulse, frequent urinations and defecations, wheezing, colic and regurgitation of food taken.

Causes

- The new born infant is stunned by the ordeal of birth, which brings with it a pressure on his brain, which is only partially protected by a still undeveloped skull.
- Another cause is his still-deficient mechanisms for maintaining body homeostasis and his undeveloped ANS. Before his birth, his homeostasis was maintained by the mother's homeostasis in the uterus.

Factors Affecting Adjustment to Post Natal Life:

1. The type of pre-natal environment.
2. The type and severity of birth experienced.
3. Pre-maturity.
4. Parental attitudes and post natal care.

Malnutrition due to poor prenatal care during pregnancy has been found to be responsible for premature birth, still-births and infant mortality. With advancing maternal age, more problems are likely to arise during pregnancy and thus more complications in the child's adjustment to postnatal life. Infants whose mothers suffer from diabetes may have more difficulties in adjustment and are responsible for a higher incidence of mortality, than infants whose mothers are non-diabetic.

5.5. PHYSICAL CHARACTERISTICS OF NEONATE

Size and Physical Appearance: The new born baby seems incredibly small. Neonates are not very attractive or cute in appearance as all the new parents expect. They like to stay curled up in fetal posture. As it was floating in amniotic fluid of the uterus for nine months before birth, their skin is exceptionally wrinkled. All his body structures are present, some ready for full functioning, others only in rudimentary form. He is a real human being, down to the last eyelash and the miniature nails on fingers and toes. All the nerve cells are present at birth, but in immature form-the brain more than doubles in size, from 350 cc. to 750 cc., between birth and age one and doubles again by age six. Even at this age, we see the beginnings of marked individual differences in behaviour. While most neonates have very little head hair, some may have abundant long hair. During the first few days, some neonates also have fine body hair, called "lanugo".

Body Proportions: New babies have characteristic body proportions, including a relatively large head chubby rounded cheeks, prominent forehead, flat and rather depressed nose and a receding chin (which makes it easier to nurse). As the child's overall size increases, parts of the body grow at different rates. The child's extremities grow much faster than the trunk, resulting in a more proportionate appearance for the body as a whole.

Head and Skull: At birth, the newborn's head is large in proportion to the rest of its body, typically one-quarter of the total body length. Its height constitutes 1/4 or 1/5 of crown to heel length, whereas in adults, the height of the head is only 1/8 of the total height of the body. Its average circumference is 13 to 14 inches (33 to 35.5 cm) - about one inch larger than the chest. The head circumference increases by about 3 inches during the first 8 months of life. The newborn's skull may appear misshapen or elongated because of molding, which occurs as the head passes through the narrow birth canal. This temporary molding was possible because the skull bones are not yet fused together; they will not do so completely for another eighteen months. As a newborn, it has six places on the head where the bones have not yet grown together; these fontanels, or soft spots, are covered by a membrane as tough as canvas. This is a temporary condition that disappears naturally in a few days. As a consequence of these proportions, the neonate appears all head and eyes. Because the cartilage in the nose is also malleable, the trip through the birth canal leaves that protuberance looking squashed for a few days.

The head may become slightly flattened if the baby is always put to sleep on one particular side. It is worth making sure that she is put on alternate sides, at least until she learns to roll herself over. The head may come back to normal shape after 1 or 2 days. In some parts of India, the baby is put in a hammock; it provides uniform pressure to all sides of the head.

The neck is so short that it is almost invisible and the skin covering it lies in thick folds or creases. The newborn's head has to rest on its chest because its neck is short and has deep creases. The newborn's trunk also occupies a large proportion of body length. In the trunk, the shoulders are narrow, while the abdomen is large and bulging. Proportionately the arms and legs of the infant are much too short for his head and trunk and kept in a tightly flexed position. The hands and feet are miniature in size. The extremities are short in comparison with other body features and the feet and hands are notable for their miniature appearance. The feet are very flat, lacking arch development, and fingernails are paper-thin in nature.

Length And Weight : Physical growth of a baby is remarkable. In the first few months of life, infants grow rapidly, gaining nearly an ounce of weight a day and an inch in length each month. During the first year of life, there is an astonishing growth spurt. At birth, 95 percent of full-term babies weigh between $5\frac{1}{2}$ and 10 pounds and the average length of the neonate (measured from head to heel) ranges between 18 and 22 inches long. Boys tend to be slightly longer and heavier than girls, and firstborn child is likely to weigh less at birth than later borns.

In their first few days, neonates lose as much as 5 to 10 percent of their body weight, primarily because of a loss of fluids by evaporation from the skin, normal micturition, defecation and respiratory exchange. This is known as **normal physiological weight loss.** When the mother's breast milk comes in or formula feeding begins, they begin to gain weight again at about the fifth day and are generally back to birth weight by the tenth to the fourteenth day. Light, full-term infants lose less weight in this period than heavy ones, and first-borns lose less than later-born. Thereafter, the newborn will gain 5 to 6 oz per week for the first month; it will double its birth weight by 5 to 6 months of age and triple its birth weight by its first birthday.

Bone Growth: The best way of estimating a child's physical maturity is to use "skeletal age", a measure of development of the bones of the body. The skeletal bones are largely connective tissue at birth. Bones and muscles develop quickly during infancy. At birth, most of the infant's bones are soft, pliable, flexible and difficult to break because they are composed chiefly of soft, pliable tissue called cartilage. Due to their softness, the bones of a newborn do not fracture easily; they are very susceptible to deformities and can readily be mis-shapened. Parents should be careful in handling children because bones can be pulled out of their sockets or deformed, as the bony tissue of the newborn is still immature.

Face: The neonate may appear chinless. The newborn's face is small, forehead is high, has a flat nose, a receding chin and when it cries, its body turns crimson. The cranial region, the area over the eyes, is proportionately much larger than the rest of the head while the chin is proportionately much too small. The eyes of a newborn are approximately one-half of their adult size, and the body as a whole is only one-twentieth of its adult dimensions. The nose is very small and almost flat on the face (due to the undeveloped bridge) , while the tiny mouth might look like a slit if the lips are narrow. Its nose is so small that the muscles inside the nostrils tend to dry up and obstruct breathing, thus making odd sounds. Drops of water in the nostrils keep remedying this. The eyes may appear swollen and they are treated after birth with antibiotic application of erythromycin or silver nitrate as a preventive measure against blindness caused by gonorrhea.

Newborns demonstrate much squinting perhaps because of the newness and initially unpleasant sensation of adjusting to a bright environment after being in the darkness of the uterus. Eye movements are slow and uncoordinated from the immaturity of the muscles that assist in focusing. The tear glands are largely non-functional at birth giving the eyes a rather glassy appearance. No tears are produced until 4 weeks of age, until the lacrimal ducts (tear ducts) are developed. The color of the iris is grayish blue in almost all white babies at birth and brown in newborns of other racial backgrounds. Final eye color emerges by about 12 months after birth.

Newborn's **mouth** is small and sharply outlined. Baby move its lips even if the areas beyond the lips are touched (rooting reflex).The neonate's mouth is usually examined closely for any defects or abnormalities, particularly **cleft palate**, the incomplete formation and nonunion of the hard palate. This condition can be corrected through surgical repair. The gums will be pink and moist.

Teeth: Natal teeth occur approximately once in every 2,000 births. They are the baby type and are usually the lower central incisors. They are deeply embedded into gums and usually drop off before the actual teeth process starts. Tongue is proportionately small and almost always kept inside the mouth.

Skin: The newborn infants have skin that is soft, thin and appears pale and wrinkled. Many newborns have a pinkish cast; it is so thin that it barely covers the capillaries through which blood flows. During the first few days, the body of some neonates are very hairy because some of the "lanugo", a fuzzy prenatal hair, has not yet fallen off. All new babies are covered with "vernix caseosa" ("cheesy varnish"), an oily protection against infection that dries within the first few days.

Pigmentation may be more pronounced in certain areas of the body, such as the earlobes, scrotum, and back of the neck; full pigmentation develops several days later. The neonate's color varies according to the amount of melamine present in the skin. **Milia**, small clusters of pearly white spots mostly on the infant's nose, chin, and forehead, may also be present at birth. These spots are caused by the retention of sebaceous material within the sebaceous glands and disappears suddenly without treatment.

Muscle and Fat Development: Increase in weight at all periods of growth is due to the development and addition to the weight of the bones, muscles and fatty tissue. Muscles play an important role in the functioning of body organs like the heart, the digestive system and so on. They are also responsible for strength and coordination of activities. Muscles develop as the infant grows. The large muscles develop more rapidly than small ones and motor abilities progress from broad to precise. However, there is continuous growth in muscle length, breadth and thickness until adulthood.

The **muscles** of the newborn infant are soft, small and uncontrolled. They have all the muscle cells they will ever have, but their strength will increase, as their muscles grow larger. At the time of birth, less development has taken place in the muscles of the neck and legs than in those of the hand and arms.

Body fat (most of which, lies just beneath the skin) increases in the last few weeks of prenatal life and continues to do so after birth, reaching a peak at about nine months of age. This early rise in the "baby fat" helps the small infant keep a constant body temperature.

The Brain: Dramatic increase in brain weight during infancy is found. At birth, the birth weight is about 12 ounces (25% of adult size) increasing to about 2½ pounds (75% of the adult size) at the end of infancy. This rapid growth rate is a continuation of the cephalocaudal direction of growth that began early in prenatal development.

The primary neuron cells of the brain were formed early in prenatal development between the 12th and 20th weeks. After birth, the majority of brain growth stems from the development of glial cells. These cells act to "myelinize" the nerve fibers of the brain.

Genitals: Maternal hormones of pregnancy present in the neonate's bloodstream may cause certain physiological anomalies. The breasts of neonates of both sexes may be swollen. This condition will disappear without intervention. The scrotum of male neonates may appear large and edematous. The scrotum should be palpated for the presence of testicles, which usually descend from the abdominal cavity into the scrotal sac during the seventh month of fetal life. Undescented testicles can be treated with a short course of drug therapy or surgery. The newborn's penis is inspected for the location of the urethral opening, which is normally just at the tip of the head of the penis under the foreskin.

The labia in the newborn female may appear swollen. A blood-tinged mucous vaginal discharge known as **pseudo menstruation** may be noted. These conditions are related to maternal hormones and disappear without treatment.

Urine is normally present in the bladder at the time of birth. The newborn should void within 24 hours after birth and 8 to 10 times a day thereafter. The initial voiding may appear rust-colored because of the presence of uric acid crystals. This condition generally disappears without treatment.

Abdomen: The neonate's abdomen appears large and flabby. Immediately after birth, the umbilical cord is tied and cut. After a few days, the blood vessels of the cord become dry or thrombosed, with a change in color from dull yellowish brown to black. By the tenth day, the dried cord falls off and the navel is completely healed. Tub bathing is avoided until the navel is fully healed.

At the time of birth, the newborn can swallow, digest, metabolize and absorb nutrients. The newborn can metabolize only simple carbohydrates, and for this reason, whole milk, which contains complex sugars, is not given to the newborn. The newborn's stomach can hold 1 to 3oz liquid; by 10 months, it can hold about 10oz. The neonate's cardiac sphincter is underdeveloped; therefore, it is important to allow the infant the periods of feeding, followed by "bubbling" or burping for the release of swallowed air.

Extremities: The newborn's extremities are short in proportion to the rest of the body and are kept in a tightly flexed position. They should be examined for a range of motion, symmetry, and reflexes. Any abnormality should be reported immediately to the physician for further evaluation. In full-term infants, the soles of the feet and palms of the hands are deeply creased. Preterm infants have only very fine lines on their palms and soles.

5.6. CHARACTERISTIC FUNCTIONING OF THE MAJOR SYSTEMS

Every system of the body undergoes some adjustment to extrauterine life of the newborn.

Nervous System: The nervous system of the newborn is less developed than an adult. The dendrites are noticeably immature in newborns. Newborns have many more neurons than adults do. As the infant grows and gains experience, neurons not needed are eliminated in a whittling down process. The central structures of the newborns' brains are noticeably immature. Myelination refers to the development of the myelin sheath, a covering consisting of a white fatty substance that grows around many of the neural axons in the body. Myelin acts as an insulator and aids in nerve conductivity. It also helps to provide nutrition for the nerve cells. Without the proper amount of Myelin, the body would be incapable of many functions such as crawling or bowel and bladder control.

Circulatory System: After the umbilical cord is clamped and cut, the infant's own circulatory system must function on its own. Blood flow in the infant's heart now actually changes directions. The infant's blood begins to flow through the heart from left to right rather than from right to left, as it had before birth. This critical change may plunge the infant's blood pressure downward and raise the heart beat to 140 counts a minute. For even the healthiest of infants, it may take ten days for blood pressure to stabilize.

Newborns are most vulnerable during their first month, and the whole first year poses special risks. Although newborns receive immunities to some diseases from their mothers before birth and after, through the mother's breast milk, their immature immune systems must nonetheless take on a host of invaders.

Gastrointestinal System: The gastrointestinal system includes the body's entire alimentary tract, from lips to arms. Although the newborn has been swallowing amniotic fluid during intrauterine life, the introduction to and ingestion of milk and the passage of the first stool are major milestones.

Intake: The infants' mouth is equipped with a shallow, rigid, hard, flat palate and a large tongue for easy grasping and compression of the nipple. The boat-shaped stomach stretches easily, causing some babies to overeat. The ready emptying of stomach contents into the duodenum may cause the baby to cry for perceived hunger about 2 hours after eating. However, breast-fed babies may need more frequent feedings than the bottle-fed babies because of the easier digestibility of breast milk as opposed to cow's milk. The intestine, which is proportionally longer than in the adult, is poorly equipped with muscular or elastic tissue. Nervous system control is also inadequate. Some digest only simple foods, not complex starches or proteins.

It is advisable to nurse the infant immediately after birth. Early-fed infants appear to experience less weight loss. The infant receives colostrum (precursor to milk), and the early sucking leads to earlier production of milk by the mother. Some health care practitioners recommend waiting about 2 hours before bottle-feeding the infant for the first time to allow the infant to adjust to extra uterine life to begin stabilizing critical functions. Glucose (sugar) water or sterile water is usually the fluid choice for this first bottle-feeding.

The full-term infant needs 140 to 160 ml of liquid per kilogram per day. Babies who are not breastfed are placed on cow's milk formula. By the second week of life, the full-term neonate needs 110 to 150 kcal/kg daily to meet the maintenance and growth needs. Because of the low fluid intake of both bottle-fed and breast-fed infants, many experience a transitory fever between the 2nd and 3rd day of life. The temperature may rise to 100 or 101 degrees. Other symptoms of dehydration may be present, such as dry skin, flushing, marked weight loss, sunken fontanels, and decreased urine output. These symptoms are readily remedied by increasing the fluid intake.

Output: The newborn frequently voids reflexively at birth when the body comes in contact with cool air. This reaction persists for several months. Failure to void within 12 hours after birth, calls for closer observation for congenital malformation, a health problem.

Stool Cycle: Most babies begin excretion of the bowel filler during the first 24 hours after birth. Its passage is frequently accompanied by the explosive sounds of "flatus" (bowel gas). Bowel movements of healthy infants vary in number, color, consistency, and general appearance. The mother's diet and the type of formula also influence the infants' stools. Within 10 hours after birth, the newborn should pass its first stool known as **meconium.** Meconium is thick, green-black, tarry, and odorless. Some infants have four to six bowel movements a day. An infant is constipated if stools are hard and can be passed with much effort. Adding some additional water or strained fruits to the diet may prevent constipation.

After the first 3 to 4 days, the color and character of the stools depend on the type of milk the infant is fed. At first, the breast-fed infant may have six to eight or loose stools per day because of the laxative effects of "colostrum". By 4 weeks of age, the breast-fed baby generally has only one or two stools per day; some breast-fed infants only defecate every other day. The bottle-fed baby usually has lighter yellow stools, which are more formed than those of the breast-fed baby in spite of adequate fluid intake. The young formula-fed infant has about four to six (foul-smelling) stools per day.

Genitourinary System: The stimulation of cold air frequently causes the infant to void. Urine output is only 1 to 4 ml/hr during the first 24 hours, for a total of about 15 to 60ml. The output gradually increases to 8 or 10 voiding per 24 hours, amounting to a daily output of about 100 to 400 ml by 3 days of life. In the neonate, the bladder is an abdominal organ, since the pelvis is still too small to hold it. The vaginal area of female babies is covered with a thin, bluish white mucous known as "Smegma". This mucous offers a protective coating for the tissues, which helps to prevent fungal and bacterial infections.

Testides: The testicles descend into the scrotum during the last month of fetal life. Therefore, the testes are palpable in the scrotal sac of 90% of full-term male infants, but only 70% of premature infants. When the perineal area is cold, however, the scrotum wrinkles and becomes smaller because of muscular contractions.

Testes that have not descended at birth usually descend within the next 3 months. If they have not descended by the age of one year , the infant may need surgical assistance. Testicles that remain undescended until pubertal years are incapable of producing viable sperm and experience an increased risk of cancer. Surgery is usually performed during the toddler years because critical emotional overtones may arise when genital surgery is performed during the preschool or early school age years.

Circumcision: Many parents choose to have their male infants circumcised (removal of foreskin of the penis), which has special religious significance to some parents. Other parents have adopted the custom for its hygienic value, to help prevent infections or to avoid the stigma of being different later in life. Some parents look on it as a sign of manhood and want the child to "look like his daddy". In 1975, the American Academy of Pediatrics found that "circumcision" has no proven medical rationale and consequently, no longer endorses the practice.

5.7 THE NEONATES' REPERTOIRES OF REFLEXES

Reflexes: A reflex is an inborn, automatic response to a particular form of stimulation. The very first movements, the fetus makes are reflexive. These involuntary, sub-cortically controlled movements form the basis for the phases of motor development. Through reflex activity, the infant gains information about the immediate environment. The infant's reactions to touch, light, sounds and changes in pressure trigger involuntary movement/activity. These involuntary movements, coupled with the increasing cortical sophistication in the early months of life, play an important role in helping the child learn more about his or her body and the outside world.

Reflexes may be classified as information gathering, nourishment seeking and protective. They are information gathering in that they help stimulate cortical activity and development. They are nourishment seeking and protective because there is some evidence that they are phylogenetic in nature. "Primitive reflexes" such as the rooting and sucking reflexes are thought by some to be primitive survival mechanisms. Without them, the newborn would be unable to obtain nourishment.

Table 5.1 The Major Newborn Reflexes

Name	Response	Significance
Babinski	Baby's fan out when the sole of the foot is stroked from heel to toe.	Perhaps a remnant of evolution
Blink	A baby's eyes close in response to bright light or loud noise	Protects eyes
Moro	A baby throws its arms out and then inward (as if embracing) in response to loud noise or when its head falls.	May help a baby cling to its mother
Palmar	A baby grasps an object placed in the palm of its hand.	Precursor to voluntary walking
Rooting	When a baby's cheek is stroked, it turns its head toward the stroking and opens its mouth.	Helps baby find the nipple
Stepping	A baby who is held up right by an adult and is then moved forward begins to step rhythmically	Precursor to voluntary walking
Sucking	A baby sucks when an object is placed in its mouth.	Permits feeding
Withdrawal	A baby withdraws its foot when the sole is pricked with a pin.	Protects a baby from unpleasant stimulation

Adaptive Value of Reflexes: Some reflexes have survival value. The rooting reflexes help a breast-fed find the mother's nipple. Babies display it only when hungry and touched by another person, not when they touch themselves. Moreover, if newborns could not suck, our species would be unlikely to survive for a single generation. Similarly, the swimming reflex helps a baby who is accidently dropped into water stay afloat, increasing the chances of retrieval by the caregiver. Other reflexes, such as Moro, probably helped babies survive during our evolutionary past.

Several reflexes help parents and infants establish gratifying interaction. A baby who searches for and successfully finds the nipple, sucks easily during feedings, and grasps when her hand is touched encourages parents to respond lovingly and feel competent as caregivers.

The helplessness of the neonate results mainly from his inability to exercise control over motor movements. Although newborns have a variety of reflexes, they do not have much control over voluntary movements. Their arms and legs jerk and flail, and they have trouble getting their fingers or hands to their mouths. When awake and in a supine position, neonates make general movements such as whole-body flexes or more localized movements of the limbs. As they gain control over their muscle activity, they become more successful at accomplishing their goals with less excess motion. Training can influence early motor development. The infant's world expands and the stimulation increases greatly when he learns to move about by the end of the first year.

5.8 EMOTIONS OF A NEWBORN

At birth, the emotions appear in simple, almost completely undifferentiated forms. They probably consist of only pleasure and pain. Emotions of a newborn are characterized by pleasantness and unpleasantness. Former is by relaxing of the body and the latter by tensing of the body. Pleasantness responses can be elicited by patting, rocking, warmth and sucking. Unpleasantness can be elicited by changing the infant's position abruptly, by sudden loud noises. Whatever the stimulus, the resultant emotion is intense and sudden. Most infants manifest with what seems to be a great deal of emotion. They cry, squirm, wiggle, kick and thrash about. It is doubtful that young infants experience complex emotional states such as joy, anxiety or disgust. Neonates express their emotions as smiles, cries, frowns, and grimaces from the very beginning of life. At first, there is only a state of diffuse **excitement.**

5.9. NEWBORN STATES

To describe the periodic variations in the newborn's day, the term state has been coined. This is relatively new concept used to describe "a behavioral condition that (1) is stable over a period of time, (2) occurs repeatedly in an individual". The newborn's state gives us clues to the way he/she is responding to the environment; it influences many physiological characteristics; and it determines how he/she will respond to stimulation. Since all babies show variations in state throughout the day, and since the abilities they show are influenced by their state at any one time, it is important to differentiate one state from another.

The following states, typical for newborn babies, combine two separate but similar classification systems. Interest in neonate sleeping pattern has been closely linked with interest in newborn states. The term "states" refers to a continuum of alertness ranging from regular sleep to vigorous activity.

Regular Sleep: Infants are at full rest; little or no motor activity occurs; facial muscles are relaxed; spontaneous eye movement is absent; breathing is regular, and it makes no movements except for sudden generalized startles. This is the low point on the arousal continuum since the infant in this state cannot be aroused by mild stimuli.

Irregular Sleep: Infants engage in spurts of gentle limb movements and more general stirring, squirming, and twisting; eye movement is occasional and rapid; facial grimaces (smiling, sneezing, frowning, puckering and pouting) are frequent; the rhythm of respiration is irregular and faster than in regular sleep. Its muscles twitch slightly from time to time but she still makes no major movements.

Drowsiness: Infants are relatively inactive; on occasion, they squirm and twist their bodies; they open and close their eyes intermittently; respiratory patterns are regular but faster than in regular sleep.

Before and after sleep, the newborn's eyes may be open, and its body is more active than in regular sleep. Breathing is irregular. Yet an infant is sensitive to such external stimuli as the sound of the radio or the sight of the mother. The incidence of spontaneous discharges-reflex smiles or startles, sucking movements, or erections-is high at certain times, low at others.

Alert Inactivity: Although infants are inactive, their eyes are open and have a bright, shining quality; respirations are regular and faster than during regular sleep. After the newborn has been fed, diapered, and burped, and is free from distressing internal and external stimuli, it may be awake for a short time with its eyes open. It may move its head, limbs, and trunk while looking at the immediate environment or at a particular "interesting spectacle," like a mobile swaying over her head. An interesting environment can initiate or maintain a quiet, alert state.

Waking Activity and Crying: Infants may be silent or moan, grunt, or whimper; spurts of diffuse motor activity are frequent; their faces may be relaxed or pinched, as when crying; their rate of respiration is irregular.

This state makes the strongest impression on anyone who spends much time with babies. It can be set in motion by intense internal stimulation, like hunger, cold, or pain, or by intense external stimulation, like restraining the baby, putting her down in the crib, or removing a pacifier from her mouth. The state may begin with soft whimpering and gentle movements and turn into a rhythmic crescendo of crying or kicking. Alternatively, it may begin and remain as uncoordinated thrashing and spasmodic screeching. Infants in this state may be too "busy" to respond to stimuli which might have elicited a reaction during sleep, drowsiness, or alert inactivity.

How States Operate

Our bodies are governed to a great degree by inner "clocks" that control our cycles of eating, sleeping, elimination, and, possibly, even mood. These biological clocks seem inborn, since they appear to contribute to the various states in infancy. This inner timing mechanism, in combination with visceral or external stimulations, takes the infant from a state of regular sleep to that of irregular sleep.

A look into a typical day in a newborn baby's life reveals that of the seventeen to twenty hours a day that the newborn sleeps, 75 percent is spent in the state of irregular sleep. She is awake and quiet for two to three hours every day, awake and active for one to two hours, and she cries and fusses the rest of her waking time-anywhere from one to four hours. Her sleep cycles range from forty-five minutes to two hours, divided into ten to twenty-minute periods of regular sleep and twenty-to forty-five-minute periods of irregular sleep. Babies have very different schedules, partly due to individual differences among the babies and also due to differences in their environments.

Environmental Conditions that Influence State

Parents have been influencing states from time immemorial. The state they most want to change is, of course, the last one, in which the baby is squalling unhappily. The quieter the newborn is, the better she will be able to maintain body weight and the better equipped the infant will be in the struggle for survival.

Feeding is one way to quiet a baby. Not unexpectedly, we learn from research that an awake baby shows more motor activity before than after feeding. We also learn scientifically that rocking a fussy infant soothes him. Research has also shown that swaddling a baby, or wrapping him or her snugly in a blanket, is also soothing. Swaddling, which is a very common practice in Russia, leads to less muscular activity and lower heart and respiratory rates.

A number of studies have yielded the finding that continuous stimulation quiets restless babies. Irritable infants have been presented with such constant stimulation as continuous rhythmic sound, a sweetened pacifier, rocking, immersing a foot in warm water, being put in warmer place, being clothed rather than unclothed, and being swaddled from neck to toes. In general, the babies crying stopped, their heart rates slowed down, their breathing became more regular, they moved around less, and they slept more, in response to all these stimuli. Findings such as these have practical value for parents and child-care professionals, especially since they flatly contradict "common sense," with the paradox that continuous stimulation actually quiets babies.

5.10 CARE OF THE NORMAL NEWBORN

After delivery the baby is placed next to the mother and leaves the labor room with the mother. Baby should be kept with the mother in the postnatal ward.

Feeding – Exclusive breast milk

– No prelacteal feeds including water, glucose water or honey

– Vitamin K injection/ orally

Clothing – Soft, white, clean clothes

– No pins, hooks or buttons, only ties.

– Easy to put on at neck and arm

– Napkins-cotton may be used instead of disposable napkins.

Care of the cord – Left open to dry

Baby bath – No bath to be given soon after delivery to ensure maintenance of temperature.

– Baby can be cleaned with oil/warm water to remove excess of vernix and meconium.

– Oil and powder are not necessary. A mild soap should be used.

In a busy, crowded ward it is wiser to avoid baby bath to prevent cross infections. At home, baby is safely bathed on extended legs in the Indian way.

Cleaning – Baby should be cleaned everyday and each time when urine or stools are passed.

– Bottom should be dipped in warm water and perineum cleaned thoroughly.

Immunization – Baby should be given BCG and the first dose of oral polio before discharge.

Sleep – A baby should sleep for 18-20 hours a day and be awake when he is hungry or uncomfortable.

– He may be awake for a few minutes during and between feeds.

QUESTIONS

SECTION "A"

Short Answer Type:

1. Who is a neonate?
2. List out the areas of adjustment of a newborn
3. Write a note on babinski reflex.
4. What is Apgar Scale?
5. What is a reflex?
6. State the factors affecting post natal life.
7. What is regurgitation?
8. Give the importance of circulatory system in the newborn.
9. Write a note on the emotions of the newborn.

SECTION "B"

One Page Answer Type:

1. Describe the characteristics of a new born
2. Write a note on the medical assessment of the newborn.
3. What are the effects of poor adjustments of a newborn?
4. Specify the various types of reflexes of a newborn.
5. Bring out the adjustments required by the newborn.
6. How will you take care of a normal newborn?

SECTION "C"

Essay Answer Type:

1. Explain the 'Newborn States' in detail.
2. Discuss about the physiological adjustments required by the newborn.
3. Examine the physical development of the neonate.
4. How do newborn infants adjust to life outside the womb?

QUESTIONS

SECTION-A

Short Answer Type

[illegible]

2. [illegible] of the new born.
3. [illegible]
4. [illegible] new born.
5. [illegible]
6. How will you take care of a premature new born?

SECTION-C

Essay Answer Type

1. [illegible]

4. [illegible]

UNIT — III

CHAPTER

6

INFANCY AND BABYHOOD

OBJECTIVES

To enlighten students about:

- Concept of Infancy and Babyhood period
- Developmental tasks
- Characteristics
- Growth and development details – physical, motor, emotional, language, social and cognitive
- Child rearing practices

6.1 INTRODUCTION

Infancy is the period of time that begins with the organism's emergence into the world as a separate being and ends with the organism's achieving a measure of independence. Infancy is the shortest of all the developmental periods and a very critical period. Infancy is the second most rapid period of growth and development, first being prenatal period. It is the stage in the life cycle between birth and two years of age. The helpless neonate becomes a walking baby. Language changes from cries to understandable speech. In Latin, the term "infans" means a "non-speaking being". Not being able to speak also implies an inability to care for oneself. Infancy, according to standard dictionaries, is an individual rather than a parasite in the mother's body.

The toddler period usually refers to the period from 1 to 2 years of age. A toddler is a baby who has achieved enough body control to be relatively independent. After the fast growth spurts of infancy, the growth rate of the baby (2 weeks- 2years) is slow and steady. Many new skills are being developed, including both fine and motor skills related to dressing, feeding, toileting, and walking. Another accomplishment during this period is related to language development. These newly acquired skills serve to strengthen the toddler's newfound autonomy

6.2 DEVELOPMENTAL TASKS OF BABYHOOD

There are basic things that must be accomplished at all ages of the life cycle to achieve success in the process of survival. So, the infant is forced to attain the developmental tasks that must be accomplished within that period of life. A series of developmental tasks challenge the baby and toddler. They are physical, psychological, cultural and social in nature. Babies who lay behind their age mates in mastering the developmental tasks of babyhood will be handicapped when they reach the early childhood years and are expected to master the developmental tasks for these years.

Physical

- Learning to Walk
- Learning to eat solid foods
- Learning to talk, foundations of speech
- Learning to control the elimination of body wastes
- Achieving physiological stability, especially in the hunger rhythm and sleep

Psychological

- Scheme of psychological development
- Acquiring a basic trust

Cultural

- Interaction with environment
- Learning to function independent of adults

Social

- Attachment behavior development
- Toilet training, self feeding
- Socialization behavior

6.3 CHARACTERISTICS OF BABYHOOD

Certain characteristics of babyhood (toddlerhood), while similar to characteristics of other periods in the life span, are of particular importance during these years. They distinguish babyhood from the periods preceding it and those that follow it. Following are the most important characteristics.

1.Babyhood is a period of rapid change

Parents as well as researchers are intrigued and amazed at the rapid rate of growth that occurs in all areas of development during babyhood. Physical changes are just as prominent as social and psychological changes during this period and the contrast in the development of individual at the end of the period to what he was like at the beginning is dramatic.

2. Babyhood Period is a Critical Stage

The period of babyhood is critical in the sense that the foundations for many behavior patterns, attitudes towards others and towards self and many patterns of emotional expression, are laid at this time. They become so firmly established that changing them may result in emotional tension and confusion.

3. Babyhood Period is Dangerous

Despite improved medical care in the prenatal and early post-natal months, the severity of diseases and the mortality rate during the babyhood/ toddlerhood years are still high. Two-thirds of all deaths in the baby's first year of life occur in the first month. After that, the mortality rate decreases rapidly. During the second year of life, accidents may prove fatal or may produce injuries that will permanently affect the course of the individual's life. The baby's strong desire to explore his environment is not held in check by knowledge of possible harm. As a result, the baby meets with many accidents some of which may be serious.

4. Babyhood Period is Appealing

The helplessness and dependency of the small baby appeal to adults and older children. The baby is easy to manage when he is helpless. As his helplessness is replaced by the ability to do things for himself, the baby is less easily managed and more resistant to adult help. Unfortunately, parents cannot or are not quick enough to accept this concept of the baby's abilities that will help them to keep pace with his development. As a result, the baby gets frustrated in his attempts, and becomes resistant and negativistic. So the appeal of helplessness is lost.

5. Babyhood Period is the True Foundation Age

Babyhood is a true foundation period of life because, at this time, many behavior patterns, attitudes, and many patterns of emotional expressions are being established. The first three years are critical in setting the pattern for personal and social adjustment. According to Erickson, how babies are treated will determine whether they will develop "basic trust" or "basic mistrust" – viewing the world as safe, reliable and nurturing or as full of threat, unpredictability, and treachery.

6. Babyhood is the time when socialization begins

Infants are taught certain basic skills considered important for functioning as independent and autonomous human beings. These skills involve learning self-regulated skills such as feeding and dressing, acquiring basic motor skills of locomotion, play, manipulation, holding objects and so on. Rules that outline and regulate acceptable behavior are taught to infants as well. The egocentrism, characteristic of the very young baby, quickly gives way to a desire to become a part of the social group. Babies show their desire to become a part of the social group by putting up protests when they are left alone and by trying to attract the attention of others in any way they can.

7. Babyhood is the Period of Decreasing Dependency

The decrease in dependency on others results from the rapid development of body control which enables babies to sit, stand and walk and to manipulate objects. The random mass movements of the infant give way to coordinated movements, which make it possible for babies to do things for themselves. Independence also increases as babies become able to communicate their needs to others. If they are not permitted to trying to be independent when they want to be, they protest. This protest takes the form of angry outbursts and crying and soon develops into negativism, one of the outstanding characteristic of the closing months of babyhood.

8. Babyhood is the launching period of Increased Individuality

Perhaps the most significant thing about increased independence is that it permits babies to develop along lines suited to their interests and abilities. As a result, the individuality apparent at birth increases as toddlerhood period draws to a close. Individuality is shown in appearance and in patterns of behavior. Even identical multiple birth babies show individuality.

9. Babyhood is the launching Period of Sex-Role Typing

Almost from the moment of birth, boys are treated as boys and girls as girls. Toys are selected that are appropriate for boys, and they are told stories about boys and their activities. The same sex-identifying traditions apply to girls. But while sex-role typing is part of a girls' early training, the pressures on her to be sex-appropriate even as a baby are not as strong as they are on a boy.

10. Babyhood Period is the Beginning of Creativity

Because of lack of muscle coordination and their inability to control their environment, babies are incapable of doing anything that can be regarded as original or creative. They are learning, however, in these early months of life to develop interest and attitudes that will lay the foundations for later creativity or for conformity to patterns set by others. And this will be largely determined by the treatment they receive from others, especially their parents. When the parent teaches them in this positive spirit, it gives them a sense not only that things are to be enjoyed but also that they will be able to manipulate them successfully.

6.4 PHYSICAL DEVELOPMENT

Infancy and puberty are two periods of rapid growth during the life span. During the first six months of life, growth continues at a rapid rate, characteristic of the pre natal period and then slows down. Throughout the first year of life, there is astonishing growth spurt. In the second year, growth is at a rapidly decelerating rate. During the first year of life, the increase in weight is proportionately greater than the increase in height, while in the second year, it is the reverse. Individual differences in the rate of growth during this time can be observed. However, it is during the second year that differences between genders and among racial groups occur.

Physical growth, maturation, acquisition of competence, and psychological reorganization occur rapidly during the first year. These changes do not occur smoothly over time but rather in discontinuous bursts that qualitatively change the child's behavior. A number of significant physical milestones in development are reached between birth and two years after birth. These include the mastery of basic motor competencies shared by all humans universally such as manual skills, locomotors (movement skills), perceptual skills, and co-ordination of sensory and motor activities.

Body Length & Weight

During infancy, changes in the overall size of the child's body are rapid-faster than at any other time after birth. By the end of the first year, a typical infant's height is 50 percent greater than it was at birth and by two years, it is 75 percent greater. Weight shows similar striking signs. Usually infants grow one inch per month for the first year. Body length increases by almost a third, and weight usually triples. A boy's height typically increases by 10 inches during the first year, by almost 5" during the second year and by a little more than 3 inches during the 3rd year, to reach 37" in all. Thus at the end of the first year, the "average" baby is 28 to 34 inches in length. Changes in length become more advanced than weight changes during the second year after birth.

During the first year, weight changes are much more dramatic than height changes. At 5 months, the average baby boy's birth weight has doubled to 16 pounds, and by one year, has nearly tripled to 23 pounds and at two years, it has quadrupled. This rapid growth rate tapers off during the second and third year; a boy typically gains about 5 pounds by his second year and 3½ pounds by his third. By the end of two years, a normal baby weighs about 19 to 25 pounds.

Boys are generally slightly longer and heavier than girls at birth and during the first two years of life, although not during the preschool years. There is an increase in birth weight with increasing birth order.

Body Proportions

After birth, the head and chest continue to have a growth advantage but the trunk and legs gradually pick up speed. The typical 2-year-old child has a potbellied appearance-a large belly and an exaggerated lumbar curve, known as lordosis. By the end of toddlerhood or third year, the child is taller and more slender, with stronger abdominal muscles and a more erect posture. Head growth slows down in comparison to the rate of growth in the body and extremities.

Bone Growth

The skeletal bones are largely connective tissue at birth, becoming cartilage and finalized bone tissue as growth occurs during infancy, childhood and adolescence. All the bones of the body originate from soft cartilage, which, over a period of time, becomes ossified or hardened into bone by the deposit of various minerals. "Ossification" is the process through which these cells are formed into hard, strong bone tissue. The bones of the body are formed in a manner by which ossification occurs first in the center of a potential bone area. Growth occurs at the tips of the bone area. An exception to this type of bone formation is that of skull bones.

Along with an increase in size, bones also increase in number. At birth, the infant has approximately 270 bones. By puberty, this number increases to about 350. In addition, they become more closely interconnected. At birth, girls are more advanced than boys in bone development. There are also wide individual differences in skeletal development .

Muscle and Fat Development

Muscle growth in infancy occurs at a faster rate than bone growth. However, muscular control is associated with maturation of nerve fibers that communicate impulses from the brain to these tissues. Willful control as opposed to random activity can be observed in infancy as the individual experiences increased myelinisation of nervous tissue in conjunction with growth of muscle fibers. As is true of the bones, different muscle groups grow at different rates. There is a general tendency for the muscles near the head and neck to develop earlier than the muscles of the torso, arms, and legs. This is an example of the **cephalocaudal** principle of development. At this time, the weight of the muscles is forty times what it was at birth.

Fat or adipose tissue develops very rapidly in infancy. These cells are formed first in the last trimester of pregnancy and continues to be produced under the skin and in other body areas for the first trimester after birth. Rapid gains in weight often accompany the production of these cells that have a long, cylindrical shape to accommodate the storage of fatty matter. The fat deposited into these cells comes primarily from the high-fat content of milk, which is the principal food source of infants. By the end of the first year, most babies have a plump, rounded appearance as a result of this process.

The Teeth

Usually beginning around 3 or 4 months, infants begin grabbing almost everything in sight to put into their mouths; but the first tooth may not actually arrive until sometime between 5 and 9 months of age, or even later. The first teeth, called deciduous teeth or primary teeth begin to erupt when the infant is about 6 or 7 months old. As these teeth emerge and grow, the cells composing the permanent teeth are formed in the infants' gums.

Usually the first teeth to appear are the two lower central incisors located central to the gum area; the two upper central incisors follow them. By age 12 months, the baby will have between six and eight teeth. The face and jaw increase in size to permit room for more teeth. At 2½ years, the child can be expected to have 20 primary or deciduous teeth, which can enable them to chew anything they want to.

Teething is not a comfortable experience for infants who also respond by being irritable and fussy. When infants are experiencing this process, they should be allowed to chew on pacifiers or other hard objects rather than on plastic objects or on a bottle nipple with milk. Major decay problems can occur when babies are allowed to go to sleep with a bottle in their mouths. Toddlers should brush their teeth at least twice a day under parental supervision.

The Nervous System

Since the cerebral cortex of the brain, which controls perception, thought, and memory-is not fully mature at birth, the infant seems to operate on a sub-cortical rather than a cortical level. Behavior is controlled by the spinal cord and lower brain centers at first. With increased cortical maturation, many reflexes present at birth gradually cease to operate. Although some sensory abilities are astonishingly keen at birth, others do not mature for some time.

The newborn's response to a nipple and sucking are all functions of the central nervous system-the brain and spinal cord (a bundle of nerves running through the back bone)- and of a growing peripheral network of nerves extending to every part of the body. Through this network sensory messages travel to brain and the motor commands travel back. The growth of the brain is fundamental to future physical, cognitive and emotional development. Dramatic increase in brain weight is found during infancy. The brain at birth, weighs about 25 percent (12 ounces) of its eventual adult weight of 3.5 pounds. It reaches 70 percent of that weight at the end of infancy and nearly 90 percent by age 3.

Vision and Hearing

The sense of sight and sound perception are equally important as touch to the infant, in receiving and processing information from the environment. Babies can see fairly well at birth and improve in their focusing ability as age increases. Looking at a human face intently testifies to the significance of this ability for the newborn. Binocular vision or the fusion of images perceived by both eyes does not occur completely until the end of infancy. The combination of poor muscle coordination with somewhat faulty depth perception may make for a clumsy infant who is mastering basic motor skills. Strabismus or the uncontrolled, independent eye movements of the newborn comes under control as eye muscles quickly mature in the early months of infancy.

Hearing becomes acute during early infancy as children show an increasing sensitivity to loud sounds. Initial assessment of the health status almost always include some testing of hearing ability in infancy. Any serious deviation in this sense perception almost invariably affects the development of others. Delayed speech, for example, may result from some type of hearing problem.

Sense of Touch and Pain

Newborns do respond to touch; a touch to the cheek produces a turning of the head; a touch to the lips produces sucking movements. Newborns can also feel pain. The important ability to connect information about vision with information about touch is evident during infancy. Coordination of vision and touch has been well documented in 6-month-olds.

Sense of Smell

Newborns can differentiate odors. The expressions on their faces seem to indicate that they like the way vanilla and strawberry smell but do not like the way rotten eggs and fish smell. In one investigation,6-day-old infants who were breast fed showed a clear preference for smelling their mothers breast pad rather than a clean breast pad.

Sense of Taste

In one study, even at only two hours of age, babies made different facial expressions when they tasted sweet, sour, and bitter solutions . At about 4 months of age, infants begin to prefer salty tastes, which as newborns they had found to be aversive.

6.5 MOTOR DEVELOPMENT

After the fast growth spurts of infancy, the growth rate of the toddler is slow and steady. Many new skills are being developed, including both fine and motor skills related to dressing, feeding, toileting, and walking. Another accomplishment during this period is related to language development. These newly acquired skills serve to strengthen the toddler's newfound autonomy.

Motor development means increasing control over the movement of the body and its parts. Motor skills are coordinated movements of the muscles and limbs. Success demands that each movement be done in a precise way, in exactly the right sequence, and at exactly the right time In addition to beginning language (sounds and crying), motor development is a form of communication and interaction between the infant and his family members who are significant in his or her life. Thus motor development and movement permeate virtually all domains of infant behavior.

6.5.1 Some General Trends In Motor Development

A number of general trends in motor development have been identified on the basis of the characteristics of children. These trends help to describe or explain the development of controlled motor development of the child – particularly during the first year or two of life.

1. **Cephalocaudal Trend:** The cephalocaudal trend relates to a directional sequence of growth and development. It implies that muscular control and coordination proceeds in an orderly sequence from head to foot. Upper body muscular control precedes lower body muscular control.
2. **Proximal - Distal Trend:** The proximal distal trend implies those parts of the body closest to the torso or centers are controlled before those in peripheral or more distal portions. Thus, control of trunk movement and shoulder functioning proceeds controlled functioning of the elbow, wrist and fingers. At the lower extremity, motor control proceeds from the hips to the legs, feet and toes.
3. **Mass–to-Specific Trend:** The mass-to-specific trend refers to the emergence and differentiation of specific patterns of movement from general or mass responses. For example, during early writing or manipulation of crayons, the child uses all feet, legs, head, trunk, lips, tongue, shoulder, elbow, wrist and fingers. The manipulation of toys with the fingers and hand emerges from total or near total body involvement. Out of general responses, specific patterns of movement develop.
4. **Bilateral-to-Unilateral Trend:** The bilateral–to-unilateral trend describes the development of one-side preferences in motor activity from bilateral activity (activity involving both sides of the body). Thus, during the early years children may eat with either or both hands, strike or kick objects with either hand or foot, or cut paper with either hand. From such bilateral activity, preferences and "handedness" develop. In general, children experiment with both sides of the body before a preference is made.
5. **Large to small Muscle Trend:** The child gains control of large muscle groups before the control of small muscle groups. In other words, gross motor control precedes fine motor control. In tossing a ball for accuracy or shooting a basketball, controlled movement proceeds from the relatively large muscles of the shoulder to the relatively small muscles of the elbow, wrist, and finger.

6.5.2 Categories of Infant Activity

The movements or activities of the infant, in spite of their random, meaningless nature, can be classified roughly into two general categories.

(A) Mass Activity: Mass activity occurs throughout the entire body when any area is stimulated, though the activity is more pronounced in the stimulated area. Normally, mass activity increases in intensity and frequency with each passing day. New born infants show,

(*i*) An amount of mass activity or general diffuse movements which seem to be caused by impulses irradiating throughout the body.

(*ii*) During the period of early infancy, these give way to an increasing number of specific and adaptive responses which emerge from the former mass activity.

(B) Specific Activities: Specific activities involve certain limited areas of the body. They include "reflexes", which are definite responses to specific sensory stimuli and which remain unchanged with repetition of the same stimulus; and "Generalized responses", which use larger groups of muscles than are involved in reflexes and which may be aroused by either external or internal stimuli.

6.5.3 Milestones of Motor Development

Motor development is marked by a series of milestones; achievements that develop systematically, or every newly mastered ability preparing a baby to tackle the next. Milestones reflect the transformation of babies from being unable to lift their heads to being able to grab things, to chase a dog and to participate actively in the play with its peers. Babies first learn simple skills and then combine them into increasingly complex systems of action, which permit a wider or more precise range of movement and a more effective control of the environment. The following table summarizes the major features of infant motor development.

Table 6.1 Gross and Fine Motor Development in the First Two Years

Motor Skills	Average Age Achieved	Age Range in which 90 % of Infants achieve the skills
When held upright, holds head erect and steady	6 weeks	3weeks-4 months
When prone, lifts self by arms	2 months	3weeks-4 months
Rolls from side to back	2 months	3weeks-5 months
Grasps cube	3 months, 3 weeks	2-7 months
Rolls from back to side	4.5 months	2-7 months
Sits alone	7 months	5-9 months
Crawls	7 months	5-11 months
Pulls to stand	8 months	5-12 months
Plays pat-a-cake	9 months, 3 weeks	7-15 months
Stands alone	11 months	9-16 months
Walks alone	11 months, 3 weeks	9-17 months
Builds tower of two cubes	11 months, 3 weeks	10-19 months
Scribbles vigorously	14 months	10-21 months
Walks up stairs with help	16 months	12-23 months
Jumps in place	23 months, 2 weeks	17-30 months
Walks on tiptoe	25 months	16-30 months

***Source** : Schiamberg L.B (1985) Human Development Second Edition. Macmillan publishing company, N.Y.*

Gross motor skills

Gross motor skills involve large-muscle activities, such as moving one's arms and walking.

1. **The Development of Posture:** Gross motor skills, as well as many other activities, require postural control. Infants need to control their heads to stabilize their gaze and to track moving objects. Newborn infants cannot voluntarily control their posture. Within a few weeks, though, they can hold their heads erect, and soon can lift their heads while prone. The tonic neck reflex position is the usual posture when the newborn lies supine (face up). A supine crying infant will often remain quiet when picked up and will then maintain the quiet alert state when propped or held in the upright positions. An upright position offers much more visual stimulation than does being on either back or stomach. By 2 month of age, babies can sit while supported on a lap or an infant seat, but sitting independently is not accomplished until 6 or 7 months of age. Standing also develops gradually across the first year of life. By about 8 months of age, infants usually learn to pull themselves up and hold on to a chair, and they often can stand alone by about 10 to 12 months of age.

2. **Learning to Walk:** Locomotion and postural control are closely linked, especially in walking upright. Walking upright requires being able both to balance on one leg as the other is swung forward and to shift the weight from one leg to the other. Infants must learn to move about in the world to "locomote". At first, unable to move independently, infants soon learn to crawl, to stand, and to walk. Once the child can move through the environment upright, the arms and hands are free. The key skills in learning to walk appear to be stabilizing balance on one leg long enough to swing the other forward and shifting the weight falling.

Figure 6.1 summarizes important accomplishments in gross motor skills during the first year, culminating in the ability to walk easily.

Figure 6.1 The sequence of Motor Events leading to upright locomotion

Development in the Second Year

In the second year of life, toddlers become more motorically skilled and mobile. They are no longer content with being in a playpen and want to move all over the place. By 13 to 18 months, toddlers can pull a toy attached to a string and use their hands and legs to climb up a number of steps. By 18 to 24 month, toddlers can walk quickly or run stiffly for a short distance, balance on their feet in a squat position while playing with objects on the floor, walk backwards without losing their balance, stand and kick a ball without falling, stand and throw a ball, and jump in place.

There are variations in the ages at which infants reach motor milestones in different cultures that are likely to depend on their activity opportunities. However, the variations are not large and milestones are reached within normal ranges.

Fine Motor Skills

Whereas gross motor skills involve large-muscle activity, fine motor skills involve finely tuned movements. Buttoning a shirt, typing, or anything that requires finger dexterity demonstrate fine motor skills. Infants must learn the "fine motor skills" associated with grasping, holding and manipulating objects. In the case of feeding, for example, infants progress from being fed by others to holding a bottle, to feeding themselves with their fingers, to eating with utensils.

The development of reaching and grasping becomes more refined during the first two years of life. Initially, infants move their shoulders and elbows crudely, but later they move their wrists, rotate their hands, and coordinate their thumb and forefinger. The developmental sequence of grasping involves initially the whole hand (palmar grasp), followed by grasping small objects with their thumb and forefinger (pincer grasp). Experience plays a role in reaching and grasping.

Factors Affecting Motor Development

Infants reach milestones of motor development at somewhat different ages. There are variations in the age at which walking begins. Some of these deficiencies seem to be attributed to cultural factors, and some are based on biologically determined individual differences. Heredity clearly plays a role in an individual infant's rate of motor development. The environment also plays a role even though in most cases it is rather limited. At some ages, first-born children score slightly better than later-borns on motor development measures. This may be because parents might be spending more time with their firstborn children and stimulating them to a greater activity.

6.6 EMOTIONS OF AN INFANT

An emotion can be defined as "feeling or affect that occurs when a person is in a state or an interaction that is important to him or her, especially to his or her well-being". An emotion is characterized by the occurrence of intense physiological responses (e.g. sudden increase in heart rate, contractions of stomach muscles, increase in blood pressure, and increase in muscle tension) in association with a specific internal need, image, thought or external stimulus.

Emotion is characterized by behavior that reflects (expresses) the pleasantness or unpleasantness of the state in which the individuals are in, or the transactions they are experiencing. Emotions also can be more specific and take the form of joy, fear, anger and so on, depending on how a transaction affects the person (for example, a threat, a frustration, a relief, and so on). It has been said that our emotions are what make us seem most human. We rage, laugh, we cry, we fear, we love. To be without emotions is to be unfeeling, perhaps, "inhuman". Having feelings is an important part of being human. Emotions differ in their intensity. They can be intense as in the case of rage or joy and subtle such as uneasiness in a new situation, or mother's joy when she holds her baby.

6.6.1 Emergence of Emotions

Infants have emotions. Initially, the infant shows emotional excitement by crying, by bodily activity in different ways, by changing their level of activity and by attending to things that interest them for short periods. However, his emotional reactions are more diffuse, less specific and defined than they will be later on. Infants' emotional expressions become more graded, subtle, and complex beyond the first year of life. As age increases, emotional reactions become less diffuse, less random, and more specific and differentiated in relation to cause, and they can be aroused by a wide variety of stimuli.

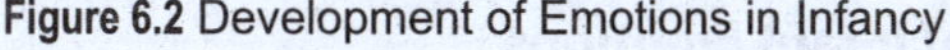

Figure 6.2 Development of Emotions in Infancy

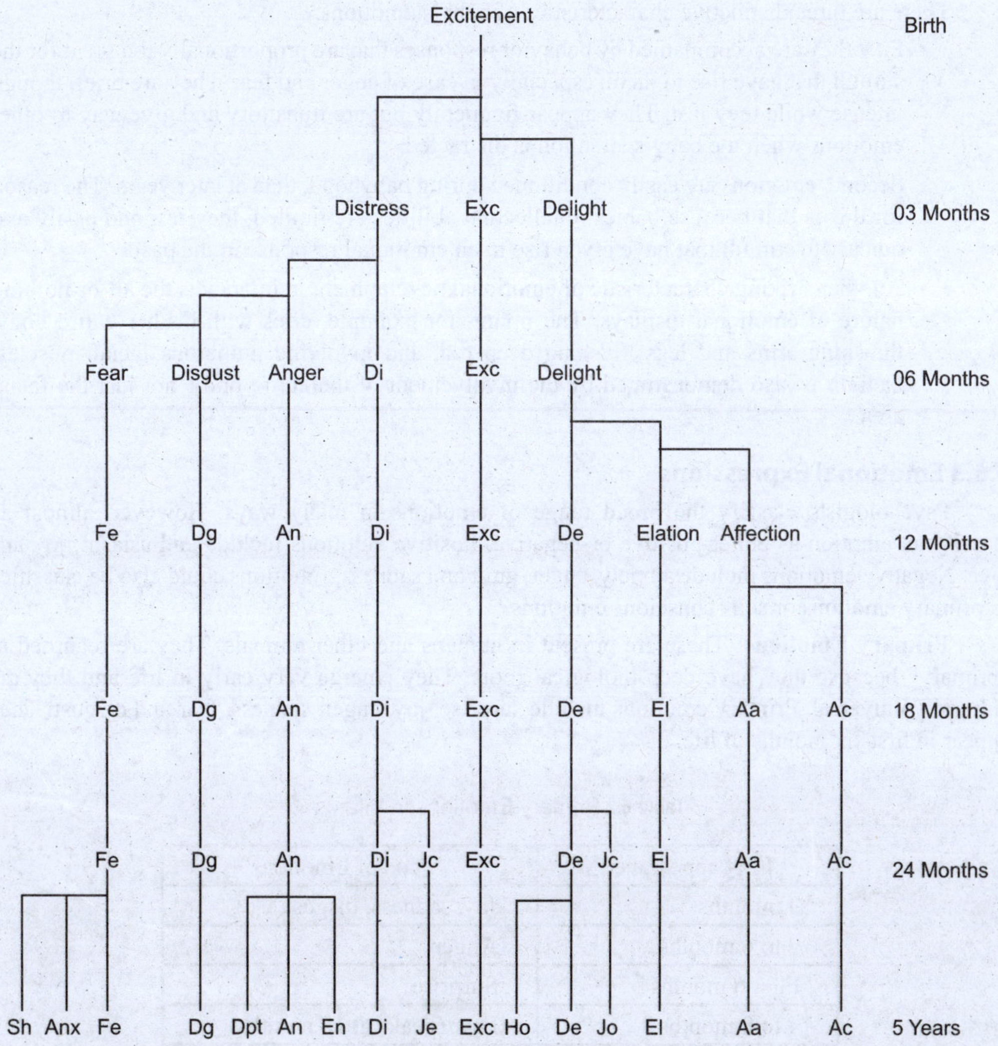

Aa = Affection for Adults	De = Delight	El = Elation	Ho = Hope
Ac = Affection for Children	Dg = Disgust	En = Envy	Je = Jealousy
An = Anger	Di = Distress	Exc = Excitement	Jo = Joy
Anx = Anxiety	Dpt = Disappointment	Fe = Fear	Sh = Shame

Bridges (1930,1937) proposed a rather more elaborate model for the observation and understanding of emotional reactivity in infants. She stated that the neonate has one basic and diffuse emotional reaction, called "excitement", which occurs in response to any intense stimulation, noxious or pleasant, and which is evidenced through general bodily reactivity, both muscular and visceral. With increasing age, the condition of excitement becomes quickly bifurcated into a pleasure versus pain differentiation. Expressions of delight become increasingly specific and can be identified behaviorally as elation, affection and joy; and distress becomes further differentiated into specific behaviors characterized as anger, disgust, fear and jealousy.

The early experiences of emotion such as those that communicate distress (crying) and delight (laughter, smiling) also are the foundation of early social interactions with caregivers.

6.6.2 Characteristics of Infant Emotions

There are three distinctive characteristics of baby's emotions.

- First they are accompanied by behavior responses that are proportionally too great for the stimuli that gave rise to them, especially in case of anger and fear. They are brief, though intense while they last. They appear frequently but are transitory and give way to other emotions when the baby's attention is distracted.
- Second, emotions are easily conditioned during babyhood, than at later years. The reason for this is that because babies' intellectual abilities are limited, they respond easily and quickly to stimuli that have given rise to an emotional response in the past.
- Another striking characteristic of emotional development in infancy is the all-or-nothing nature of emotional displays. The infant, for example, cries with his/her entire body, thrashing arms and legs, flushing deep red, and involving numerous facial muscles. Delight is also demonstrated by the involvement of the entire body, not just the facial area.

6.6.3 Emotional Expressions

Psychologists classify the broad range of emotions in many ways. However, almost all classify an emotion as either positive or negative. Positive emotions include enthusiasm, joy and love. Negative emotions include anxiety, anger, guilt and sadness. Emotions could also be classified as primary emotions or self- conscious emotions.

Primary Emotions: These are present in humans and other animals. They are regarded as "primary" because they have deep biological roots. They emerge very early in life and they are culturally universal. Primary emotions include surprise, joy, anger, sadness, fear and disgust. They appear in first six months of life.

Table 6.2 Primary Emotions in Infants

First appearance	Type of Emotion
3 months	Joy, sadness, disgust
2 to 6 months	Anger
First 6 months	Surprise
4 to 8 months	Fear (peaks at 18 months)

Self-Conscious Emotion: These are emotions that require self-awareness. Sometimes called "secondary emotion", self-conscious emotions emerge later than primary emotion. They are not apparent in animals and may not be culturally universal. Self-conscious emotions include empathy, jealousy and embarrassment, which just appear at about one and half- to-two years and pride, shame and guilt which just appear at about two and half years of age. The ability of infants to communicate emotions permits coordinated interactions with their caregivers and beginning of an emotional bond between them.

Some common emotions of the infants are:

Smiling: Smiles and laughter are infants' most irresistible means of communicating. Two types of smiling can be distinguished among infants.

Reflexive smile: During the first 2 weeks of life, infants ordinarily smile when they are drowsy or sleeping lightly rather than when they are awake. These smiles are called reflexive smiles, as they do not occur in response to external stimuli or triggered by social stimulation. Instead, they come from completely internal events within the brain i.e., the infant's rising and falling levels of arousal. They are therefore, called endogenous smiles. In the second two weeks of life, smiles can be coaxed from infants by gentle stimulation while they are awake. At the end of the first month, bouncing and other forms of moderate stimulation coax those smiles from the infant. These smiles do not really signify pleasure or sociability in the infant.

Social smile: Perhaps the most important emotional development is the first social smile. Social smiles are the bright-eyed, alert smiles, which infants give to the people around them. It is a smile that occurs in response to an external stimulus, typically a face in the case of young infant. Social smile does not occur until two months of age although some researchers believe that infants grin in response to voices as early as three weeks of age. When infants are about one-month-old, they begin to show exogenous smiles in response to events in the outside world. They smile when heads nod at them silently or speak in a high voice, when lights blink, and when they perceive rhythm or repetition.

By 3 months, infants smile when they see a human face, a doll, or other familiar object. Now, their smiles are truly social. When babies are 4 months-old, they smile at a moving face. The 5-month-old smiles after he has done something like move a ball or mobile and then shown his mastery by moving it again. His smiles show that he takes pleasure from learning and doing.

Crying: Crying is another powerful means of communication. Crying is most important mechanism newborns have for communicating with their world. The sound or sight of an infant crying galvanizes most people into action. Crying is the baby's way of calling for attention. This is the only method of communication until he learns to smile, gurgle, babble and form words. It has a complex set of functions and meanings.

Babies have at least three types of cries.

Basic Cry: Hunger is one of the conditions that incite the basic cry.

Anger Cry: Lack of attention for a long duration may arouse the anger cry.

Pain cry: It is stimulated by a high intensity stimulus. Most adults can determine whether an infant's cries signify anger or pain. Parents can distinguish cries of their own baby better than those of another baby.

Holding and lifting an infant has a calming effect. Crying babies who were picked up and put on the shoulder, were likely not only to stop crying but also to open their eyes and watch about. Sucking also has a calming effect. But if an infant is crying because of hunger, feeding is much more effective.

Whether caused by pain, hunger, cold, fatigue, frustration, overstimulation, incongruity, or fear, crying is not good for babies. It saps their energy, increases the pressure on their brains, removes oxygen and adds white cells to their blood. In newborns, crying may even return blood circulation to its fetal direction. Even so, the question of whether it is best to respond every time a baby cries remains controversial. Experts in child care give conflicting advice.

Wariness and Fear: Fear typically first appears at about six to eight months of age and peaks at about 18 months. Prior to that time, he exhibits wariness(suspicion), which may be defined as a more general negative reaction to the unknown or unfamiliar; fear is a more specific reaction to a particular stimulus. They cling to their parents, burst into tears, scream, or scoot away.

Two fears that have been of particular interest are the fear of being separated from the caregiver or attachment figure, known as **separation anxiety**, and the fear of stranger, known as **stranger anxiety**. Infants experience fear of being separated from their caregivers resulting in "separation protest" – crying when the caregiver leaves. Separation protest tends to peak at about 15 months.

The most frequent expression of an infant's fear involves "Stranger Anxiety", which usually emerges gradually. It first appears at about 6 months of age in the form of wary reactions. By age 9 months, the fear of strangers is often more intense and it continues to escalate through the infant's first birthday. It appears that when infants have a sense of security, they are less likely to show stranger anxiety.

Rage and Anger: Scientists now generally agree that anger cannot be measured reliably in infants less than about 7-months-old. Rage is what appears when a young baby's bottle is taken from her and she cries. Rage is a more general reaction-in this case, a general reaction to disappointment-while anger is typically defined as a specific reaction to a particular object or person. Anger is a more sophisticated response and does not show itself in infants until they are about 7-months-old.

6.7.SOCIAL ORIENTATION

Early social experiences play a dominant role in determining the baby's future social relationships and patterns of behavior toward others. And because the baby's life is centered around the home, it is here that the foundations for later social behavior and attitudes are laid.

As socioemotional beings, infants show strong interest in the social world and are motivated to orient to it and understand it. From early in their development, infants are captivated by the social world. Young infants stare intently at faces and are attuned to the sounds of human voices, especially their caregiver's. Later, they become adept at interpreting the meaning of facial expressions.

In the first few months of life, the human infant gives positive responses to almost all social objects. By three months of age, he gives some signs of discriminating the strange person, not by negative or withdrawing responses, but by sobering, staring, and cessation of movement. By six months of age, negative and withdrawing responses appear in some infants. From an early age, then, the infant organism can differentiate between the familiar and the novel. Although in general, any organism tends to prefer what he has become accustomed to, the process is especially clear in the case of social attachments. In fact, it is a basic requirement; attachments are built up by familiarity.

Face-to-face play often begins to characterize caregiver-infant interactions when the infant is about 2 to 3 months of age. The focused social interaction of face to face play may include vocalizations, touch, and gestures. Such play is part of many mother's motivation to create a positive emotional state in their infants. Due to such positive social interchanges infants respond differently to inanimate objects , such as puppets. At this age, most infants expect people to react positively when the infants initiate a behavior, such as a smile or a vocalization. As early as 2 to 3 months of age, infants also show more withdrawal, negative emotions and self-directed behavior when their caregivers are silent and unresponsive. The frequency of face-to-face play decreases after 7 months of age as infants become more mobile. In the second year of life, infants develop the ability to crawl, walk, and run. They are able to explore and expand their social world. These newly developed, self produced locomotor skills allow the infant to independently initiate social interchanges on a more frequent basis. Even though infants as young as 6 months of age show an interest in each other , their interaction with peers increases considerably in the last half of the second year . The following table indicates the usual social behaviour pattern of babies.

Table 6.3 Common Social Behaviour Pattern of Babies

Age group	To adults and other babies
Two to three months	• Babies can distinguish people from inanimate objects and they discover that people supply their needs. • They wish to be with people but not being left alone. • At this age , babies show no preference for any one person.
Four to five months	• Babies like to be lifted by someone around them. • They respond in various forms to scolding and smiling faces and to friendly and to angry voices.
Six to seven months	• Babies are able to differentiate between "friends" and "strangers" by smiling at the former and showing fear in the presence of the latter. • It is also the beginning of the "attachment age" – the time when babies become strongly attached to their mothers or mother-substitutes. • The baby smiles at other babies and shows concern in their crying.
Eight to nine months	• The baby attempts to imitate the speech, gestures, and simple acts of others.
Nine to thirteen months	• The baby reacts to the warning "no-no". • Babies attempt to explore the clothes and hair of other babies, imitate their behavior and vocalizations, and cooperate in the use of toys.
Thirteen to Eighteen months (in case of response to adults - from sixteen months only)	• Negativism, in the form of stubborn resistance to requests or demands from adults is manifested in physical withdrawal or angry outbursts. • Fighting over toys decreases and the baby shows more co-operation during play and a willingness to share.
Eighteen to twenty four months (in case of response to adults - from twenty two months only)	• The baby shows more interest in playing with other babies and uses play materials to establish social relationships with them. • The baby cooperates in a number of routine activities, such as being dressed, fed, and bathed.

Social Referencing

This involves "reading" emotional cues in others to help determine how to act in a particular situation. The development of social referencing helps infants to interpret ambiguous situations more accurately, as and when they encounter a stranger and need to know whether to fear the person. Infants become better at social referencing in the second year of life. At this age, they tend to check the context and characteristics of the strangers.

6.8. LANGUAGE DEVELOPMENT DURING INFANCY

Sequence of Early Language Development:

Before babies can use words, they make their needs and feelings known through sounds that progress from crying to cooing and babbling, then to accidental imitation and then deliberate imitation. These sounds are known as "prelinguistic speech". Infants also grow in the ability to recognize and understand speech sounds. Babies typically say their first word around the end of the first year, and toddlers begin speaking in sentences about 8 months to a year later. Prelinguistic speech is the forerunner of linguistic speech.

Preliminaries to Language

Early Vocalization: Crying, Cooing, and Babbling

Infants are noisy creatures, crying, cooing, and making a variety of other sounds even in the first weeks of life. These noises gradually become more varied over the first months of life. Babies actively produce sounds from birth onward. Babies' sounds and gestures go through this sequence during their first year. Usually, by the end of the first year, the infant is able to use single words. Screaming and crying occur during first six months of life; however, these are not considered real language.

Crying: Babies cry even at birth and crying can signal distress. However, there are different types of crying that signal different things. Crying is a newborn's only means of communication. Crying is the most noticeable sound uttered by the newborn. Variations on the basic rhythm include the "angry" and "pain" cries. Different pitches, patterns and intensities signal hunger, sleepiness or anger. Although it serves as the infant's primary means of communication, crying cannot be considered true language. Young infants also produce a number of other sounds including yawns, sighs, coughs, sneezes, and belches. Although infant crying may lead to an adult response, there is no evidence that the infant is aware of the meaning of its cries.

Cooing; Babies first coo at about 1 to 2 months. These are pleasure sounds made in the back of the throat that often sound like cooing or gurgling. They usually occur during interaction with the caregiver. Around their third month, infants begin making cooing sounds when they are happy, and squealing-gurgling noises and making vowel sounds like "ahh", which they sustain for 15 to 20 seconds. At about 3 to 6 months, babies begin to play with speech sounds, matching the sounds they hear from people around them.

Babbling: Babbling (the playful repetition of sounds) usually occurs during the second six months of life and represents a limited form of communication and is often mistaken for a baby's first word. Babies between four and six months of life, emit a simple consonant-vowel combinations, such as "ba, ba, ba, ba" that, they repeat in rapid succession. By about 6 months, and the infants begin to use wide range of sounds, including a lot of what we would call 'consonants' such as k and g, l. Frequently, the baby combines a consonant sound with a vowel sound and produces a kind of syllable, such as ba and ga. When infants babble, they typically explore all the possible sounds they can make by changing the force of the airstream as it passes their vocal cords and by varying the positions of their tongue and mouth. Babbling is not real language, since it does not hold meaning for the baby, but it becomes more word like.

Gestures: Infants start using gestures, such as showing and pointing at about 8 to 12 months of age. At nine months, the infant points out to an object, sometimes making a noise to show that she wanted it. Between 9 and 12 months, it learned some conventional social gestures. For example, they may wave good-bye, nod to mean "yes", show an empty cup to ask for more milk, and point to a dog to draw attention to it and shaking her head to signify no. By about 13 months, she uses more elaborate representational gestures; for example, she would hold an empty cup to her mouth to show that she wanted a drink or hold up her arms to show that she wanted to be picked up.

Symbolic gestures, such as blowing to mean hot, or sniffing to mean flower, often emerge around the same time as babies say their first words, and they function much like words. By using them, children show an understanding that symbols can refer to specific objects, events, and conditions. Gestures usually appear before children have a vocabulary of 25 words and drop out when children learn the word for the idea they were gesturing and can say it instead. Gesturing seems to come naturally. Learning gestures seems to help babies learn to talk.

Language development continues with accidental imitation of language sounds. Babies hear and then imitate by themselves making these sounds. At about 9 to 10 months, infants deliberately imitate sounds without understanding them. Once they have a repertoire of sounds, they string them together in patterns that sound like language but seem to have no meaning.

First Words: Sometime around the first birthday, the child achieves a milestone in language; the utterance of the first word. At about 8 to 12 months of age, infants often say a first word indicating their first understanding of words, thus initiating linguistic speech - verbal expression that conveys meaning. The appearance of the first word is a continuation of their communication process with their parents, often by gesturing and using their own special sounds. For now, an infant's total verbal repertoire is likely to be "mama" or "dada".

By 13 months, most children understand that a word stands for a specific thing or event, and they can quickly learn the meaning of a new word. Addition of new words to their *expressive* (spoken) vocabulary is slower at first, but as children come to rely more on words than on gestures to express themselves, the sounds and rhythms of speech grow more elaborate.

The infant's spoken vocabulary rapidly increases once the first word is spoken. The average 18 months-old can speak about 50 words, but by the age of 2 years, can speak about 200 words. This rapid increase in vocabulary that begins at approximately 28 months is called the **vocabulary spurt**. The timing of a child's first word and vocabulary spurt varies. The ages for the first word of individual children ranged from 10 to 17 months and for their vocabulary spurt from 13 to 25 months.

Two-Word Utterances or First sentences

By the time children are 18 to 24 months of age, they usually utter two-word utterances, about 8 to 12 months after they say their first word. However, this age range varies greatly. A child's first sentences typically deal with everyday events, things, people or activities. To convey meaning with just two words, the child relies heavily on gesture, tone, and context. The wealth of meaning children can communicate with a two-word utterance are great.

In fact, in every language, a child's first combination of words have this economical quality; they are telegraphic. Telegraphic speech is the use of short words without grammatical markers such as articles, auxiliary verbs, and other connectives. Sometime between 20 and 30 months, children show increasing competence in syntax, the rules for putting sentences together in their language. They become somewhat more comfortable with articles (a, the), prepositions (in, on), conjunctions (and, but), plurals, verb endings, past tense, and forms of the verb to be (am, are, is).

6.9 RECOGNITION, MEMORY AND PERCEPTION

Recognition: Even though infants cannot describe what they remember, they do often indicate recognition of particular objects, people, and activities. Familiar people, such as mothers, bring forth a special response in one-year-olds, who may coo suddenly at the sight of them, stretch out their arms to them, and even crawl or walk to them if they know how. Less familiar people, such as neighbors or the family doctor, tend not to produce responses like these and in fact may even produce active distress.

Memory: Memory is the retention of information over time. Memory or the storage of information by cognitive process is assessed by the infant's response to the introduction of stimulation. Presumably, because of the very short memory span of attention, most stimuli are initially responded to as a novel stimulus. As the infant is stimulated, the pulse rate and respiration will increase; however, breathing and heart rate will slow, and body movements will be greatly reduced, as the infant focuses energies toward maximal exposure toward a stimulus. If a ripple is in the baby's mouth, sucking will stop. The attention of a young infant is complete. The one-year old baby who has just begun to crawl has a far more limited memory (yet memory it has) than a brother or sister of four.

Infant Perception: Perception refers to how the brain organizes and interprets sensations. Perception operates relatively automatically. Children acquire a number of perceptual skills during infancy. Each corresponds to one or another of the five human senses: vision, hearing, touch, taste, and smell. The first two, vision and hearing, account for the large majority of research about infants' perception.

Visual Perception: Infants-even newborns just two days old-could discriminate between human faces and abstract patterns. At all ages studied (birth to six months), infants showed a clear preference: they stared at a picture of a human face almost twice as long as at any other stimulus picture. Young infants, it seemed, were inherently interested in people.

When infants get to the age of two or three months, their perceptual interest shifts to complexity and curvature. At this age an infant prefers looking at a pattern of many small squares rather than at one of just a few large squares. And he prefers looking at curved lines to looking at straight ones. These qualities, too, are provided by human faces, but not by faces alone. Young infants prefer near objects-things at about one meter or less-to objects that are farther away.

Generally, young infants-about three months-show constancy only for simple shapes. Older infants-around eight months-can also recognize complex forms such as faces or abstract drawings even when they are presented at sidelong or tilted angles. Whatever the timing of their appearance, when babies acquire the constant perception of shape and size, it helps them to distinguish familiar objects from novel ones and to begin seeing the world as predictable and secure. Gradually, mother is mother and father is father whether viewed from the side or from the front and whether viewed from ten feet or two feet. Shape and size constancies also help infants learn about new, inanimate objects more efficiently.

Auditory Perception: Infants respond to sounds even as newborns; under certain conditions infants can indeed organize the sounds they hear, and in this sense they can hear as well as perceive what they hear. For example, infants just two-days-old can locate sounds, as shown by the way they orient their heads toward the noise of a rattle. But they often take much longer than older children or adults before responding. Although infants can locate sounds, their skill at doing so has certain limitations. They are better at locating relatively high-pitched sounds, such as that made by a foghorn.

For the first few months of life, infants locate sounds only by the differences in loudness of the sounds when they reach each ear. This allows only fairly crude judgments about the direction of a sound (during the newborn period, of course, a baby may not need very precise judgments). By about the fourth month of life, however, infants begin using an additional source of information that increases their accuracy considerably-namely, the slight differences in when a sound arrives at each ear. A sound originating off to the left arrives at the left ear a few thousandths of a second sooner than it arrives at the right ear. The difference in timing in fact reflects the direction of the sound fairly precisely.

Depth perception: It refers to a sense of how far away objects are or appear to be. Infants begin having this kind of perceptual skill about as soon as they can focus on objects at different distances, at around two or three months of age. Later on in infancy, children use their perceptions of depth to orient themselves in three-dimensional space. Eighteen-month-olds come to believe that their spatial environment remains still or fixed even when they themselves move.

6.10 COGNITIVE DEVELOPMENT DURING INFANCY

From an early age, human beings think and communicate their thoughts to others. As perceptual skills develop, children begin to put them to cognitive uses. Jean Piaget (1896-1980) believed that children are naturally curious. They constantly want to make sense of their experience and in the process, construct their understanding of the world. Although children's understanding of the world is often incomplete, it is valuable to them because they make the world seem more predictable.

Newborns know nothing about the world around them. But they are equipped with reflexes, senses and curiosity which make them ready and eager to begin making sense of the multiple sensations and events that surround them. The infant's pace of cognitive development is dramatic. It is capable of satisfying his or her curiosity about its world through such basic activities such as sucking, grasping, listening and staring. However, within a short span of two years, the infant is capable of anticipating future events, remember, and imitate the actions of others. By age 2, they have learned a great deal about

- Objects- that some make noise, others move, they can play with some while some are not to be touched.
- People-that some are familiar and trustworthy that others are strange and unpredictable.
- Experiences- playing with water or sand is enjoyable while visiting a hospital/doctor is unpleasant.

Even more impressive, they have learned to communicate, initially with gestures, body movements and sounds and then with words- a few by age one and a hundred or more by age 2.

All these achievements are part of "cognition", that is, the interaction of all the perceptual, intellectual and linguistic abilities that are involved in thinking and learning. Cognition is the activity of knowing and the process through which knowledge is acquired and problems are solved. Human beings are cognitive beings. Discussion of cognitive development of children seeks to inquire into the process by which children grow in knowledge and in the ability to perceive, think and understand, and then utilize these abilities to solve the practical problems of everyday living.

What is Cognition?

"Cognition" comes from a Latin word meaning "to know", "to become acquainted with", and "to perceive". "To cognize" simply means, "to become aware of". Therefore, cognition is any activity of becoming or being aware of something. Cognition "refers to the inner processes and products of the mind that lead to "knowing". The overt indication that there is awareness (cognition) may be a verbal statement, or it may be simply a nonverbal behavior.

Cognition includes all the mental activities of attending, learning, imagery, sensation, perceiving, remembering, retention, recall, problem solving, reasoning, thinking, symbolizing, categorizing, all verbal behavior and understanding-through which we gain and use knowledge about our world. They are all processes central to our understanding of human nature.

Cognitive development

Cognitive development refers to the growth and refinement of these intellectual process. Mental development is a process that begins at least as early as the day the infant is born and probably earlier. The motor and sensory skills serve as the basis for cognitive development.

In infancy, cognitive development is closely linked to the development of sensation and perception because these capabilities provide the foundations for early thought. The infant begins to comprehend his world cognitively, which involves moving, sensing, feeling and thinking. Discussion of cognitive development of children seeks to inquire into the process by which children grow in knowledge and in the ability to perceive, think and understand, and then utilize these abilities to solve the practical problems of everyday living (Rice, 2007). The infant begins to comprehend his world cognitively before he can speak. Piaget feels that intelligence is the ability, to adapt to the environment and that the development of this ability passes through a series of maturational stages.

Piaget's Theory of Cognitive Development

Piaget thought that, just as our physical bodies have structures that enable us to adapt to the world, we build mental structures that help us to adapt to the world. Adaptation involves adjusting to new environmental demands. Piaget also stressed that children actively construct their own cognitive worlds; information is not just poured into their minds from the environment. He sought to discover how children at different points, in their environment think about the world and how these systematic changes occur.

Processes of Development

Through careful observation of his own three children-Laurent, Lucienne and Jacqueline and inquisitive interviews of other children, Piaget changed our perceptions of the way children think about the world. What processes do children use as they construct their knowledge of the world? Piaget argued that these processes are especially important in this regard; schemes, assimilation, accommodation, organization, and equilibrium (Santrock, 2007).

Schemes

Piaget (1954) said that as the child seeks to construct an understanding of the world, the developing brain creates "schemes". According to Piaget, children understand the world with "schemes," which are psychological structures that organize experience. Schemes are mental categories of related events, objects, and knowledge. These are actions or mental representations that organize knowledge. Schemes change constantly, adapting to children's experiences. During infancy, most schemes are based on actions. That is, infants group objects based on the actions they can perform on them. For example, infants suck and grasp and they use these actions to create categories of objects that can be sucked and objects that can be grasped.

In Piaget's theory, behavioral schemes (physical activities) characterize infancy, and mental schemes (cognitive activities) develop in childhood. A baby's schemes involve simple actions that can be performed on objects such as sucking, looking and grasping. Older children have schemes that include strategies and plans for solving problems. For example, a 5 year-old might have a scheme that involves the strategy of classifying objects by size, shape, or color.

Assimilation and Accomodation

To explain how children use and adapt their schemes, Piaget offered two concepts: assimilation and accommodation.

Assimilation: "Assimilation occurs when new experiences are readily incorporated into existing schemes". Imagine a baby who has the familiar grasping scheme. She will soon discover that the grasping scheme also works well on blocks, toy cars and other small objects. Extending the existing grasping scheme to new objects illustrate assimilation.

Accommodation: "Accommodation occurs when schemes are modified based on experience". Accommodation occurs when children adjust their schemes to fit new information and experiences Soon the infant learns that some objects can only be lifted with two hands and that some cannot be lifted at all. Changing the scheme so that it works for new objects (e.g. Using 2 hands to grasp heavy objects) illustrate accommodation.

Assimilation and accommodation operate even in very young infants. Newborns reflexively suck everything that touches their lips; they assimilate all sorts of objects into their sucking scheme. By sucking different objects, they learn about their taste, texture, shape, and so on. After several months of experience, though, they construct their understanding of the world differently. Some objects such as fingers and the mother's breast can be sucked, and others, such as fuzz blankets, should not be sucked. In other words, they accommodate their sucking scheme.

Organization: To make sense out of their world, children cognitively organize their experiences. Organization is Piaget's concept of **grouping isolated behaviors into a high order system**. Items are grouped into categories. Every level of thought is organized. Continual refinement of this organization is an inherent part of development. For example, a boy who has only a vague idea about how to use a hammer may also have a vague idea about how to use other tools. After learning how to use each one, he must relate these uses, or organize his knowledge, if he is to become skilled in using tools. In the same way, children continually integrate and coordinate the many other branches of knowledge that often develop independently.

Equilibrium and Equilibration

Equilibration is a mechanism that Piaget proposed to explain how children shift from one stage of thought to the next. The shift occurs as children experience cognitive conflict, or disequilibrium, in trying to understand the world. Eventually, they resolve the conflict and reach a balance, or **equilibrium of thought**. Piaget believed there is considerable movement between states of cognitive equilibrium and disequilibrium as assimilation and accommodation work in concert to produce cognitive change. For example, if a child believes that the amount of a liquid changes simply because the liquid is poured into a container with a different shape- for instance, from a container that is short and wide into a container that is tall and narrow-she might be puzzled by such issues as where the "extra" liquid came from and whether there is actually more liquid to drink. The child will eventually resolve these puzzles, as her thought becomes more advancing. In the everyday world, the child is constantly faced with such counterexamples and inconsistencies.

Equilibrium and Stages of Cognitive Development

Assimilation and accommodation are usually in balance, or equilibrium. Children find that many experiences are readily assimilated into their existing schemes but that they sometimes need to accommodate their schemes to adjust to new experiences. This balance between assimilation and accommodation is illustrated by the baby with the theory about lifting the objects. Periodically, however, this balance is upset, and a state of disequilibrium results. That is, children discover that their current schemes are not adequate because they are spending much time accommodating and much less time assimilating. When "disequilibrium" occurs, children recognize their schemes to return to a state of equilibrium, a process that Piaget called **"equilibration".** To restore the balance, current but now-out moded ways of thinking are replaced by a qualitatively different, more advanced set of schemes (Kail and Cavanaugh, 2007).

Periodically children reach states in which their current theories seem to be wrong much of the time, so they abandon these theories in favor of more advanced ways of thinking about their physical and social worlds.

Stages of Development

Assimilation and accommodation always take the child to a higher ground. Piaget theorized that individuals go through four stages of development. A different way of understanding the world makes one stage more advanced than another. Cognition is qualitatively different in one stage compared with another. In other words, the way children reason at one stage is different from the way they reason at another stage. Each of Piaget's stages is age-related and consists of distinct ways of thinking. Piaget believed that there are four stages of cognitive development: sensorimotor, preoperational, concrete operational, and formal operational (Santrock, 2007).

Piaget's four Stages of Cognitive Development

In Piagetian theory, the growth of intelligence is divided into four major periods or stages-sensorimotor stage, preoperational stage, concrete operational stage and formal operational stage. Piaget believed that humans progress through these four distinct stages of cognitive development because of the interaction of biological maturation and experience,

1. The sensorimotor stage (birth to 2 years)
2. The preoperational stage (2 to 7 years) - Preschool and early elementary school years
3. The stage of concrete operations (7 to 11 years)–Middle and late elementary school years
4. The stage of formal operations (11 years or later and beyond)—Adolescence and adulthood

These stages represent qualitatively different ways of thinking and occur in an "invariant sequence"–that is, in the same order in all children. However, depending on their experiences, children may progress through the stages rapidly or slowly; the age ranges associated with the stages are only average. During these four stages, the exploratory behavior of infants transform into the abstract, logical intelligence of adolescents and adulthood.

Another important aspect of Piaget's theory is that in each stage, children actually create a series of active "experiments" on their environments and, as a result of these experiments; they construct new views of the world for themselves. It may be difficult for adults to understand that children's thinking is different from adult thinking not only in the amounts of information that children possess, but more importantly in ways that they know things. Piaget believes that infants are not only influenced by the environment but infants also influence the environment and construct personal views of it.

The sensorimotor stage

The first of Piaget's four stages of cognitive development is the "sensorimotor stage", which commences from birth and extends up to approximately two years (Papalia et al. 2004). At the beginning of this stage, newborns have only a few patterns of actions or reflexive patterns with which to work such as grasping, sucking and crying. The child's capacity in symbol usage, language, imagery and concept formation is limited. Therefore, child's adaptations do not involve extensive use of symbols or language. With inadequate brain maturation the infant can learn about the world only through sensory means such as taste, touch, and motor means such as movement and so on. Piaget believed that infants and toddlers "think" with their eyes, ears, hands and other sensorimotor equipment (Berk,2006). Hence, Piaget (1954; 1963) labeled the first stage of cognitive development as the sensorimotor period because it involves learning to respond through motor activity to the various stimuli that are presented to the senses.

During the sensorimotor stage, infants learn about themselves and their world through their developing sensory and motor activity. They cannot yet carry out many activities inside their heads.

Sub stages of the Sensorimotor Stage

Piaget divided the sensorimotor stage into six sub stages: (1) simple reflexes (2) first habits and primary circular reactions (3) secondary circular reactions (4) coordination of secondary circular reactions (5) tertiary circular reactions, novelty and curiosity and (6) internalization of schemes. They act as stair-steps leading from simpler to more advanced levels of sensorimotor intelligence. The age ranges for these stages are approximate. More important is the order in which the stage occur (Stewart et al, 1988).

These six sub stages flow from one to another as a baby's schemes, organized patterns of behavior, become more elaborate. During the first five sub stages, babies learn to coordinate input from their senses and organize their activities in relation to their environment. They do this by the processes of organization, adaptation, and equilibration. During the sixth and last sub stage they progress from trial-and-error learning to the use of symbols and concepts to solve simple problems.

Sub stage 1: Practice, Repetition and Use of Existing Reflexes (Birth to 1 month):

The first stage occurs between birth and one month of age. Throughout most of Stage I, the behavior of the infant is largely reflexive, that is, infants respond to the world largely in terms of the inborn reflexes that they are born with (e.g., crying, grasping, sucking, and specific movement of head, trunk, legs and arms). Reflexes are simple innate behaviors that all normal babies can produce at birth, such as sneezing, blinking, crying, grasping, sucking and specific movements of head, trunk, legs and arms. The newborn practices reflexive actions like sucking, grasping, looking and listening. For example, whenever an object is placed in the mouth of an infant, the infant sucks it regardless of what it is (e.g., bottle nipple, blanket, rattle).

Piaget regarded newborn reflexes as the building blocks of sensorimotor intelligence. These include the rooting and sucking reflexes, which the infant has at birth. Even though reflexes are inborn reactions to stimulation, they are adaptive. Adaptive behavior is intelligent behavior. Reflex behavior is adaptive and therefore, is intelligent, since it enables the infant to survive and allows later learning to take place. Intelligent reflex behavior forms the basis for later intelligent activity. The infant relies on these reflexes to provide much of her/his motor behavior at this time.

During this sub stage, the infant's behavior is essentially into exercising innate skills. In this sub stage, sensation and action are coordinated primarily through reflexive behavior. The reflexes provide the earliest behaviors that the infant has for dealing with its environment. The infant relies on these reflexes to provide much of her/his motor behavior at this time. These reflexes soon become modified by experience. This stage involves a systematic and increasingly less awkward use of natural reflexes.

In Piaget's words, this is a time of **reflexive exercise.** Neonates begin to gain some control over their inborn reflexes and become more efficient. They engage in a behavior even when its normal stimulus is not present. For example, newborns suck reflexively when their lips are touched. They soon learn to find the nipple even when they are not touched, and they suck at times when they are not hungry. Thus, infants modify and extend the scheme for sucking.

By the end of this stage, the infant can distinguish between objects. When hungry, for example, the infant may actively suck milk-producing nipple and repel other objects placed in its mouth. Such behavior was not present at birth. The infant changes from a passive recipient of stimulation that elicits the reflex to an active seeker of stimulation. It is easier to see the infant as an active stimulation seeker as she gets a bit older. She babbles. If her babbling brings attention from her parents, cuddling and smiles, she will be able to do more and more.

Object Permanence

At this stage, infants begin to develop the notion that objects are separate from themselves. When they drop their rattle, they stare at their fingers, a bit perplexed. But within moments, they have gone on to something else. They do not search for objects they cannot see; out of sight is literally out of mind. They do not realize that objects are permanent; a realization Piaget called **"object permanence".**

Sub stage 2: Primary Circular Reactions (1 to 4 months)

The second stage begins with the alterations in reflexive behaviors. Several new behaviors appear that represent such changes. They are

- Hand-mouth coordination, which develops and is reflected in repeated thumb-sucking.

- Eye coordination, which is the ability of the eyes to follow moving objects.
- Eye-ear coordination, which is reflected in the ability of the infant to move its head in the direction of sounds.

Much of this early cognitive growth comes about through circular reactions, in which an infant learns to repeat pleasurable or interesting behavior or actions originally discovered by chance. Initially, an activity produces a sensation so enjoyable that the baby wants to repeat it. For example, by chance, when a child's thumb touches the mouth, triggering the sucking reflex, it results in a pleasurable sensation. As this is a pleasurable act, the baby tries to repeat it and the repetition leads to the baby learning how to suck on her/his thumb. Piaget called these repetitions of what begins as random or reflexive actions as **primary circular reactions.** These actions are referred to as **"primary"** because they occur first in relation to the infant's body and as **"circular reactions"** because they are repeated to become habitual behaviors. As maturation proceeds, anything the baby grasps is brought to the mouth to be sucked upon as well. These actions involve hand-eye and hand-mouth coordination abilities.

Sub stage 3: Secondary Circular Reactions (4 to 8 months)

Prior to Stage 3, the infant's behavior is oriented largely toward the self. It repeated his/her primary circular reactions for the joy of the action themselves. In addition, the infant cannot distinguish itself from the objects of the environment, nor can it coordinate eye-hand movements. During Stage 2, behavior was random and was not designed to attain an object or goal. During stage 3, however, all these change.

During Stage 3, the infant's behaviors are increasingly directed to events or objects beyond its own body. Piaget called such repetitions **Secondary Circular Reactions** because it happens outside the child's own body. The repetition is a circular reaction like the ones in the previous stage, but with an important difference. Now the circular reaction is oriented to external objects and events rather than to the baby's own body. Actions shift now from the body (primary reactions) to the physical environment (secondary reactions). Infants can now sit up and become skilled at reaching for and manipulating objects. These motor achievements play a major role in turning their attention toward the environment. In this simple way, the infant learns to act upon the surroundings and make things happen.

Using the "Secondary Circular Reactions", they try to repeat interesting events that are caused by their own actions. Improved control over their own behavior also permits infants to imitate others' behavior more effectively. However, 4 to 8 month-olds cannot adapt flexibly and quickly enough to imitate novel behavior.

Object permanence

In the first two stages of infant cognition, objects often seem to disappear from baby's mind if it loses contact with it or no longer touches them. By stage 3 they will look for an object briefly if they have been unlatching it carefully or manipulating it just before hand. This skill is being mastered, however, as the infant can recognize and recover objects if they are only partially hidden or covered. Further experiences allow the baby to discover the independent existence of objects when they are removed from view, as shown by attempts to uncover objects or to look for when they were taken away.

Sub stage 4 : Coordination of Secondary Circular Reactions (8 to 12 Months)

By the time infants reach the fourth sub stage, they have built on the few schemes they were born with. Schemes are the basic building blocks of cognitive development. As a result, new behavior patterns emerge from existing ones as the infant learns new ways to solve problems and intact with the surroundings. An infant may learn, for example, that she/he can search for an object he/she has seen being hidden and grasp the object once it has been located. They will crawl to get something they want, grab it, or push away a barrier to it (such as someone else's hand). They try out, modify, and coordinate previous schemes, to find one that works. This sub stage marks the development of complex, intentional or goal-directed behavior. Behavior is more deliberate and purposeful as infants coordinate motor activities with sensory input. Thus, infants will look at and grasp a rattle, or see a toy. Finally, play extends to practicing the means in the babies' new means-end action sequences.

Retrieving hidden objects is evidence that infants have begun to master "object permanence" understanding that objects continue to exist when they are out of sight. However, awareness of object permanence is not yet complete.

Sub Stage 5 : Tertiary circular reactions- The Discovery of New Means through Active Experimentation (12 to 18 months)

A new power learned by the infant is the ability to produce new events. These refinements in cognitive development are shown by the baby's first efforts in learning the cause-and-effect nature of certain actions. Toys are dropped or thrown repeatedly since the infant observes that they always fall, make certain sounds, or produce particular actions when treated in this manner. The exploration of their environment by manipulating objects and discovering the effects of their behavior through trial-and- error experimentation is a hallmark of development during this time.

The infant still makes accidental discoveries of action that produce pleasing sensation. But it no longer repeats these accidentally discovered actions exactly. The infant varies them somewhat as it repeats them. He/she experiments to find out in what respect an object, event or situation is new. The infant intentionally accommodates to find new solutions for new problems. As it tries out new behavior patterns to reach some goal, he/she is learning by trial and error, which leads to new complete acts of intelligence. The 12-18 month-olds deal with the world in this way; they are far better sensorimotor problem-solvers than they were before. For example, they can figure out how to fit a shape through a hole in a container by turning and twisting it until it falls through.

Sub stage 6: Mental Representation (18 to 24 months)

In sub-stage 5, the infant arrived at new means for problem solving through active experimentation. Sub-stage 6 provides evidence that the child has moved from a sensorimotor level of intelligence to a mental "representational level of thinking". By "representation" is meant the "ability of the infant to symbolize objects or events mentally". In Stage 6, the invention of means for problem solving is suddenly apparent, suggesting to Piaget that such invention occurs through representation and mental activity. One sign of this capacity is that 18 to 24-month-old arrives at solving new problems suddenly rather than through the laborious process of trial and error. Instead, it can now solve problems and find solutions mentally. Thus, they begin to develop insight into how to solve problems. This development is accompanied by a growing ability to use word symbols (language) in dealing with people and situations.

Representation results in several other capacities:

First, skills with mental representation, makes true object permanence possible. It enables older toddlers to solve advanced object-permanence problems involving "invisible displacement" - finding a toy moved out of sight, such as into a small box while under a cover. An infant or toddler will search for a toy even after it has been fully hidden.

Second, it permits deferred imitation-the ability to remember and imitate the behavior and actions of other people even after they are not in front of him, at a significantly later time than when he experienced it-sometimes days or even weeks later.

By stage 6, the infant has considerable understanding of the nature of objects, their relationships and some understanding of causality. It develops the ability to picture events in his mind and to follow them through to some degree. In other words, he can think. Finally, it makes possible make-believe play, in which children act out every day and perform imaginary activities. As the sensorimotor period draws to a close, mental symbols become the major instruments of thinking.

Learning Abilities of Newborns

An infant is always learning. For example, a 5-month-old learns that a new toy makes a noise every time it is shaken. Infants are born with many mechanisms that enable them to learn from experience. This learning can take many forms, including habituation, classical conditioning, operant conditioning and imitation.

Imitation: Infants are capable of imitations. A 10 month-old may imitate an adult waving her finger back-and-forth or imitate another infant who knocks down a tower of blocks. Over the course of the first year of life, infants are able to imitate a rapidly expanding range of behaviors.

CARE OF THE INFANT

6.11 CHILDREARING PRACTICES

Childrearing Practices consist of feeding, weaning, sleep and rest, toilet training, immunization, clothing and bathing. The biological and psychological challenges facing neonates and their parents were about establishing effective feeding and a predictable step-wise cycle. In the course of accomplishing these tasks, infants and parents engage in significant social interaction, laying the foundation for cognitive and emotional development.

Feeding: The neonate is seldom very hungry immediately following delivery. Infants' sucking and swallowing, and rooting reflexes enable them to search for and secure their food. Breast-fed and bottle-fed infants thrive equally well. First feedings are either sweetened water or colostrum. Colostrum is a sweet, thin fluid that is produced by the breast for two to three days before milk comes out. Milk is generally not tolerated well for a day or two, although it then becomes the only necessary source of nutrients for the first few months of infancy. Healthy breast milk is by far the best food a baby can have and every mother should make up her mind that she will suckle the baby herself. In some hospitals, infants are placed at the breast immediately in the delivery room. This practice has a number of positive effects for both mothers and infant.

Actual breast milk appears on the third day after delivery. Mothers who cannot or do not wish to breastfeed can bottle feed with formula. Bottle-fed infants are usually given nothing by mouth for the first few hours of life. The first feeding begins with glucose and water, if this is tolerated, the infant progresses to the formula of choice. Bottle-fed newborns require a feeding every 3 to 4 hours at first and then according to the individual hunger patterns. The caregiver should never prop the bottle and leave the infant unattended. The baby should never be allowed to sleep with a bottle that contains anything other than water. Putting juice or milk in a nighttime bottle can lead to "bottle-mouth syndrome; dental caries", caused by sugar in the milk or juice that weakens the tooth surfaces. By 8 or 9 months, infants are ready to be weaned; that is, they can accept the cup in place of the bottle or breast.

Human milk is ideally suited to the developmental needs of the human baby. There is no doubt that milk manufacturing companies have contributed considerably to a decline in breast feeding. However, the situation is gradually changing and many educated mothers are breast-feeding their babies with help and support from health personnel and a feeling of sense of pride and achievement.

Besides its nutritional significance, breast milk elicits a number of immunological effects that may be very important for health in the long term. There is considerable evidence that bottle-fed babies have more infections–gastro intestinal and respiratory problems than do breast-fed ones. Different forms of instant feeding may result in defective immunity function.

The nursing mother's diet has to be balanced and nourishing. It should include meat, fats, cheese, shell eggs, fish, raw salad, fresh fruits, green vegetables and milk. A glass of milk during mid-morning and another before bedtime is advisable. It is necessary for nursing mothers to increase their fluid intake, as this will necessarily increase the milk supply. The best guide for quantity of fluid intake is her own quantity of thirst. Finally, the mother should take care that she has sufficient periods for rest and pleasure pursuits.

To summarize, the feeding routines of the mother are

- Lift and 'pot' the baby.
- Washing her hands carefully after doing this.
- Cleanse nipples with cotton wool soaked in water.
- Put baby on breast, and after about 10 minutes help to expel any air, he has swallowed.
- Finish feed.
- Bring up wind again.
- Cleanse nipples

How long to continue Breast Feeding? It is now accepted that mothers should, if possible, breast-feed their babies certainly for the first four to six months. Weaning from breast milk and introduction of a full mixed diet should come about gradually and with the least discomfort to the mother.

Advantages of Breast-feeding: It is the most suitable and natural milk for the baby nature has provided. It is ever warm, readily available, and almost bacteria-free and can simply be transported along with the mother. It is a far cheaper method of feeding, involves much less work as with artificial one, where food has to be prepared and bottles cleaned and sterilized. There is no need for boiling bottles, teats, bowls and spoons.

Breast feeding brings the baby and mother together. It promotes attachment or bonding between mother and child. Baby loves to be cuddled and talked to. The mothering is good for growth and it is believed even for the development of personality and behavior. Close contact with the mother's normal bacteria and factors in the milk, such as antibodies; help to impart immunity to the infant. Another significant advantage of this approach is the responsiveness of the infant to the mother at this early time, which helps to foster a more positive mother–infant relationship. Therefore, long-range as well as short-range effects may be noted by fostering early contact and breast-feeding.

The breast-fed baby has a much greater resistance to infection, less liable to be constipated than bottle fed one. Infections in the baby, particularly diarrhea is far less in breast-fed babies. Breast feeding promotes the production of "Colostrum", which is the precursor of breast milk, rich in antibodies and is present in the mother's breast from as early as seventh month of fetal life. It contains more protein, salt, and carbohydrates but less fat than regular breast milk. In addition to these nutrients, it contains immunoglobulin to help protect the newborn until its own immune system is more developed.

Breast feeding hastens the "involution" of the uterus to its non-pregnant state, by stimulating uterine contractions and helping to restore muscle tone in the uterus. It helps the mother to gradually lose weight by drawing on the store of fat which her body has laid down during pregnancy. The baby's brain grows very rapidly in months after birth. The brain is largely fat and breast milk is rich in special fat needed. Human milk is also very rich in lactose which serves as a good supply of galactose needed by developing brains. Mothers who breast-feed their babies have a longer period of 'amenorrhea'. This helps to delay the next pregnancy thus increasing spacing between one child and next. Finally the mother regains her figure more quickly.

General problems in Breast- Feeding

1. **Sore Nipples:** Sometimes mothers experience extreme soreness of the nipples so that feeding the baby becomes a painful ordeal. When this condition occurs, the baby should not suck from them until they are healed. The following precautions will help to keep them free from soreness.
   - Never allow baby to lie with nipple in his mouth after he has finished feeding.
   - While feeding, see that he takes the brown circle behind the nipple into his mouth, as well as the nipple.
2. **Breast Abscess:** If the breast becomes red and very painful, one should take medical advice at once and the baby should be fed only from the breast which is healthy.
3. **Flat or Retracted Nipples:** Flat nipples can be made more prominent by frequently pulling out in both horizontal plus vertical directions, during the last month of pregnancy. This problem of retracted nipples is quite uncommon.
4. **Cracked Nipples:** The nipple may develop cracks because of the delicate tender skin, particularly if baby sucks for a longer time. The nipple should be cleaned with water and protective cream should be applied.
5. **Leaking:** While the baby is feeding from one breast, milk begins to flow from other breast. This can be stopped by pressing the nipple with a hand or handkerchief. The leaking will gradually become less.

Artificial feeding: If it is essential that your baby should be artificially fed, the main problem is what type of feeding shall be given. A substitute to breast milk in case of any serious condition of the mother is the cow's milk. Cow's milk contains as much protein as human milk. Since it is not easily digested by the infant, water is added to dilute protein and to aid in the excretion of waste products. The extra water reduces the number of calories per ounce, requiring the addition of some form of sugar to elevate the calorific value to 20 calories per ounce, the same as breast milk. However, the amount of sugar must be carefully regulated because too much of sugar in a formula can cause loose stools and too little may lead to constipation.

Unless there is any reason for urgency, changing from the breast to the bottle should take about five weeks, replacing one breast feed at a time with a bottle feed. The easiest way to explain the various stages in switching over from breast or bottle-feeding to more or less solid foods is to detail them month-by-month. The main thing to remember is that each change must be made very slowly and each new food introduced only as a small quantity at that time. If he appears to dislike a new food, never force him, but only introduce a little of it at the time, mixed up with one that he is already accustomed to, by gradually increasing the amount of the new food while decreasing the old.

Difficulties in feeding

Overfeeding: Overfeeding occasionally occurs in both breast- fed and artificially-fed infants. In former case, the baby is overfed because he takes too much food during the 24 hours, and in the latter, unsuitability of the milk mixture that may be too strong for them. It should be stressed that it is never advisable to feed a baby too strictly according to the instructions on tin or packet food, nor too strictly according to any charts.

Underfeeding: Here the stools tend to be dry, crumbly and small and there is often definite constipation. In addition, the baby will not be gaining sufficiently in weight and his skin will have a dry and wrinkled appearance. If underfeeding is caused through an insufficiency of breast milk, everything should be done to stimulate secretion of milk.

Constipation: Breast fed babies often have only one motion in two or even three days. However, if motion when passed is normal, in color, consistency and odor, there is no indication of constipation at all. True constipation occurs far more frequently in artificially fed infants. Natural methods of curing trouble are by giving more fruit juice or water or giving a little extra sugar. When these have to be resorted to, use only a mild laxative, such as fluid of magnesia.

Diarrhea: The causes of diarrhea can be too much fat or sugar in diet, baby may have caught a chill in his tummy or infection of mouth such as thrush. In severe cases, medical advice should be sought. Frequent sips of warm boiled water to which glucose has been added, at the rate of one teaspoonful of glucose per glass, can be given.

Weaning: Weaning is taking off the breast milk and introducing a new food to an infant. It should be done gradually, one feeding at a time. The noon bottle is usually a good feeding to eliminate first; and the baby should not be too tired or hungry to attempt learning the use of a cup. Liquid supplements such as animal milk, fresh fruit juices and soups from green leafy vegetables are good substitutes at around the 6th month, when the frequency of breast feeding is reduced to 3 or 4 times per day. Milk is also a poor source of vitamin C and supplementation with fruit juice is essential .Fish liver oils are good sources of vitamin A and D. Therefore, infants should be given a few drops to $\frac{1}{2}$ teaspoon per day mixed in small quantity of milk.

The ideal time to start introducing semisolid food is when a baby is ready to sit up, swallow and eat and taste other foods. The infant's nutritional needs can be met during the entire first year by breast-feeding or by using iron-enriched formula. However, many pediatricians recommend the introduction of solid foods after the 5th month. After six months, as the increasing needs of calories and protein of growing children cannot be met by diminishing output of mother's milk, cereals, vegetables, and meat should be added to the diet. Mashed food is started around the 7th or 8th month of life. Well-cooked, mashed cereals like rice, rice flour, rice flakes and ragi flour mixed with milk and sugar can be given. Cooked, mashed vegetables like potato, green leafy vegetables and carrots can be introduced to get vitamins and minerals and colour in the diet. All the fruits, with the exception of banana which is mashed, must be stewed and served for one year old baby. Thereafter, it is given simply stewed, with the addition of a little sugar and lime juice for flavor. A small amount of hard boiled yolk of egg is given to start with and if the infant tolerates, the amount may be gradually increased.

These foods have been known to cause allergic reactions in many infants. It is best to introduce only one new food at a time for several days to detect any adverse reaction. A rule of thumb is to add 1 to 2 teaspoonfuls of each new food, gradually increasing the amount to one tablespoon of each food item for each year. The year-old baby eats three meals per day.

When the baby starts cutting his teeth, it is time to start chopped and lumpy solid supplements such as cooked cereals, pulses and vegetables. Solids like idiappam, bread, chapathi, rice and dal can be given after the child gets used to semi-solids. Home made or commercial processed foods can be given as weaning foods prepared by using cereals, pulses, nuts and jaggery with or without milk products.

Sleep and Rest: The neonate sleeps a great deal, as much as 20 out of 24 hours. The faster the rate of growth, the more sleep is required. By one year of age, the baby will need only about 12 hours of sleep in a day. The newborn's sleep pattern is not continuous but is characterized by periods of light sleep marked by stirring movements and noises. Sleep patterns may be interrupted by discomfort and hunger. A bedtime routine will help to establish a nighttime sleeping pattern. This consistent approach to bedtime helps to lower anxiety and make the infant feel more secure. Early on bed, help infants learn to distinguish day from night by interacting more during the day hours and by keeping the talking, cuddling, and interactions to a minimum at night. Infants should be placed awake in their cribs so that they learn to soothe themselves and fall asleep on their own. During the first year, most infants require both morning and afternoon naps to replenish their stamina.

During the daytime, provided the weather is suitable, the baby should be put out of doors as much as possible with the pram hood down, unless it is very cold and windy. When it is necessary to sleep indoors, the room should be well aired and fresh, with the windows open. The cot, if it is in a room with another child, should be placed so that the air comes to the baby first. It is not necessary to draw the curtains or darken the room. The newborn baby will sleep well in daylight or darkness, and this is obviously a useful habit to encourage.

SIDS

Sudden infant death syndrome (SIDS) is responsible for the death of about one out of every 500 babies, most commonly between the ages of 1 and 4 months. Although the exact cause of SIDS (also known as "crib death") is still unknown, recent research indicates an association between SIDS and sleep patterns. Death usually occurs between midnight and 6 A.M. The American Academy of Pediatrics recommends as a preventive measure that healthy infants sleep on their backs and sides and not on their stomachs. Recently it has been suggested that parents should offer a pacifier to infants to lessen the risk of SIDS. In addition, infants should be put to sleep in cribs that meet current safety standards. Parents should not use soft materials like quilts, comforters, or pillows in the sleeping area. Co-sleeping arrangements in the parents' bed may pose the danger of suffocation or entrapment for the infant. In these cases, special care must be taken to avoid placing the bed against a wall or using a railing or headboard that may cause the infant's head to become trapped between these surfaces.

Toilet training: Toilet training is a task that a child cannot successfully undertake until he has grown physiologically to the point where he is ready for it. This varies widely with each individual child. Do not be in a hurry to start. If begun before the child is physically ready, it is like asking something of her that she is simply not mature enough to give. One cannot make her use a pot and attempt to force training, as it will incite the child to experience successful defiance only.

Early initiation of toilet training is likely to be associated with rebellion against the training. Until the close of the first year, bowel and bladder functions remain a completely involuntary process. Therefore, early training is largely a waste of time. In addition, premature training may cause unnecessary frustration for the mother. The child may become hostile towards the parent if the training is severe. It should be remembered that no matter when "training" is started, the child is unlikely to be entirely reliable on her own in the daytime before her third year. If started early, she will take longer to learn; if you start later, she will learn faster and reach the same point at the same time.

All babies gradually gain the control of their bowels and bladders as they grow. During the first year, the child does not pay much attention to these functions, the child may pass stool soon after the stomach is full, (i.e.) after a feed. During the first year, the mother has to anticipate and keep the baby clean. Around one year the child may be allowed to sit on a pot or in a toilet seat. It is important to train the baby to pass the stool at a particular spot so that it gets accustomed to the thought that it should not defecate at any other place in the house. Elimination control constitutes an important type of socialization training during infancy.

In the first half of the second year children gradually become more conscious of when a bowel movement occurs. They may pause in what they are doing or change facial expression momentarily though they are nowhere near ready to notify a parent. The second year of life usually is the time when most parents begin to make major socialization demands upon the child. They begin to impose restrictions on activities the child normally finds pleasurable; they demand that he inhibits certain kinds of behavior that he enjoys. The child is asked to delay bowel and bladder elimination until he can get to an appropriate place. When the mother initiates toilet training with her child, she becomes a "teacher", expecting him to assume some independence and responsibility for his own care.

Balking: Early in the second year, they have an increasing urge to do everything for themselves, in their own way, and using the potty may seem too much of the parents' scheme so they just hold the movement at least until they can get away from the seat, which symbolizes giving it up, and giving in. If the resistance persisted for many weeks children might hold back not only when on the seat but for the rest of the day if they could manage it. This is a psychological type of constipation. Balking is more apt to occur in the first half of the second year than in the second half. This is a reason for waiting until about the middle of the year to start training and for letting children feel that it is they who have decided to control their bowels and bladders, rather than they are giving into parental demands.

Loud praises and exaggerated enthusiasm are inadvisable because they attach too much importance to this routine behavior. Similarly, angry scolding and constant naggings should also be avoided.

Sometimes a child gradually or suddenly gets into a spell of unusually hard movements that is painful to pass. The child who has once been hurt may dread a repetition and fight against toileting again. It may become a vicious circle, because if the child succeeds in holding back the movement for several days, it is more likely to be hard. It is important to notify the doctor promptly if the child begins to have hard movements, so that he can be helped with change of diets and medicine .

Bladder Training: The first sign of readiness is your child's learning of the momentary control of overcoming urine. Somewhere around her second birthday, the child will learn to take charge of her coming urination at an earlier stage, by recognizing her full bladder and lightening the muscles of her abdomen. Now she can delay the flow for several minutes and she can walk without losing control. She is therefore, ready to make for the pot if she wants to. After a few days or weeks of occasional casual successes, take the child out of nappies when she is at home and awake. Do not make a big thing of it or she may feel demeaned by having the nappy back on for outings, naps and nights. Be sympathetic about the frequent accidents.

During this stage, it is a good idea to introduce the child to the lavatory as well as the pot. She might like to pee in the place where elders do. One may show the child how easy it is to go behind a bush in garden. Once she is more or less reliable at home in the daytime, abandon nappies as part of her regular clothes. She can have them on for naps and at night, but that is all. Although there will still be pools, giving up nappies is important.

While bowel training is established by the age of about 2 years, bladder is controlled by 2.5 at day and night. Staying dry at night also varies with children. They become dry at night between two and 3 years of age, and few of them between 1.5 and 2 years, and in some cases by 3 or 4 years. A routine and regular habit training in all the baby's activities will be beneficial to her healthy development. As she grows older, although the nature of her routine will alter slightly, it is still as necessary as ever that she should be trained in regular ways. Her day should be arranged so that she has regular hours for sleeping, for play, fresh air and exercise and regular hours of feeding.

Immunization

Immunity means that individual develops resistance against a disease and does not suffer from it. Infants and children are susceptible to many diseases. Immunization is a method of raising a child's resistance to certain diseases by inducing his body to produce antibodies or by introducing antibodies directly into his body. Other names for immunization are inoculation and vaccination. In active immunization, a substance containing modified disease germs or a substance produced by the disease germs is introduced into the body, usually by injection; such a substance is commonly called vaccine. In response, the body produces antibodies to fight the germs. Passive immunization involves the use of a serum already containing the disease fighting antibodies. The immunized child is protected against the disease only as long as these antibodies are in blood stream and active. Thus, protection given by passive immunization is temporary; the usual period of effectiveness is from 4 to 6 weeks.

Precautions regarding vaccination

1. Baby should be well: It should be free from any illness as the fever and other manifestations of vaccination are liable to be confused with those of illness.
2. Family or Previous History of Fits: Any previous and family history of convulsive fits must be notified to the doctor. Because 'P' part of the DPT vaccine can induce or precipitate convulsive fits.
3. Complete vaccination from one centre: As every vaccination centre has its own routine and standards, immunization should preferably be completed from same centers only. Haphazard vaccination should be avoided.
4. Vaccination record: Immunization card, which is provided to parents, must be carefully kept and brought at every visit.
5. Next visit: Date of next visit given by the doctor should be honored. Booster doses are as important as first three doses.
6. No Medicine before and after the Vaccination: Stop the usage of all medicines or postpone the immunization, if required, as certain medicines can challenge the efficacy of these injections.

All these vaccines are instituted to prevent diseases and not treat them. The common diseases against which infants could be protected are :

1. Small Pox 2. Tetanus 3. Polio 4. Tuberculosis
5. Diphtheria 6. Whooping Cough 7. Measles.

Table 6.4 Immunisation Schedule

IAP Recommended immunization schedule for children aged 0-6 years (with range), 2012

Age		6 wk	10 wk	14 wk	18 wk	6 mo	9 mo	12 mo	15 mo	18 mo	2-3 yr	4-6 yr
Vaccine	Birth											
BCG	BCG											
Hep B	Hep B1	Hep B2				Hep B3						
Polio*	OPVO	IPV1	IPV2	IPV3		OPV1	OPV2	IPV B1				OPV3
DTP		DTP1	DTP2	DTP3					DTP B1			DTP B2
HIB		HIB1	HIB2	HIB3					HIB-booster			
Pneumococcal		PCV1	PCV2	PCV3					PCV-booster		PPSV	
Rotavirus**		RV1	RV2	RV*2								
Measles							Measles					
MMR									MMR1			MMR2
Vericella									Vericella1			Vericella2
Hep A								Hep A1			Hep A2	
Typhoid											Typhoid	
Influenza						Influenza (yearly						
Meningococcal											Meningococcal	
Cholera									Cholera 1 & 2			
JE							JE					

Some of the common reactions found in children could be any of the following such as swelling, tenderness and redness along with pain at the site of prick, fever, irritability and refusal of feeds, fretful sleep, vomiting and loose motions due to slight digestive disturbances, rashes or convulsive fits.

Clothing: A good mother must give adequate attention to the newborn's clothing with special reference to diapers or napkins, popularly known as nappies. Cotton fabric nappies are washable and ready for use repeatedly. The other type is the readymade, disposable and sterile, available from sophisticated markets.

There are four ways of folding a nappy. First type are the triangle nappies. After folding the nappy into a triangle, it should be put under baby's buttocks. One corner should lie between his legs. The other two corners should lie around the baby's middle. The three corners should be joined with a safety pin in the front. Second is the oblong nappy in which there are two ends at the back. The corner of the front should be brought up between the legs and then joined to the ends of the back with safety pins. Third, the so-called twisted nappy is more or less same as oblong nappy. But, it should be twisted before bringing up between the legs and then the ends of the back should be joined to the ends of the front with safety pins. Fourth one is the kite nappy, where the sides of the nappy are so folded that it becomes wide on the top and narrow at the bottom. Using safety pins, the front and back ends should be joined.

One has to be careful when the pin is used. Two fingers of the hand should be slipped between the nappy and the baby's skin so that the pin does not prick him. Sharp end of the safety pin should be always away from infant's body.

The nappy should be changed as soon as it is soiled. An exceptional baby may not care if he is wet but most of them do become restless and cry. The infant's buttocks should never be rubbed with the nappy. Rather it should be washed or cleansed with cotton soaked in baby oil. One should not forget to make the area dry, sprinkle powder on it before putting on another nappy.

Nappy Washing: Before beginning to wash, remove loose stools from dirty nappy in the toilet by scraping or raising it in the flush. It is a good idea to put the used diapers or nappies in a basin containing water and soap or detergent. Napkins should either be boiled daily or else washed in a special preparation such as 'Napisan' or 'Milton'. They can be placed immediately in a bucket containing 'Napisan'. As an alternative extra precaution, the washed nappies may now be put in dettol solution for 20 to 30 minutes. Squeeze the water out, let nappies dry and finally iron them. The use of dettol helps to prevent occurrence of nappy or diaper rash.

Diaper liners: The paper or treated cloth-made, if available are certainly of help in protecting the nappy from getting wet. These are placed between baby's skin and the nappy. They are of special help during traveling.

Protective pants: These again are of very special help when one is traveling with the baby. They should not be too tight, should not be used in the presence of nappy rash, should be replaced frequently and be sterilized in same way as nappies. These pants are waterproof, made either from rubber or from plastic.

The Clothes Babies Need

- Night gowns are entirely practical and can be worn also during a baby's period of awake and even during visits; short ones may be preferable for a hot climate.
- Two styles of vests- pullover and wrap-over.
- Small round bibs are useful for keeping drool off the clothes as well as the mess made during solid feeds.
- By 6 months, when babies can move about in their cots, most mothers find it more practical to put them to bed in sleeping bags than to try to keep blankets over them.

- Caps, bonnets and mittens are used for outdoors.
- Blankets for extra warmth when necessary.
- Waterproof sheeting of plastic or rubber preferably large enough to tuck in around the mattress.

A baby's clothes should be loose, comfortable and should allow free movement. Tight dresses or sweaters with tight necks and sleeves make life miserable for a child. Tight elastic in their underwear or on their socks or stockings make them feel very uncomfortable. Nowadays zippers are 'in' and traditional buttons are 'out'. Nevertheless, small children do not wear underwear beneath their shorts; zippers are in direct contact with delicate skin of genitalia. This skin often is caught and injured. Hence, preferably use buttons in front of the shorts. "Velcro" is a novel fastener used on the two edges of a garment, so that it sticks to each other.

Parents are always prone to over clothing babies. They are always scared that the child will catch a chill if left exposed. This is probably true in winter. However, over clothing results in all types of rashes including heat rash. If baby's skin is moist and there is perspiration under his armpits, probably, it is due to too many clothes. Also, woolen should not be worn next to the skin. A vest or cotton underskirt or petticoat beneath the sweater is ideal. Thus babies' clothes are good when they are loose and fit easily, if they are cheap but imaginative, attractive, comfortable, durable and washable. Cotton, terracotta, and poplins are good materials.

Bathing : To give the baby a bath at home, you will need a good size wash basin or a baby tub. The water should be comfortably warm and should fill half or three fourths of the basin or tub. The room should be warm and free of draught. The fan should be switched off. First the baby's face and head should be washed. The baby can then be put in the tub while supporting his head properly. If the baby's buttocks are soiled with stool, he should be cleaned before being put in the tub. The baby's skin is very delicate and only a mild soap should be used. A shampoo or soap should be used for the head and a soft brush can be used for the hair.

After the bath, the skin should be dried gently and the clothes put on. Pat the skin dry rather than wipe it. Most mothers like to use talcum powder because it smells nice. It may be stacked in the skin folds and irritate the skin. If at all it is used, it should be used sparingly. Powder should not be put on the cord. While powdering his neck or chest, it should be made sure that it does not go too near his nose as there is danger of his inhaling it. Until the cord comes off and the navel becomes dry, it is better not to put the baby in the tub, but to pour water over him, avoiding the cord area. Alternatively, the baby can be sponged.

The Indian-style bath is quite good for all babies. The mother sits and keeps the child on her outstretched legs and gives a complete bath in that posture. A pot of water, a small bottle of oil, a plate with the 'dhal-powder,' (which is very soft), and generally non-irritating and non-allergic, is kept by her side. The mother is either assisted or generally helps herself in giving this bath. The national habit of a daily bath of the baby is good and is practiced by all mothers irrespective of their social or economic status. Only a certain amount of education of the mother is necessary so that she avoids the injurious practice of putting oil into the nose, eyes, and ears of the child at the time of bath. However, occasionally clean oil should be put in the ears of the child as it softens the wax that can be easily removed by someone who knows this job.

Applying the oil over the raw umbilicus is also unnecessary as this sometimes infects the umbilicus, causing delay in drying. Wiping simply with sterile cloth and applying the dusting powder either medicated or non-medicated, is sufficient.

Oil Bath: Generally oil bath is given to all young babies in Indian homes, which is a nice stimulating thing to the baby as there is a mild massage after oiling of the body. A soft wash of all the pores of the body with a mild 'Special protein powder' to take off the oil and the dirt with a warm water bath, will be refreshing.

It is a wise practice to get everything ready and assembled before the baby is lifted from the cot or pram. The materials to be assembled are: powder, ointment, cotton wool, bath and face towels, blunt-pointed scissors, strong safety pins, face and body flannels, a good super fatted baby soap and a hairbrush, along with his day clothes, and a change of napkins, his pot and the mother's waterproof apron. The room in which he is to be washed should be warm and the bath should be placed at a height that can comfortably be reached while sitting down. If an enamel bath is used, one should be careful not to have this too near to a fire, as it will get very hot and could burn the baby.

Put some cold water in the bath and then add hot water until the bath is about half-full at a temperature of about 95 to 100 degree F; otherwise, the bottom of the bath will hold the heat and the baby would receive a hasting burn on his buttocks. If the thermometer is not available, the water can be tested with bare elbow, so that it should feel comfortably warm.

Oil Massage: In India, oil massage is credited with all kinds of beneficial effects. The body can be massaged with mild oil like sweet oil, or some body oil to prevent the skin from becoming dry. Massage is stimulating for the skin-it improves its texture and stimulates circulation. In summer, a gentle massage can be given with oil or powder. A vigorous oil massage generates too much heat and the baby may feel some discomfort.

Mix Dhal Powders for Bath: These powders are a mixture of various dhal like green gram, bengal gram and a trace of turmeric powder along with a few fragrant flowers that are generally used in the country. Some children may get allergic to these powders, in which case a soft soap may be used.

Care of the Eyes, Ears, Nose and Mouth: Nature takes care of keeping the eyes, nose, mouth and ears clean.

Ears: The outer canal of the ear only should be cleaned with a small towel or washcloth, but the wax inside the ears should not be tried because that is meant to protect the ear. No water should enter the ear as it may cause infection and ear ache. The ears can be dried by putting or twisting the fine end of the towel and introducing it into the outer canal. It should not be pushed too much inside.

Eyes: The eyes can be washed and the eyelids gently wiped with a washcloth. Oil or any surma or kajal should not be applied in the eyes , as it may contaminate and sometimes cause eye troubles. Eyes are constantly bathed by a steady flow of tears to lubricate and to disinfect the area. Therefore, it is not necessary to put any oil drops, when they are healthy.

Nose: The nose should not be rigorously cleaned either. The dry crusts can be removed with a washcloth or with slightly moistened cotton wick rolled between the two hands.

Mouth: The mouth does not need any special care. If there are any white patches in the mouth (thrush), it indicates a fungal infection and it means the teats or breasts (nipple) are not kept clean as they are the sources of infection to the mouth of the child at that age. The white patch may also be due to the milk residue over the tongue; it can be gently cleaned once or twice in the day.

Topping and Tailing: If the baby has his bath in the morning, he will require another wash before his bedtime and 6'O clock feed. As for the bath, it will save delays if all the necessary things are kept ready before hand. The babies' nightclothes and change of napkins and the toilet articles required, such as soap, washing flannels, powder, cotton wool, towels etc, and his pot should be placed nearby. In addition, a bowl of warm water is required.

The baby should be undressed and laid on his back on the mother's lap, which is protected by a water-proof apron covered with a large towel. His nose and ears should be cleaned as done in the morning. His face and neck should be washed, followed by washing his hands and under the arms. Then he should be dried thoroughly and powdered on his neck and under the armpits, after which his night dress should be worn. The mother should make a good lather of soap in her hands and clean the babies' buttocks thoroughly, washing all round the napkin area and down the grains, followed by thorough drying and powdering. His hair should be brushed with a soft baby brush, and his finger and toe nails cut, if required.

Sore Buttocks: If the baby is bathed and 'topped and tailed' regularly in this way, his skin will keep in good condition and free from sores or rashes. It should be remembered however, that whenever a soiled or wet napkin is removed , the baby's buttocks should be bathed, thoroughly dried and powdered if they are to be kept free from soreness and rashes. When washing the napkins, all the soap should be rinsed thoroughly, as otherwise this will make the baby's skin red and sore.

It does sometimes occur, however, that the baby's buttocks do become sore in spite of all the care. He might have been left too long in a damp napkin, or there may be some error in his feeding which is causing his urine to be too strong. If this should happen and the baby develops red and inflamed buttocks, water should not be used on the sore area; instead they should be cleaned with olive oil. Before putting on a clean napkin, the buttocks should be smeared with a good zinc and castor oil ointment or cold cream.

QUESTIONS

SECTION "A"

Short Answer Type:

1. Write a note on overfeeding.
2. Trace the factors affecting language development of children.
3. What is weaning?
4. Specify the vaccines to be given to the child during his 1st year.
5. Mention any six advantages of breast feeding
6. What is emotion? Give examples
7. How will you inculcate good eating habits in children?
8. Explain any two problems of breast feeding.
9. How would you help a two year child to overcome temper tantrums?
10. Specify foods recommended for a lactating mother.

SECTION "B"

One Page Answer Type:

1. What are the special measures to be taken in bottle-feeding?
2. Bring out the characteristics of babyhood.
3. How will you inculcate good feeding habits among child.
4. Discuss briefly the importance of immunization schedule.
5. Write a note on supplementary feeding and list some foods?
6. Describe the language development taking place during babyhood?
7. Write short notes on toilet training.

8. Give the immunization schedule. Write about the nature of disease for which vaccines are recommended.
9. Discuss the perceptual skills in infancy.
10. Discuss about the cognitive development during the first two years.
11. Write about the characteristics of children's emotions.
12. Examine the problems of breast feeding.

SECTION "C"

Essay Answer Type:

1. Explain the care of infants with regard to toilet training, feeding, clothing, sleeping and immunization .
2. Discuss the social and cognitive development of the infants.
3. Trace the motor developments of an infant in detail.
4. What are the characteristics of infants? Discuss about their physical development.
5. Discuss about the baby's vocabulary during infancy?

UNIT — IV

CHAPTER

7

EARLY CHILDHOOD (2-6 YEARS)

OBJECTIVES

To enlighten students about:

- Concept of early childhood period
- Developmental tasks
- Characteristics
- Growth and development details – physical, motor, emotional, language, social and cognitive.
- Physical and psychological hazards during the period

7.1 INTRODUCTION

Childhood begins at the conclusion of babyhood, the age when dependency is practically a thing of the past and is being replaced by growing independence. It begins approximately by the age of 2 years, and extends to the time when the child becomes sexually mature, at approximately 13 years for an average girl and 14 years for an average boy.

Childhood is subdivided into two separate periods – early and late childhood. The period of early childhood begins with the final stages of infancy, and ends around age six, when children are ready to embark on their school career and enter kindergarten. Late childhood follows from 6 years to the time the child becomes sexually mature. The significance for placing the dividing line between early and late childhood at 6 years is that, it is not influenced by physical but by social factors. During these years, marked changes take place in both physique and psychology of a child.

Movement, constant activity, bursting enthusiasm keeps the early childhood years in action. Boundless energy, constant curiosity, and growing mental maturity all characterize children from 2-6years of age. By the age of two, typically children walk and talk and eagerly explore their environment, gradually acquiring greater mastery over their physique. The years of early childhood represent a time of emerging competencies within an expanding world for the individual. It is a time of increasing knowledge of the environment and development of an attitude that serves as the foundation of many future learning experiences. It is an exciting time when a child's personality and attempts at establishing social interactions first appear and when individual differences are noticed more frequently in a variety of ways.

7.2. DEVELOPMENTAL TASKS OF EARLY CHILDHOOD

In early child hood, there is an expansion in vocabulary and other elements of language development that allow the child to perform unlimited tasks. The developmental tasks for early childhood as prescribed by Hairghurst are enumerated in broad terms as follows:

- Learning to talk.
- Learning sex differences and sexual modesty.
- Forming simple concepts of social and physical reality.
- Learning to relate one's-self emotionally with parents, siblings and others.
- Learning to distinguish right from wrong and developing a conscience.

7.3. CHARACTERISTICS OF EARLY CHILDHOOD

There is a persistent feeling, derived from Freudian personality theory, that childhood is the formative period for attitudes, beliefs, values, and habits that persist throughout life. The individual comes to be characterized by several traits that are notable to development prior to entrance into the public school system. The names used by parent, educators and psychologists reflect the important characteristics of this period.

1. *It is a time of discovery:* Early childhood period is marked by high energy levels and an exuberance for learning. The young child is intensively pre-occupied with discovering herself as a person, her abilities to do things and make things happen, herself as a family member and what her family is like, the power to communicate with others, and with the thought that there is a much larger world beyond the doorstep.

2. *It is a"Troublesome Age":* Early childhood is considered to be a "problem age" or "troublesome age" by parents. Freed from the pressure of their older sibling's domination, the two- and three-year old race from one activity to another. Watchful parents or caregivers need to chase back and forth with them to keep up with each other's activities. Childhood behavior problems become more frequent and troublesome than the physical care of babyhood. This behavioral problem during the childhood is due to development of distinctive personalities and demand for independence which are incapable of handling successfully. Children are often obstinate, stubborn, disobedient, jealous, negativistic and antagonistic.

3. *It is a "Toy Age":* Young children spend most of their waking time playing with toys. Toy play reaches its peak during the early childhood years and then begins to decrease when children reach the school age.

4. *It is a "Pre-school age":* Early childhood is referred to as "*pre-school age*" by educators, in order to distinguish it from the time when children are considered to be old enough both physically and mentally to enter formal schooling.

5. *It is a time of curiosity:* Early childhood is the time when children are learning the foundation of social behavior. Psychologists consider this period as "*Pre Gang Age*". Children are encouraged to develop routine habits of everyday living that parents hope will be sustained in later years of life. The major development that occurs during early childhood centers around gaining control over the environment by asking questions and by imitation of speech and actions of others. Therefore this age is also called as "*Questioning Age*" or "*Imitative Age*".

6. *It is a time when social roles and interaction patterns are first learned:* The child should come to value other children's presence in play activities and derive much pleasure from these ventures. Sex-role commences at some point early in this period along with learning a number of other social roles that exist in the individual's environment.

7. *It is a period of emerging competencies and self awareness:* Apart from being imitative, most children show more creativity in their play during early childhood than at any other time in their lives and hence are considered as "*Creative Age*". One of the most important attitudes that young children should develop is the feeling that they can become involved in their environment. As the young child experiences a variety of interactions with parents, siblings, relatives and others she discovers her own personal capabilities and limits.

7.4 PHYSICAL DEVELOPMENT

Physical development which is increase in bodily tissues, is considered important as it influences a child's attitude towards herself. Growth in childhood proceeds at a less frantic pace than

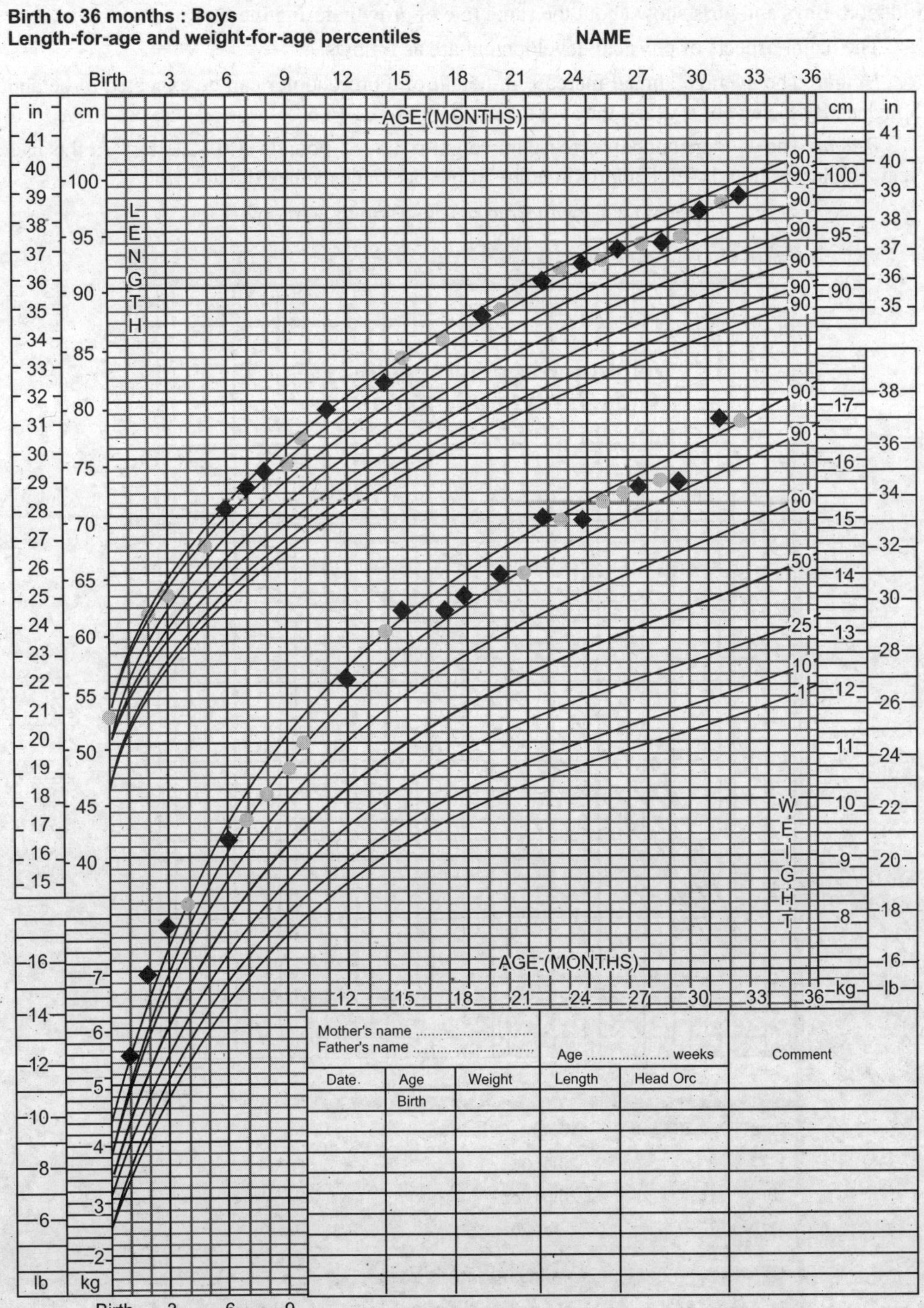

Figure: 7.1 Growth Rate of Boys(Birth to 36 months)

in infancy. Children during this period grow about another 12 inches and continue to gain weight at the rate of about 5 pounds (2.3 kg.) a year. During the pre-school years, children start to lose their baby fat, grow taller, thinner and develop muscle. As abdominal muscles develop, the toddler potbelly tightens, losing its babyishness. The child's heart beat and breathing rates decrease, and average body temperature falls. Growth hormone deficiency may occur during infancy or later in childhood. Boys and girls show about the same rate of growth during these years.

The major aspects of physical development are as follows:

Height: The average annual increase in height of a preschooler can be expected to be about 2.5 inches. By the age of 6 years, the average child measures 46.6".

Weight: The average annual increase in weight is 3.5 – 5 pounds (1.6 – 2.3 kg). At the age of 6 years, children should weigh approximately 7 times as much as they did at birth.

Figure: 7.2 Growth Rate of Girls(Birth to 36 months)

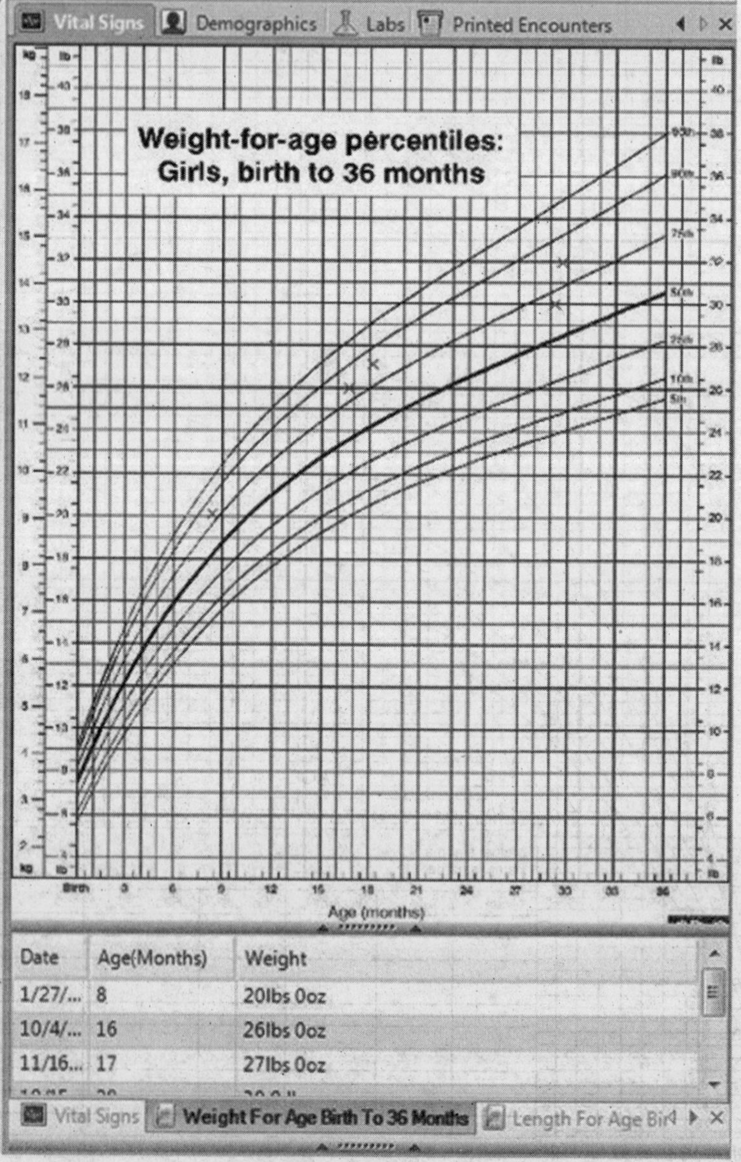

Bodily Proportions: Bodily proportions change markedly and the baby look disappears; facial features look small but they become more pronounced and neck elongates. There is a gradual decrease in the stockiness of trunk and the body tends to become cone shaped with a flattened abdomen and chest and shoulders that are broader and squarer. The rounded bodies of infancy give way to the slimmer torsos of early childhood, muscles begin to form, bones begin to harden, and continued brain development provides a foundation for a world of symbolic promise. The head growth is slow. Arms and legs lengthen and hands and feet grow bigger. By about age 6, the legs make up almost 45 percent of body length.

Body Build: Children who tend to be endomorphic or flabby with fat body build, have more adipose than muscular tissue; those who tend to be mesomorphic or sturdy, with muscular body build, have more muscular than adipose tissue; and those with ectomorphic or relatively thin body build have both small muscles and little adipose tissue. Girls have more fatty tissues and boys have more muscular tissues.

Teeth: At the beginning of this period, children usually have all their baby teeth; at the end of this period children begin to lose them. All milk teeth are erupted during the first 4-6 months of this period and by the last half years almost all of them are replaced by permanent teeth. By age 3, all the primary or deciduous teeth are in place. The first baby teeth to appear are the front central incisors. Dentists stress the importance of regular care due to the influence of nutrition and other factors on the development of the permanent teeth at this time in life.

Nervous and Muscular Systems: Nervous system grows rapidly during babyhood and it slows during the 3-4 years of age. Development of immature to mature cells occur at this stage. These changes coordinated by the maturing brain and nervous system, promote the development of a wide range of motor skills. Myelination in the areas of brain related to focusing attention develops slower in this period. Rapid growth of frontal lobe during this period helps the child to gain cognitive skills.

Skeletal Development: Bone development consists of growth in bone size, change in the number of bones and composition. Cartilage turns to bone at a faster rate than before, and bones become harder and stronger, giving the child a firmer shape and protecting the internal organs. The increased capacities of the respiratory and circulatory systems build physical stamina. The developing immune system, keeps children healthier. As the ossification process is not yet complete, the bones, joints, ligaments and tendons are more flexible in the early part of this period.

Sensory Organs: As the eyeball does not complete its growth until puberty, young children tend to be far-sighted. Vision and focusing ability improves considerably as children grow through these years. The need for corrective lenses become more noticeable in early childhood. About 5 per cent of children of this age group begin to wear eyeglasses. Hearing problem affected only a small number of preschool children. About 2 per cent of children of this age have some type of hearing difficulty (U.S. Dept. of Health Education, and Welfare, 1978).

7.5 FACTORS AFFECTING PHYSICAL DEVELOPMENT

There are many factors which affect the growth of the children. Any abnormal physique development may lead to widen a feeling of inferiority about self.

Nutrition: An individual's personality and social development can be strongly influenced by the experiences of feeding. Eating habits, food preferences, and social interaction patterns are formed at mealtimes in early childhood. Preschoolers eat less in proportion to their size than infants do. As growth slows they need fewer calories per pound of body weight. Preschoolers who are allowed to eat when they are hungry and are not pressured to eat everything given to them are more likely to regulate their own caloric intake than the children who are fed to schedule. One kind of severe malnutrition that children in this age suffer is a protein deficiency called kwashiorkor.

As children move through the preschool period, their eating patterns become more environmentally influenced, like those of adults. To avoid overweight and cardiac problems, young children should get only about 30% of their total calories from fat, and less than 10% of total from saturated fat. Lean meat and dairy foods should remain in the diet to provide protein, iron and calcium. Milk and other dairy products can now be skimmed or of low fat.

Obesity: Obesity, or extreme overweight, is defined in childhood as having a body mass index (BMI)-comparison of weight to height- at or above the 95th percentile for age and sex. Obesity today is more common among preschoolers (especially girls, who tend to be less active than boys) than twenty-five years ago. Overweight children, especially those who have overweight parents, tend to become overweight adults and excess body mass can be a threat to health. A tendency to obesity is partly hereditary, but it also depends on fat intake and exercise.

Obesity causes pulmonary problems such as sleep apnea, high blood pressure and cholesterol in later ages. Obese children are 3 times more prone to develop hypertension than non-obese.

Oral Health: By age 3, all the primary teeth are in place. The permanent teeth, which will begin to erupt at about age 6, have started developing by now. Use of fluoride and improved dental care is recommended to prevent the incidence of tooth decay for this age group. Disadvantaged children still have more untreated cavities than other children.

Child Abuse: Abused children often were underweight at birth and therefore as infants, cried often, matured slowly, needed special feeding and care, looked thin and pinched. It is a part of a vicious cycle set in motion by both child problem (irritability, unattractiveness, aggressiveness) and parent problem (ignorance, impatience, inadequacy). It passes from one generation to next.

Heredity and Environment: Research indicates how the interaction of heredity and environment produces the different rate and kinds of physical growth. Genetic elements or hereditary elements are of immense importance to the regulation of growth. The genetic growth plan is given at conception and functions throughout the growth period.

Psychological Disturbances: Stress can produce negative effects on physical development, beginning with prenatal period. During the early childhood years, children experience the trauma of leaving home for preschool and kindergarten, adjusting to new adults and peers.

Socioeconomic Status: Children from different social classes differ in average body size at all ages. Children of the professional classes are one inch taller at age 3 and 2 inches taller at adolescence. The difference seems to stem from nutrition, sleep, exercise and recreation.

**Secular trends:* During the past hundred years the tendency has been for children to become progressively larger at all ages. This is especially true in Europe and America.

Note: This brief overview of physical development again illustrates the importance of the bio-psychosocial model. However, the role played by nutrition and socioeconomic status, the interaction among biological, psychological, and social influences testifies to the power of the bio-psychosocial model in explaining development.

Sleep Patterns and Problems: Sleep patterns change throughout the growing-up years. Young children usually sleep more deeply at night than they will later in life. Bedtime may bring on them a form of separation anxiety and the child may do all he or she can do to avoid it. Regular, consistent sleep routines can minimize this common problem. Children should not be put to sleep by feeding or rocking as this may make it hard for them to fall asleep on their own.

About 20 to 30 % of the children in their first four years engage in bedtime struggles lasting more than an hour and wake their parents frequently at night. Five experiences tend to distinguish children with these problems. One is sleeping in the same bed with parents; it is simply more tempting and easier to wake someone in the same bed than in the next room. The other four conditions signal family stress-the family is likely to have experienced a stressful accident or illness; or the mother is likely to be depressed, or to have mixed feelings about the child, or to have recently changed her schedule so as to be away for most of the day.

Walking and talking during sleep are fairly common in early childhood. Although sleepwalking itself is harmless, sleepwalkers may be in danger of hurting themselves. However, persistent sleep problems may indicate an emotional, physiological, or neurological condition that need to be examined.

Children of this age normally recognize the sensation of a full bladder while asleep and awaken to empty it in the toilet. Children who are bed wetters do not have this awareness. Fewer than 1% of bed wetters have a physical disorder though they may have a small bladder capacity, nor is persistent enuresis primarily an emotional, mental or behavioral problem - though such problems can develop because of the way bed wetters are treated by playmates and family.

7.6 MOTOR DEVELOPMENT

Stand, walk, or run - we tend to take the accomplishment of the 6-year-old for granted, but a great deal of neuro-muscular development had to occur before these motor skills became so effortless. The capacity to gain control over the different muscles of the body refers to motor development. We are concerned here with two types of motor skills - gross (using the large muscles) and fine (using the small muscles of the hands and fingers). The following table summarizes the development of motor skills.

Table 7.1 Development of Motor Skills

AGE	GROSS SKILLS	FINE SKILLS
1.	Runs, climbs stairs, jumps from object(both feet)	Throws ball, kicks ball, turns pare, and begins to scribble.
2.	Hops, climbs stairs with altering feet, jumps from bottom step.	Copies circle, opposes thumb to finger, scribbling continues to improve.
3.	Runs well, skillful jumping, begins to skip, pedals tricycle.	Hold pencil, copies square, walks balance beam.
4.	Hops about 50 feet, balance on one foot, can catch large ball, good skipping.	Colors within lines, forms letters, dresses and undresses self with help, eats more readily.
5.	Carries bundles, begins to ride bicycle, jumps rope, chins self, can catch a tennis ball.	Ties shoes, uses scissors, uses knife and fork, and washes self with help.

With gratitude to perceptual and motor development, 3-and 4- year-old children can hold crayons, copy triangles, button their clothes, and unlace their shoes. The ability to engage in diversified and strenuous activities are primary, due to rapid muscular growth. Children vary in adeptness, depending on their genetic endowment and their opportunities to learn and practice motor skills. Co-ordination in skills prior to muscular development was proportionate to overall body growth. Approximately, 75% of child's weight gain is due to muscular development. As muscular and skeletal growth progresses, it makes the child stronger. Infants and toddlers are quite capable of controlling their movements in relation to a stationary world. What they will master during childhood is the ability to move capably in a changing environment – when a ball is moving toward them, or when they must navigate on a crowded sidewalk.

In a finely tuned sequence, which no one has to teach them, children move from the pincer movements of infancy to random scribbles to skillful creations. In analyzing children's art, it is important to remember that their drawings are the expression of what they are capable of doing. That is, the early childhood youngster is limited in eye-hand co-ordination, motor ability, and manual dexterity, but their drawings, as crude as an adult may think they are, tell us much about a child's personality and emotional state.

Artistic expression seems to peak by the end of early childhood period. During these years, children begin to paint and hold the brush with thumb and fingers. They hold the paper in place with the free hand. They give names to their drawings and begin to show representation.

Children's drawings not only are good clues to their motor co-ordination but also, as we will see, provide insights into their cognitive and emotional lives, another example of how a bio-psychological perspective helps us to understand. These, then, are the early childhood years which are exciting, rewarding, and yet, challenging.

Handedness: Early childhood may be regarded as a critical period in the establishment of handedness. The reason being, during this period, children are tended to shift from the use of one hand to the other and asked to concentrate on learning skills with one hand as the dominant hand and other as the auxiliary or helping hand.

The children who attend pre-school i.e. nursery schools or kindergartens, are less likely to develop left-handed tendencies than children whose early childhood years are spent mainly in homes. The reason is that, in pre-schools and childcare centers, teachers and other care takers are advised to encourage the use of right hand in children. Many parents believe that handedness is hereditary and as a result, when they see their children using their left hand, they assume that they are naturally left handed and do nothing to encourage them to learn new skills with their right hands.

Few skills require both hands to play an equally important role in carrying out an activity. Therefore, young children are taught on the movements made by the dominant hand and those by the auxiliary hand. For example in case of crayoning, the dominant hand uses the crayon and the auxiliary hand holds the paper.

7.7 FACTORS AFFECTING MOTOR DEVELOPMENT

The factors affecting motor development are as follows:

- Economic status: It has been reported that children from poor economic environment generally master skills earlier and in large numbers than children from more favored environment.
- Sex Difference: In preschool years, boys come under pressure to learn play skills that are culturally approved for members of their own sex whereas it is not so in the case of girls.
- Social behavior: The most important people in the pre-schooler's life are their family. The children try to please others, but if they are expected too much, they might rebel. Pre-schoolers spend a lot of time playing with fantasy friends and stories.

7.8 EMOTIONAL DEVELOPMENT

Self-conscious evaluation of emotions- pride, shame, and guilt- first appear in $2\frac{1}{2}$ yrs. Expression of these emotions indicate that children are beginning to acquire and are able to use societal standards and rules to evaluate their behavior. Parents, teachers, and other adults can help children understand and control emotions.

Positive Emotions

- **Joy:** Young children derive joy when they are physically fit. Unexpected noise, playing pranks on others and accomplishing what they think as a difficult task add to their happiness. They express their joy by smiling or laughing, clapping their hands, jumping up and down or hugging the object or person that has made them happy.

- **Affection:** Older children become more demonstrative and express their affection for their loved ones verbally. But while they are still young they express it by hugging, patting and kissing the objects of their affection.
- **Curiosity:** Curiosity is the interest shown towards something unusual or new in a person's environment. Anything new excites the curiosity of children .Their first response to this curiosity takes the form of sensory motor exploration; later as a result of social pressures and punishment, they respond by asking questions.

Negative Emotions

- **Anger:** Children give vent to their anger through temper tantrums. Conflict over play things, thwarting of wishes and vigorous attacks from another child result in crying, screaming, stamping and jumping up and down.
- **Fear:** Conditioning, memories of unpleasant experiences, stories, pictures, radio and television programmes and movies with frightening elements arouse fear in children. At first, a child's response to fear is panic. Later responses become more specific and include running away and hiding, crying and avoiding frightening situations.
- **Jealousy:** Jealousy is a feeling of angry resentment towards other people. The birth of a brother or a sister causes jealousy in a child. Sibling rivalry is the most common cause of jealousy among preschoolers. This results in aggressive behavior or triggers regression. Children vie for the attention of the parents, for which they may resort to thumb sucking and other babyish activity.
- **Grief:** When young children lose something or someone they love they become sad. Typically, they express their grief by crying and by losing interest in their normal activities including eating.
- **Envy:** Children often complain about what they have or express a wish to have what another person has. This is because they often become envious of the abilities or material possession of the other child.
- **Anxiety:** A painful uneasiness of the mind towards anticipatory expectations of sickness is anxiety. It is a mental condition that creates fear, and a general state of mind that all is not well. It is mostly found around three years. An anxious child is usually unhappy and irritable and highly sensitive. Such a behavior can lead to adjustment problems.

7.9 LANGUAGE DEVELOPMENT

Language development is an integral part of cognitive development. Thinking cannot occur without symbols- that is, there must be some mentalistic device that represent objects and behavior and that can be manipulated in abstract fashion. Therefore, children will now be able to transform the mental image with words of appropriate meaning instead of using actions like crying, grabbing, hitting or biting.

Language is the most obvious symbol system; and preoperational thought develops together with the child's acquisition of this mode of behavior. Initially there is difficulty in "knowing" a word. Parents and especially mothers are the child's first models for the learning of words and phrases. Television and books also play an important role. The child's speech will be clear enough to understand and he will be able to name basic colors, days of the week and other time related words.

There is the implication that the verbal skills have increased for present-day children as compared to those of the recent past. It plays a part in the development of memory and the predictability of intelligence. Language is not involved in the development of logical thinking in children. From about 18 months to about 3 years, early childhood youngsters resemble language machines, accessing their languages at a phenomenal rate. The size of children's vocabularies grow extensively during the preschool years. Between the late twos and the mid threes, children's language blooms into fluent grammatical conversion so rapidly, sentence length increases steadily and because grammar is a discrete combinational system, the number of synaptic types increases, exponentially doubling every month, reaching the thousands before the third birthday. .

Cognitively, it is the time of Piaget's preoperational period, which roughly extends from 2-7 years, and it traces a child's mental odyssey during these years. According to Piaget, the level of intelligence of infancy and early childhood being representational thought, through its symbolic capacity can grasp an entire sequence of events and is not confined to a one-by-one analysis. Imagine the possibilities: the child uses words to refer things, people and events that are not physically present. The child can refer to both past and present. Many of these early childhood youngsters will also experience some form of preschool education. Finally, these are the years when children acquire their language so rapidly that we refer to them as the "language explosion".

Communication skills: The major tool and vehicle of socialization is language. The development of communication skills is based on a child's effective use of language. Throughout early childhood, children experience numerous refinements and advancements in their ability to use language effectively in communicating with others. Talking and the beginnings of verbal communication occur in early childhood. Speech development parallels motor development. As the neuromuscular systems mature and lay the foundations for motor skills, they also lay the foundation for speech skills. If a child is deprived of opportunities and guidance, his speech ability will be lower than his potential, and that of his age mates. Acquiring adequate communication skills in early childhood involves building the vocabulary, mastering pronunciation of words, combining individual words into complex sentences, understanding and correctly using appropriate grammatical structure, and developing listening skills.

The emergence of language skills as a unique facet of development in infancy and early childhood is closely associated with physical development. When infants and young children hear language, it is recognized and used to amplify pro-existing language structures. Second, imitation of others' speech is considered to have a significant role in language development. This may explain how vocabulary is acquired. Third, infants and young children are influenced by reinforcement of their attempts to learn language skills. A smile, a hug, and positive verbal praise are used by parents to reinforce correct language form and so on. Fourth, the level of cognitive development may determine how language works to influence concept formation and comprehension.

Tasks in learning speech skills

The major tasks involved in learning to speak are:

1. Increasing comprehension
2. Building a vocabulary
3. Mastering pronunciation and
4. Combining words into sentences.

1. *Increasing Comprehension*

The first step for communication is the ability to understand what others say. Normally, a young child can understand most of what others say to him either through comprehension of the words used or the gestures and facial expressions that accompany the words spoken. When he enters school, the child would have enough comprehension to understand the instruction given to him and to understand the meaning of stories read to him and the songs sung or taught.

The child's comprehension is influenced greatly by his attentiveness to what is said. Children who are the only child in the homes or who have older siblings have been found to be more attentive listeners than children from larger families or those whose ordinal position is that of the first-born. In short, "the more intelligent the child, the better listener he is".

2. *Building a vocabulary*

The child's vocabulary increases rapidly due to direct teaching of words and his/her curiosity about a particular word. The young child not only learns new words everyday but also meanings for old words; also a child of this age does not easily understand words that sound alike but have different meanings.

In addition to building up a vocabulary that will be of general use, young children learn many words of courtesy, such as 'Thank you', 'Please' or 'I am sorry'. He also acquires a vocabulary of colours so that at the age of five years he can distinguish blue, green, yellow and white. He learns the meanings of numbers so that by the age of five years, he can count up to hundred.

By the time children are five or six years old they can distinguish between coins. The pre-school child knows and uses such words, which denote time as 'morning', 'afternoon', 'night' and seasons such as 'winter' and 'summer'. Many young children pick up slang or even swear words from their older brothers and sisters, their parents or their playmates. Children often use these words in parrot-like fashion without any comprehension of their true meaning or context.

The range of a child's vocabulary at different ages will depend not only on his intelligence but also upon the opportunities he is given and his motivation to learn. Girls, at every age have been reported to have larger vocabularies than boys.

3. *Pronunciation*

A young child's pronunciation improves rapidly depending upon the correctness of the model he imitates and the guidance he receives in correcting mispronunciations. Learning to pronounce all words correctly is difficult for a child, but certain sounds and sound combinations have been reported to be especially difficult for the young child than vowels and diphthongs. Among the consonants, which are difficult to pronounce, are *z, w, d, s, t*. The difficult consonant blends are *st, str, dr* and *fl*. Some of the easier consonants to pronounce are *t, b, p, m* and *n*; the easy vowels are *a, e, i* and *u*.

4. *Sentence formation*

The formation of sentences follows a fairly definite and predictable pattern in early childhood. Two to three-year-old children usually use short sentences of three or four words. These sentences have an excess of nouns but lack verbs, prepositions and conjunctions. Many of the child's early sentences are incomplete. After three years, complete sentences of six to eight words appear frequently in a young child's speech. All parts of speech are then used.

Young children tend to increase the length of their sentences by combining two or more simple sentences with the conjunction 'and'. Young children of today speak in longer and more accurate sentences than did young children of the past generations. Several factors account for this change. The media and the growth of various trends of teaching in nursery schools afford more opportunities for language inspiration outside the home. Stimulating environments for children at home and the modern permissive treatment of the society with its greater acceptance are some of the other facilitating factors.

7.9.1 *The factors influencing how much a child can talk*

Intelligence: Bright children and those from the higher socio – economic groups usually use longer, more complex and better constructed sentences than children of the same age who come from less favorable environments or who are not so bright.

Type of discipline: Children, who grow up in homes where discipline tends to be permissive, talk more than those whose parents are authoritarian and who believe that "Children should be seen but not heard".

Ordinal position: First born children are encouraged to talk more than their later-born siblings as parents have more time to talk with them.

Family size: Only children are encouraged to talk more than children from large families as their parents have more time to talk to them. In large families where the discipline is likely to be authoritarian, it prevents the children from talking as much as they would like to.

Socio-economic status: In lower-class families, family activities tend to be less organized than those in middle and upper-class families. There is also less conversation among the family members and less encouragement for the child to talk.

Racial status: The poorer quality of speech and conversational skills of many young black children may be due in part to the fact that they have grown up in homes where the father is absent, or where family life is disorganized because there are many children , or because their mother must work outside the home.

Bilingualism: While young children from bilingual homes may talk as much at home as children's from monolingual homes, their speech is usually very limited when they are with members of their peer group or with adults outside the home.

Sex-role typing: As early as the pre-school years, there are effects of sex-role typing on children's speech. Boys are expected to talk less than girls, but what they say, and how they say it, is expected to be different. Boasting and criticizing others, for e.g., are considered more appropriate for boys than for girls, while the reverse is true of rattling.

7.9.2 Speech disorders

The term, 'speech disorder' refers to a serious form of erroneous pronunciation. Some disorders of pronunciation come from organic causes such as nasal obstructions, malformations of the teeth, jaws, lips or palates or a tongue-tied condition. However, most come from emotional disturbances. McCarthy (1960) has pointed out: 'Evidence is accumulating in the literature indicating that most articulatory disorders which do not have an organic basis are associated with neuroticism in the parents and poor quality of parent-child relations.'

Some young children develop speech disorders in addition to errors in speech. The three most common forms of speech disorders, which children tend to develop during early childhood are:

(*a*) **Lisping:** Lisping or letter sound substitution, for example, s for z ; and w or d for r are a few of the most common speech disorders of early childhood; for example, some children say 'rip' for 'ship'. During the transitional stage when the first tooth falls and the second is yet to appear there is likely to be a gap in front of the jaws where the second teeth will eventually cut through. At this time, there is often a slight lisp, which unless corrected as the new teeth develop, may become established into a habit.

(*b*) **Slurring:** Slurring is an indistinctness of speech caused by inactivity of the lips, tongue or jaw. The inactivity may be due to the child's timidity but it more often arises from excitement and a desire to tell things quickly because they are important and he is excited about them. As speech in the preschool years has not yet become habitual, the child must give conscious attention to what he is saying, to what words he will use and to how he will combine them into sentences. If he tries to speed up, he runs his words together causing slurring. Later, when he has mastered the tasks of speech, he can talk quickly and distinctly.

(*c*) **Stuttering:** Stuttering is a repetition of sounds, syllables, or even words. It is often accompanied by deadlocking of speech usually referred to as 'stammering' in which case the individual is unable to produce any sound for a time and then suddenly sounds come out in a torrent. Like slurring, stuttering is caused mainly by nervous and emotional tension. Between the ages of two and four years, slow, repetitious speech is more or less the characteristic of all children. Stuttering also occurs frequently between fifth and sixth years. This period represents an important break in the child's life. Stuttering in a minor form is part of the early speech pattern of all children.

7.10 SOCIAL DEVELOPMENT

Social and mental development in early childhood is characterized by the widely expanding world and awareness of people and things. Essentially, it is thought that young children should :

(1) develop an awareness of the self as an individual;

(2) acquire an identity as a member of some social group; and

(3) begin to apply labels that evaluate their self-concept. Young children learn how they are similar as well as different from others, which marks the beginning of an idea of "I" and "ME."

Social development means acquisition of ability to behave in accordance with social expectation. There is a rapid development of social contact in this period due to increased motor and language skills. Play is an important part of social development. By the age of 3-4 years they learn to adapt themselves to others and cooperate in group play activities. As a general rule, the child is breaking away from the home environment, establishing himself in the broader social environment of the school and neighborhood. Children find social contact with members of their own sex more pleasurable than those with members of opposite sex. There are two types of social behavior, namely, positive or social and unsocial or negative behavioral patterns. Positive social behavior patterns like imitation, rivalry, co-operation, sympathy, empathy and sharing and the unsocial behavior patterns, such as, negativism, aggressiveness, egocentrism, destructiveness, prejudice are common among these age groups. Parents begin more actively to socialize and discipline the children, trying to shape and mold them into mature, responsible, productive, functioning members of the society.

Research indicated six categories of social behaviors that change with increasing age during preschool years:

1. Dependency directed towards peers increases; dependency directed towards adults decreases.
2. Sympathy and altruism increases (empathy, also increases).
3. Ascendancy (tendency to take the lead) increases.
4. Competition increases, particularly under conditions inviting comparative evaluation of performance with others.
5. Quarreling decreases, but quarrels tend to last longer.
6. Aggressive activity increases but tends to decline after the nursery school years are over.

Social Behavior Patterns

Imitation: Children imitate the attitudes and behavior of a person whom they especially admire and want to be like. Young children imitate older siblings and vice versa.

Rivalry: Children feel an urge to outdo others at home and outside, as early as the fourth year.

Co-operation: Children at the end of third year learn to socialize and co-operate with their peer group. Their inclination to play with other children increases.

Sympathy: Play contacts develop sympathetic attitudes in children. This helps in understanding the feelings and emotions of others.

Empathy: Empathetic attitude can be identified in a child only in later childhood. An empathic response is one in which the emotion of the person observing, to some extent. match with the one who is being observed.

Sharing: Sharing and caring will win social approval. Children learn this while playing with friends. They share what they have, especially toys, with others. Generosity then gradually replaces selfishness.

Unsocial Behavior Patterns

Negativism: The habit of contradicting elders starts between 3 and 4 years of age and then declines. Physical resistance gradually gives way to verbal resistance. Children sometimes pretend not to hear or understand requests.

Aggressiveness: The physically aggressive behavior that begins by the age of 2, normally declines by the age of 4 giving way to verbal attacks like name calling, battling or blaming others. Boys tend to be more aggressive to peers than girls. They also are more likely to play rough, mock-fight and have aggressive fantasies than girls.

Ascendant behavior or Bossiness: Children become more authoritative at the age of 3. Girls tend to be bossier than boys.

Egocentrism: Social interaction and the anxiety of children to win the acceptance of others helps them to overcome their self-centered attitude.

Destructiveness: The children display their temper by destroying anything within the reach, whether their own or someone else's possession. The angrier they are the more widespread their destructiveness.

Prejudice: Most pre-school children become diffident in the company of playmates of another race because of language problems.

Sex antagonism: Boys withdraw from girlish activities when they are 4 years old due to social pressure. Many of them, then, engage in aggressive behavior, which antagonises girls.

7.11 COGNITIVE DEVELOPMENT

The mental development that occurs in early childhood is exciting and dynamic as children explore their environments, develop ideas, learn solutions to problems, participate in imaginary play, and gain a unique understanding of the world and how it operates.

During the early childhood years, three brain growth spurts appear; at ages 2, 4 and 7. At 4 years of age, children understand much more about the world around them. They probably experience some type of preschool world, which they enjoy because they find pleasure in interacting with others. They are beginning to decide which of their playmates they like and which they don't: most importantly, they are learning why they like some and dislike others. They can jump, chase others, and PLAY! With their steadily growing cognitive abilities, they imagine all kinds of playmates and engage in fantastic activities.

The nature of the changes occurring during the early childhood years is interesting to trace. The great task of the early childhood years is to form connections. Children of these years gobble up information from the outside world through their eyes, ears, nose, and hands and translate into nerve impulses.

A shift occurs in intellectual development at about two years after birth, which Piaget (1967) calls the change to the preoperational period in cognitive development. Thought now focuses on internalizing the environment by an increasing use of symbols. At about age four until age six, children enter a transitional period characterized by intuitive thought. There is an increased preoccupation with classification and the beginnings of logical processes. Children make judgments based on a limited understanding of operations and rules and with minimal cues and information. Piaget calls this period the intuitive stage of preoperational thought. Piaget uses several concepts to indicate the changing nature of thought as is found in later stages of development. These concepts include egocentrism centeredness, lack of reversibility, inability to solve conservation problems, preoccupation with classification, and precausal thinking.

Another facet of preoperational thought is the tendency to attribute life to inanimate objects. This is termed animism. Intuitive thought leads children to believe that things have conscious thoughts and motives just as they do. The moon follows the child when walking at night, the sun is friendly because it is bright and warm, a chair bumps into the child rather than vice versa, are examples of animistic thought. These thought experiences help to prepare children for later learning of cause and effect relationships.

In the early pre-school years, young children may have trouble telling the difference between what is real and what fantasy is. With increased ability to ask questions in words, they understand people, objects and situation rapidly. The child will obey commands but does not understand why things are right or wrong. The child also learns fish before perch or bass, car before Chevrolet or Ford, house before bungalow or mansion. Some of the child's vocabulary is learned this way- milk and water are acquired before liquid, apple and orange are learned before fruit, mother and father before parents, and the like.

7.11.1 Concepts Developed

Anything that interferes with normal growth and development is likely to lead to cognitive deficits and a lowering of IQ. Concepts may develop rapidly by emphasis on the development of a number of concepts, as information for entering the first class in school is laid either at home or in the nursery school. The child should begin to understand ideas, such as size, numbers, days of the week and time. Some of the major concepts acquired by the preschoolers are:

(*a*) Concept of living and Death: As young children ascribe living qualities to everything, it is difficult for them to comprehend the meaning of death. To them anything that 'goes away' or disappears is 'dead'.

Animism: could be understood in 4 stages:

I. In the first stage, everything is alive (unless broken or damaged) for children between four and six years of age;

II. In the second stage, everything which moves is alive for six and seven-year-old children;

III. In the third stage, everything that moves by itself is alive for eight to ten-year-old children;

IV. In the fourth stage, life is reserved for animals and plants, or animals alone, by ages eleven or older.

(*b*) Concept of space: Long distances are unrelated to his body and so are still very difficult to be judged accurately. But they develop their ability to judge shorter distance due to their play activity. The child's ability to perceive difference in form gradually increases from 2-6 years.

(*c*) Concept of weight:The child is yet to estimate exclusively in terms of size until he learns that different materials have different weights. A large ball of cotton, for example would be judged heavier than a rubber ball of smaller size.

(*d*) Concept of time: Young children have no idea of the length of time. Hours are learned, then half-hours and quarter hours. Time is first conceived as a sequence in relation to activities, than as outstanding divisions of time, such as morning and afternoon, followed by an understanding of the day of the week, of the seasons of the year and there after calendar and clock time. By the age of 4 or 5years most of the children know the day of the week, month, season or the year.

(*e*) Concept of self: By three years, the child will know whether he is a boy or a girl and know different parts of the body. He/she can point out his/her nose, eyes, mouth, hair etc.

(*f*) Concept of aesthetics: They like pictures of familiar people and animal doing familiar things. The younger the child the more they like colors which are bright and gaudy.

(*g*) Concept of music: Liking for music or rhymes are strong among young children. They prefer song or music with definitive tunes or rhythm.

7.11.2 Creativity

The tendency to be creative in everyday life may have roots in certain inborn traits; reinforcement and learning are factors that also operate to influence creative expressions. Creativity enriches human life and stimulates thinking and mental development, encourages self-expression, enhances exploration of the self and the environment, and motivates initiative behavior.

Young children can be encouraged to express and explore their creative efforts in several ways,

(1) by receiving proper attention from adults and being accepted as individuals

(2) by being provided with adequate space, time, and materials that encourage creative growth

(3) by participating in experiences that enrich and stimulate creative expression

(4) by receiving positive reinforcement for creative efforts.

Types of activities in which creativity occurs most readily for young children are art- and music-oriented such as modeling, painting, block building, singing, playing instruments, and so on. Each of these activities allows new explorations of the young child into discovery of her/his own unique ability, thereby to create – a valued individual in people of all ages.

7.12 HAZARDS OF THE EARLY CHILDHOOD

Like the hazards of babyhood, those of early childhood can be physical, psychological or both.

Physical hazards: The physical hazards of early childhood have psychological as well as physical repercussions, especially such hazards like illness, accidents and awkwardness.

- *Mortality*: Deaths start to decline rapidly in the latter part of babyhood and decline even more rapidly during early childhood.
- *Illness*: Young children are highly susceptible to all kinds of illness, though respiratory illness is the most common.
- *Accidents*: Most young children experience cuts, bruises, infections, burns, broken bones, strained muscles or similar minor disturbances resulting from accidents. Although most accidents in early childhood are not fatal, many of them leave permanent physical or psychological scars.
- *Unattractiveness*: As early childhood progresses, children become increasingly unattractive, reaching a low point as they emerge into late childhood. First, as the body changes shape, children begin to look skinny and gawky. Second, their hair becomes coarser and less manageable and this gives them an unkempt appearance. Third, there are gaps in the mouth where baby teeth have fallen out and the permanent teeth which have erupted seem proportionally too large and the fourth, young children care more about having a good time than about keeping neat and clean. The result is that they frequently look dirty and ill groomed.
- *Awkwardness*: Awkwardness in early childhood may be due to brain damage at birth, mental deficiency or some physical cause by environmental obstacles or by lack of

opportunities to practice. As a result motor development is delayed and children give the impression of being "awkward "as compared with their age mates.

- *Obesity*: Young children who are 20% or more above the norm for their ages and body builds are regarded, as "obese ". Obesity is a health hazard and obese children are more far likely to develop diabetes and to experience heart and blood pressure problems.
- *Left-handedness*: Left-handedness can affect children's educational success or their social adjustments. Many parents believe that left- handedness is a hazard and try or force their left-handed children to use their right hands. This can also be hazardous because it emphasizes their difference, which they often interpret as inferiority, especially when parents use punitive approaches to force them to use their right hands.

Psychological hazards: Every major area of the child's behavioral development has association with its potential hazards which can affect personal and social adjustments.

Speech Hazards: Speech is a tool for communication and essential for social belonging. Children, who unlike their age-mates, cannot communicate with others, will be socially handicapped and this will lead to feelings of inadequacy and inferiority. The quality of young children's speech is so poor that what they say is unintelligible and their ability to communicate with others is even more jeopardized than if they had not listened to what was being said to them. Bilingualism is a serious handicap to the social development of young children. Children who speak foreign language in their homes and know only few words in English cannot communicate with their age mates in play, nor can they comprehend what their age-mates are trying to communicate to them.

Emotional Hazards: The major emotional hazard of early childhood is the dominance of the unpleasant emotions, especially anger. If young children experience too many of the unpleasant emotions and too few of the pleasant ones, it will distort their outlook on life and encourage the development of unpleasant conditions. Another serious hazard to good emotional development is the development of too strong an affection for one person.

Social Hazards: When young children's speech or behavior makes them unpopular with their peers, not only will they be lonely but, they will be deprived of opportunities to learn to behave in peer approved manner. Young children may and often do develop unhealthy social attitudes.

Play Hazards: When children lack play-mates, either because of geographic isolation or because they are not accepted by the children who are available for them to play with, they are forced to engage in solitary forms of play. Equally serious is the fact that, because most young children enjoy watching television more than other forms of solitary play; children who lack play-mates often spend proportionally too much of their play time in front of the television screen.

Conclusion: Early childhood is the stage characterized by many emerging abilities, traits, and competencies leading to an increasing self-awareness and integration of the individual into the family unit. During early childhood years, although the rate of physical growth slows somewhat, it still continues at a steady pace. Physical and motor skills become more refined. Cognitive development during these years leads to a world of representation in which children are expected to acquire and manipulate symbols. Brain lateralization seems to be well established by the age of 5 or 6. As children come to the end of the early childhood period, several language milestones have been achieved. Language gradually becomes a powerful tool in adapting to the environment.

BEHAVIOUR PROBLEMS IN CHILDREN

The term "behaviour problem" is used to designate a deviation in behaviour from the one expected or to which makes difficult and unsatisfactory for the child and his parents. Bracken ridge and Vincent (1965) consider behaviour problems as those forms of behaviour, which indicate that something is wrong with the child himself or with the environment in which he lives. In Varma's (1964) view, behaviour problem is nothing but a deviation from accepted pattern of behaviour on the part of an individual in society. A child who may be considered normal in one part of the world may be considered as one with behavior problem in another part of the world. Family's expectations, whether the action is disruptive and what is expected from an average child of that age determined whether a child has 'good' behavior or a 'bad' one. Children learn to behave in a certain manner by observing other people.

Hurlock has classified the common types of problem behaviour into following 4 groups, according to the way in which they interfere with the child and endanger his well being. Those which affect

- the child's efficiency
- physical well being
- social Adjustment
- the feelings of inferior or inadequacy

In different children, the reactions vary. For e.g., if a baby is annoyed by interference with his movement or play, he will cry or crawl to his mother for help and protection. If a young child is annoyed he will react by biting, kicking, or abusing. However, problem behaviour although normal for a child to develop, should not be ignored.

In general, the behaviour problem appears as thumb sucking, nail biting, bed wetting, aggression, destructiveness, lying, temper tantrum, stealing, selfishness, abnormal fears, jealousy, use of bad languages, truancy, and eating too little or exorbitantly.

CAUSES OF BEHAVIOUR PROBLEMS

The causes of behaviour problems, particularly in emotional sphere, have been explained. Thus a variety of theories stated the following:

- A child suffers from genetic weakness or defect that makes him vulnerable to stress
- A child's problem stems mainly from a conflict between his basic drives and a forbidding environment demanding that he inhibits the expressions of his drives.
- The problem behaviour comes about through learnt or conditioned ways of behaving that impair the child's adaptation to his environment.
- Some problems arise as a consequence of inability or failure to meet cultural demands such as failure to meet standards set at school.

Table 7.2 Ways of Handling Behavior Problems

Behavior Problems	Possible Meaning	DO NOT	DO
Hurts other children	Troubled feeling, Anger	• Punish or hurt him. • Make him feel bad. • Act angry.	• Separate quietly the other children. • Divert his attention. • Take away the hurting objects calmly and firmly. • Teach the child that is something we just do not do. • Help the children play happily together again.

			• Prevent hurting episodes by helping the child feel loved, by giving him other onsets for feeling.
Destroying Things	Feelings of helplessness, jealousy, boredom, wanting attention, excitement, exuberance, curiosity.	• Scold, yell, shout, or tell him he is bad • Preach at him • Punish, spank or hit him.	• Remove destroyable things from the child's reach. • Provide him a good place for play. • Expect some wear and tear from things. • Substitute something else for what is being destroyed. • Expand the child's world by taking him to see and explore new areas. • Provide things to pound and smear and cut and tear. • Teach him firmly what he may and may not do.
Uses bad language	Try something new. A joke, imitation, getting attention, letting off steam.	• Get excited. • Feel shocked or embarrassed • Scold or punish. • Lecture at him • Over emphasize the bad language.	• Relax, understand what it means. • Tell him calmly to stop. • Try shimming some other word with it for fun or often another. • Simple substitutes give him healthy outlets for his feelings.
Does not share	Too young or too little. Need for experience in owning and sharing.	• Snatch from him. • Scold or hurt him. • Tell him you do not like him. • Do not play favorites in settling a dispute.	• Help him share and like it. • Be sure he has things that are all his. • Let him know what it means to own things. • Be a fair arbiter in his squabbles with other children. • Love him, help him to feel secure. • Provide experience as he is ready for them.
Sucks his thumb or fingers.	Need for sucking. Need for loving, cuddling, assurance and comforting. Fatigue, hunger, dissatisfaction, insecure feeling, boredom.	• Force or restrain. • Punish or scold • Coax, threaten or bribe. • Show excessive anxiety • Tie fingers or smear them with bitter medicine.	• Provide sucking satisfactions. • Give more satisfaction, love, attention, pleasure. • Find out what he wants and needs and provide them as best as you can. • Relax. Thumb sucking rarely lasts, and is not serious. See it as a sign that the child is unhappy or dissatisfied at the moment.
Nail biting	Fearfulness, Need for love, boredom, insecure feeling	• Punish or scold. • Force or threaten • Tie fingers or smear them with bitter medicine.	• Provide secure feeling to the child • Show love and affection • Divert attention • Provide ways of developing self confidence to the child.

Masturbates	Natural exploration curiosity. Boredom, need for love, comfort, and security.	• Punish, or shame. • Tie his hands. • Threaten • Be too anxious.	• See that he has plenty of interesting things to do. • Answer his sex questions freely and frankly. • Never fail to love him. • Help him make friends. • Provide opportunities for free play.
Demands attention	Feels let out, insecure, unloved, boredom.	• Scold or punish • ignore or isolate him. • Ridicule him • put him to shame infront of you.	• Give him a fair measure of attention. • Show interest in him as a person. • Provide interesting things to do, share yourself with him.
Fears	Previous painful experiences. Fear of new situations, such as entering a new school. Strangeness. Need for his parents closeby. Feeling unloved and guilty.	• Force the child to come out of his fears. • Shame, threaten or make him to do the feared thing.	• Try to get the child to verbalize his fears. Listen to them without being critical, help him think through the realities rationally. • Reassure and comfort him. • Make the feared place or situation a happy one. • Teach him caution for real dangers and hazards. • Show him love and comfort. • Encourage his efforts to be big. • Help him to help himself. • Avoid fearful experience or prepare him for them.
Steals	Ignorance of property rights. Unsatisfied needs and hunger. Rebellion. Hostile feeling, imitation.	• Make him feel "bad". • Scold or shame. Punish or reject. • Take from him something to make up for the theft. • Humiliate him before others.	• Let him own things and get a sense of mine and yours. • Help him earn and get what he needs and wants. • Be kind, understanding, and not too rigid. • Provide creative outlets for his interests. • Help him make real friends.
Tell lies	Fear of punishment. Exaggeration, Imagination, unable to distinguish between reality and fantasy, Attention seeking, Avoiding stressful situations, Imitating the behavior of the adults around him	• Preach or pro-punish or shame or reject. • Make him apologize or get upset.	• Relax and try to understand. • Give him attention for what he does and necessary support with imagination. • Help him discover the differences between fact and fantasy. • Tell him the truth.

Runs away from home	Boredom, exploration, independence, anger, rebellion	• Make a scene. • Try or make over to him. • Punish or tie him up. • Remove privileges. • Avoid restricts.	• Find him and see why he went away. • Provide attractive alternatives within his limits if possible. • Let him know you like him. • Help him grow up in many ways and take him to trips. • Let him take responsibility around home. • Gradually, remove restrictions, as he is able to take care of himself.
Refuses to eat	He is not hungry. Dislikes particular food. Feels unwell. Independent. Wants Attention. Imitation.	• Force him to eat the food. • Make a scene. • Punish or reward. • Threaten to put on an act. • Divert him	• Be casual and calm. It will not hurt him to miss one or two foods. • Introduce new foods only a bit at a time and along with favorite foods. • Let him rest for sometime. Later feed with something else interesting and attractive. • Help him learn how to feed himself. • Enjoy food yourself. • Give him the time to take the food as he shows interest and readiness.
Bedwetting	He is not ready for training yet. Too early to effort train. Resistance or rebellion. Insecurity, fear.	• Make an issue. • Threaten/shame or punish • Bribe or reward. • Insist that he tells you when he should go to the toilet. • Tell him you do not love him.	• Accept the child as gracefully as you can. • Expect some accidents. • Give him some affection freely let him know you have confidence that he will do better some day. • Help him become independent in other ways and encourage him to grow up.

HOW TO MANAGE BEHAVIOUR PROBLEMS?

Behaviors that are appreciated or rewarded may make the children repeat them again and again and the behaviors that are ignored or warrant punitive actions are normally dropped off. It is the consistency of the parents that helps the child to decide, whether to continue a behavior or not. Rewarding a behavior at one time and punishing the child for it on another, may just confuse the child and your child may develop behavior problem. Sometimes, we may have to decide whether the behavior is not a problem depending on the child's age and stage of development. Ignoring unwanted or 'bad' behavior is the best way to stop it in the long term as some children just repeat the actions as they crave for your attention, whether it is positive or negative.

When more drastic steps are needed to make the child stop a certain behavior, you may use the time-out method as a way of punishment. Explain once but do not discuss bad behavior again and again. Reinforce good behavior by giving rewards. Reward system works best for children above two years of age and it may take about two months to make the children understand how it works. Parents need to be patient. Keeping a diary and targeting at just one or two behaviors to change at once makes it easier for kids and parents too. Behaviors you choose can include brushing teeth before going to bed, keeping toys and books in their place and good table manners. Rewards can be simple fun activities that you share with your children such as an extra bedtime story, allowing children to delay their bedtime by half an hour to watch their favorite cartoon, a preferred snack or points for older children that they can collect and use to get a special toy or favor from you. Before the child switches from a doing one thing to another, tell him beforehand, such as in five minutes, playtime will be over or it is dinnertime in another ten minutes. Punishments and shouting at children may just make them rebellious or they may repeat the behavior to get your attention, which they may crave for more than any reward. Simply, do not give them the reward that they would have got, if they had behaved in the desired way.

QUESTIONS

SECTION "A"

Short Answer Type:

1. Define early childhood.
2. Mention the characteristics of early childhood.
3. Why early childhood is called as a pre-school age?
4. Explain about the name used by psychologists for early childhood.
5. Why preschool age is considered as a questioning age?
6. Why early childhood is considered as an imitative and creative age?
7. Explain about the height and weight changes of early childhood.
8. Explain any two factors affecting motor development of early childhood.
9. Explain any two emotions of early childhood.
10. What are the positive emotions of early childhood?
11. According to early childhood, explain the concept of death, space and time.
12. Write about any two psychological hazards of this period.
13. Write a note on the causes, prevention and remedy for thumb sucking.
14. How can nail biting be controlled in preschoolers? Mention the causes for this problem.

SECTION "B"

One Page Answer Type:

1. Explain the characteristics of early childhood.
2. Write about the physical development of preschoolers.
3. Explain motor development and factors affecting motor development of early childhood.
4. Explain the emotional development of early childhood, with few examples.

5. Describe the social behaviour patterns of early childhood.
6. Explain unsocial behaviour patterns of early childhood.
7. Examine the intellectual development of early childhood.
8. Write about the developmental tasks of the preschool period.
9. Write a note on the causes, prevention and remedy for any two behaviour problems in children.

SECTION "C"

Essay Answer Type:

1. Explain the characteristics and physical development of early childhood.
2. Examine the motor development and emotional development of early childhood.
3. Explain social development and cognitive development of early childhood.
4. Briefly discuss the developmental changes of language in early childhood period.
5. Describe the hazards of the early childhood period.
6. Discuss the common behavior problems existing in children. Suggest suitable remedies.

CHAPTER

8

NURSERY SCHOOL EDUCATION

OBJECTIVES

To enlighten students about:

- Concept of Nursery/Preschool education, its need and importance
- Types of Preschool
- Objectives of Preschool education
- Requirements essential for a preschool
- Preschool building
- Selection of Play Equipment for Preschool
- Principles of Programme/ Curriculum planning
- Preschool teacher
- Records and registers
- Importance of preschool teacher and parents' Cooperation

8.1. INTRODUCTION

The most commonly used term for a preschool in India is Nursery school. A critical learning period for all children is the time from birth until they enter kindergarten. Many may wonder the need for preschool education. Preschool education is the foundation for a child's education. The skills and knowledge (including aptitude and attitude) that a child develops in the preschool years has a great impact on a child's success when formal schooling begins. According to many educationists and child psychologists, preschool serves as a platform to develop many skills, namely,

- Visual
- Listening
- Language of reading
- Mathematical
- Manipulation

8.2. THE NEED AND IMPORTANCE OF PRESCHOOL EDUCATION

During the preschool years children have a rapid physical, mental and social growth. They gather information and form them into patterns of knowledge that become integrated with their life. They begin to work and play cooperatively with other children. In their play, they show skills and ingenuity. These are the years of the 'flowering of the self'. As the rate of growth and development is fast, any stimulation along these lines will have its maximum effect during early childhood.

This stage is also crucial in terms of the child's development of interests, attitudes and values. The extent of ultimate development and achievement is practically fixed by the experiences the child has already undergone during this period. Rapid growth at the preschool stage necessitates the provision of a suitable environment for optimum development.

The preschool child, whether he be two and a half, three, four or five years old is one who needs space to be vigorous, alone and or part of an active group, for his happiness, concern and self-expression. He needs materials, which are appropriate to his size, ideas and feelings. He needs an understanding adult to help him to help himself, to explore manually and verbally, and to learn the lessons of life from both people and objects.

Many families are not in a position to provide such an enriching and stimulating environment to children because they themselves live in deprived conditions and they do not know how to give the desirable stimulation to their children. The more experiences the child receives at this stage, the richer will be the dividend. Preschools with good management, able personnel, enough space for free movement and proper equipment to play are the source of these experiences.

Due to economic pressures, impact of education, social and family changes, many mothers have chosen a career outside the home, to supplement the family income, meet the national goals, and face gender equity. Numerous dynamic changes have lead to .the disintegration of joint family system into the nuclear family system due to various reasons. This has lead to the problem of leaving their children at home. Space constraint for a developing toddler is another major issue. Preschool children love to have more of physical activities, for which space is required. With our rapid population growth and people moving to cities, the living space in towns is limited today. Families live in small apartment or even single rooms where there is hardly any space for children to move about, play and run. Kindergarten, nursery school or such preschool is an answer to the problem.

Many mothers, both educated and uneducated, do not appear to understand the significance of the demands of growth in early childhood. They either tend to baby their children too much or ignore them. Thus, even in educated homes, the environment may not be fully satisfying and challenging for the optimum growth of children. Persons, who are trained and experienced in guiding young children, are those in nursery schools, who are in a better position to meet these needs. These persons, together with the parents, will be able to achieve better results.

Preschool provides an enriching environment for the holistic development of the child. In short, preschool involves the following

P – physical and gross
R – ready to learn self-help skills
E – emotional and aesthetic
S – social and attitude
C – confidence
H – happiness
O – overall coordination
O – organizing oneself
L – language of speech

The core concept of preschool program is to strengthen the foundation of children in their early childhood age with care and education that helps child development in proper way. Below are the highlights of the educational program.

- The basic concept of preschool education is to make children understand and get quality care and learning by which they can examine historical perspective, theories of curriculum and different approaches to preschool education.
- The principles of child development up to six years of age regarding the major milestones within areas like language, physical, social, emotional, personal, motor, cognitive and moral development are framed through the syllabus of preschool program.
- The program also covers various techniques of working with children that fulfills their development needs.
- Emphasis is given to promote good health and nutritional habits in almost all early childhood development program curriculum. This can be achieved only if the teachers and also parents take this very seriously.

8.3. TYPES OF NURSERY SCHOOLS

Nursery schools vary greatly. One type of school may emphasize social and personal growth, getting along with others and gaining a feeling of mastery over the environment. Another may stress the importance of training the senses and developing motor abilities. Still another may emphasize cognitive growth in one of two ways. The cognitively oriented school may follow Piagetian format by structuring the programme to encourage the children to discover the world around them and to learn from their own experience. The second cognitive approach emphasizes the teaching of academic skill and uses a behavioural new point involving repetition and reinforcement. Many preschools claim to have goals in all these areas, so putting one school in a particular category can be difficult. Even nursery school can sometimes be classified based on their goals and programme.

Traditional Nursery School: The traditional nursery school emphasizes on social and emotional development and may not follow any specific educational theory. Activities may include story-time, listening to music, moving to music, involving in all types of artistic endeavors and field trips in the neighbourhood, and the children are encouraged to co-operate and share. Some Piagetian influence may be in evidence, as teachers create situations in which children can learn through self-discovery.

Montessori School: Montessori schools, which use the approach developed by Maria Montessori at the beginning of 20th century, have gained popularity all over the world. They stress the importance of educating the senses because Montessori believed there is a close relationship between senses and intellect. Training the senses play the ground work for reading and writing, passing fingers across the letters with the eyes shut and listening to the name of the letter and training them with the index finger and then with pencil. The Montessori pupil learned the sound of the alphabet with touch, sight and muscular coordination. He had to learn how to write before reading. Every activity in Montessori school has an educational purpose. For instance, when children color, they do implement art to create something beautiful. Many Montessori activities are self-correcting so that children can proceed at their own rate and no pressure is placed on them. There is no punishment for not finishing an exercise. In Montessori classroom, each item has its proper place and children are expected to keep their classroom clean and pick up and keep back the articles by themselves. The teacher must be specially trained in the Montessori method.

Montessori method is not without critics. Play is considered unimportant and this troubles many educationists who consider play to be an important part of child's development. Understanding one's emotion is also not a primary goal in this method. Social interaction is present but it is not stressed as neither children do not act out plays nor does a teacher tell story.

Piagetian Pre-School: Piaget's ideas of learning through doing are in contrast to Montessori method. Piagetian based Pre-School stresses on play as learning activity. During play, children are exposed to viewpoint of others, which challenge their egocentric view of the world. Developing curiosity, independence and self-confidence, learning to co-operate and gaining physical control of the environment are definite goals. In Piagets' preschool, children are not given formal instruction, instead teachers act as guides helping the children discover things through active participation. Children are exposed to wide range of materials and help them gain experience in classification and seriation.

Englemann-Berciter Approach: Nowhere is the goal of academic growth addressed as much as in the programme developed by Engelmann and Berciter known as DISTAR. In this programme, the children are taught the concepts that are considered necessary by the educational staff. The teacher has an objective and presents the material in a standardized fashion to a small group of children for about 20 minutes or so with periods of rest, music or other activities, alternating with instructional periods. The exchanges are rapid and teacher reinforces the children for correct answers. This is the teaching approach based on the idea that children can be taught desired concepts if the material is presented clearly and appropriately. For e.g., the children may be taught the concepts of equality, that both sides of an equation must be equal. The teacher may present the concept in an appropriate way and ask the children questions and give much positive reinforcement for the correct responses. Englemann and Berciter argue that the disadvantage for the children is the requirement for additional help in cognitive areas, especially language. Their programme is an attempt to provide such cognitive training.

A preschool in India is known by the terms Nursery school, Balwadi, Anganwadi, Laboratory nursery school, Montessori school, etc.

Nursery school: The most commonly used term for a preschool in India is Nursery school. In general usage, a preschool situated in an urban area is referred to as nursery school. In rural areas, preschools are referred to as Balwadis.

Balwadi: It is a preschool situated in a rural area. State governments, CSWB and voluntary agencies usually run Balwadis with financial help from Social Welfare Board. Invariably, all balwadis provide free meals to children. Education is provided free in Balwadis (mainly non-formal through play way method). The medium of instruction is the regional language. A large number of Balwadis also provide crèche services for children below 2 years. Babies from 6 months of age are provided custodial care and children above 2 years are given non-formal education.

Anganwadi: It is the basic institution through which the ICDS programme is carried out. The programme provides a package of services to women and children, which includes periodic health check-ups, referral medical services, monitoring of growth, immunization, supplementary feeding, non-formal preschool learning opportunities and nutrition and health education for pregnant and lactating women. The institutional means through which these services are provided is the Anganwadi, which are situated (for every population of 1000) in rural and tribal areas and urban slums.

In an Anganwadi, non-formal education is given to children of preschool age. It is given normally for 3 hours a day. Children are taught songs and stories. No rigid curriculum is followed. Three hundred days a year, food is prepared and distributed to children below 6 years. This supplementary food helps in preventing deficiency diseases in children.

Laboratory Nursery school: The main objectives of these schools run by Home Science departments in various instituitions aim at the all round development of the child through non-formal education. It is basically run to facilitate the Home Science students to observe the various aspects of child development. The school will have special provision for observation booths from which the nursery children can be observed without being aware of .

8.4. THE OBJECTIVES OF A PRESCHOOL:

The promoters of the preschool education movement in different countries at different times have put forward various objectives, aiming at the all-round development of the child – physical, social, emotional and intellectual. The objectives are:

- To provide a happy, safe and caring environment for all the children
- To provide the highest possible standard of care and education in a stimulating environment enabling children to develop into happy, healthy individuals, encouraging them to respect others.
- To work closely with parents in order to provide the best care for their child, always maintaining complete confidentiality.
- To provide a range of well planned opportunities through a broad curriculum so that children can learn through play.
- To achieve the 'Early Learning Goals' which form the basis of the 'Foundation stage' in the following areas of development:
    - Personal, Social and Emotional development
    - Communication, Language and literacy
    - Problem solving, Reasoning and Numeracy
    - Knowledge and understanding of the world
    - Creative development
    - Physical development
- To help children to become independent, self-motivated and confident and allow them to progress at their own rate of development through the Early Years Foundation stage and into Key Stage one where appropriate
- To monitor every child's progress and development by careful observation and completion of development records.

Based on the objectives, **the various development activities kindergarten teachers and preschool institutes focus on are as follows:**

8.4.1. Physical Health and Care

This area consists of five sub-domains:

- Motor Development
- Physical Development
- Health and Personal Care
- Nutrition and Feeding
- Safety

Motor Development

Motor development has three distinct components: gross motor skills, fine motor skills, and sensorimotor skills. Gross motor skills are characterized by movements of the large muscles of the body and include such movements as rolling over, walking, jumping, and climbing. Fine motor skills involve the ability to coordinate smaller muscles including the muscles of the hands, fingers, and face that allow for movements such as grasping, cutting, picking up food, or intentionally winking.

Sensorimotor skills involve the ability to use and integrate the senses (sight, hearing, smell, taste, and touch) to support activity. These skills provide a foundation for behavior, learning, and overall development for young children.

Physical Development

Children should have access to free time, play opportunities, adequate space, and challenging materials to pursue their physical development needs. Physical competence allows children to participate in group activities and maintain attention to, and interest in tasks necessary for the learning process. The various elements of physical competency and development includes stamina, energy, strength, flexibility, coordination and endurance.

A child when he joins the nursery school is still a toddler. He often falls down when he walks or runs; he cannot climb steps without support, as his muscles are not fully developed. The nursery school provides suitable indoor activities like tearing, cutting, pasting, drawing, painting, threading beads etc. for fine muscular co-ordination and outdoor activities such as climbing, jumping, sliding, swinging, and pedaling for the large muscular development of children. Physical fitness is the objective of such activities and programs.

Health and Personal Care

Prenatal care, personal hygiene, and basic personal care are essential to a child's physical health. Children's physical health is impacted by access to medical and dental care, nutrition, healthy sleep patterns, and opportunity for physical activity and active play. Recognizing and addressing acute and chronic illness is essential to sustain healthy physical development. Various social and environmental risks (e.g., firearms, lead, pesticides, inadequate or unhealthy water supplies, violent homes and neighborhoods, water safety) also impact children's physical well-being.

Nutrition and Feeding

Preschool offers an excellent opportunity to supplement the home diets of children and overcome the nutritional deficiencies, if any. Through well-planned meals, the nursery school can make up the imbalance in the diets, meeting 1/3rd of their daily requirements. Children eat a variety of nutritious foods which encompass far more than food groups and nutrients recommended for children. Attitudes, self regulation, culture, and general areas of development are entwined with food and feeding.

Safety

Safety includes protecting children from exposure to harmful substances and situations and helping children learn to avoid harmful objects, environments, and circumstances. Though young children can learn safety rules and regulations, know when and how to ask for help, and recognize the boundary between safety and danger, they cannot be expected to keep themselves safe. Young children's physical well-being is dependent on adult-provided safety.

8.4.2. Establishing Healthy Habits

Early childhood is a prime time to instigate children begin healthy habits or behaviors that will promote a healthy lifestyle. We need to teach kids to stay healthy. In order to develop healthy habits, two things must be remembered. First, learning becomes more meaningful when the experience is woven into the children's daily experiences. Second, learning experiences must be repeated often enough until the lessons become a natural and integral part of their lives.

Some of the good habits include

In any preschool program, children are taken to toilet and for washing hands at regular intervals. Then children are told about the necessity of brushing teeth, combing hair or taking bath through free conversation, stories and puppetry. These activities help children to develop proper health habits. The children are encouraged to do their own work and be self-reliant.

Good Handwashing

In a well-planned preschool, children learn the healthy habit of using the toilet regularly and washing their hands. Good hand washing requires three elements-- soap, water and friction. Everyone should wash hands before and after eating, using the bathroom, handling nappies, blowing into a handkerchief or tissue, cleaning, doing art projects, or playing with toys. Proper hand washing will significantly reduce transmission of infections.

Getting Enough Sleep

Another healthy habit that kids develop is to get enough sleep. Studies show that lack of sufficient sleep can contribute to inattention, hyperactivity, and disagreeableness among children. Most children's sleep requirements fall within a predictable range of hours based on their age. However, there is no magical number of sleeping hours required as each child would have his own distinct sleep needs.

Eating Healthy

A further healthy habit is to eat healthy food. Good nutrition is a wonderful foundation for wellness. Everyone needs to eat a variety of food, from vegetables and fruits to milk, cheese, fish, chicken, meat, and nuts, to rice and grains. A balanced diet is one that includes all the food groups. It should be made sure that they drink plenty of water.

Exercise

Most kids are active and so they are encouraged to stay healthy by developing their love for exercise and activities that make them move. Physical activity should be increased by reducing sedentary time (e.g. watching television, playing computer/ video games or talking on the phone.) All children age 2 and older should participate in at least 30 minutes of enjoyable, moderate-intensity activities every day. Researchers Say: Yoga is Good for Kids

8.4.3. Satisfying the Educational Needs

A young child is very curious and he is always asking questions. Much depends on how his questions are answered and his curiosity is satisfied. A good preschool aims at satisfying the educational needs of the young child by providing the atmosphere, teaching equipment and materials which are challenging and stimulating, by allowing each child to understand the world in which he lives, and by fostering new interests through opportunities to explore, investigate and experiment. A child can take in many things if they are properly explained to him. At the same time, the objective should be that the kindergarten child should be encouraged to investigate and draw his own conclusions rather than remain satisfied with ready answers. This will help him to understand the world in which he lives to foster new interests. The educational programme in the nursery school provides opportunity for:

- Better perception of various concepts such as color, texture, number, size and shape, days and time
- Expansion of vocabulary through the practical use of new words
- Thorough use of language due to careful monitoring of pronunciation
- Creating an interest in reading by the use of books, experiences such as listening to and

telling stories.

- Helping the children to learn by repeating and participating in the recitals of rhymes and songs
- Developing memory power through repetition of songs, stories and associating the events with objects and persons, and
- Encouraging independent thinking as the child is motivated to communicate his ideas in his own way.

8.4.4. NURTURING EMOTIONAL GROWTH

A child has hardly any control over his emotions when he comes to school. He can hardly wait for his turn and is often unable to take 'NO', but by proper and careful guidance by the kindergarten and preschool teacher, he gains better emotional control by the time he leaves the nursery school. Guiding the child to express, understand, accept and control his feelings and emotions can develop approval, acceptance and emotional maturity. Emotional development during the preschool years encompasses self-concept, self-regulation, and a better understanding of emotions and how to express them.

To help foster emotional development in young children, activities that allow the child to take control over, and name his / her actions and feelings are encouraged. It is important to promote a positive, healthy self-image. The child will be praised for self-regulation tasks such as using words to express negative emotions instead of hitting or biting.

Cultivation of Positive Emotions

The preschool can help to develop positive emotions such as trust, love, and a sense of belonging, achievement, tolerance, equality and dignity of labor through providing a variety of activities such as painting, gardening and carpentry work. A few illustrations are given below.

(a) Trust:

During early years, children learn about love by being loved. They learn the role of rules in a community by having rules set at home. They learn about consequences, fairness, tolerance, altruism, justice, giving, sharing, and caring during their years in the most important community—the family.

"Likely as not, the child you can do the least with will do the most to make you proud." - Mignon McLaughlin

Trust can be developed in children in the preschool in three main ways:

(*i*) Planning the environment and arranging the equipment in such a manner that a child can take them independently and carry them to the place where he wants to play. When a child gets used to independence, he begins to trust his ability and the environment. These, in turn, will lead to the development of initiative.

(*ii*) Assuring the child of the teacher's help when he needs it, and allowing him to act on his own initiative.

(*iii*) Helping the child even without the verbal request, because the teacher had discerned the need.

(b) Love and Affection

Love moves the world and hate stagnates it. Love is the strongest emotion that brings happiness into each one's lives. To nurture the children into becoming good human beings, the preschool teacher must inculcate in them the emotion called Love. And what is love? It may be defined as affection, devotion, fondness, admiration, compassion, attachment, dedication, and so on. When children learn to live by these emotions, then we do away with all the negatives that cause our destruction.

Children learn to love others by being loved first. Foreseeing danger and preventing it can show the fact that they are loved in many ways in the preschool, for example, the comfort a child receives from the teacher, when he is hurt either physically or mentally, also helps to develop love and affection. To narrate a case, Sheela is climbing a tree and the teacher cautions her to get down; she does not pay heed to and soon encounters a fall. The teacher rushes and helps her to clean the wound and says that she feels sorry for her. The child was touched. But, if the teacher had said, 'I told you not to climb up', the child would have felt hurt and started shedding tears.

The other ways of developing love and affection in children are:

- Allowing them to care for pet animals like rabbits in natural surroundings.
- Telling stories like the 'lion and the rat', and the 'ant and the pigeon', and
- Showing visuals through recorded discs or players about pictures of mothers, birds and animals caring for their young ones.

(c) Sense of Belonging:

Allowing the children contribute to group living and group activity creates the sense of belonging, which boosts the concept of self -'ego'. For example, when the teacher wants to engage the children in a drawing activity, she can request one child to distribute the books of everyone in the class or if a teacher is planning to teach about the concept of colours, she can request each child to get one object each of various colours, so that the children enjoy and participate, while their sense of belonging also improves.

In his book "Miseducation: Preschoolers at Risk", the author asserts that "a child who does not develop a strong sense of belonging during this period (three to four year old period) may develop a sense of alienation that will later make it difficult for the person to become an active group member and make it more likely that he or she will be something of a loner." He continues to say that families who value and model cooperation, encourage young children's sense of belonging to and acceptance by peer groups. Teachers and parents can be strong role models of cooperation as they partner to work through problems and plan preschool activities.

(d) Accomplishment:

The sense of accomplishment a child gets through his play activities helps the child to gain confidence for further participation. For example, if a child is asked to wrap letters on a tree (model), he does it by telling the name and sound of the letter, in a continuous fashion. If he is cheered each time he does it correctly, the entire ordeal goes on smoothly, with the feeling of accomplishment.

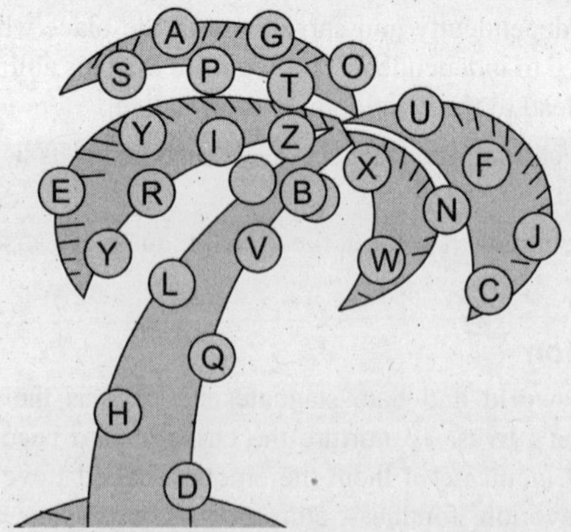

(e) Tolerance and Empathy:

The teacher can encourage the child to be kind and gentle and to make the concepts of diversity and acceptance more "real" and meaningful in many ways. In the preschool, she serves as a child's conduit to the world, and therefore, the way she interacts with others is important. Using what the child already knows and loves, such as books, music, blocks, dolls, dress-up clothes, or other toys — is the easiest, and most natural way to expand the child's knowledge about her own family culture, as well as those that are different from hers. It can be as simple as introducing items and games from different cultures into the child's play. A few tips are to

- *Persuade to Play outside.* Because kids tend to meet more children in outdoor play spaces, outdoor play provides more opportunities for children to learn to be comfortable around with all the different kinds of people.
- *Encourage the child to both give and receive during play.* Being able to receive a kind thought or deed or share a special toy is another way children learn about compassion.
- *Make gifts for relatives and friends.* It may be for a birthday, holiday, or simply because the child likes them. Encourage the child to send a card to a classmate who is sick.

(f) Equality and Dignity of Labour:

A nursery school, with the objective of developing 'self help' policy and independence to children can offer suitable opportunities. For example, the child can be made to carry their own plates into the kitchen after a meal, have them put washed and get them to put their toys away after playtime sessions and involved in spreading or folding the mats for sleeping. In the process, they will earn respect for those expected to perform these tasks for them, responsibility and independence, even at home. At the same time, when their house staff is on leave, it will become easier for the children to manage things and give a helping hand. These experiences create the attitudes of 'dignity of labour', and also a respect for public property.

Preschool also helps in channelising the negative emotions such as fear and anger.

TUMBLING NEGATIVE EMOTIONS

(g) Anger

Anger is an emotion that every child needs to learn to cope with. Children's anger presents challenges to teachers committed to constructive, ethical, and effective child guidance. Let us see about the components of children's anger, factors contributing to understanding and managing anger, and the ways teachers can guide children's expressions of anger.

Three Components of Anger: Anger is believed to have three components.

- **The Emotional State of Anger:** The first component is the emotion itself, defined as a feeling experienced when a goal is blocked or needs are frustrated. Several types of stress-producing anger provocations that young children face daily in classroom interactions are conflict over possessions, physical assault such as pushing or hitting another child, verbal conflict (a tease or a taunt), rejection by peers, issues of obedience, which often involve asking or insisting that children do something that they do not want to do--for instance, wash their hands with reference to media advertisement.
- **Expression of Anger:** The second component of anger is its expression. Some children vent or express anger through facial expressions, crying, sulking, or talking, but do little to try to solve a problem or confront the provocateur. Others actively resist by physically or verbally defending their positions, self-esteem, or possessions in non aggressive ways. Still other children express anger with aggressive revenge by physically or verbally

retaliating against the provocateur. And some children use adult seeking, looking for comfort or solutions from a teacher, or telling the teacher about an incident.

Teachers can use child guidance strategies to help children express angry feelings in socially constructive ways. A major challenge for early childhood teachers is to encourage children to acknowledge angry feelings and to help them learn to express anger in positive and effective ways.

- **An Understanding of Anger:** The third component of the anger experience is understanding--interpreting and evaluating--the emotion. Because the ability to regulate the expression of anger is linked to an understanding of the emotion and because children's ability to reflect on their anger is somewhat limited, children need guidance from teachers and parents in understanding and managing their feelings of anger.

(h) Fear:

All children have fears at some point in their life and it is usually considered to be a normal part of development. It should not be ridiculed. These fears are abnormal only if they are persistent or keep the child overly preoccupied with the subject that is feared so that it interferes with normal activities, if the child cannot be reassured or distracted away from the fear (becoming a phobia), or if it is an irrational fear. Whether or not a fear is irrational depends on a child's age and developmental level. For example, it is normal for a 2 year old to be afraid of sitting on the potty, but it would be irrational for an 8 year old to have the same fear.

Preschool age children normally have simple fears of animals and insects, monsters and ghosts, getting lost, loss of a parent and of bedtime. They may also develop a fear after a triggering event, such as falling in the water or being chased by a dog. They may also increase during times of stress (new baby, while moving, divorce, etc.) As a child learns more about the world, the list of things they fear tend to grow. Some fears are real and some are imaginary.

Some children are more fearful of things, even common things, than others and this is usually a function of his type of temperament. Also, children who have parents of attitude being very anxious or fearful, or who tend to overreact to things, often have the same reactions in similar situations. The preschool teacher must recognize the fear and help the child to get over it.

Helping the child to deal with fear includes taking their feelings seriously, encouraging them to talk about their anxieties, telling them the facts and giving them the opportunity to confront their fears at their own pace and with the teacher's support.

Suggestions to a teacher for helping a preschool child includes:

- Let the child know that you take their fears seriously
- Give the child truthful information on topics such as death or war, and let them know you are willing to answer any questions
- Encourage the child to confront the object of their fear, such as dogs, one step at a time at their own pace. For example, perhaps start with pictures, then try a very small gentle dog that is tied up, so that the child decides how close to get
- Allow the child some control. For example, if they are afraid of intruders, make the child responsible for enquiring a stranger when he enters the classroom
- Daily routines and rituals give a child a sense of stability and security, and may ease general anxiety

8.4.5. Expansion of Social Development

Desirable social attitudes are developed by encouraging the children to share play materials or food with each other, wait for their turn and take care of the school property. Here the objective is focused on social behavior of every child.

The nursery school encourages healthy group participating by providing materials, which enable the children to enjoy sharing and playing together. It teaches children their rights and privileges in being a member of a social group and encourages them taking care of the property belonging to others. The preschool helps children to work in groups and conform to the group demands. Responsibility and other desirable social attitudes and good manners are cultivated through the relationships with the peer group and with adults.

8.4.6. Invigorating Visual Appreciation

There are many beautiful things around in the environment but unless the children's attention is drawn to these, they do not notice them. The children are encouraged to appreciate beauty in the environment, such as pretty flowers, colorful butterflies, or a beautiful view. In today's global warming situations, it is the duty of preschool teachers to educate children and make them aware of such things. The experiences conducive for the aesthetic expression and appreciation are those which provide:

- Opportunity to express ideas and to experiment with color, balance, symmetry, pattern and design through a variety of media such as paint, clay and blocks;
- Opportunity for imagination through the shared enjoyment of books, songs and stories; and
- Opportunity for finding beauty in nature through excursions, nature walks and appreciation for the right things at the right time.

8.4.7. Inspiring Language Development

The language development of the child depends, to a great extent, on the opportunities he gets to speak language or listen to correct speech. Through storybook reading, free conversation, puppet play, etc. new words are introduced to the children and these new words are used again and again till they become a part of their active vocabulary. The children in the nursery school are encouraged to talk in a group, describe his experiences and join on the spot story-making activity.

Above are some of the very important objectives focused on childhood education program by most of the nursery, kindergarten and preschools around the world.

8.5. REQUIREMENTS ESSENTIAL FOR A PRESCHOOL

Proper building with compound: Since a preschool can be a child's play group area, pre-primary education center or just an activity center, the basic and most important requirement is children's security when they are away from their parents. It is the responsibility of preschool owner to have a well planned building, villa or any home that has proper compound around, so that children should not be able to jump and run around. The school building should be in compliance with fire and safety laws and regulations as evidenced by reports of annual school fire and safety inspections as conducted by appropriate local authorities. It should also be in compliance with rules established by the state board of education regarding school food services.

Play ground or garden: Every preschool has a special activity method of teaching children which is quite famous, known as 'play way method' which includes outdoor games too. A nice play ground or a garden attached to the nursery will attract more parents.

Proper urinal / bathroom facilities: Now this is one of the very important point to be considered as priority while starting a preschool / kindergarten in any location of the world. As the kids are very young to understand the toilet manners, it should be part of the daily preschool timetable. It can be a headache if one forgot to notice how well it is found in the premise.

Beautiful and safe interiors: The nursery should be beautiful with nice interiors and safety equipments. The furniture and look and feel of a newly started kindergarten should be the best. It should attract children as well as parents. It should have happy looking colorful pictures, and charts, along with no edge of furniture pointed that can harm children and so on.

Legal formalities: To start a preschool in India as commercial business, the legal formalities such as certifying from the Municipal Corporation (Government Body) and the appointment of a certified ECCE (Early Childhood Care Education) teacher has to be checked out.

Preschool curriculum planning: The syllabus to be taught to the children, knowing the list of holidays, list of indoor and outdoor games / activities, fees structure, evaluation, preschool timetable, qualified staff members and teachers and also non-teaching staff like maid, must be noted ahead in the preschool curriculum.

Location of the preschool: Property planning to start a preschool is a must and most important. One should be careful to remember that it involves children and every parent prefers the nearest and best location. The play area is preferable in the ground floor of any building and should be spacious enough.

8.6. THE PRESCHOOL BUILDING

The building or the physical plant which houses the preschool may be stimulating or stilling and may be conducive or inhibiting to the development of children. The prerequisite for the achievement of the objective, 'gracious living' is a clean, pleasant and well-maintained building. Children spend most of their time during the day in the preschool rooms or grounds. Naturally the surroundings are bound to exert a far-reaching influence on their growth and health. Therefore, the school building, its situation, design, lighting and ventilation all have important roles to play in the behavior and welfare of the children.

8.6.1. Essentials of a good building

(*i*) *Ambiance*: The ambiance greatly influences a child's health, attitudes and development of personality. A preschool, therefore, cannot be built anywhere and everywhere, if it is to fulfill its functions efficiently. If the aim of the preschool is to bring about mental, moral and physical development of children, the school building must be located amidst desirable surroundings. On the other hand, unclean surroundings are detrimental to the mind and body. It can cause adverse effects on character formation. There is vast distinction between the outlook of a person raised in clean, healthy and adequate surrounding and the one who had spent his childhood in crowded, dirty and unclean surroundings.

(ii) Location: The location of a building includes

(*a*) Neighborhood

(*b*) Soil

(*c*) Aspect and Elevation

(a) Neighborhood

The neighborhood of a preschool must preferably be a refreshing environment, without stagnant pools, swamps, sewers or other settings, which are sources of disagreeable odor, mosquitoes, flies and harmful microorganisms. There should be a good water supply. The preschool may be located at a short distance from the towns to get fresh air and have less risk of epidemics. This will also reduce the cost of the land to be purchased or of the building to be rented. The preschool must be closer to a road, but well back from the road and not on its brink. It should not be in close proximity to a burial or cremation ground. The vicinity must be such as to permit any future expansion. It must be a place away from the problems of industrial noise, dust, smoke and pollution. It should also avoid the physical danger of factories, railroads or bus service.

(b) Soil

The type of soil makes the school building strong, safe, congenial and educational. The important criteria in selecting the site with regard to soil conditions is that it should be a raised area and a dry one having natural drainage free from water logging.

(c) Aspect and Elevation

Considering the main features of aspect and elevation for the preschool, the facing of the building to the south is the most ideal. Corridors can be planned on one side of the building to enable free access of light. Planting trees and shrubs on the other side will help to serve as sun-breakers, especially in tropical countries like India. Vegetation provides shade and wind breaks and cools the air. It attracts wildlife, provides loose parts for the children to play (leaves, cones and twigs), provides landmarks and builds in seasonal change and beauty. Plants with prickly foliage, nettles, thorns, and barbs should be avoided.

8.6.2 Building plan:

The preschool building plan would vary as per the type of nursery school. The following suggestions help in developing a suitable blue print.

(*a*) The building plan should adhere strictly to the rules of sanitation, hygiene, ventilation and lighting. It should permit sufficient entry of sunlight and fresh air to all the parts of the building.

(*b*) The facility should include not less than thirty-five square feet (3.3 sq.m) of indoor space for each child in the program. Safe play space, including both indoor and outdoor play space, totaling not less than sixty square feet (5.6 sq.m) for each child using the space at any one time, shall be regularly available and scheduled for use. The minimum requirements of play area, toilets, and washrooms must be met.

(*c*) A single-storey building is preferable for convenience and safety.

(*d*) First aid facilities and space for temporary placement or isolation of injured or ill children should be provided.

Considering the various requirements for a preschool and its smooth progression, a suitable building space ideally would be as in the following table. On coinciding with the budget allotted, the number of play rooms in the school (one or two), along with a kitchen and washrooms, could be decided. Keeping the requirements in view, we can consider a plan for the building for a preschool, with the minimum requirements of space met. It consists of two play-rooms measuring 7m x 8m, a kitchen cum store-room 5m x 5m and a wash cum latrine of 5m x 3m and an outdoor area of 100 sq.m. If funds do not permit, the number of playrooms can be reduced to one. The details of the built up space is given in the table.

Table 8.1 Space Requirement of a Preschool

Types	Plinth area of built up Space	Total area
Preschool with two play rooms	218 sq.m.	318 sq.m.
Preschool with a single play-room	164 sq.m.	264 sq.m.

Figure 8.1 Sample Plan For A Preschool Building

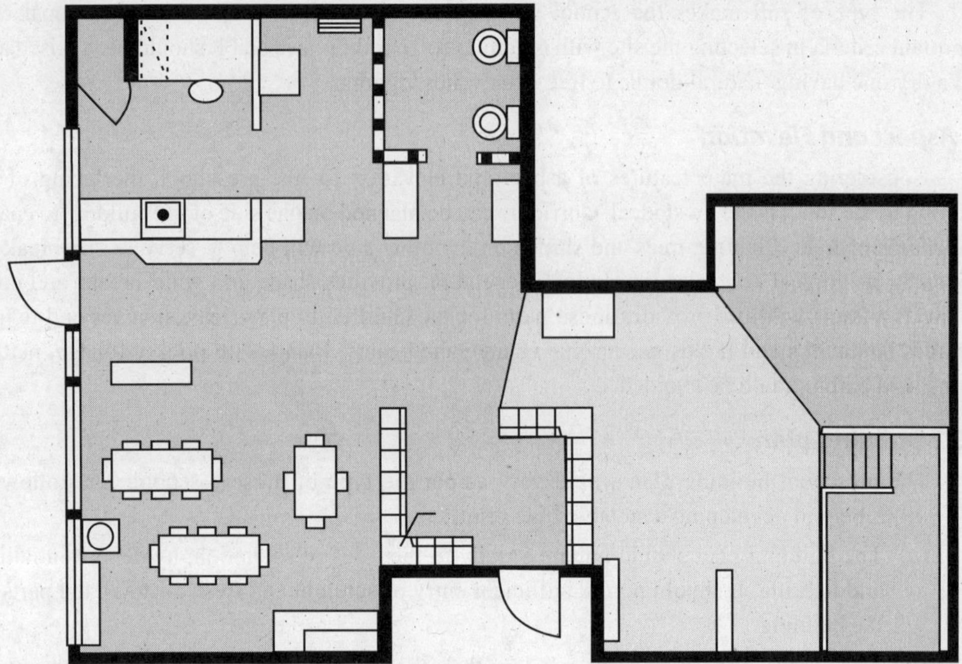

8.6.3. Room Requirements for a Preschool

A preschool room should be designed for children to engage in large and small group activities while further enhancing ever-growing independent and self-help skills. A preschool room should have a large carpeted area for group socialization. Distinct and well-defined areas (e.g. science and discovery area, literacy area), as visible by the placement of furniture and equipment, will allow for self-directed guidance and facilitate the flow of activity within the room. A larger bathroom space and cubby area, with child-size amenities, will further enhance self-help skills. As always, room size, wall colour, natural lighting, and providing a variety of textures within an inclusive setting, continue to be paramount. The room considerations are

- A play activity room for not more than 24 children with an unobstructed floor area of 2.8 m^2 per child.
- Space for washing, dressing, toileting, space for isolation, storage.
- For programs 6 hours and more per day, the room shall have an unobstructed glazed window area equivalent to not less than 10% of the floor area; and storage for beds and linens;
- space for eating, resting (children and staff);
- food preparation area; and
- storage for outdoor equipment.

Activity areas or playrooms

They are the key areas where children's program take place. They must be designed to ensure safety, provide clear supervision by staff at all times and contain a range of program areas that are age appropriate and support learning. The room should be designed, finished and furnished to encourage children to be engaged in a safe and comfortable environment.

The room should include a variety of open spaces along with smaller more intimate spaces. The space should be designed to be flexible and support a variety of activities such as quiet and active play, creative play, resting, and eating. The finishes, colours, layout, furnishings and staff amenities need to be carefully considered to support these various activities. The design should encourage children to both explore the room, engage in different activities while providing the clues and the design elements that allow other activities to occur simultaneously.

The shape of the room is important: Avoid rooms with sharp or acute angles that limit program flexibility. Rooms that are "L" shaped can be difficult to supervise and long narrow rooms may limit natural light. Rectangular rooms lend themselves more readily to activities of the children than square ones. The room should have both visual and spatial connections to adjoining activity areas. By altering the height of the room and providing some semi-secluded areas, quiet activity space can be created.

Unobstructed floor and wall space that is well organized, efficient and convenient for staff accessing and/or putting equipment away is important.

Walls: Walls with a variety of pleasant colors can add beauty and a feeling of spaciousness if properly selected from primary colors such as red, blue and yellow. They should be skillfully used to challenge the imagination of children and yet not over stimulate them. Ceilings at heights ranging from three meters and above are desirable to relieve noise and provide for freedom of movement.

The wall space should be utilized well to promote preschool activities. An abundance of 'pinning space' at the eye level of the child is desirable in order to have picture boards. The arrangement of windows and doors should allow large spaces for bulletin boards, for attaching things to pull on and for blackboards. The walls should be coated with a suitable, washable, porous material to deaden the noise. Make-shift movable walls provide for a wide variety of activities and better use of space.

Floors: Suitable floors for a preschool should be durable, easy to clean, and maintain. If installing sheet flooring material and vinyl tile in various colours and patterns is considered, it is very pleasing. The floors shall have a finish that is slip resistant and facilitate good sanitary maintenance. They must be hard to withstand wear and help to reduce or absorb sound.

Windows and doors: Sufficient cross ventilation through open windows is desirable, depending upon the climatic conditions of the given area. Natural light and views are a high priority. Openable windows are preferred even when building is air conditioned. Window openings should be at a higher level, out of children's reach.

Exterior windows promote engagement with the outside world. Windows that open into corridors or in-between the rooms help children to see themselves as part of a larger community. They also permit visual surveillance by staff from adjoining rooms. Light can be "shared" from one room to the next by enlarging existing windows or cutting out windows between rooms, however, it will not be counted in the calculation of direct light. Each room must have clear window glass that is the equivalent of 10% of the floor space to ensure natural light.

The windows should be low enough to enable a child to look out and should be fitted with shades or blinds. They should be easily operated. Translucent shades or venetian blinds help in regulating the light. They shall be provided with a regulator preventing them from opening more than 100 mm (4") where it is possible for a child to access the window or for all windows located above the first floor. Consider making the upper portion of the window a minimum 1000 mm (3') above the floor level.

Include small trees and deciduous trees in landscape design to provide shade from the sun. Provide awnings for shade. An overhanging shade may help to regulate the glare. All windows need to be fitted with guards, screens or both; the windows in the areas used for preparing and eating food must be screened to keep off flies and mosquitoes. It should be ensured that there is sufficient shade for metal surfaces (e.g. slide) that will otherwise become too hot for children to use if constantly exposed to the sun.

All doors should be light in weight so that children can handle them easily. The heights of door knobs should be within easy reach of the children and of the type that he can readily turn without being hurt.

Artificial Lighting: Florescent lighting is the most efficient and cost effective form of artificial lighting. If they are to be used, it is recommended that bulbs selected should provide the most natural colour mix. Fixture covers can lessen the glare of florescent lighting. Wherever possible florescent lighting should be supplemented with incandescent lighting operated by a separate switch.

Light needed for specific tasks or atmosphere, as well as those with dimmer switches for sleep and/or quiet areas should be provided. Each room should have its own light switch. Adults should be alert to control the light during the changing conditions through the day, ensuring an ample quantity of good light evenly distributed over the room.

Children's Washroom

Water facilities are essential for the cleaning of activities in the preschool. The toilet and washing facilities should be easily accessible from both the indoors and outdoors. One toilet for every ten children is essential. . Care must be taken to see that the sinks and toilets are equipped with disposal drains.

- If the washroom contains not less than two toilets, the room shall be designed so that toilets and sinks are not visible from the entrance to the room.
- Locate mirror, and soap dispenser at a height suitable for children.
- Toilet fixtures with seats varying at heights from 10 inches to 12 inches from the floor are desirable.
- The ideal counter height for preschoolers is 550 mm (1 ft 10 in).
- Child height toilets provide more autonomy to the preschooler and removes fear of falling.
- Avoid toilet cubicles that may hinder staff assistance, visual surveillance, and interactions between children.
- Ensure that water taps are at accessible height to the children

Spatial consideration of the washroom should enable

- the children direct access from play activity room
- privacy and independence for children
- supervision by staff without leaving the playroom
- convenience to outdoor play areas.
- the usage of a centrally located washroom, giving access from both rooms, when there are two activity rooms

Entry

The main entry should be designed to both provide a welcoming environment and a necessary level of supervision and security. Ideally the entry should lead directly to the child care facility; this reduces the amount of circulation space and improves supervision.

General Storage Space

Planning for and providing ample storage for both materials and equipment is important. Well designed and adequate storage contributes to the organization and accessibility to things needed for each program and group of children. Keeping the space uncluttered improves the flow of movement from one activity space to another and minimizes children interrupting the play of others.

A well-planned closed storage area is a vital component of a child care centre and yet the amount of space allocated for it is underestimated. This area provides a place for staff to safely store materials and equipment, as well as items used on a rotation basis. If there is not sufficient closed storage, items tend to clutter the hallways and at times, part of the activity rooms. Not only is this dangerous, it adversely impacts upon the most needed program space for children. In addition, it is difficult to maintain control of inventory, equipment and materials unless they are stored in an organized manner. The necessary prerequisites are lockable storage space for linen, books, teaching aids, records, toys, indoor play materials and equipment, cleaning materials, hazardous substances, and other equipments.

Cabinets designed to store equipment or personal belongings intended to be accessible to children should be low to promote children's independence. The design of moveable storage units contributes to program flexibility. These should be equipped with drawers and open shelves according to the specific plans for use. Provision of adjustable and fixed shelving is appropriate. Storage cupboards should be durable and easy to maintain with laminate finish and solid hardwood or vinyl edges. Storage rooms should be ventilated to eliminate odours and dampness and also to keep free from insects and cobwebs.

Kitchen

Kitchens can be designed either as a full on-site meal preparation area or as a receiving kitchen to which a caterer would deliver meals and snacks on a daily basis. During the functional planning stage of the centre, discussion should include the type of meal service anticipated, so that the kitchen space can be designed appropriately. Consideration of capital costs, operating costs, and availability of community catering services have to be planned ahead. Garbage and recycling areas should be convenient to the kitchen and away from play areas to avoid smells, insects, wasps, and rodents.

Exterior Design and Play Elements

The play space should have provisions for

- Hard surface area where wheel toys can be used and balls bounced.
- Grassy plot for playing, running and romping.
- Spot for pets, gardens and digging.
- Sand box for sand play and manipulative activities and space for water play.

The children should have access for both active play and quiet play.

- **Active Play:** The active play area of a playground should consist of both a physical play area and a social play area. This will allow children to have the opportunity to develop gross motor skills and to socialize with other children. The equipment in the physical play area should provide challenges which promote children's overall development without creating hazards. The design of this area should allow for sequential movement from activity to activity.
  - **Physical Play Area:** Play equipment and furnishings must be provided in numbers that are adequate for the licensed capacity of the centre. A range of type and design that meet the needs of the children enrolled should be included with concern for all ages and with respect to their developmental levels and the type of program

offered at the centre. Play equipment should be arranged so that children are able to approach, use, and exit from the equipment safely.

- **Social Play Area:** A well-shaded social play area should be inviting and comfortable, for which a landscaped enclosure to produce such an effect is ideal.□ Including a non-climbable playhouse and other structures to encourage imaginative play could be considered. □An outdoor storage cupboard or box is ideal for storing loose materials in the social play area. Ensure that the children are under total supervision while playing here.
- **Quiet Play:** The Quiet Play Area also requires a balance between some shade for lengthy play in the sandbox and some exposure to the sun that will allow the sand to dry quickly after rain. Children can enjoy a quiet time out of doors for reflection, to discover the wonders of nature, or to read a book. The main elements for a quiet play area are sandplay, blockplay, seats, grass, and shade. □To accommodate block play, a soft surface can be provided conveniently near the building, so that noise can be controlled.

If several groups of children use the area and the space is limited, a schedule for using the playground should be provided so that all children are not outdoors at the same time. The outdoor area should be securely fenced with a non-splintering material and kept in good repair, with a gate that can be locked. Fences to be designed are to be non-climbable and aesthetically pleasing. It is to be ensured that there are no sharp edges or points protruding through the top of the fence.

8.7 PLAY EQUIPMENT

Play equipment is among the basic needs of a preschool. Play gives children emotional satisfaction. It keeps them occupied and prevents boredom. Play materials give the child opportunities for exploration and keep him happy and help to reduce his strains and anxieties. It has great intellectual value. It helps children learn, practice and develop new skills all the time. It teaches them to use their hands and coordinate them with their eyes. Play helps children to observe, concentrate and experiment. It teaches them how things are made and work, and how to take care of their possessions. It aids them to cooperate with others and develop friendly relationships. It helps them to learn to be honest, to lose with equality and team spirit. Outdoor play gives scope for exercise in the fresh air and thereby improves health and strength.

SELECTION OF PLAY EQUIPMENT

Toys are the tools for play and childhood is the age of toys. They need to be chosen carefully in order to facilitate learning. In selecting toys, parents, teachers and other adults must bear in mind the following points:

(*a*) The price of the play materials should be proportional to the value of play and to the expected life of the toy. A toy which is expensive but can remain in use for a long time, can actually be cheaper and more economical in the long run.

(*b*) The play equipment should be suitable to the age and maturity of the child, although developmental stages among children of the same age can vary.

(*c*) The size of the toy must be proportionate to the control, competence and safety of the child. Until the age of five years, the child needs simple large play materials. As his manual dexterity matures, he will be able to handle smaller and finer things.

(*d*) Toys should be sturdy and durable. Toys for long-term use must withstand hard wear and tear. It is important that children are helped to learn the important personal relationship of companionship with a toy, as well as, how to deal with delicate objects and protected from the sorrow of having a toy broken unintentionally.

(*e*) One of the basic principles involved in the selection of toys is safety. Although there is no absolute safety against accident and injury, reasonable precautions should be taken to avoid dangerous toys and materials. It is important to see that the toys themselves, or parts which can be detached are not sharp to hurt the child; that they are not so small that they can be inhaled or swallowed; that they are not easily flammable and that the paint does not come off.

(*f*) Simple toys usually hold more challenges than the complicated ones and have more different uses. The construction and the mechanism of the toy must be easy to understand and manipulate.

(*g*) In the choice of play materials, attention should be given to equipment that involves the use of large and small muscles and things that stimulate imagination, creativity and concentration. Children like best, the toys with which they can imitate familiar, adult activities.

Very few preschools can afford to have expensive equipment and materials. Much depends on the imagination, resourcefulness and creativity of the teacher. If resourceful, she can have a good collection of equipment and work materials for children's activities from the materials in the environment. Instead of selecting sophisticated and expensive equipment, the imaginative teacher should always go in for sturdy and easily replaceable play things. She should be constantly in search of new equipment and materials that will challenge the children. She should be well informed about the indigenous materials available in the surroundings and what could be bought from the market. Proper arrangement of play equipment would facilitate their use.

All the materials should be arranged attractively in the room and placed on low open shelves, so that children may take them out themselves. In this way, children will learn that there are fixed places for things to be kept and that they may take out any item they like from the storage places but they should put it back in place when the play is over. This, in turn, will help the children to learn to use and care for equipment and materials.

Proper care, maintenance and replacement of worn out equipment deserve constant attention from the preschool teacher. At the end of each term, the teacher should condemn worn out equipment and try to replace them. She should repair the broken toys, repaint the old and make them attractive, new and usable again. For this repair work, she can solicit the help of parents, who are good with tools. Many parents may like to contribute play materials to the school when their children grow up. The teacher can explore this possibility also.

8.8 THE PRESCHOOL PROGRAMME

"Foundation for children lies in what his early childhood education program teaches. The concept of kindergarten and preschool program is a set of uniquely developed programs that gives every child an opportunity to grow smarter physically and mentally." The true meaning of preschool education is to teach one to think for oneself. To live successfully, both knowledge and thinking are essential. Education trinity is knowledge, intelligence and thinking. Every preschool program must ensure that in addition to carefully selected and trained education, caregiver's links with family, home culture and home language are a central part of the program policy.

8.8.1. Importance of a good curriculum in preschool education :

With the advent of Internet in a great scale, teaching methodologies have undergone drastic change. Awareness about the importance of education has also increased. Playschools, preschools and nursery schools have emerged in a big way. Considering the busy lifestyle of parents and increasing number of nuclear families, preschools/nursery schools have become the first educational choice for the parents. With both father and mother working, especially in urban cities and metropolitans, parents have got no better alternative than sending their kids to early childhood education programs.

Though parents always play a major role in the child's learning process, preschools and kindergarten classrooms actually develop all the basic and essential skills of a child. It is a known fact that children learn at the fastest pace when they are between 0-6 years of age. This conclusion makes preschool/ nursery school early childhood curriculum development a very important issue. The different activities conducted in a preschool are specified as the programme or curriculum of the preschool. Meticulous planning is required in carrying out wholesome and appropriate learning programmes for these children. The goals for a preschool programme are short-term and long-term ones.

An ideal preschool or nursery curriculum in India should fulfill all the needs and requirements of toddlers. Because of the early age of preschoolers, curriculum should include a varied blend of songs, poems, reading, preschool worksheets, and writing and math exercises along with colorful preschool activities of fun. The various activities must help the child to develop better interpersonal relationships, acquire good sensory experiences, and kindle his curiosity regarding his physical surroundings, so that he is stimulated intellectually, develop his large and small muscles, and get opportunities to build up his language. Such pattern of curriculum help children in learning and developing their skills in all the fields. Children are quite captivated by playful activities and colorful objects. Thus, a proper preschool curriculum development helps in increasing good social skills and focuses on improving motor skills of the kids.

Curriculum development process must take into consideration all the aspects of a child's personality. The individual child is the basis for planning the programme for the group. Their abilities and maturation stages are very different and plans should be made accordingly. Celebration of national and community festivals and functions should find a place in the programme.

8.8.2. PRINCIPLES OF A PRESCHOOL PROGRAMME

There are a few principles to be followed while planning a preschool programme. They are :

- *The curriculum of a preschool programme should be such that it meets the objectives of preschool education* : A good early childhood curriculum places emphasis on learning through play, and therefore gives equal importance on the physical, cognitive, emotional and social development of the child.
- *The ultimate aim of a preschool curriculum is to cater to the individual needs of a child and develop his self-esteem through various methods*: The curriculum should be so framed to meet the growth norms of children at specific ages. The activity, which is appropriate for one stage of development, may be inappropriate for another. Planning above the development level of a child will frustrate him. Planning below his level will bore him. The readiness of the children must be determined and the plans built upon it.
- *The curriculum should be flexible to suit the requirements of the children:* The plans for the day should not be rigid. Allowance should be made for changes and additions, but by writing down the activity for the day, the teacher is aided to plan thoroughly. For example, if the school has arranged a new guest (magician) suddenly to entertain the children, the teacher should not hesitate to deviate from her regular schedule, so that the child will not miss the entertainment and feel happy to have visualized the show.
- *The curriculum should be planned cooperatively by all personnel involved:* If a copy of the plan is posted on the notice board, all the staff members can be aware of the activities planned for a particular day. Each day, before the preschool begins, the teachers should meet together for a few minutes and go over the plans for that day. In this way, they can make the day meaningful to the children.

- *The preschool activities should include both individual play as well as group activities:* Children should be given choice to participate in whatever they like. The program can help bring out the individual potential of the child, for example, assembling puzzles, but should not make the child less sociable. While children need to have freedom for self-development, there are values in being a member of a group. Therefore, there should be at least one activity, which will bring the children together as a group each day. Through interacting with other children, a child learns about interests and ideas of others. He also gains a more realistic self-concept, tries new techniques and adequately expresses himself verbally.
- *The program should include a combination of active and quiet play:* The preschool curriculum should have activities to meet the energetic child's vigour. They like to play in the sand pit, jungle gym or sliding board. But the teacher should check on the duration of active play so that a child must not get exhausted. So, the outdoor game should be limited and followed by some indoor activity like colouring or craft work. Similarly, a child cannot continue in quiet activity for a very long time. He may become restless. Therefore, a quiet activity should be followed by active play.
- *The preschool programme should be more purposeful:* The curriculum for the preschool children provides for teaching interrelated aspects simultaneously. The plans for each day should include free play (both indoors and outdoors), creative time for children to explore materials and express their feelings, sessions of music and story and eating time for snack or lunch. Intellectual stimulation, social relationship, muscle development and opportunities for language development need to be interwoven into these activities. By maintaining the required adult:child ratio, the activities planned for the children will become more purposeful, if not, the curriculum will not be suitable. Whatever the children are taught, should be associated to their familiar community, so that they learn some social skills needed by the society.
- *The programme should balance between free play as well as guided activities:* When the toddlers happen to get exposed to some new experience or activity, they learn to manipulate on their own. For example, if a child finds a new mechanical toy, he may throw it, bang it on the floor, insert various objects into and out of it, but may not be able to operate it initially.. He may still use it as a pushing toy. Gradually, with some cues given by the teacher, such as, using the key found along with the toy, or pressing a button, the child may learn to start the device aptly. Therefore, the teacher should help with basic guidelines and then allow freedom to experiment on their own.
- *The preschool programme should provide for hands-on skills experience:* The child's understanding is at a sensory-perceptual level, during the preschool stage. Providing the children with opportunities for exploring, grouping and segregating, enables first-hand experience. This gives better understanding to gain knowledge for the kids. Children learn many aspects through play-way method. Therefore, the programme should be based accordingly.

A good preschool curriculum should offer many learning opportunities correlated with children's readiness and interests. Good teaching does not just happen – it is the result of careful planning and foresight. Creative and meticulous planning is required in carrying out wholesome and appropriate learning programmes for preschool children. The goals for a preschool programme are short-term and long-term ones.

Long-term planning: This involves planning a programme that could cater to the entire academic year, during which the teacher must consider about the learning activities, equipments and play materials required, budget allocated and other extra-curricular facilities. This plan is developed based on the important goal of the preschool in mind, and the steps to be taken to achieve the final goal. One has to wisely decide about the ways to procure the requisites, cost effectiveness, physical and financial constraints, and the ultimate motive.

Short-term planning: To attain the target of the long term curriculum, the teacher has to divide the plan into various smaller entities, and determine the period and duration of the year when it has to be conducted. For example, the children should have more of classroom activities only, which are mostly oral and fun based in the first term. This helps the children to get acquainted with the new environment outside the home. Gradually, some amount of writing, outdoor visits and experiments can be introduced in the second or third term. By now, the children get accustomed to the nursery school and the other children.

Short term planning includes weekly planning which consists of daily planning for the whole week. The various materials, aids, objects required for each day's activities, the essential communication with the parents, if required, and the individual needs of the children in that particular class, are all taken into consideration. The alterations should be done as and when necessary.

Table 8.2 The daily programme for a preschool

Hours	Activities
8.00-8.10	Arrival of the teacher
8.10-8.30	Arrival of the children
8.30-8.45	Morning Prayer & Mini Exercise
8.45-9.30	Independent Work (creative activity)
9.30-10.00	Group work(drawing/colouring)
10.00-10.15	Break- recess time
10.15-10.45	Music, Rhymes
10.45-11.30	Writing work
11.30-12.00	Reading / oral classes
12.00-12.45	Lunch break
12.45-1.00	Large group activity/reading
1.00-2.00	Nap/Quiet Activities
2.00-2.15	Break- recess time
2.15-2.45	Story Session
2.45-3.30	Outdoor play activities
3.30 onwards	Dismissal-bags

Taking into account the age, interests and abilities of the children enrolled, a flexible schedule can be planned as given in the table.

8.8.3. ACTIVITIES AND PROGRAMS

Some of the activities mentioned in the curriculum for preschool education can be described as follows:

Music: Music is one great way for children to vent out their feelings. Developing an appreciation for music will be a life-long asset. Sound is found all around the world, such as the chirping of birds, the drizzling of the rain, beat of the vessels in the kitchen, the ticking of the clock, the sound of specific music on television shows or advertisements, and the ringing of the telephone bell, the hooting sound of vehicles and so on. Every sound is music to a listening child.

A child can be encouraged to use instruments, such as strings and percussion to help him in large or small muscular activities. Music can change his temper, mood and expression. By helping the children observe the activities around them, such as walking of a duck or the ticking of a clock, they can be helped to gain concepts of rhythm, incorporate music in their lives and appreciate many things, which ordinarily go unnoticed. When a child enjoys playing music along with other children, it promotes his social development.

Literature (Language, stories and books)

There are 10 reasons for literature to be included in the curriculum of the preschool children .

- It serves as a foundation for academic excellence, in general.
- It aids in better communication skills.
- It is a good exercise for the brains, as it strengthens brain connections and actually builds new connections.
- Reading improves concentration in toddlers, along with which comes a stronger self-discipline, longer attention span, and better memory retention, all of which helps the child when she enters school.
- Language enhances a child's vocabulary, enabling him to learn new words as well as automatically get the knowledge of sentence formations and ways of using words and language effectively.
- Storybooks help to develop a child's imagination, from the description of characters, places and things read in the story and the pictures accompanying it.
- Stories also teach children to develop empathy. The child identifies with the character in the story and imagines himself to be in the same situation.
- Literature helps to share experiences and thereby build good social relationships.
- Books opens the vision of children to the outside world. It promotes aesthetic appreciation for the children .
- Reading relaxes the body and calms the mind. Unlike the television , computer, any electronic media or games in which the bright lights affect the eyes, reading enables quieter activity.

Science-based literature should be chosen carefully with attention to both literacy and science concerns in mind. With these considerations in mind, Zeece (1999) recommends choosing books with the following criteria in mind:

- current, factual content;
- clear and simple explanations;
- depth and complexity of subject matter closely matched to the developmental and interest level of children in the group;
- beautifully presented illustrations and narrative;
- content consistent with overall philosophy of the program; and
- completeness and ease of use allowing children to answer questions and/or explore ideas effectively.

Science Experience

Young children are naturally curious and passionate about learning. In their pursuit of knowledge, they are prone to poking, pulling, tasting, pounding, shaking, and experimenting. "From birth, children want to learn and they naturally seek out problems to solve".

They want to know what makes the wind blow, how trees grow, why fish have fins, and where turtles go in the winter. They may not want adults to give them the answers but would like to be the discoverers, the experimenters, and the theory builders. They don't want science to be something that is imparted to them; they want it to be something that they do. They want to be scientists; not just consumers of science. They may ask their own questions, collect their own information and arrive at new and wonderful ideas. These "desires" should outline the foundation of an early childhood science curriculum.

By observing, listening, exploring and performing, the various concepts of physical and biological science could be learnt by the toddlers in their preschool activities. Knowledge about equipments, animals, plants, human beings, food patterns and so on are gained through proper inclusion of this information in the preschool curriculum.

Science experiences kindle the curiosity of preschool children, enabling the idea of exploring, experimenting, raising issues and trying to get solutions for their problems. The children gain these attributes through proper first- hand-experiences, and together all these aid in improving their all-round development. The children also become aware of various tools, models and equipments, and learn the art of manipulating them.

Development of Scientific Thinking could be promoted by

(a) Science as Active Exploration

Science for young children should involve asking questions, probing for answers, conducting investigations, and collecting data. This approach allows children to become engaged in the investigative nature of science and to experience the joy of having wonderful ideas.

(b) Discovery Learning

Developing new concepts or ideas is an active process and usually begins with child-centered inquiry, which focuses on the asking of questions relevant to the child. While inquiry involves a number of science-related activities and skills, the focus is on the active search for knowledge or understanding to satisfy students' curiosity. A far more important objective is to help children realize that answers about the world can be discovered through their own investigations.

(c) Science Goals

Desired goals of science in the early childhood curriculum include what we hope children will attain or achieve. Adults should support the children sincerely in practicing and applying these skills in a variety of activities throughout the day, by providing a variety of materials and settings that invite experimentation.

In the New Approach to Science, Science is viewed as active exploration, where the teacher is viewed as facilitator. The topics of study are based on child interests and related to their experiences. The curricula is designed so as to blend with other areas of study.

Some of the science concepts typically taught during the Preschool Years* according to Kilmer & Hofman (1995) are:

- **Systems (groups or collections having some influence on one another)** e.g.: parts of the human body; ecosystems (where animals and plants live interdependently)
- **Models (representations of real objects or phenomenon)** e.g.: word descriptions or drawings; physical models
- **Constancy and Change (how things change over time)** e.g.: seed to plant; different seasons; growth and decay
- **Scale (focusing on characteristics and comparisons)** e.g.: size; distance; quantity; weight
- **Patterns and Relationships (structure and organization of matter)** e.g.: properties of materials; alike and different comparisons; patterns in nature
- **Cause and Effect relationships(explanations for phenomena)** e.g.: shadows; freezing/ melting; gravity
- **Structure and Function (relationship between characteristic and action)** e.g.: makeup of plants and animals; tools; eating utensils
- **Variations (discontinuous and continuous properties)** e.g.: sounds; colors
- **Diversity (variety of types)** e.g.: seeds; leaves; living organisms

Excursion

An excursion well planned and conducted can help in the developmental progress of preschool children. The place selected for the excursion should suit the type of background, number, age and interests of the children. The place should have been visited by the teacher prior to the excursion, so that it will help in the right planning of the programme. Proper mode of transport is important for the trip, to reduce fatigue for the children. While arranging for transportation, safety of the vehicle and the requisites of the driver (such as his license, insurance, etc.,) should be ensured. The duration of the trip should not be too much or too little. It should give ample space for nurturing the curiosity of the children, without creating tiredness.

The importance of planning excursions for children are

- To give them live experiences of the various concepts they are learning, to suit their developmental level

- To construct good relationships among their peer group by creating group experiences
- To help in broadening the ideas and concepts they have learnt
- To have fun and joy, with thrilling experiences
- To make them conscious of certain issues happening in the world around them
- To develop and improve their curiosity and creativeness

8.9 TEACHING AND NON-TEACHING STAFF IN A PRESCHOOL

8.9.1 The Role of a Nursery School Teacher

An important role of the nursery school teacher is to identify the developmental stages of every child in her class and plan for various experiences. To acquaint children with music, literature or scientific experiences, the teacher should be initially familiar with many songs, stories and books available in the market so that she can pick and choose, what is essential. To enhance the habit of reading, the teacher should display colourful books in one corner of the classroom, so that the children become curious to take them and read. The teacher should have good principles in selecting books for the nursery children.

The teacher should persuade children to use musical instruments and help them to be creative rather than be monotonous. She should kindle their love for music by repetition of the musical notes in various activities of the school program, such as storytelling, dramatic play or during exercise. She should help the children in releasing their pent up emotions, like anger, antagonism, fear, joy or appreciation, by providing them such music experiences.

Similarly, storytelling is another way in which a teacher can interact with the children and develop better interpersonal relationships. The children could be taught various moral values through this form. But, the duration spent in story telling should be flexible according to the interests of the children. If they are happily responding, the teacher can continue, if not, she can make the session short.

To foster scientific thinking, teachers should view young children as active learners and give them varied opportunities to explore and experiment. Children need access to materials that they can take apart and the tools to assist them in doing so. They need places where they can dig in the dirt and dip water from a pond. They also need magnifying glasses, measuring tools, buckets, and frequent access to the natural world. Such opportunities will allow children to construct meaning and develop understandings that are not only valid but also valuable to their on-going intellectual development. An environment that fosters scientific thinking is one that gives young children the time, space, and materials to exercise their curiosity. It also gives them the freedom to engage in child-centered explorations, experimentations, and explanations.

Sufficient adult supervision is essential during excursions and therefore, atleast, one teacher for five children is ideal. One teacher should stay back in the school premises, if one or two children do not participate in the excursion. If necessary, a few parents' help could be sought to handle the varied nature of children during the excursion. It is customary to ascertain the permission of parents with a circular for allowing their child for the trip.

Children should be well prepared about the excursion, only a few days ahead, to avoid distraction in the classroom. They could be given an outline about what they will be observing, how to behave during the visit and how they can enjoy. During the next classroom session, the teacher should discuss about the trip with the children, to assess its usefulness. Some suggestions for the places of visit for preschool children could be parks, zoo, aquarium, gardens, musical events, flower shows, and circus.

8.9. 2. Qualities of an Ideal Preschool Teacher:

A class managed by an ideal preschool teacher should be full of lively, interested and positive children who can achieve high standards. A child's preschool experience is his or her introduction to the world of education. As a preschool teacher, it is her responsibility to provide kids with a safe, fun environment where they can express themselves creatively, make new friends and adjust to spending part of the day without their mommies and daddies. Teaching preschool is certainly not easy, although most teachers say the job gets easier with experience. Nonetheless, there are a number of essential qualities that make a successful preschool teacher.

A good teacher will be a friend, an elderly playmate, a guide, a mother or a sister. The teacher plays an important role in molding and shaping the personality of the child. They will be interested and have lots of self – discipline and self confidence. The normal adult- child ratio in a preschool is expected to be around 1:15. To play their part effectively, the teacher is expected to possess these qualities:

1. A teacher should have **calmness** which consists of spiritual humility and intellectual purity i.e her mind should not be possessed by obsessions, complexes, prejudices or superstitions and must have an objective outlook.
2. Educational qualifications may vary by state, but most states require that preschool teachers hold at least an associate's degree and, in many cases, a **bachelor's degree.** A background in education is essential, and a good candidate for a preschool teaching position will have taken higher education classes in the fields of psychology, childhood development, education, classroom management, and curriculum.
3. Quality of a teacher in preschool depends also on the amount of her **love for the teaching profession;** the teacher should feel the importance of her profession. She should use various teaching aids and adopt proper methods of teaching.
4. **Experience** working with young children is one of the keys to being a successful preschool teacher. Often the best preschool teachers are those who grew up around younger siblings, have worked in camps and schools or have raised children of their own.
5. A good preschool teacher should also have a good **memory power.** Being intelligent is a must, but a good quality of a teacher lies in her memory power as she handles many students at one time. She should never enter class without preparing herself. However able and experienced is the teacher, she could never succeed without her preliminary preparation.
6. The success of a class teacher in the class also depends on the **art of questioning.** Fewer commands should be given to the students and when given, they must be stuck to; otherwise they lose their effectiveness.
7. Preschool teacher should work on their **voice quality;** the voice of a teacher should be clear, moderately pitched and well modulated. A thin low voice develops dullness and monotony in the class. A very high-pitched voice or a shrill must be avoided as it distracts the minds of the students.
8. "While books can teach, only personality can educate", says an educationist. Children imitate the dress, habits, manners, and voice of their teachers. The teacher has to be concerned with the total development of the child. A good teacher will make it a point to be **punctual** in every work.
9. A teacher must understand the needs of both the children and their parents. As the link between home and school, **communicating** effectively with parents is crucial to developing a good relationship with the children and helping them grow.
10. Teachers in a preschool should not show undue favor to someone. All should be equal in her eyes. **Partiality** to some students will lead to frustrations among others.

11. **Management** of a classroom full of young children can be very challenging. The teacher has to gain the respect of the children without scaring them. She should be their friend but should also treat them as an authority figure just as their parents. A successful preschool teacher is able to control a classroom while always keeping things educational and fun. Organization is extremely important.
12. She has to deal with a large number of students having a low and high power of understanding. She may have to repeat her lessons many a time for the sake of the less intelligent children. She should not be irritated in doing so. A good teacher should always possess required **patience** to make them understand gradually.
13. A teacher should **never laugh** at her pupils. She should laugh with them and also see that they laugh with her and not at her.
14. Above all, to be a successful preschool teacher, one should really believe in what she is doing. The teacher should **care tremendously** about the progress and well-being of each and every child in the classroom. Teaching preschool can be tiring and stressful, but it is also incredibly rewarding in the end. A bad experience in preschool can really compromise a child's educational future, so the teacher should always do her best to encourage children and foster their learning. On the other hand, no teacher is perfect and therefore, one should not get too discouraged when she makes mistakes now and then.

8.9.3. Other Personnel:

The number and nature of other personnel involved in a preschool vary according to the type and location of a preschool. **Preschool assistants** are those persons involved in the classroom activities along with the children, helping them to do their work, maintaining cleanliness in the classroom, and assisting the teacher in carrying out her routine. The assistant guides the children while they are having lunch or playing. They should be persons having patience and knowledge about the needs of children, so that they can take care of them. **A cook** is also essential for certain preschools such as the laboratory nursery school or those run as Balwadis and anganwadis. The preschool teacher plans the menu and under her supervision, food is prepared and served. The persons handling food should maintain perfect hygiene and have some awareness of nutritious and tasty food. If the required formal training is not possessed by the cook, sufficient in-service training should be given. Most of the preschools may have another **helper** who is required to keep the premises clean. She needs to take care of cleaning the toilet or wash room, as well as the classroom floor effectively.

8.10. RECORDS AND REPORTS FOR A PRESCHOOL

While planning about the administration of a preschool, it is essential to remember the records and registers that have to be maintained. Records are useful to improve one's understanding of children in the preschool, as well as the effective management in running the school. The recording of data regarding academic performance and developmental aspects of normal and deviant behavior of children by the preschool teacher, will be of great use for future reference. The knowledge about health status of children, dietary and other major setbacks in the family background, along with skills acquired by the child are all of great importance for the welfare of the children, in their succeeding classes. Evaluation of the various talents of the children, the preschool personnel and aids used for curricular and extra-curricular activities can guide in enhancing the progress of the preschool. Records help in modifying the curriculum and they are also a good source of data for research. Records normally maintained in the preschool are:

Admission Record: This register maintains details regarding the date of enrollment of the child into the school, along with age, sex, religion and mother tongue and so on. Other background information about the child such as father's name and occupation, the economic status of the family, and the number of siblings are also obtained. On one corner of the admission form, the date of registration and number on the waiting list at the time of registration is recorded. Similarly, at the time of withdrawal, the date, age and reasons for withdrawal are recorded.

Attendance Record: The details regarding attendance of children as well as the staff employed are maintained in two different registers. An analysis of the reasons for long absenteeism of the children, if any, can be studied and necessary remedial measures be taken.

Health Record: The systematic recording of height and weight measurements of every child, with other information on dental and nutritional defects are made note of in the health record. In addition, they are to give information regarding the immunization record of the children. In case, the required vaccinations had not been given to the child, the parents are advised to get these done, before the child is sent to school.

Stock Record: Proper details about the various items maintained in the preschool is recorded in this register. Consumables such as crayons, chalk piece box, uniform material and more permanent items such as furniture, blackboard, etc, and other materials like mats, toys, are entered in different type of register each, with the date of purchase and cost of the item. This would be of great use in the future, to plan for the curriculum and budget of next academic year.

Record of teacher's assessment of each child: Individual data about the advance of each child in academics, behavior, creativity, skills and all round development is noted periodically, along with the comment of the teacher. This record helps to bring out the potential of the child in its later years or to spare more attention regarding certain specific areas.

Record of group experience: The teacher maintains the entry of various activities conducted in the preschool, mentioning the participation of every child. When children are taken for field visits and excursions, it is made note of in this register, so that it will be useful to judge the awareness of the children and also ascertain some of his good qualities and bad behavior.

Other Records: Information about the record of home visit of the teacher with the date and purpose, record of parent-teacher meetings held in school, record of information gathered informally by the teacher regarding the child, such as his sickness, habits, interests, discipline enforced at home and so on are entered in this register. Such details give a clear picture of the child and his family so that it helps in further research when required.

8.11. IMPORTANCE OF PRESCHOOL TEACHERS' AND PARENTS' CO-OPERATION

"Children learn from both, preschool teachers in school and parents at home. A proper co-operation between teachers and parents is a key for a healthy child growth and early childhood education". Therefore this co-operation becomes so important.

8.11.1.Home school relations

There was a time when teachers regarded parents as a necessary evil in education. But now, it is understood that the family has a noteworthy role in the development of the personalities of children. Only when the teacher works through the parents, she can create a healthy and favorable environment in the preschool. The modern educator seeks the active interest and co-operation of parents in the education of their children. The new school realizes the importance that home and school share a mutual interest and responsibility in the child's total living and that without co-operation of home and school, they cannot be successful in educating the child. The result is that parents and teachers must meet in small or large groups to discuss their common problems. In some schools, parents assist in the office and classroom; they participate in field trips and many other social and community undertakings.

8.11.2.Home visits

Home visits, sending return materials, individual conferences or counseling, parents meetings, observing and participating in the school programme and other means can be used effectively in parent education. As the home is the basic social instituition, home visits are one of the effective methods used in parent education programme from time immemorial. The basic objective of home visit is to help establish a friendly rapport with the parents and children. The second purpose is to make the parents see that the teacher's zeal is focused on the welfare of their child. A friendly social visit will make the child, as well as the parents feel comfortable. Thus the home visits and the information collected thereby about the home background of the children is necessary for the guidance of the child.

8.11.3. Individual Meetings / Interviews with parents:

It is the duty of the preschool teacher to educate the parents also. Teachers should help the parents to gain confidence in themselves to play the role of parenthood effectively, and to learn more about their children. The teacher is perhaps the best agent through whom new trends could be communicated to the parents. For this purpose she should arrange special lectures, cinema shows, exhibitions etc. in the school, and the parents should be invited. The parents may have their own special problems that they want to communicate to the teachers. It is only when there are free and frequent connections between the parents and the teacher that all the problems concerning the education of the child can be solved. Even a shy parent who does not express himself in public forum may be willing to talk when met alone. Teachers need to get co-operation from the parents in order to discharge their duties. Every preschool has the obligation to integrate its educational programme with the child's education at home. In the interest of pupils, a teacher should have intimate relationship with parents by organizing Parent- Teacher Associations (PTA). Parents and teachers are associates in this great task, and therefore should work together to make it a success. The ways in which the cooperation of parents- teachers take place depend on the main objective of the preschool, its type and socio-economic status.

If these goals are achieved, the children will have a nourishing, rich and full life in the school and at home.

QUESTIONS

SECTION "A"

Short Answer Type:

1. What is the need for pre-school education?
2. What is meant by adult-child ratio?
3. What is meant by records and reports for a pre-school child?
4. What is meant by home school relations?
5. Discuss the motor development during the preschool stage.
6. Plan a day's schedule for a nursery school.
7. Role of teacher- Explain.
8. Write about the daily programme for a pre-school child.
9. List out some play equipments for the pre-schoolers.

SECTION "B"

One Page Answer Type:

1. What are the aims and objectives of a preschool?
2. Explain the plan of the pre-school building.
3. Write a short note on selection of play equipment.
4. Bring out the responsibilities of a pre-school teacher.
5. List out the planning programmes for children.
6. Plan a programme for a pre-schooler.
7. Explain any six principles of programme planning in a nursery school.

SECTION "C"

Essay Answer Type:

1. What are the principles of a pre-school programme?
2. Write in detail about the selection of a site and building for a preschool.
3. How does a nursery school promote the overall development of a pre-school child?
4. Discuss the social and language development in pre-school stage.
5. Describe the various types of preschools in India.
6. Examine the various records and registers maintained in a preschool.
7. Elaborate on the importance of parent-teacher co-operation.

UNIT — V

CHAPTER

9

LATE CHILDHOOD (6-12 YEARS)

OBJECTIVES

To enlighten students about:

- Concept of late childhood period
- Developmental tasks
- Characteristics
- Growth and development details – physical, motor, emotional, language, social, cognitive and moral
- Physical and psychological hazards during the period

9.1 CONCEPT OF LATE CHILDHOOD PERIOD

The middle to late childhood years span the period between preschool period and adolescence. It is defined as a period that falls from about 6 to 12 years for girls and from 6 to 14 for boys. It is summarized as the school years because almost all over the world children at this age go to some kind of school or receive some kind of education. Children in the age group 9 to 12 years (late childhood) are becoming "pre adolescents." There are greater refinements in behavior and conspicuous strides in maturity. Children become marked by self-confidence during these years. Children are eager to learn, they apply their knowledge of numbers, words, and concepts more and more effectively, pick up on skills quickly, and begin to think logically as long as what they are thinking about is not too advanced. This is a turbulent time in development when growth trends begin to speed up and the behavior of children seem to deteriorate.

Children become critical of adults and especially their parents. They rebel against performing routine chores and tasks and often strive for unreasonable independence from adult controls. Relation with peers becomes intense. The importance of peer groups increases for the individual during this stage and social skills also develop rapidly as children are usually found in the group of selected peers. Failure to be recognized or accepted by peers can be a crushing experience for children at this age. Girls may discover the attraction of boys and become preoccupied with getting their attention. Boys show a slower growing interest in girls but reciprocate that of girls by showing off, teasing, and demonstrating their daring behavior. Towards the end of this period, sexual differences become more pronounced. Children see their parents as helpful, teachers as fair, and their friends as loyal. They develop a concrete sense of right or wrong. However, some children face difficulties such as learning disabilities or change in family structures.

9.2 DEVELOPMENTAL TASKS

During the years of middle childhood, as the child meets the world, he is moved by what Havinghurst means 3 outward pushes.

1. The social thrust from the home to the peer group environment
2. The physical thrust into a world of games and of work demanding neuromuscular skills, for legs, handwriting, and
3. The intellectual thrust into the world of adult ideas, symbolism and communication.

Out of these pushes, emerged the developmental tasks of middle childhood, which are

- Learning physical skills necessary for ordinary games
- Building wholesome attitudes toward oneself as a growing organism
- Learning to get along with age – mates
- Learning an appropriate masculine or feminine role
- Developing the basic skills of reading, writing and arithmetic
- Developing concepts necessary for daily living as tools of thought
- Developing conscience, a sense of morality and of values
- Achieving personal independence
- Developing the ability to choose and
- Developing attitudes towards social groups and institutions.

9.3 CHARACTERISTICS OF LATE CHILDHOOD

Parents, educators and psychologists apply various names to late childhood and these names reflect the important characteristics of this period.

1. It is a "*quarrelsome age*": Many parents regard late childhood as the "troublesome age" the time when children are no longer willing to do what they are told to do and when they are more influenced by their peers than by their parents and other family members. Many parents regard late childhood as the "quarrelsome age"- the time when family fights are common and when the emotional climate of the home is far from pleasant for family members.

Parents must now change their style of interaction with the child to be an effective caregiver. Personal adjustment of the adults in the family are focused on revising goals set earlier in life and establishing new ones for the future. The period is one of challenge for the entire family; the individual during middle childhood thus faces a number of basic tasks in developing as a person.

2. It is an "*elementary school age*": Educators call late childhood as "elementary school age". It is the time when the child is expected to acquire the rudiments of knowledge that are considered essential for successful adjustment to adult life.

Educators also regard late childhood as a "critical period" in the achievement drive - a time when children form the habit of being achievers, underachievers or overachievers. The tempo of developmental change slows in the period of middle childhood which begins at about the age of six and continues until the individual is twelve. Here, the teacher becomes a powerful influence in the individual's development .

3. It is a "*gang age*" and "*creative age*": Psychologists label late childhood as "*creative age*". It is a time for a child's active discovery of the world and while making things and getting experience with such activities, friends become very important to an individual.

This age group is considered as "*gang age*", as there is a gang spirit in which the major concern is the acceptance by the age-mates in a gang. There is a team spirit in play activities and creative works.

4. Late childhood is also frequently called the "*play age*", not because more time is devoted to play than at any other age, which would be impossible after the child enters school- but rather because there is an overlapping of play activities characteristic of younger years and those characteristic of adolescence.

9.4 PHYSICAL DEVELOPMENT

In contrast to the rapid increase in height and weight during the first years of life, physical development takes place in a less dramatic rate and proceeds at a slower pace during middle *childhood*. The secular trend is generally based on improved nutrition, although emotional stress tends to interfere. Boys and girls who mature earlier showed greater self-confidence, more matter of factness, and more maturity in social situations and late maturing individuals were expressive, talkative, eager, and attention-getting. The fact remains that children are maturing earlier than few decades ago, which means that the period of childhood is growing shorter.

Sex difference in physical growth relatively varies slightly in early years, but become more pronounced in late childhood. Because boys begin their puberty growth spurt approximately a year later than girls, they tend to be slightly shorter and lighter in weight than girls of the same age until they too become sexually mature. Girls also get their permanent teeth slightly earlier than boys, while boy's head and face grow larger than girls. Children double their strength capabilities during these years because of greater number of muscle cells, and boys tend to be stronger than girls. Changes in proportions are among the most pronounced physical changes in middle and late childhood

Pattern of physical development in late childhood are assessed by the following factors:

Height and weight changes: Both boys and girls can be expected to grow about two to three inches each year during middle childhood. The average height for boys is slightly greater than that of girls throughout the period. However, girls' average height between ten and twelve years exceeds that of boys. At the onset of puberty, an average 11 year old girl has a height of 58" while an average boy of the same age has 57.5" as height .

By 6 years of age, most children are about seven times their birth weight. Weight increase is at the rate of 3-5 (1.3 – 2.3 kg.) or more pounds annually. The average 11 year old girl weighs 88.5 pounds (40.1 kg.) and an average boy of the same age weighs 85.5 pounds (38.7 kg.). Girls begin the process of attaining sexual maturity roughly two to three years before this process begins in boys. The average age of menarche (experiencing the first menstrual period) is reported to be about twelve and a half years in girls.

Body proportions: Body shapes of individuals are characterized by a greater proportion of body fat to muscle among females, while the opposite is true for males. Facial disproportions disappear as the mouth and jaw become larger, the forehead broadens and flattens, the lips fill out, and the nose becomes larger and acquires more shape. The trunk elongates and becomes slimmer, the neck becomes longer, the chest broadens, the abdomen flattens, the arms and legs lengthen and hands and feet grow larger but at a slow rate. Children are tremendously active physically and gradually display a steady improvement in motor coordination. Unhappily, all children are not so fortunate. By the end of the middle childhood period, the youngster's body is more in proportion and is more like an adult.

Muscle fat: The increasing level and desire for physical activity in middle childhood reflects the increasing size and strength of a child's muscles. Gain in weight is due to increase in size of skeletal and muscular systems, as well as size of some organs. Muscle mass and strength gradually increases as "baby fat" decreases in middle and late childhood. Throughout the middle years, boys have more muscle tissue, and girls have more fat; muscle growth tends to be extremely rapid , not only in changing composition but also becoming more firmly attached to the bones. Despite these advances, the muscles at times continue to remain immature in function. The fitness and development of muscles depends not only on good physical care, rest and activity but also upon their structure and the use that is made of them. Proper nerve and muscle development provides increasing steadiness of movement, speed, strength and endurance.

Body size and type, muscular strength, and athletic ability serve as criteria for acceptance by the peer group among boys. Developmental maturity is associated with prestige and acceptance among girls.

Dentition: One of the most apparent physical changes in middle childhood relates to dentition, or the process of losing existing teeth and erupting new ones. The primary or deciduous teeth that erupted during infancy and early childhood are lost during the school-age years, when the permanent teeth begin to replace the primary teeth between the ages of six to thirteen. Except for the third molars ("wisdom teeth"), all permanent teeth should have come by the end of middle childhood. Also, the loss of baby teeth and the emergence of permanent teeth change the shape of the lower jaw. Girls' permanent teeth erupt earlier than boys' in keeping with the generally more rapid rate of development in girls.

Bone development: Earlier, the child's bones were soft and spongy consisting mostly of cartilage, but now the mineral salts give hardness and rigidity to the bones. As a child approaches sexual maturity in the latter years of middle childhood, the rate of bone development will quicken in response to stimulation from the sex hormones than being produced in large quantities. Bone growth occurs at the ends of epiphyses producing changes in length. Growth in the outermost edges of bones of periosteum produces changes in width. Throughout the years of childhood, cartilaginous tissue at the epiphyses continues to be replaced by the process of ossification, or the depositing of minerals and other substances which give bones their hardened condition and strength as well as their final mature shape. This process of bone development continues until the individuals' twenties. In addition, females lead males in the rate of bone development throughout the growing years of childhood until maturity is reached.

Brain development: Most of the brain's development occurs during the prenatal stage of an individual's life. Myelination is the process that brings nerve and brain cells "on line" to function efficiently. Essentially, it involves the depositing of fatty matter around these cells. During middle childhood the reticular formation of the brain should complete its myelination process. This brain structure is responsible for maintaining the stages of attention, consciousness (wakefulness), and sleep. The second feature of brain development in middle childhood is the organization of the brain's functioning.

Heart: The heart grows at a very slow pace although by the school years, its weight has increased approximately five times. The heart is now smaller in proportion to body size than at any other point in the person's lifespan. The heart rate, relatively greater through the early years, declines gradually during the later years. Rates of respiration also exhibit a decrease, shifting from 20-30 inhalations/minute during the pre-school period to approximately 17-22 inhalations in the middle years.

Two important aspects that can have an impact on this age group are:

I. Nutrition

The physical picture of the middle childhood youngster is one of energy and growing motor skills. Parents often worry that the child is not eating enough, but given the slower growth rate of these years, less food is needed. Rather, it is the quality of the food that is important; junk foods and excessive fats and sugars are to be avoided.

Vegetarian diets are in many ways desirable, but care must be taken that nutrients such as iron and zinc are obtained. Also, some fat is necessary, and if the fat content of a diet falls below 20 percent, growth can be stunted. At the other extreme, obesity has many adverse consequences.

II. Obesity

With a slower growth rate, children need fewer calories. Although their need for protein, vitamins, and minerals remain high, some children begin to accumulate empty calories from high-sugar and high-fat foods. Thus, obesity, with its social, psychological, and medical consequences, looms on the horizon. Recent research indicated that children who are overweight between the ages of 10 and 17 years will probably have a lifetime problem regardless of whether their parents were thin or fat. To help their children avoid obesity, parents should follow several safeguards. They should carefully monitor their children's time spent watching television; the sarcastic label "couch potato" is, unfortunately, all too true, given the tendency to munch while watching.

- Encourage appropriate physical activity on a year-round basis.
- Serve as much fruit and vegetables as possible.
- Watch fat intake because it is the most concerned source of calories.
- Start early to make children aware of what they're eating.
- If a child is overweight, don't become obsessed with it; remember that obesity may well be a genetic problem.

Variables such as genetic influence, health, and nutrition may also cause wide fluctuations in the growth of these children. Two youngsters may show considerable physical variation and yet both are perfectly normal. Consequently, although most children achieve the major development milestones, development may well differ among cultures, subcultures, and ethnic groups.

9.5 MOTOR SKILL DEVELOPMENT

The elementary school age children, eager to participate in strenuous activities that require large muscle movement are now able to become proficient in many new areas. Motor skills continue to develop and become refined and extended in middle childhood. A study by Goodenough showed that speed of response increases steadily throughout these years, along with increase in strength. By this age, however, children in most non-literate and transitional societies go to work, and this coupled with more household labor, especially for girls, leave them little time and freedom for physical play . They spend more time in free, unstructured activities, such as rough-and-tumble play and informal games, and more time in organized sports. At times, vigorous play that involves wrestling, kicking, tumbling, grappling and sometimes chasing, often accompanied by laughing and screaming are also common. This kind of play peaks in middle childhood; the proportion typically drops to about 5 percent at age 11, about the same as in early childhood.

Boys around the world engage in rough-and-tumble play more than girls do, a fact generally attributed to a combination of hormonal differences and socialization. Exercise-or lack of it- affects both physical and mental health. It improves strength and endurance, helps build healthy bones and muscles, helps control weight, reduces anxiety and stress, and increases self-confidence.

To help children improve their motor skills, they should participate in organized athletic programs which offer the chance to try a variety of sports. It should gear coaching to building skills rather than winning games, and should include as many children as possible rather than concentrating on a few star athletes.

Motor development through the middle childhood period is characterized by steady, regular improvements in coordination and performance. Williams and Stith (1980) identify eight basic components of motor development during this period.

- Strength, or the ability to exert force,
- Flexibility- refers to the degree of freedom in bending or moving the body.
- Impulsion -relates the rate of beginning body movements from a stationary position.

- Speed -is the rate of movement once body action is started.
- Precision -in motor development involves dexterity and accuracy of movements.
- Coordination, -or the ability to use muscle groups together to accomplish specific movements, is closely associated with precision.
- The ability to balance.
- The ability to display rhythm -increases slowly during middle childhood until about age eight. Girls exceed boys in rhythmic movements involving the feet.

By 6 years, most children can skip-rope and begin to ride a bicycle and by 7 years- most begin to perfect the movements necessary for catching, throwing, swimming and hitting baseball. They develop flexibility in different parts like wrist, legs etc. Their speed of movement and balancing ability is professionalized. The motor skills acquired at this stage are categorized into self-help skills, social help skills, school help skills and play skills.

Self-help skills: Older children of this age are able to eat, dress, bathe and groom themselves with almost as much speed and adeptness as an adult, without much attention from elders.

Social-help skills: These skills relate to helping adults such as making beds, dusting and sweeping at home and emptying wastebaskets and cleaning chalkboards at school and also in helping to prepare for play activities.

School help skills: The child develops skills required for drawing, writing, painting, clay modeling, dancing, sewing, cooking and woodworking.

Play skills: Grown up children learn to throw and catch balls, ride a bicycle, skate and swim better than in preschool school stage.

There is a similar increase in strength with age. Thus, among measures of motor development there is a tendency for the stronger to be taller, faster, and healthier than the weaker child. Differences may arise for children who feel that they are physically different from others such as being short or tall, thin or fat. Being different from a group frequently represents a potential hazard to the child's social and emotional development and adjustment. The physical differences of some children, which occur from differences in rates of maturation, may become a prominent problem.

Box 9-1 Common Motor Skills of Middle Childhood

Common Motor Skills of Middle Childhood

Upper region body skills

Children may be expected to learn skills involving the hands, arms, and back. These include writing, playing musical instruments, performing household chores (washing dishes, sweeping floors, and so on), and using tools, cooking, and drawing, for example.

Lower region body skills

Children improve in their ability to use their legs, thighs, and feet, as in running, hopping, jumping, and dancing, for example.

Total body skills

Some motor skills involve use of the major muscle groups of the entire body such as those found in swimming, playing ball games, skating, and related activities.

9.6 EMOTIONAL DEVELOPMENT

Patterns of emotional development:

General pattern of emotionality follow a predictable course, but pattern for different emotions are likewise predictable. Temper tantrums, for example, reach their peak between 2-4 years of age and are then replaced by more mature patterns of angry expressions such as sulkiness and general orneriness. Occasional minor stealing is common among children. It is not a sign that anything is seriously wrong but it should be dealt with. Increased understanding and ability to deal with complex emotions such as pride and shame, increased ability to suppress or conceal negative emotions and use of self-initiated strategies for redirecting feelings is observed in this stage. The consequences of emotional development are as follows:

- Emotion prepares the child for action
- Emotional tension disrupts motor skills
- Emotion serves as a form of communication
- Emotion interferes with mental activities
- Emotion acts as source of social and self evaluation
- Emotion colors children's outlooks on life
- Emotion affects social interactions
- Emotions leave their mark on facial expressions
- Emotion affects the psychological climate
- Emotional response when repeated develops into habits.

Emotional development could be learnt by trial and error, by imitation, by conditioning(which is learning by association), or by training from adults (to encourage pleasant emotions and discourage unpleasant ones)

Characteristic feature of children's emotions:

- Emotions are intense
- Emotions appear frequently
- Emotions are transitory: Young children rapidly shift from laughter to tears, from anger to smiles or from jealousy to affection.
- Emotions change in strength
- Emotions can be detected by behaviors and symptoms.

Anger

The immediate causes of anger shifted with increase in age. Older children showed an increase of problems of social relationships; and developmental changes in expression of anger showed less and less random behavior and more aggressive behavior directed toward something or someone. These causes of anger relate to people and the characteristics of people. Even more specifically it was the child's peers who often made him angry. As children grow older, they alter their way of expressing anger, and show it through sneers, sarcasm and so on till they are able to stir up anger in other children.

A derivative of anger, *annoyance*, becomes more prominent in later childhood. Annoyance is an emasculated form of anger and it frequently expresses more aptly the general kind of emotional response given during these years than does anger itself. In addition, the older child may be observed to express his anger in sulkiness, quarreling, fussiness and being generally disagreeable.

Fear

Fear is still found much among children of this age. A large proportion of the fears shown in childhood persist into the adult years. Those that showed the greatest persistence were fear of animals, of bodily harm through such dangers as fire, illness, or drowning, of the supernatural, of the dark, and of being alone. Intelligence, sex, socio-economic status, physical conditions, social contacts and the personality of the child play a role in the variation of fear among children.

Anxiety

When we use the term "anxiety" in the emotional-state sense, we are referring to the arousal that occurs when a situation is perceived as being potentially embarrassing, degrading, or guilt-provoking, and in which there is, consequently, a threat to our self-concept or self-image. The kind of pervasive apprehensiveness that we term "anxiety" is likely to occur in our interactions with others or when we are uncertain about the way things will turn out.

A person who lacks anxiety also lacks concern for the thoughts and feelings of others and as a consequence, is likely to be without empathy. Too much anxiety, on the other hand, leads to an intense self-concern and interferes with good social adjustments. In contrast too low-anxious children have been observed to do better on simple tasks, but poorer on more complex ones.

Children's anxiety is found to increase somewhat with maturity. Cloaks for childhood anxiety are:

1. **Boredom:** Anxiety makes children bored, restless and disturbed and they cannot concentrate on anything long enough to become interested in it.
2. **Ill-at-ease:** Whether alone or with others, anxious children feel insecure and show their anxiety by nervous mannerisms and speech problems.
3. **Out-of-character behavior:** A friendly child who is anxious may show a streak of cruelty or usually a kind child may commit a brutal act.
4. **Excessive eating:** Anxious children almost always become nibblers of sweet and as a result become overweight.
5. **Excessive use of Mass Media:** Anxious children tend to use television and other mass media more than their age mates.

Affectively Pleasant Emotions:

Younger children tend to stress a holiday or a birthday or other occasions when they received special attention and gifts more than the case with older children. Children of all ages were apt to mention visiting friends, the return home of relatives, and the like. The oldest – age boys get a sudden upsurge of interest in literally going to places such as parks and recreational centers and in traveling. Older children placed more emphasis on the pleasures of self-discovery and self-realization, opportunities for self-improvement, and for vocational preparation. Girls, again, were more concerned with social relationship than boys.

With increase in age, the importance of social relationships and the opportunities for self-realisation become large. The period of later childhood, in terms of the affectively pleasant emotions, is the period of self and social discovery.

Periods of heightened emotionality

Heightened emotionality may arise whenever the children face problem in adjusting to new situations. It may arise either from physical or environmental causes or both. Physical conditions contributing to heightened emotionality are the home climate, child training method enforced, relationship with family members, relationship with peers, over protectiveness, and parental aspirations. The psychological conditions are anxiety, poor intellectual development (owing to fatigue, poor health or development), and poor health due to malnutrition, irritating condition, chronic changes, asthma, diabetes or glandular changes at puberty. The environmental causes could be stress or portal attitudes.

9.7 LANGUAGE DEVELOPMENT

Language is a vital aspect of cognitive and emotional development. Learning to speak properly is important, as speech is an essential tool in socializing and plays an important role in accepting an individual among his peer group and society. Without language as a means of communication, social interaction would be nearly impossible. This linguistic skill is improved or acquired by an individual with the help of his parents and from the world outside the family in the form of television, radio, bool.s and peers. Multi linguistics is also developing now-a-days.

The various areas of improvement observed in late childhood are

1. **Speech improvement:** This is enabled by the following three aspects:
   - Vocabulary building: The vocabulary during late childhood grows rapidly, according to the educational opportunity and intellectual maturity the child gains at this stage. It improves based on family environment and the systematic teaching in school, reading, conversations with others and exposure to media. They build up vocabularies which they use in their speech, writing and in their use of computers. First graders, on an average, know about 20,000 to 24,000 words. By the time a child completes his sixth grade, he may know approximately 50,000 words. Not only do older children learn new words, they also tend to learn new meanings for old words. Girls, generally build up larger vocabularies than boys. There are special vocabularies which the children of this age learn – those which have special meanings and limited uses. They are etiquette vocabulary, color vocabulary, number vocabulary, money vocabulary, time vocabulary, slang-word and swear word vocabulary and also secret vocabulary. Sex differences and socio-economic differences play a great role among these children in learning special vocabulary.
   - Pronunciation: Errors in pronunciation are less common at this age than earlier. A new word may be incorrectly pronounced for the first time but after hearing once or twice, children are generally able to pronounce correctly.
   - Forming Sentence: A six year old child should have command of nearly every kind of sentence structure. From 6 until age of 9 or 10, length of sentence will increase. Generally, after the age of nine, children start using shorter and more compact sentences.
2. **Improvement in comprehension:** "World view" expands from home to neighborhood and local community. This age group needs to feel independent and free to express themselves. These children have a need to know and understand "why." Perhaps the most important aid to improved comprehension is due to the budge from egocentric speech to more socialized speech. This is also added by the guidance from school environment.
3. **Content of Speech:** This varies from child to child depending on his level of socializing and the group to which he belongs. The greater the size of the group, the greater will be the content of speech. Mostly, older children talk more in the form of boasting, more commonly found among the boys. Another form of increased content is to make criticisms and make fun, of peers or even adults.
4. **Amount of Talking:** There is a gradual decrease in talking as childhood continues. The characteristic chatterbox stage of early childhood is replaced by more controlled and selective speech. This may be due to the fact that children realize that unnecessary talking is not appreciated and sometimes they are shy of being ridiculed or criticized. Usually, girls tend to talk more than boys and children of upper socioeconomic groups also talk more than their counterparts.

The importance of reading

The importance of reading in our society is found in school for knowledge, on computers for practical usage, at home for pleasure. A discussion of language development from infancy through the middle childhood years shows that language and reading are not simultaneous accomplishments. Rather, reading is built on solid language skills and facilitated by advancing cognitive abilities. For example, children (and adults) are rather limited information processors. Consequently, we are faced with the dilemma of understanding how good readers distribute their attention across the many processes needed for efficient reading. It is a formidable task. Children must learn to identify letters, connect them to sounds, de-cipher spelling patterns, and finally, comprehend what all of this means. The key to this complex process seems to be that good readers process printed words automatically and use their cognitive processes for comprehension.

The features for the middle childhood stages of language development are seen as follows:

- Stage 1 – 6 to 7 years: Children learn the relationship between letters and sounds and begin to read simple text. They usually experience direct instruction in letter-sound relations (phonetics) and use high-frequency words in their reading.
- Stage 2— 7 to 8 years: Children demonstrate greater fluency in reading simple stories. They combine improved decoding skills with fast mapping to meaning in their reading selections.
- Stage 3— 9 to 13 years: Reading is now used as a tool to obtain knowledge (science and social science textbooks, novels, magazines).

9.8 SOCIAL DEVELOPMENT

Social development means acquisition of ability to behave in accordance with social expectations. Becoming socialized involves three processes, which although they are separated and distinct, are so closely inter related that failure in any one of them will lower the individual level of socialization. They learn not to look bored, even though they may be bored; not to talk about tabooed subject in presence of those who disapprove and not to look pleased when someone they dislike is hurt.

School-age children are faced with the central problem of developing a sense of industry as opposed to a sense of inferiority, according to Erikson (1950).

The noteworthy uniqueness in the social development of this period are as follows:

1. **Creation of childhood gangs:** Upon beginning schooling, children enter the "gang age"- an age when social consciousness develops rapidly. It is characterized by interest in peer activities, an increasingly strong desire to be an accepted member of a gang and discontent when children are not with their friends. Even one or two friends are not enough for older children. They want to be with the gang, because only then will there be a sufficient number of individuals to play the games and sports they now enjoy and to give excitement to their play.
2. **Over sensitiveness:** A common outgrowth of susceptibility to social approval and disapproval is over sensitiveness. The tendency to be easily hurt by peer or siblings or parents and to interpret what others say and do as hostile, is a measure of the children's desire for social acceptance. Over sensitiveness is seldom used outside the home because other children can see through it too easily.
3. **Suggestibility and contra suggestibility:** Others like easily influencing a person who is suggestible over sensitiveness; suggestibility is an outgrowth of craving for attention and social approval. Contra suggestibility means thinking and acting contrary to suggestions from others. While accepting in a more or less unquestioning manner the suggestion of peer group, older children begin to revolt against adult and to act in direct contradiction to them.

4. **Good sportsmanship:** Good sportsmanship is ability to cooperate with others to the extent of submerging individual personalities and promoting spirit of the group. Good sportsmanship entails a willingness not only to co-operate with others but also to share. Children who want to be considered "good sports" must be generous with their material possessions whether in school or games.
5. **Responsibility:** Closely related to good sportsmanship is responsibility and willingness to assume one's share of load. Children who learn to assume responsibility at home not only make better adjustment with peer group but also are likely to be selected for leadership roles.

Characteristics of children's gangs:

- Children's gangs are play groups.
- To belong to a gang, a child must be invited.
- Members of a gang are of the same sex.
- At first, gangs consists of three or four groups of older children and become interested in sports.
- Boys' gangs more often engage in socially unacceptable behaviors than girls' gangs.
- Popular gang activities include games and sports, going to the movies and getting together to talk or eat.
- The gang has a central meeting place, usually away from the watchful eyes of adults.
- Most gangs have insignia of belongings; for example, the members may wear similar clothes.

Favourable Effects of Gang formation

- Gang helps children to learn to get along with age-mates and to behave in a way that is socially acceptable to them.
- Gang can help children to develop a rational conscience.
- Through gang experience, children learn appropriate social attitudes, such as how to like people and how to enjoy social life and group activities.
- Gang can help children's personal independence by giving them emotional satisfaction from friendships with peers.
- Competition during gang age is developed; competition takes three forms of rivalry among group members- for recognition within group itself, conflicts between gang and rival gangs, and organized agencies of society.
- Helps to build up solidarity and feelings of loyalty.
- At times, lead to hostility and quarrelling within gang thus serving to weaken the group and loyalty of each member.

Unfavourable Effects of Gang formation

- **Parent child conflicts:** Many older children spend more of their time with their gangs than with their families and in so doing, they fail to carry their load of home work or family responsibilities. When parents object to this, parent-child friction develops and with it, the emotional ties between them weakens.
- **Sex antagonism:** Some older children may prefer a member of the opposite sex as a friend and may find some of the play activities of the opposite sex more enjoyable than the play activities considered appropriate for their own sex; but, fearing unfavorable

attitudes on the part of their fellow gang members, they do not want to be seen playing with girls.

- **Prejudice:** Discrimination is expressed on the basis of race and later as children approach puberty, on religion and socio-economic differences.
- **Treatment of their companions:** Once older children have formed a gang, they are often cruel to those whom they do not regard as friends. Much of their secrecy that surrounds gangs is designed to keep out the children, the members whom they do not want as friends. The tendency to be cruel & callous towards all who are not gang-mates, generally reaches a peak around the eleventh year.

Sometimes the quarrel with a gang-mate is only temporary and play relationships are soon re-established. At other times, the strained relationships persist and the child who is the target of the gang antagonism is made to feel unwelcome as a playmate and as a result, may be dropped from the gang.

Factors contributing to variations in social group influences:

- **Acceptability to the group:** Popular children and those who see possibility of gaining group acceptance are influenced more by group and less by their families than children who do not get along well with their peers. Children who see slight chance of being accepted by group have little motivation to confirm to its standards.
- **Security of status:** Children who feel secure in the group will feel free to express any disagreement they have with judgments of other group members. Those who feel insecure, in contrast, will conform closely and will follow other group members.
- **Type of group:** The influence of group comes from social distance-the degree of affective relationship between group members. In primary group (family or peer group) bonds of inter group relation are stronger than in secondary (organized play groups or social clubs).
- **Different members of group:** Within a group the greatest influence usually comes from leader and least from those who are least popular.
- **Personality:** Children who suffer from feeling of inadequacy or inferiority are more influenced by group than those who have greater self-confidence and greater self acceptance.

9.9 COGNITIVE DEVELOPMENT

Between the time when children enter school and the time they reach adolescence is called late childhood. Childhood worlds are expanding from close family ties to outward relationships with friends, teachers, coaches, care givers and others outside the family. As a child develops, there are considerable changes in his mental abilities which includes imagination, memory, creativity, questioning and perception. 6-8 year olds can rarely sit for longer than 15-20 minutes for an activity. Attention span gets longer with aging.

The younger child's thinking is limited by his/ her rigid egocentricity in perceiving, assimilating, and accommodating information about the environment. By way of contrast, the school-age child is characterized by an increasing flexibility in processing information and reaching decisions as well as the increasing ability to delay a response while considering several alternatives for a possible solution. They can also develop a plan to meet desired goal. In the school-age years, however, the development refinements of children include an improved ability to be reflective and to acquire a more efficient memory and a greater command of language skills. The school-age child's flexibility of thought also is shown in an improving ability to classify, group, comprehend several parts of a whole, and understand that there are invariant and unchanging elements in the world.

An important cognitive skill acquired during middle childhood is called "*reversibility*", which permits a child to fully understand basic relationships between objects and events. It involves the ability to return to a beginning point in a process or to understand that a process can be reversed. "*Conservation*" is another significant cognitive skill acquired in middle childhood. Children demonstrate their understanding of conservation when they comprehend that something has not changed in its essential properties even though its shape, arrangement, or physical appearance has been altered.

In this stage, intelligence is demonstrated through logical and systematic manipulation of symbols into operational thinking and concrete words. At about age 7, according to Piaget, children enter the stage of concrete operations, so named because children can now use mental operations to solve concrete or actual problems. Experience plays a major role in this stage. They have a better understanding of spatial concepts, of causality, of categorization, of inductive reasoning and of conservation.

If children discover pleasure in intellectual stimulation, being productive and seeking success, they will develop a sense of competence. Children begin to read and write early in middle childhood and will be skillful in reading and writing by the end of this period.

School children remember a lot of new information and logical relations among things. Their remembrance is high compared to preschoolers due to use of deliberate strategies for remembering, such as rehearsals, organizing information into systematic categories, imagination, knowledge and elaboration.

Girls on an average get consistently higher scores than boys on tests of verbal abilities, and boys on spatial abilities. The openness of classes and classrooms and teacher's expectations of students' performance, all affect a child's learning.

Box 9-2 National Association for the Education of Younger Children (NAEYC)

According to a research done by (NAEYC 1986), it is found that

- Most five-year-olds can begin to combine simple ideas into more complex relations. They have a growing memory capacity and fine motor/ physical skills. They have a growing interest in the functional aspects of written language, such as recognizing meaningful words and trying to write their names.
- Six-year-olds are active learners and demonstrate considerable verbal ability. They are interested in games and rules and develop concepts and problem-solving skills from these experiences. Hands-on activity and experimentation are necessary for this age group.
- Seven-year-olds become increasingly able to reason, listen to others, and show social give-and-take. Spatial relationships and time concepts are difficult for them to perceive.
- Eight-year-olds combine great curiosity with increased social interest. During these early grades, children can learn from the symbolic experiences of reading books and listening to stories;
- Nine-year-old may be somewhat self-conscious and prefer group activities to working alone. They are beginning to understand abstractions as well as cause-and-effect relationships. Most are operating at a concrete level.
- Ten-year-old may be experiencing bodily changes and rapid growth spurts. These changes cause periods of frustration and anger. Generally, ten-year-olds are interested in and enthusiastic about places and problems in the news. They want to know what events caused these problems, where they occurred, and the reasons for them.

- Eleven-year-olds are generally in a period of transition between childhood and adolescence. More decision making is required of them. They tend to be sociable and need opportunities to express feelings and opinions.

Recent research testifies to the advances made in the cognitive neurosciences. Whether it is learning to walk, talk, read, or make new friends, the brain is ready to supply a child with all of the neural firepower needed to be successful. The task of those adults who are around children during these electrifying times is to provide the appropriate stimulation that will make them want to participate in this enticing world, thereby adding new connections and strengthening those already present.

The various concepts developed at this stage are:

Concept of Life: While some older children find it difficult to understand that many things which move- a river, for example - are not alive, they become increasingly aware that movement is not the sole criterion of life.

Concept of Death: Children who experience the death of a family member or pet have good understanding of the meaning of death and the emotional weighting of their concepts of death is colored by the reactions of those around them.

Concept of Bodily Function: Until children begin to study hygiene in elementary school, many of their concepts about bodily functions are inaccurate and incomplete, especially true of internal bodily functions.

Concept of Space: The child's concepts of space and time also change during middle and late childhood. The conservation of relationships of speed do not appear until around seven or eight years of age. By using scales and rulers, children learn meaning of ounces, pounds, inches, feet and even miles. A factor analysis revealed that boys tended to exceed girls in spatial ability. This may possibly be due to the greater participation in construction activities during play.

Concept of Numbers: Numbers take on new meanings as older children use money and work out arithmetic problems. By the time they are nine or ten years old, children understand number concepts to 1,000 and beyond.

Concept of Money: Children begin to understand the value of various coins and bills when they start to use money. Economic content in the early years of education should relate to events in children's lives as they examine buying, selling, and trading transactions, the process of making goods and services, and the origin of materials and products in their everyday lives. By age seven, children have formulated fairly accurate conceptions of work, wants, and scarcity and evidence the capability of developing a method for making decisions.

Concept of Time: The rigid schedule of school day enables children to develop concepts of what they can accomplish in a given period of time. Social studies in school and mass media help them to develop concepts of historical time.

Concept of Sex role: Not only do boys and girls develop clear concepts of approved sex roles, but before childhood is over they may also learn that the male role is apt to be considered more prestigious than the female role.

Concept of Beauty: Older children tend to judge beauty in terms of group standards, rather than according to their own aesthetic standards.

9.10 MORAL DEVELOPMENT

In middle childhood the individual is confronted with one of the most significant challenges in life: the task of developing a conscience or acquiring the values society deems necessary to govern one's behavior. Schools, teachers, Scout groups, youth organizations, religious groups, and others contribute to children's development of good character. Good moral or character development may include:

(1) The promotion of honesty and integrity

(2) Conformity to group standards

(3) Service to others

(4) The development of self-control

(5) Consideration for the needs of others over self

(6) The demonstration of consistency, initiative, and persistence in tasks and related aspects.

According to Piaget, moral relativism replaces moral inflexibility. For example, to a five-year old, lying is always bad, while an older child realizes that in some situations, a lie is justified and, therefore, not necessarily bad. 'Moral' comes from the Latin word 'mores' meaning, 'manners', 'customs' and 'folkways'.

9.10.1 Phases of moral development:

If true morality is to be attained, moral development must take place in two distinct phases: first, the development of moral behavior, and second, the development of moral concepts. Social pressures, how children feel about themselves, the way in which they are treated by family members and peers, desires at the moment and many other factors influence how children will behave when a choice must be made.

1. Development of moral behavior:

Moral behavior means behavior which conforms to the moral code of the social group. Moral behavior is controlled by moral concepts, the rules of behavior to which the members of a culture have become accustomed and which determine the expected behavior patterns of all group members.

Children can learn to behave in a socially approved manner through trial (puzzles) and error, through direct teaching or through identification. Of the three, direct teaching and identification are not only the best methods but also the most widely used.

2. Development of moral concepts:

The second phase of moral development consists of the learning of moral concepts or the principles of right and wrong in an abstract, verbal form. This of course is too advanced for a young child. Training in moral principles must therefore wait until the child has the mental capacity to generalize and to transfer a principle of conduct from one situation to another. As a result, general concepts are gradually learned as the child becomes able to recognize a common element in a variety of situations.

As pre-school children are incapable of abstract thinking, they define 'good behavior' in terms of specific acts such as 'obeying mother' or 'helping others' and 'bad behavior' in terms of not doing these things. By the time children are 8 or 9 yrs old, their concepts become more generalized. They realize for e.g. 'stealing is wrong' rather than that it is 'wrong to steal a ball'.

9.10.2 Kohlberg's Stages of Moral Development

Kohlberg suggests three general levels of moral development, each of which is composed of two stages. As cognitive growth occurs, individuals are able to solve more complex moral questions. The first level of moral development is experienced in early childhood and continues through the majority of the middle childhood years. The second stage occurs in the later years of middle childhood and goes through adolescence and adulthood.

Box 9-3 Kohlberg's Stages of Moral Development

	Levels	Stages
Level 1	Pre – conventional	1. Obedience and punishment orientation. 2. Self - interest orientation.
Level 2	Conventional	3. Interpersonal accord and conformity 4. Authority and social–order maintaining orientation.
Level 3	Post- conventional	5. Social contract orientation 6. Universal ethical principles

Pre- conventional

The pre- conventional level of moral reasoning is especially common in children, although adults can also exhibit this level of reasoning. Responders in the pre-conventional level judge the morality of an action by its direct consequences. The pre-conventional level consist of the first and second stages of moral development. In stage one, individuals focus on the direct consequences that their actions will have for themselves. For example, an action is perceived as morally wrong if the person who commits it gets punished. The worse the punishment for the act , the more 'bad' the act is perceived to be.

Stage two espouses what's in it for the self, right behavior being defined by what is in one's own best interest. Stage two reasoning shows a limited interest in the needs of others, but only to a point where it might further one's own interests, such as you scratch my back, and I'll scratch yours. In stage two, concern for others is not based on loyalty or intrinsic respect. Lacking a perspective of society in the pre-conventional level, this should not be confused with social contract (stage five), as all actions are performed to serve one's own needs or interests.

Conventional

The conventional level of moral reasoning is typical of adolescents and adults. Persons who reason in a conventional way, judge the morality of actions by comparing these actions to societal views and expectations.

In stage three, the self enters society by filling social roles. Individuals are receptive of approval or disapproval from other people as it reflects society's accordance with the perceived role. They try to be a good boy or good girl to live up to these expectations.

In stage four, it is important to obey laws, dictums and social conventions because of their importance in maintaining a functioning society. Moral reasoning in stage four is thus beyond the need for individual approval exhibited in stage three; society must learn to transcend individual needs. If one violates a law, perhaps everyone would; thus there is an obligation and a duty to uphold laws and rules.

Post conventional

The post conventional level, also known as the principle level, consists of stages five and six of moral development. Realizations are separate entities from society which now becomes salient.

In stage five, individuals are viewed as holding different opinions and values. Along a similar vein, laws are regarded as social contracts rather than rigid dictums. Those that do not promote general social welfare should be changed when necessary to meet the greatest good for the greatest number of people. In this way democratic government is ostensibly based on stage five reasoning.

In stage six, moral reasoning is based on abstract reasoning using universal ethical principles. Laws are valid only in so far as they are grounded in justice, and commitment to justice. Carried with it is an obligation to disobey unjust laws. Right are unnecessary as social contracts are not essential for demonic moral action. The resulting consensus is the action taken. In this way, action is never a means but always an end in itself; one acts because it is right and not because it is instrumental, expected, legal or previously agreed upon.

9.10.3 Discipline

Discipline refers to teaching children character, self-control, and moral values and behavior. It can be a powerful tool for socialization with the goal of developing self-discipline. There are two types of behaviorist techniques of disciplining, namely, 'reinforcement' and 'punishment'.

Parents sometimes punish children to stop undesirable behavior, but children usually learn better from reinforcement which can be an external factor such as candy, money, toys or stars and internal factors such as praise, hug or privilege. Corporal punishment is defined as use of physical force with the intention of causing a child to experience pain, but not injury, for the purpose of correction and controlling.

In late childhood, not only new techniques of discipline but also shifts in emphasis on the different aspects of discipline are essential. Changes in the three essential elements of discipline – education to build up moral concepts, punishments for intentional wrong doing and reward for right behaviour must meet the developmental needs of the older child. When children are young, they like to feel that parents know best. By late childhood, they rebel against their parents and parental standards. Too strict discipline is liable to lead the child to misbehave, to prove to himself and his friends that he is independent. On the other hand, too lenient discipline will confuse the child and create a feeling of insecurity. Long-term consequence is more important than the immediate consequences of discipline.

Role of discipline in moral development

1. **Aids in building moral code:** For the older child the teaching of right and wrong should emphasize the reasons why certain patterns of behavior are acceptable while others are not and should help the child understand special concepts into more generalized form.
2. **Rewards:** Praise or special treat for handling a different situation well, will have a strong education value as they show children that they behaved correctly and they also motivate children to repeat the approved behavior. Rewards must be appropriate to child's age and level of development.
3. **Punishment:** Like rewards, punishment must be appropriate and administered fairly, otherwise it may arouse resentment on the child's part. Punishments must also motivate a child to conform to social expectants in future.
4. **Consistency:** Good discipline is always consistent. What is right today is right tomorrow and next day. A wrong act should receive the same punishment every time it is repeated and right act the same reward.

9.10.4 Development of conscience

One of the important developmental tasks of late childhood is developing a conscience. By conscience is meant a conditioned anxiety response to certain types of situation and actions which have been built up by associating certain acts with punishment . Conscience is a type of 'internalized policeman' which motivates the child to do what he knows is right and thus avoid punishment.

'Guilt' is a special kind of negative self- evaluation which occurs when an individual acknowledges that his behaviour is at variance with a given moral value to which he feels obligated to conform. 'Shame', by contrast, is an 'unpleasant emotional reaction of an individual to an actual presumed negative judgment of himself by others resulting in self-depreciation vis-à-vis the group'. Shame, thus, relies on external sanctions alone, though it may be accompanied by guilt. Guilt, by contrast, relies on both internal and external sanctions.

With the development of shame and guilt, an older child develops a willingness to confess or admit misbehavior. This may be to relieve the tension caused by shame and guilt, or it may be a method of gaining forgiveness which will lighten the punishment. Shame is thus a powerful agent in the development of moral behaviour.

Factors which influence conscience development

The effectiveness of a child's conscience as a motivating force in directing his actions into channels that will lead to moral behaviour, will depend on the type of punishment he has been accustomed to receive. The punishment the child receives influences parent-child relationships which in turn influence the development of conscience. When parents are warm and understanding, children resist temptations better than when parents are cold and punitive. The child, because of affection for his parents, thus becomes insulated against misbehaviour. As girls have a closer relationship with their parents at this age than boys, they have a stronger motivation to live up to parental expectation than boys. A combination of the wholesome forms of punishment and wholesome parent- child relationship can be regarded as conscience -building devices.

9.11 HAZARDS OF LATE CHILDHOOD

The hazards of late childhood are both physical and psychological.

Physical hazards

1. **Illness:** Since vaccines against most childhood diseases are now available, older children suffer mainly from occasional colds and stomach upsets which rarely have any lasting physical effects. The psychological effects of illness in late childhood, however, can be serious. Illness upsets the body homeostasis, which in turn makes children irritable, demanding and difficult to live with. If they are sick for a long period their school work may suffer and they may fall behind their peers in the learning of play skills.
2. **Obesity:** With a slower growth rate, children need fewer calories. Although their need for protein, vitamins, and minerals remain high, some children begin to accumulate empty calories from high-sugar and high-fat foods. Thus, obesity, with its social, psychological, and medical consequences, looms on the horizon. Recent research indicated that children who are overweight between the ages of 10 and 17 years will probably have a lifetime problem regardless of whether their parents were thin or fat .
3. **Sex – inappropriate body build:** Girls with masculine body builds and boys with girlish physiques are likely to be ridiculed by their peers and pitied by adults.
4. **Accidents:** Older children are more cautious, and when this happens it develops into a generalized shyness that affects social relationships, school works and personalities.
5. **Physical disabilities:** Most disabled children are inhibited and ill at ease in social situations. As a result they make poor social adjustments and this, in turn, affects their personal adjustments.
6. **Awkwardness:** Awkwardness and clumsiness prevent the older children from doing what their playmates do or from keeping pace with them in play.
7. **Homeliness:** Homeliness can be and often is a hazard if other people react unfavorably and communicate their feelings by the way they treat homely children. As older children as a group are less appealing than babies or even young children, adults tend to be more critical of them and less tolerant of their normal, but often annoying behavior. Older

children interpret this as reflection, an interpretation that can have a harmful effect on their developing self - concepts.

Psychological hazards

Psychological hazards have a powerful influence on children's personal adjustments and on their developing personalities.

Speech hazards:

1. A smaller than average vocabulary handicaps children in their school work as well as in their communication with others.
2. Speech errors, such as mispronunciations and grammatical mistakes, and speech defects such as stuttering or lisping, may make children so self conscious that they will speak only when necessary
3. Children who have difficulty speaking the language used in their school environment may be handicapped in their efforts to communicate and may be made to feel that they are different.
4. Ego-centric speech, critical and derogatory comments and boasting antagonize their peers.

Emotional hazards:

Children are considered disagreeable and unpleasant if they show emotional expressions such as temper tantrum, anger and jealousy.

Social hazards:

There are five types of children whose adjustments are affected by social hazards. They are children neglected by their peer group, voluntary isolates, geographically or socially mobile children (in games), those with racial or religious prejudice, and followers who want to be leaders become resentful and disunited group members.

Moral hazards:

Six hazards are commonly associated with the development of moral attitudes and behavior in late childhood.

- The development of the moral code based on peer or mass media concepts of right and wrong which may not coincide with adult.
- A failure to develop a conscience as an inner control over behavior.
- Inconsistent discipline which leaves children unsure of what they are expected to do.
- Physical punishment, that can trigger moderate aggressiveness in children.
- Peer approval of misbehavior sometime is so satisfying that such behavior becomes habitual.
- Intolerance of wrong doings of others.

Hazards of personality development:

The two serious hazards in personality development are the development of an unfavorable self-concept which leads to self rejection, and secondly, the carryover from early childhood of egocentrism, which gives the children a false sense of their own importance.

Middle childhood youngsters moved away from a sheltered home environment and into a world of new friends, new challenges, and new problems. Whether the task is adjusting to a new sibling, relating to peers and teachers, or coping with difficulties, youngsters of this age enter a different world. But the timing of their entrance into this novel environment is intended to match their ability to adapt successfully, to master those skills that will prepare them for the next greater development epoch, adolescence. With their entrance into a widening world, middle childhood youngsters require those skills that will enable them to cope successfully. Inevitably, they face times of turmoil, which, as we have seen, can come from internal or external sources.

With all of the development accomplishment of the previous six or seven years, youngsters want to use their ability, which means that they sometimes experience failure as well as success, especially in their schoolwork. Physically active, cognitively capable, and socially receptive, much is expected of these children, especially in school, as we shall see.

Figure 9.1 Cognitive Skills and Motor Skills of the late childhood years

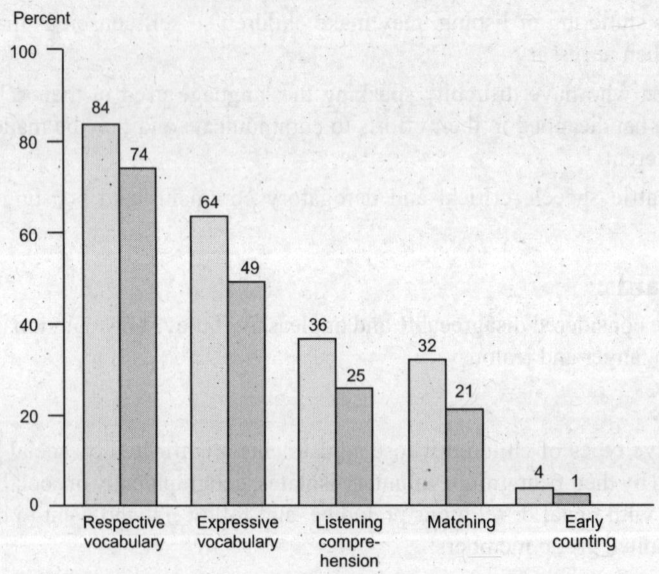

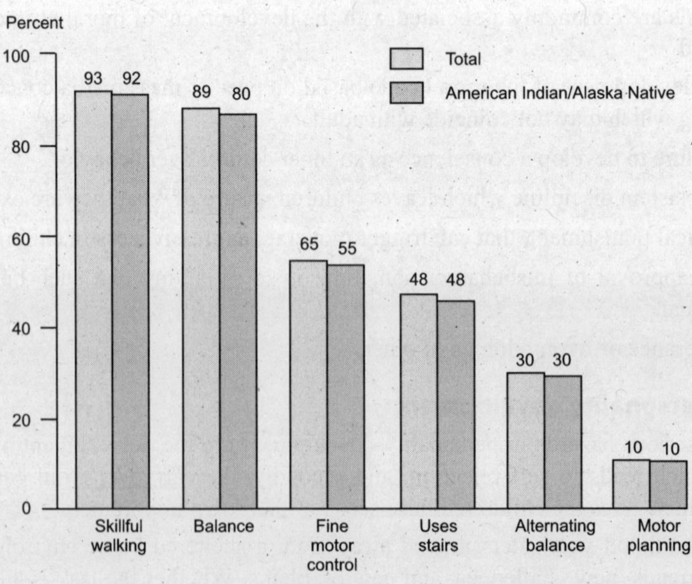

QUESTIONS

SECTION "A"

Short Answer Type:

1. Why is late childhood stage called as elementary school years?
2. Give an account on developmental tasks of late childhood.
3. Describe motor skill development during late childhood years.
4. Give the characteristics of late childhood stage.
5. Why is late childhood stage referred to as 'gang age'?
6. Give the characteristics of children's gang.
7. Write a note on the cognitive development of late childhood stage?
8. What are the common misdemeanors of late childhood?
9. What is the role of discipline in moral development?
10. Give the difference between moral and immoral behaviour.
11. What are the unfavourable effects in social development of late childhood stage?
12. How is speech improved in late childhood stage?

SECTION "B"

One Page Answer Type:

1. Discuss on the physical development of late childhood stage.
2. What is catharsis?
3. What are hazards of late childhood stage?
4. Write about the emotional development in late childhood stage.
5. How does improvement in comprehension and vocabulary building take place?
6. What are the psychological hazards of late childhood years?
7. Give few categories of concepts developed in late childhood.
8. Mention about the language development of late childhood

SECTION "C"

Essay Answer Type:

1. Discuss in detail about Kohlberg's stages of moral development.
2. What are the areas of speech improvement in late childhood ?
3. Give an account on language, emotional and moral development in late childhood.
4. What are the periods of heightened emotionality? Why?
5. Describe the social and moral development of this stage.
6. Give an account of the physical and motor development of the middle childhood period.

UNIT — VI

CHAPTER

10

ADOLESCENCE (12-18 YEARS)

OBJECTIVES

To enlighten students about:

- Concept of adolescence period
- Developmental tasks
- Characteristics
- Growth and development details – physical, motor, emotional, language, social and aagnitibe
- Problems of adolescence
- Parent-Adolescent relationship
- Juvenile delinquency

10.1 INTRODUCTION

The adolescent stage in human development is a relatively recent social invention. G. Stanley Hall (1904) is usually credited with formalizing the concept of "adolescence". He believed that individuals passed through stages in their development that reflected the social evolution of the human species. Development from birth to maturity followed a primitive to civilized pattern. Adolescence, in Hall's view, came to represent a "storm and stress" period that reflected the unsettling turbulence of growth in modern societies.

The teenage years which can be traumatizing to all who are involved, are known as adolescence. As you go through this time period you not only feel differently, but you also think differently as well. The term adolescence comes from the latin word 'adolescere', meaning ' to grow' or 'to grow to maturity'. It is a long developmental transition period from childhood to adulthood, which can include major interrelated physical, mental, and psychosocial changes.

Definition:

Adolescence is a period of biosocial transition between childhood and adulthood (Kuppuswamy, 1981), when rapid changes take place. The individual's physical, mental, social, moral and spiritual outlooks undergo rapid and revolutionary changes during adolescence than during infancy or childhood. During adolescence the individual wants to take independent decisions in various situations of his experience. Lerner (2002) characterized the adolescent transition as being distinguished by four traits;

- Relative plasticity- the potential for change
- Relationism – the multiple levels of the individual's relationships with others
- Historical embeddedness - in the context of the historical time in which it occurs
- Diversity and individual difference - the emphasis is on the variety of ways individuals learn to cope with themselves and their environments

The stage of adolescence is categorized into two basic periods, namely, early adolescence and late adolescence. Studies on changes in behaviour, attitudes, and values throughout adolescence have revealed that these changes are more rapid in the early than in the latter part of adolescence

1. Early adolescence involves the initiation and completion of the physical changes associated with puberty and ends at about ages sixteen;
2. Late adolescence begins as the physical changes are completed and extends through the eighteenth birthday or the age of legal maturity, which is a very short period.

The dividing line between early and late adolescence is somewhat arbitrarily placed at around seventeen years - the age when the average adolescent enters the senior year of high school.

10.2 DEVELOPMENTAL TASKS

The developmental tasks that individuals encounter in adolescence center on acquiring and refining more advanced skills, abilities, and attitudes that lead to preparation for adulthood. Adolescence is viewed culturally as a transition between two broad stages in the life cycle. Adolescents are similar to what sociologists term 'a marginal man', referring to the situation in which individuals are caught between the demands and expectations of two different cultures. The adolescent is neither a child nor an adult. Conflicts occur for the adolescent because of the uncertainty of how to behave while knowing that present behavior could not be fully tolerated as mature and acceptable behavior of an adult. The nature of adolescence as a transition period from dependence to independence is a major emphasis of this time of life.

Havighurst classifies the tasks of adolescence in terms of peer influence, movement towards independence and autonomy and the attainment of an ethical code and system of positive value. The first two tasks are associated with peer relationships, the next six with the thrust towards independence and self-responsibility and the last two towards achieving the traits that characterize the good man and the good citizen. The important developmental tasks in adolescence are

- Achieving new and more mature relations with age mates of both sexes.
- Achieving a masculine or feminine social role.
- Accepting one's physique and using one's body effectively.
- Desiring, accepting and achieving socially responsible behavior.
- Achieving emotional independence from parents and other adults.
- Achieving assurance of economic independence through actual work experience or through educational planning for such independence.
- Preparing for an economic career.
- Preparing for marriage and family life.
- Acquiring a set of values and an ethical system as a guide to behavior – developing an ideology.
- Developing skills necessary for civic competence.

Adolescents, however, appear as an ubiquitous age group in society perhaps because of the degree to which our culture admires youthfulness as a healthy, dynamic, and attractive period in life. Adolescence can be best described according to characteristics that distinguish development at this time of the life cycle.

10.3 CHARACTERISTICS OF ADOLESCENCE

1. *Adolescence is an important period:* It is a period of rapid physical and psychological change, where metamorphosis in an individual's life occurs. It is one of the periods when both the immediate effects and long term effects are important. Dramatic changes in body proportions, physical size and sexual maturation coincide with changes in attitudes and behaviours such as heightened emotionality, feelings of inadequacy, shifts in values, and heightened egocentricity. Most physical changes occur in early adolescence, while psychological changes occur throughout the period. Some periods are important for their physical and some for their psychological effects.

2. *Adolescence is a transitional period:* The physical changes that take place during the early years of adolescence affect the individual's behavioral level and lead to re-evaluations and a shifting or adjustment of values. During any transitional period, the status of the adolescent in the modern society is vague and he becomes confused with his role. He is treated as a child and when he acts like a child he is reproved and told to "act his age", and while he attempts to act like an adult he is often accused of being "too big" for his age.

3. *Adolescence is a period of change:* During the adolescent period (early) rapid mental developments occur. These give rise to the need for mental adjustments and the necessity for establishing new attitudes, values and interests. It is a period during which marked changes occur in duties, responsibilities, privileges and relationship with others. Under such conditions, changed attitudes towards self, parents, peers and others cause irritability. There are five almost worldwide accompaniments of the changes that occur during adolescence.

- Heightened emotionality is a major issue, which is generally more pronounced in early than in late adolescence. The force in which it is reflected depends on the rate at which the physical and psychological changes normally occur more rapidly during early adolescence.
- Next, the impact of sexual maturity makes young adolescents insecure of themselves, their capabilities, and interest. They have severe flux in their feelings which are often aggravated by the ambiguous treatment they receive from parents and teacher.
- While getting accustomed to the change in their bodies, their interests and in the roles the social group expects them to play, fresh problems arise for young adolescents, who consider these to be the greatest in the world. Until they have solved their problems to their satisfaction, these adolescents will be worried all the time.
- When the interests and behavior patterns change, so do values. What was vital to them as children seems less important to them now that they are near adults. For example, most adolescents do not consider the policy of being honest always, as now it is no more accepted by a large number of friends who have gained popularity. They now recognize that accomplishment is more important than the principle.
- Lastly, most adolescents are ambivalent regarding the changes; while they want and demand independence, they often fear the duties that go with independence and have doubt about their capacity to cope with these duties.

4. *Adolescence is a problem age:* In childhood, seeking help from parents and teachers was acceptable, but now he feels that his parent and teachers are 'too old' to understand and help him. Therefore, an adolescent is found to be more problematic, than at other ages. Studies show that problems are numerous and for the most part centre around physical appearance and health, social relationships in the home and outside relationship with members of the opposite sex, school work, plans for the future, including education, choice of vocation, selection of a life mate, sex and moral behavior, religious and finances.

5. ***Adolescence is a time of individual emancipation:*** It is a time of search for identity. Western cultural pattern emphasizes the teenage years as appropriate for establishing one's independence as a mature person. The adolescent becomes an emancipating child who attempts to achieve a new self-definition in many different ways. In the early years of adolescence, conformity to the group is still important to boys and girls. Gradually, they begin to crave for identity and are no longer satisfied to be like their peers in every respect, as they were earlier.

One of the ways adolescents try to establish themselves as individuals is by the use of symbol in the form of cars, clothes and other readily observable material possessions. They hope in this way they could attract attention to them and be recognized as individuals while, at the same time, could maintain their identity with the peer groups.

6. ***Adolescence is a dreaded age:*** Popular stereotypes influence the self concepts and attitudes of adolescents towards themselves. The stereotypes have also functioned as mirrors held to the adolescent by society, reflecting an image of himself that the adolescent gradually comes to regard as authentic and according to which he shapes his behavior.

7. ***Adolescence is a time of experimentation, idealism, conflict, and uncertainty:*** The culture of youth dictates that one tries to understand adolescence in psychological and social terms rather than in other ways. Because our culture has created the unique characteristics and expectations of adolescence, there are certain issues central to this period of development including

- Tension between self and society (an attempt to define who one is and where one stands in relation with others)
- A high value placed on movement and action of the self, others, and the culture,
- A tendency to band with other youthful subcultures that maintain a deliberate social distance from established social order.

These unrealistic aspirations change to increased rationality when they become older (late adolescent) adolescents. As a result they suffer less from disappointment and disillusionment than they did when they were younger. There is a focus on gaining freedom to explore and to examine a wide variety of attitudes, values and behaviors as well as life styles. Because there is still intellectual maturation occurring in this period, many behaviors seem hypocritical, insensitive, egocentric, unrealistic and troublesome to adults.

Adolescents are focused psychologically on certain preoccupations. These include identity crystallization, autonomy, alteration of stimulation with boredom, being sociable with one's age group, experiencing physical maturation and achieving a variety of environmental experiences.

Because of these preoccupations, interests, concerns, and activities, this stage is characterized as unique from others in the life cycle. Adolescents have a very broad interest in variety, freedom, sexual play, fashion, experiences exploring life and emotions, novelty, and excitement. These interests find expression in such activities as dating, sports, arts and crafts, dancing, and participation in organized youth programs, "hanging around," travel, and so on.

8. ***Adolescence is the threshold of adulthood:*** As adolescents approach legal maturity, they are apprehensive to discard the stereotype of teenagers and to create the impression that they are near adults. They begin to concentrate on behavior that is associated with the adult status, such as smoking, drinking, using drugs, and engaging in sex, as they believe that this behavior will construct the reflection they want.

10.4 PHYSICAL DEVELOPMENT

The teenage years are characterized as a time of rapid physical change leading to physical maturity. These patterns are especially notable in the rapid changes in height, weight, muscle growth, and maturation of sexual organs associated with puberty. They also are associated with the psychological effects stemming from concern about one's appearance and body build, emotional sensitivity, and other factors.

Height and weight changes: Puberty is defined as the period of rapid growth. The approach of puberty at about age eleven in girls and age twelve in boys signals the beginning of numerous physical and psychological changes. Puberty, or the process through which the reproductive organs mature, causes rapid increases in height and weight known as the adolescent growth spurt. These rapid changes occur over a period of about three years. Approximately thirteen centimeters (about five inches) in additional height gains are experienced by girls and about eighteen centimeters (approximately seven inches) by boys through the age of fourteen.

Weight gains average about 30 pounds (13 kgs.) for girls and about 45 pounds (20 kgs.) for boys over this same age period. Most gains can be expected to be completed by age fourteen for girls and age fifteen for boys. Heights gained precede weight gains in early adolescence. Most weight gains occur toward the second half of this part of adolescence and are due to rapid increases in muscle mass and size. During the puberty, the bones grow longer and change in shape, proportions and internal structure. The cartilage and fibrous tissue that made up the bones in childhood are replaced by a harder tissue created by the conversion of cartilage into bone. This is brought about by the thyroid hormone. By 17 years, the girls' bones are mature or nearly mature in size and ossification, whereas for the boys, skeletal development is complete approximately two years later.

Age of maturity affects the growth spurt of those who begin late. There is slight tendency for early developers to have a longer duration than later developers. Late maturing girls have completed with the result that they are generally taller at maturity than are the girls who started to mature earlier. As growth in height and weight is nearly complete at the time of menarche, late maturing girls have a longer time in which to grow.

Body Proportions: The various parts of the body gradually come into proportion. Changes that occur in the proportions of the body follow a dramatic course similar to the increases in height and weight. The extremities of the body grow earlier and more rapidly than other areas of the body at the beginning of puberty. These rapid increases in proportion give the young adolescent the appearance of being "all hands and feet." The calves and forearms begin to increase next, followed by the trunk area involving the hips, chest, and shoulders. Most height increases come from growth of the trunk areas rather than growth of the legs. Adolescents who look attractive and have favourable body image are likely to have greater favourable self-image and be happier, and also socially successful than unattractive adolescents with poor body images.

Sex Organs: Both male and female sex organs reach their mature size in late adolescence, but are not mature in function until several years later. The reproductive systems of boys and girls at adolescence enlarge and mature into those of sexually mature men and women. The primary sexual characteristics – genitals and associated structures- have been in existence since birth, but at puberty they become functional. Girls begin to menstruate and then to ovulate, boys to ejaculate semen.

Sexual maturation :

Puberty is the developmental event in which a child becomes a sexually mature individual. Puberty is experienced by boys and girls in a different maturational sequence as well as time. Although individual differences are very noticeable in the ages at which puberty begins and ends worldwide, there is a trend toward an earlier age at which both sexual maturity is begun and achieved.

When does puberty start?

Change in hormonal balance occurs first, but its beginning is difficult to pinpoint. Skeletal growth, genital growth, pubic hair, breast development, voice change, growth spurt—are all inconvenient to measure. Menarche has been suggested as the major turning point for girls. Menstruation in girls is a significant physical event that produces psychological effects. Menarche is an event related to an emerging identity as a woman, a newly acquired ability to reproduce, and a change in the relationship with the mother . Hormonal changes actually precede menarche by about two years, or as early as 8 or 9 years of age. Sometimes the first ejaculation is suggested as the beginning of adolescent puberty for male.

Just as the body proportions and size generally undergo a rapid increase in growth during adolescence, the event of puberty produces rapid changes in the growth of the reproductive organs. Menstruation is highly variable in duration and length for about the first year, which is a period of adolescent sterility. Although a girl may be menstruating irregularly during this time, ovulation or production of viable egg cells does not yet occur.

With the appearance and regulation of the menstrual cycle, other sexual developments occur in girls. The hips become enlarged and widened as a result of the growth of the pelvis. The breasts begin to develop shortly after the widening of the hips with the nipples showing increases in size before the mammary tissue enlarges. Public hair appears next after the enlargement of the hips and breasts commences. Growth of hair at other locations on the body is associated with the menarche but is lighter in pigmentation and softer in texture except at the armpits and on the legs (because of the practice of shaving these areas). Voice changes are noticeable in girls at this time but breaks in tone and pitch are uncommon. In both boys and girls the glands that are located in the armpits also become active at this time resulting in the production of perspiration and changes in body odor. Similar glands located on the face also begin to function at this time, sometimes accompanied by acne, which can result from lack of hygiene, infection, or other causes.

Despite the fact that puberty is primarily thought of as a physical change in an adolescent, the psychological impact can be significant. Too many girls experience menarche without being properly prepared. As a result, an event in a young girl's life that should be remembered as the exciting, positive beginning of the transition to adulthood is instead viewed as a negative, sometimes frightening experience. The same is no doubt also the case for a male's first ejaculation. Accurate and accessible information about the changes our bodies undergo benefits adolescents, for whom physical changes often lead to sexual activity.

Psychological effects of puberty

Hurlock (1980) lists several psychological changes in early adolescence that are associated with or are a result of the physical changes produced by puberty:

- A desire for isolation, which teenagers demonstrate at times by withdrawing from interaction with peers and family and devoting much time to daydreaming, being alone, and craving privacy;
- Heightened emotionality, which is demonstrated by emotional outbursts of anger, pouty behavior, and crying easily;
- Excessive modesty, which is shown through a heightened sensitivity and embarrassment about changes that are occurring in the body;
- Lack of coordination due to an inability to adjust quickly to rapidly changing body size and proportions;
- Heightened insecurity, which appears in the form of decreased self-confidence, and may also be due to changes in the behavioral standards set up by parents as well as a decreased level of strength and energy.

Other effects at early stages of puberty include a peak in self-doubt, avoidance of responsibility, resentment of parents, and anxiety about social relations. Emotional tension peaks by mid-puberty. Throughout the period, individuals shift their interactions increasingly away from parents and toward peers. Girls may react more strongly than boys to the rapid body changes because they experience the changes of puberty earlier than boys but recover quicker and establish a stable pattern of behavior sooner.

The secular trend

The secular trend refers to the decreasing age of the onset of puberty, including a significant drop in the average age at which females in a particular country reach menarche. Earlier puberty affects other development factors such as sexual attraction. Today, the average age of menarche is 12.5 years, about the same as it was in 1955. For white girls, the average age is 12.9, for Africa-Americans, 12.2. Most researchers feel that improved nutrition and sanitation are responsible for the trend and that we are now at a period of leveling off.

10.4.1 Development of primary and secondary sex characteristics:

The female sexual system

The parts of the female sexual system are defined as

- Bartholin's glands. A pair of glands located on either side of the vagina. These glands provide some of the fluid that acts as a lubricant during intercourse.
- Cervix. The opening to the uterus located at the inner end of the vagina.
- Clitoris. Comparable to the male penis. Both organs are similar in the first few months after conception, becoming differentiated only as sexual determination takes place. The clitoris is the source of maximum sexual stimulation and becomes erect through sexual excitement. It is above the vaginal opening, between the labia minora.
- Fallopian tubes. Conduct the ova (egg) from the ovary to the uterus. A fertilized egg that becomes lodged in the fallopian tubes, called a fallopian or ectopic pregnancy, cannot develop normally and if not surgically removed will cause the tube to rupture.
- Fimbriae. Hairlike structures located at the opening of the oviduct that help move the ovum down the fallopian tube to the uterus.
- Hymen. A flap of tissue that usually covers most of the vaginal canal in virgins.
- Labia majora. The two larger outer lips of the vaginal opening.
- Labia minora. The two smaller inner lips of the vaginal opening.
- Mons pubis or Mons veneris. The outer area just above the vagina, which becomes larger during adolescence and on which the first pubic hair appears.
- Ova. The female reproductive cells stored in the ovaries. These eggs are fertilized by the male sperm. Girls are born with more than a million follicles, each of which holds an ovum. At puberty, only 10,000 remain, but they are more than sufficient for a women's reproductive life. Usually, as only 1 egg ripens each month from the mid teens to the late forties, a women releases fewer than 500 ova during her lifetime.
- Ovaries. Glands that releases one ovum each month. They also produce the hormones estrogen and progesterone, which play an important part in the menstrual cycle and pregnancy.
- Pituitary gland. The "master" gland located in the lower part of the brain. Not strictly part of the sexual system, nevertheless it controls sexual maturation and excitement and monthly menstruation.
- Ureter. A canal connecting each of the kidneys with the bladder.
- Urethra. A canal leading from the bladder to the external opening through which urine is excreted.

- Uterus. The hollow organ (also called the womb) in which the fertilized egg must implant itself for a viable pregnancy to occur. The egg attaches itself to the lining of the uterus, from which the fetus draws nourishments as it matures during the nine months before birth.
- Vulva. The external genital organs of the female.

The male sexual system

The parts of the male sexual system are defined as

- Cowper's glands. Located next to the prostate glands. Their job is to secrete a fluid that changes the chemical balance in the urethra from an acidic to an alkaline base. This fluid proceeds up through the urethra in the penis, where it is ejaculated during sexual excitement just before the sperm also may be found in this solution, sometimes called preseminal fluid. Therefore, even if the male withdraws his penis before he ejaculates, it is possible for him to deposit some sperm in the vagina, which may cause pregnancy.
- Prostate gland. Produces a milky alkaline substance known as semen. In the prostate the sperm are mixed with the semen to give them greater mobility.
- Epididymis. A small organ attached to each testis. It is a storage place for newly produced sperm.
- Foreskin. A flap of loose skin that surrounds the glans penis at birth, often removed by a surgery called circumcision.
- Glans penis. The tip, or head, of the penis.
- Pituitary gland. The "master" gland controlling sexual characteristics. In the male it controls the production of sperm, the release of testosterone (and thus the appearance of secondary sexual characteristics such as the growth of hair and voice change), and sexual excitement and maturation.
- Scrotum. The sac of skin located just below the penis, in which the testes and Epididymis are located.
- Testes. The two oval sex glands, suspended in the scrotum, that produce sperm. Sperm are the gene cells that fertilize the ova. They are equipped with a tail-like structure that enables them to move about by a swimming motion. After being ejaculated from the penis into the vagina, sperm attempt to swim through the cervix into the uterus and into the fallopian tubes, where fertilization takes place. If one penetrates an egg, conception occurs. Although the testes regularly produce million of sperm, the odds against any particular sperm penetrating an egg are enormous. The testes also produce testosterone, the male hormone that affects other aspects of sexual development.
- Ureter. A canal connecting each of the kidneys with the bladder.
- Urethra. A canal that connects the bladder with the opening of the penis. It is also the path taken by the preseminal fluid and sperm during ejaculation.
- Vas deferens. A pair of tubes that lead from the Epididymis up to the prostate. They carry the sperm when the male is sexually aroused and about to ejaculate.

10.4.2 Internal organ changes

There are a number of changes in the functioning and structure of internal organ systems that are associated with adolescence. Blood pressure levels off, pulse rates decrease, and basal heat production falls rapidly after menarche in girls. Changes in the blood are also noted in adolescence. The number of red blood cells and the amount of hemoglobin in the blood increases throughout childhood. This ceases at puberty for girls but continues for boys during adolescence and may be due to the increasingly higher levels of testosterone in boys that is associated with greater blood volume, greater muscle mass, and high metabolic rates. The central nervous system reaches full maturity in adolescence. Brain waves become adult like and head circumference enlarges slightly, indicating a small additional increment in brain size. Sensory organs experience change in adolescence as well. Eye abnormalities are much less prevalent in adolescence than in middle childhood. About 15 percent of adolescents studied have some type of ear abnormality, reducing hearing sensitivity at all frequencies. The average number of decayed, missed, or filled teeth also increases steadily through adolescence.

Facial acne is the most frequently observed skin condition at this time of life and its incidence increases rapidly during the period, especially among boys. This condition is a chronic inflammation of the oil glands and hair follicles located on the face area. Treatment ranges from daily washing with special soaps to creams that remove oil and provide antibacterial action. More extreme methods include X-ray treatment, vitamin A therapy, and skin-peeling techniques. After puberty, boys tend to improve in running and jumping after age thirteen while girls show decline in performance of these skills. Boys have a definite advantage over girls in throwing skills throughout adolescence.

Other common changes are found in

(*a*) Digestive system — The stomach becomes longer and less tubular, the intestines grow in length and circumference, the muscles in the stomach and intestinal walls become thicker and stronger. The liver increases in weight, and the oesophagus becomes longer.

(*b*) Circulatory System — The heart grows rapidly during adolescence by the age of 17 or 18. The length and thickness of the walls of the blood vessels increase and reach a mature level.

(*c*) Respiratory System — The lung capacity of girls is almost at a mature level at age 17; boys reach this level several years later.

(*d*) Endocrine System — The increased activity of the gonads at puberty results in a temporary imbalance of the whole endocrine system in early adolescence. The sex glands develop rapidly and become functional though they do not reach their mature size until late adolescence.

(*e*) Body Tissue — The skeleton stops growing at an average age of 18. Tissues other than bone continue to develop after the bones have reached their mature size.

Factors influencing physical development

(*a*) Nutrition and Obesity — Nutrition has an important influence on the quality of growth in adolescence as well as the timing of puberty and general health status. Teenagers will, of course, eat more during the growth spurt. Adolescent eating habits are notoriously poor as almost every parent can testify. Teenagers typically eat too many empty-calorie or junk foods such as potato chips, pizza, soft drinks, pastries, candies, and so on that contain mostly starches and sugars, all of which results in fat deposition. Poor relationships with parents were linked with increased dieting in girls. Anorexia nervosa, or bulimia nervosa is common in this period.

(*b*) Hereditary — A child or adolescent is more likely to be obese if one or both of his parents are obese. Many of the adolescents have low calorie needs because of physical inactivity and this inactivity causes them to accumulate fat.

(*c*) Malnutrition — It appears to delay the growth spurt, and a poorly nourished child grows slowly and do not grow into average size. Deficiencies in any of the elements required for growth – vitamin, minerals and protein can have adverse effects on energy level, resistance to disease, behavior, emotion and appearance.

(*d*) Health and Illness — Health generally improves as age increases, with fewer illness and abnormalities being observed than in earlier years. Boys exceed girls in number of total illnesses. Cardiovascular conditions are more prevalent in adolescence than in childhood. Neuromuscular and joint conditions occur at greater frequencies, however, than cardiovascular problems. Childhood infectious diseases continue to occur frequently throughout adolescence. Teenagers are reluctant to discuss many health-related issues with parents, however, such as venereal disease, death, and mental illness. They feel, on the other hand, the need to involve parents in discussions about sexual matters. Teenagers are stereotyped at practicing generally poor health habits such as using drugs, smoking, drinking, and eating improperly, and so on. Physical illness is often associated with life stress and other measures of psychological illness.

(*e*) Smoking — It affects overall physical development. It is started mostly by peer group influence; some use it as an outlet of feeling though it is a negative one.

(*f*) Use of drugs and alcohols — The use of certain of these substances by adolescents constitutes health problem, both physical and mental. The misuse of drugs among adolescents and young adults is one of the greatest concerns today. In reading mass-media accounts, one can gain the impression that drug misuse is at epidemic proportions. Drugs used more commonly by adolescents include alcohol, tobacco, marijuana, hallucinogens, inhalants, barbiturates, amphetamines, and other related substances and their effects are felt on body and mind. Peer and adult models have a decided influence on the initiation of adolescent drug use. Alcohol and tobacco are used more frequently than other drug agents by teenagers.

(*g*) Attractiveness — Every boy is interested in masculinity and the majority of girls want to lose weight. Most of them become obese because of humiliating rejection, social isolation, physical inferiority and feeling of depression.

(*h*) Acne — Acne appears to be a natural occurrence during adolescence; it is due to increased secretion of the sex hormone- androgen. This may worry adolescents, as they feel that facial skin is said to be a canvas in which the surface reveals its emotions.

(*i*) Cultural and class difference — Cultural differences and related social class distinction account for discrepancies in the rate of growth; those in higher status seem to grow more.

(*j*) Hormones — Hypo secretion of the anterior portion of the pituitary cause a person to remain child like in size, while hyper secretion makes growth spurt to gain in proportion.

(*k*) Pregnancy — Adolescent girls who become pregnant are likely to experience a greater-than-usual number of complications that are physical, psychological, and social in nature. Teenage pregnancies usually are considered to be of high risks.

(*l*) Accidents and injuries — The incidence of serious accidents and injuries increases steadily through adolescence. Boys exceed girls in experiencing a greater number of these injuries as age increases through adolescence. Accidental death rates also increase considerably during adolescence with males dying in greater number than females.

(*m*) Suicide — The second leading cause of death among adolescents is suicide. The causes of adolescent suicide include:

- Feelings of social isolation;
- Stress due to strained relations with parents or in reaction to parental abuse;
- Drug abuse;
- Alienation from society;
- Depression;

- High suggestibility to suicide ideas;
- Internalized, self-directed aggression;
- A need to communicate a desire for help.

School counselors and psychological counseling is very effective in helping adolescents to recover feelings of self-worth and purpose during stressful periods when suicide often is contemplated.

10.5 EMOTIONAL DEVELOPMENT IN ADOLESCENCE

Adolescence is a period of heightened emotionality ie., intensified emotions. The criteria to decide whether or not an individual is experiencing heightened emotionality is how he reacts emotionally as compared with the usual pattern, which is expressed in the form of his/her behavior. Emotional fluctuations in early adolescence are due to variability of hormones, stress, eating patterns, sexual activity and social relationships. Moods become less extreme as adolescents move into adulthood.

Adolescence is labeled as a period of equilibrium – times when insanities, tension, indecision and similar forms of behaviour are readily recognized. Expression of heightened emotionality is specified in the form of nervous habits such as oral thumb sucking, nasal wrinkling of the nose, hirsutal – scratching the head, or facial expression.

Heightened emotionality results from the necessity of breaking old habits, thoughts and actions and establishing new ones and while the adjustment is taking place, the adolescent is emotionally disturbed. After the adjustment has been made the adolescent settles down, which are the products of environment and social factors. Social experiences of more mature behaviour, social adjustment to the other sex, school failing, vocational problem, religious doubt, unfavourable family relationship are the obstacles that prevent the adolescent from doing what he desires.

Common emotional pattern in adolescence

The most important emotional pattern of adolescence includes fear, anger, worry, jealousy, envy, grief, affection, joy and curiosity.

1. **Anger:** Adolescents get angry when teased, ridiculed and criticized by a friend, or during unfair treatment and punishment by parents or teachers. The more common form of anger response is sulkiness or being a disagreeable individual, who refuses to talk and do what he is expected to do.
2. **Fear:** Adolescents fear about school and subject, fear about illness, or staying alone in the house. The response in adolescence is rigidity of the body accompanied by trembling and perspiring.
3. **Worry:** It is the type of fear that comes from imaginary causes. There is an element of reality in it but it is exaggerated. It is specific in that it is related to the persons, thing or situation. Tests and exams in schools are the chief source of worry connected with school work. Young adolescent girls worry about the appearance, difficulty in making friends, clothes, and money, whereas boys worry more than girls about ability and money. There are two common emotional responses to worry - the first consist of verbalising worries to peers and teachers in the hope of gaining their sympathy and help and the second going around with a worried and harassed look disregard of the present situation.
4. **Jealousy:** An young adolescent is jealous of peers who have privilege and more independence or who are more successful in school work and athletics than they are and also of their classmates who are more popular than themselves. The decreased security they feel with their relation with peer groups, the more likely they are to be jealous of those whose acceptance seem assured.

5. **Envy:** Adolescence may be envious of a classmate whose clothes and home are superior to hers. The envious adolescent may criticize and make fun of the possession of others.
6. **Grief:** Most grief in adolescence may come from loss due to death, divorce, absence of the person to whom he/she has strong emotional attachment or breaking of relationship-friendship (i.e.) which enabled the adolescent benefit and learn from those concepts and mistakes made as a growing child. Thinking is flexible because problems can be dealt within the present and future, and further more the adolescent can make use of rational and logical thought processes.
7. **Affection:** It is a pleasant emotional state of mind. Stimulus to affection is aroused by people inside home and rarely by animals. The affection is shifted from people inside home to outside home with whom the relationship is less frictional. Usual response is happiness in the presence of people who are liked.
8. **Curiosity:** For most of the adolescents the chief source of new interest is their own and their friends' sexual maturation. They are also curious about scientific phenomenon, the world affairs, sports, religions and moral issues. Books containing information about sex are eagerly read by both boys and girls.

10.6 SOCIAL DEVELOPMENT

An adolescent's social behavior is an enigma to many adults. The individual strives for unreasonable autonomy in adolescence but behaves in many hypocritical ways. Much of an adolescent's behavior centers on several developmental tasks that are central to psychological well-being. Erikson speaks of a sense of identity versus role confusion as the critical psychosocial issue of adolescence development. Cognitive or mental development enters a final phase in adolescence. Teenagers have characteristic ways of perceiving and understanding the world as well as experiencing a shift in problem-solving activities. Moral development in adolescents reflects these cognitive changes as teenagers confront crucial decisions that affect their behavior. How much adolescents know, how they think, and how will they write is determined to some extent by what they are taught in school, be that mathematics, creative writing, and computer programming, shopping and home economics.

One of the most difficult developmental tasks of adolescents relates to social adjustments. These adjustments must be made to members of the opposite sex because adolescents spend most of their time outside the home with members of peer group. It is understandable that the peers would have a greater influence on the adolescent's attitude, speech, interest, appearance and behavior than the family has. To identify themselves with an adult, the young adolescent wants to do what adults do when they are in such a situation, for eg., smoking, drinking, driving, using narcotics, engaging in sexual activities which are a symbol of adult status.

Social grouping

Friendship is based on similarities and shared interest. They comfort each other when they are sad, angry or in trouble. Adolescent girls' friendships are more intimate and exclusive than boys. The most common grouping in adolescence includes chums, cliques, crowd, organized group and gang.

- Chums (close friend) – They are the inseparable companions and confidants. They are often people who know each other from childhood. Usually they are of same sex and have similar interest and abilities.
- Cliques – Cliques are usually made up of groups of close friends. At first they consist of members of the same sex but later include both boys and girls. Their activities consist of going to the movies, attending athletic contest, studying together, going to parties, talking and telephoning to each other when parted.

- Crowds – Crowds are made up of cliques and groups of close friend. They develop interest in parties and dating grows. The major interest centers on talking, playing, listening to records, eating, drinking, and going to movies.
- Organized groups – Formally organized groups are planned by school, churches, community to provide social activities for all adolescents but especially for those who lack membership in cliques or crowds. Participants are not selected by their peers but come together because of common interests. Many adolescents lose interest in organized groups by the time they are 16 or 17 year old.
- Gangs – There are boys and girls who are poorly adjusted to school and also have few friends among their classmates. They spend their time in street corners. Majority of adolescent gangs spend their time in antisocial behaviour, seeking revenge on those who have not accepted them.

New values in selecting friends and leaders:

Adolescents no longer select their friends on the basis of ready availability at school or neighborhoods as they did during childhood, and the enjoyments of the same activities is not much important in friendship selection. For most young adolescents, popularity means having a large number of friends. As they grow older, the kind of friends they have become more important than the number. By now, they know what they want in their friends and so they insist upon the right to select them without adult interference.

As adolescents feel that the leaders of their peer group represent them in the eyes of society, they therefore want leaders of superior ability who will be admired and respected by others and who in turn will reflect favorably on them. The quality of a leader is to make a good appearance, should be nice looking, very stylish, and above average in intelligence. They must come from a family of higher socio economic status than who are non-leaders. Other qualities to be present in them are dependability, royalty, a wide range of interest, self confidence, ready to extend a decision, good sportsmanship, and sociability, sense of humor, ethnicity, good adaptability, smartness and co-operativeness.

Highlights of social and mental development in adolescence appear in the box below.

Box 10-1

Social And Mental Characteristics Of Adolescence

- Usually have two or three close friends.
- Is a member of a clique in early adolescence; enjoys crowd participation in late adolescence.
- Beginning of interest and participation in heterosexual relationships.
- Enjoys organized games and sports activities.
- May experiment with drugs, alcohol, smoking, and various types of sexual behavior.
- Has idealistic attitudes and opinions about almost every topic.
- Beginning of exploration of vocational interests and preferences.
- Moral development is closely related to cognitive development.
- Emerging ability to use logic and reasoning as well as abstract thinking.
- Greater flexibility in thought but remains egocentric.

Sociogram: It is a means of presenting simply a graphically structured relationship existing at a given time among members of a given group. According to Best (1963), sociometric choices that are represented graphically on a chart is known as Sociogram.

Sociometry: It is the technique for describing social relationships that exist between individuals in a group. In an indirect way it attempts to describe attraction and repulsion between individuals.

Peer relations

Important debates have existed in the field of adolescent psychology concerning the value and influence of peer and parental relationships during adolescence. The role of peers as a source of activities, support, and influence increases greatly. Perhaps it is for these reasons that adults and the media have been interested in and anxious about the role of the peer group. Brown (1990) described four specific ways in which the peer group changes from childhood to adolescence.

- As previously mentioned, adolescents spend much more time with peers than do younger children. As early as sixth grade, the early adolescent begins withdrawing from adults and increases time spent with peers. During high school, middle adolescents spend twice as much time with their peers as they spend with parents.
- Adolescent peer groups receive less adult supervision and control. Teenagers try to avoid close supervision by parents and teachers, and are more independent, and find places to meet where they are less closely watched. Even at home, teenagers seek privacy and places where they can talk to friends without being overheard by parents and siblings.
- Adolescents begin interacting more with peers of the opposite sex. Although boys and girls participate in different activities and friendship groups during middle childhood, the sexes mix increasingly during the adolescent years. Interaction with members of the opposite sex seems to increase at the same time as adolescents distance themselves from their parents.
- During adolescence, peer groups become more aware of the values and behaviors of the larger adolescent subculture. They also identify with certain crowds, which are groups with a reputation for certain values, attitudes, or activities.

It is well known that teenagers, especially girls, spend a lot of time talking to their peers, much of it over the telephone. Peer relationships were the most frequently discussed topic (46 to 60 percent), followed by family problems (10 to 20 percent) in various public forums.

Functions of peer groups

In contrast to the popular view that peers are a negative influence during adolescence, peer influence serves important social and psychological functions. When adolescents do not have the chance to be part of a peer group, they miss out on important learning experiences. Kelly and Hansen (1990) described six important positive functions of the peer group.

The group can help teens to:

(1) Control aggressive impulse.

(2) Obtain emotional and social support and become more independent.

(3) Improve social skills, develop reasoning abilities, and learn to express feelings in more mature ways.

(4) Develop attitudes toward sexuality and gender-role behavior.

(5) Strengthen moral judgment and values. The adolescent has to evaluate the values of peers and decide what is right for him or her. This process of evaluation can help the adolescent to develop moral-reasoning abilities.

(6) Improve self-esteem. It is clear that the formation of intimate friendship is an important adolescent goal. One of the most important aspects of these friendships during adolescence is the growing trend for them to become sexual.

10.7 COGNITIVE DEVELOPMENT

Adolescence is a complex process of growth and change. Because biological and social changes are the focus of attention, changes in the young adolescent's ability to think often go unnoticed, yet growth spurts in the parietal and frontal lobes of the brain, as well as subcortical regions, make possible tremendous changes in the quality of a teenager's thinking. It has recently been discovered that there are actually two growth spurts, one at around 12 and 13 and a second in the later teen years. It is during early and middle adolescence that thinking ability reaches Piaget's fourth and last level—the level of abstract thought. Culture & gender can also influence cognitive development.

Gender also plays a role in the definition of formal operations. Gilligan, (1982), contends that this gender difference also leads to distinctions in the development of thinking about morality. A sex difference is noted in which boys have been found to increase in intelligence test scores in adolescence while girls experience decrease as a group. This may be the result of the pressures experienced by many girls to conform to a cultural stereotype about appropriate sex-role behavior. Teachers generally rate girls higher than boys in overall academic performance, however. This difference may reflect the disadvantages boys encounter in academic work from having a shorter attention span, more aggressive and restless behavior, and so on.

An individual emerges from the middle childhood stage by viewing the world in absolute terms. Issues and behavior are seen in terms of polar extremes. Something is definitely either right or wrong to do, people are treated either fairly or unfairly, and someone is either good or bad. A major developmental task of the adolescent is to reconcile this approach to categorizing values and behavior by developing an ability to perceive gray areas and to develop a rationale for understanding rules of conduct.

Critical Thinking

The distinction between convergent and divergent thinking is helpful here, because critical thinking is made up of these two abilities. Convergent thinking is used when we solve a problem by following a series of steps that close in on the correct answer. Divergent thinking, on the other hand, is just the opposite. This is the type of thinking used when the problem to be solved has many possible answers. In summary, critical and creative thinking are similar in that they both employ convergent and divergent production, except that, critical thinking aims at the correct assessment of existing ideas, whereas creativity is more aimed at the invention and discovery of new ideas.

Robert Sternberg (2000a, 2000b) said that the intelligent person can recall, analyze, and use knowledge, whereas the creative person goes beyond existing knowledge, and the wise person probes inside knowledge and understands the meaning of what is known. It should be noted that these conclusions appear to hold true not only for adolescence but also for all periods of the lifespan.

Mental disorders

Adolescents suffer from a wide range of mental health disorders that affect their normal development and functioning. The most common of these mental health disorders are anxiety disorders (13 percent of children 9 to 17years), depression (8 percent of adolescents), and attention defect hyperactivity disorders (3 to 5 percent of school-aged children) (Child and Adolescent Mental Health Government Guide, 2002). Other disorders adolescents can experience are eating disorders, autism and other pervasive developmental disorders, conduct disorders, and substance abuse disorders. Many teens are not treated for mental disorders, as their parents and even their doctors often hope they will "grow out of it."

The transition from junior high school to high school can be a stressful time for adolescents. The stress may come from many different sources, such as peers, parents, siblings, and teachers. It is a time when more emphasis is placed on grades and academic achievement. It is also a time of increased pressure to date and experiment with cigarettes, drugs, and alcohol. The more the teen felt a sense of belonging in the school and the higher the teen's GPA, the easier the transition.

A number of factors that may affect adolescent mental health issues are age, gender, culture, poverty and genetics, to name a few. In addition, the diagnosis and treatment of adolescents' mental health disorders are very important for the long-term development of the youth. The failure to treat these mental health issues can lead to a range of academic, social, emotional, and behavioral problems as well as suicide and delinquency (Child and Adolescent Mental Health Government Guide, 2002). In conclusion, adolescence is not a time of turmoil and distress for most teens. Rates of mental disturbance among teens are very similar to rates of disturbance among adults. As you will recall, however, adolescents (and adults) are experiencing increasingly high levels of daily stress.

10.8 MORAL DEVELOPMENT

Moral development in adolescence parallels and reflects the shifts and refinements in cognitive skill development at this time in life. The idealism that emerges in adolescence is moral egocentricity as teenagers discover the discontinuity and hypocrisy of the adult world. Adolescents become very dogmatic and self-righteous, in keeping with their level of cognitive development. They see themselves as moral reformers of their parents and the world in general proposes that individuals move through three basic levels of moral development. The first is the Pre conventional stage which occurs in early childhood. The second is the Conventional stage which is experienced initially in adolescence and continues through adulthood. The third is termed Post conventional morality and is characterized by understanding a universal basis of individual choice in determining the ethicality of issues.

Late adolescence may find some individuals experiencing a regression in moral development to that found more commonly in middle childhood This apparent regression may represent the individual's attempts to deal with moral conflicts at this time in life. These conflicts may revolve around a number of issues occurring in late adolescence that reflect the determination of vocational and educational directions, personal goals, and the reconciliation of family and personal expectations. This situation is often remedied when reaching more advanced levels of moral reasoning by about the age of twenty-five.

The adolescents frequently seeks higher moral standard for him and for others that can be reached at all times. The adolescents are usually more willing to accept the blame than in the childhood. He/ she has a strong sense of fairness and intolerance to those whose behaviour falls below his/her standard. This leads to friction and quarrelling misdemeanors. As adolescents grow old, their behavior confirms to more social standards.

Misdemeanor – Common school misdemeanors (misbehaviour) include annoying the teacher, bullying classmates, smoking or drinking in the school ground, cheating, destruction of school property and truancy and vandalism. Home misbehavior consist of going out without telling parents, going to forbidden places, staying out beyond the set time, being rude, attacking the siblings, functioning away from home. Other common misdemeanors include annoying members of opposite sex, of their own sex who belong to another clique, and being unnecessarily noisy when they get together as a group. As such, misdemeanors are common among boys than in girls.

Personal adjustment

When the environment is characterized by affection, respect, co-operation, and tolerance, adolescence will develop a wholesome self-concept. This will be reflected in good adjustments to life. If the adolescence is to improve his personality and if he is to improve his personal adjustment, there are three essential requirements that must be fulfilled.

- He/she must have characteristic assessment for himself/herself and for the strength and weakness.
- He/she must have a stable self- concept. (Usually the self concept is unstable during puberty and early years of adolescence). However it normally becomes increasingly more stable as adolcscence progresses. An adolescent with a good self concept and a higher level of self esteem and fewer feelings of inadequacy, contrast the adolescence with unstable self concept who shows such qualities as introversion; dominance seeking, hypersensitivity and other problems.
- He/she must have a good self acceptance. Self acceptance leads to behaviours which makes others like him/her. When an adolescent does not like what he sees, he develops a self rejecting attitude. Self rejection leads to behaviour which makes others dislike and reject him.

Maladjustments

It is more common in adolescents to have poor social and personal adjustment. Many adolescents do show poor work in school and on the job. Mostly they have few friends and almost all are quarrelsome and unhappy at home and in their social relationship outside home.

Danger signals of maladjustment:

- Irresponsibility and dependency on others.
- Extreme feeling of inadequacy and inferiority.
- Aggressive physical or verbal attacks on others.
- Over use of defense mechanism such as rationalization and use of alcohol and drugs.
- Excessive worry, anxiety and insecurity.
- Over concern or lack of concern about appearance.
- Hypersensitivity.
- Other signals are temper tantrums, show–off type, shyness, smoking, depression, withdrawing, delinquency, cheating, destructiveness, disobedience, showing fear over persons, inquisitiveness, and truancy.

10.9 ADJUSTMENT PROBLEMS AMONG ADOLESCENTS

Adjustment is the outcome of an individual's attempt to deal with stress and meet their needs to maintain harmonious relationship with themselves and their environment. The efficiency with which the adolescents adjust or attempt to master and transcend the challenge of life by utilizing a variety of techniques and strategies is crucial to them. Many adjustment problems first occur during the adolescent years when they are unable to adjust with psychological or social stress. Their maladjusted behaviour occurs when they fail to perform the functions demanded by their position in life. Adjustment problems among adolescents could be seen in five major areas, namely, Home, Health, Social, Emotional and Educational.

- **Home:** Family plays an important role in establishing healthy adjustment problems of adolescents. Family helps the adolescents to fulfill their personal needs, and teaches them cultured patterns of behaviour. The psychological climate of the home is extremely important in all phases of human development. Rebellion, the stereotypical hallmark of adolescent behavior, results not because it is a destined part of adolescent development but because of a home environment that is patriarchal, authoritarian, and unhappy. Lack of understanding and empathy between parents and teenagers is likely to disrupt family harmony and breed conflicts. When the relationship of young adolescents with family members deteriorate as adolescence progresses, the fault usually lies on both sides. Parents refuse to modify their concepts of their children's abilities as they grow older. As a result they treat adolescent sons and daughters much as they did when they were younger.

Common Causes of Family Friction During Adolescence:

The majority of these disagreements focus on the teenager's personal conduct and activities and the degree of freedom that he or she deserves to have in conducting her or his own affairs. Conflict however, most often results when parents resort to coercive control methods to resolve disagreements.

Immaturity in family relationships, as shown by quarreling with family members, criticizing them constantly, or making derogatory comments about their appearance or behaviour, is especially common during the early years of adolescence. Poor family relationships are psychological hazards at any age, but especially so during adolescence because at this time boys and girls are typically unsure of themselves and depend more on their families for a feeling of security and guidance to master the developmental tasks.

Specifically, the causes are :

Standards of Behavior: Adolescents often consider their parents' standards of behavior old-fashioned and resent having to conform to standards different from those of their peers.

Methods of Discipline: When adolescents regard disciplinary methods used by their parents as "unfair" or "childish" they rebel. Authoritative disciplinary methods of parental control in which the adolescent is consulted about family matters and given a fair share of economy and discipline primarily on a verbal basis are effective and rewarding.

Relationships with Siblings: The adolescent may be scornful of younger siblings and resentful of older ones, leading to friction with them as well as with parents, whom they may accuse of "playing favorites".

Feeling Victimized: Adolescents often become resentful if the socioeconomic status of their families makes it impossible for them to have the same status symbols - clothes, cars, etc.- their friends have, or if they must assume many household responsibilities or if a step-parent comes into the home and tries to "boss" them.

Hypercritical Attitudes: Family members resent adolescents' hypercritical attitudes toward them and the general pattern of family life.

Family Size: In medium sized families – three to four children – there is more friction than in small or large families.

Immature Behavior: Parents often develop punitive attitudes when adolescents neglect their school work, shun their responsibilities, or spend their money foolishly. Adolescents resent these critical and punitive attitudes.

"Latchkey Problems": The new and more active social life of adolescents may result in the breaking of family rules concerning time to return home and the people they associate with, especially members of the opposite sex.

"Generation Gap": is an even more important problem between adolescents and their parents. This gap is partly the result of radical changes in values and standards of behaviour that normally occur in any rapidly changing culture and partly the result of the fact that many young people now have greater educational, social and cultural opportunities than most of their parents had when they were adolescents. Thus it is more correctly a "Cultural Gap" and not entirely due to different chronological age.

Elkind (1974) describes conflicts between parents and adolescents as a product of the growth toward maturity by both groups. He states that there are three types of arrangements between parents and adolescents that govern and regulate child behavior: the bargain, the agreement, and the contract. Conflict results either between the adolescents or the parents or both. Relations between parents and teenagers may become tense as teenagers come to expect and demand freedom that violate these contractual agreements with parents. Grinder (1973) identifies three reasons that may explain why parents have difficulty in recognizing the adolescent's needs to achieve recognition as a maturing, responsible individual:

(1) Cultural impoverishment of the parents,

(2) Personality constrictions of the parents, and

(3) Anticipating events that the teenager will confront in his/her future,

Elkind relates to parents' conflicts over recognition that their increasingly autonomous child is removing their "need to be needed" in showing less dependence on them for guidance and care. Adolescents also attempt to influence the mother more than the father. Mostly, it includes use of leisure time, television viewing, choice of travel site, car and appliance purchases, menus, planning for family social activities, family decisions, personal appearance, and changing jobs. Much of the conflict between parents and teenagers ultimately relates to the adolescents' use of and strivings toward autonomy and identity. Teenage sons as well as daughters and their parents agree on a number of topics that should be discussed between them. Sons and their parents agree that topics such as birth control, sex, drugs, alcohol, diet should be openly discussed, but most of all, they want their parents to share more of the personal concerns with them such as health problems, marital problems, and costs of health care.

Parents likewise find it difficult to accept their adolescent children's objections to the restraints they regard as necessary and they may be impatient with their failure to assume responsibilities they feel are appropriate for their age. When family relationships are marked by friction, feelings of insecurity are likely to be prolonged, and adolescents will be deprived of the opportunity to develop poise and more mature patterns of behaviour. This militates against good social adjustments. These sources of irritation generally reach their peak between 14 and 15 years, after which there is generally an improvement in parent– adolescent relationship.

Ways of Improving Communication between parents and adolescents:

- Parents need to recognize the continued importance of their relationship with their adolescents. Although the parent-child relationship undergoes transformation during adolescence, the adjustment of adolescents depends in good measure on the quality of their relationship with their parents.
- Children are more vulnerable to adjustment problems in adolescence than in childhood. Parents need to anticipate that their adolescent requires increased support during periods of transition, such as entry into high school. Adolescents need to feel that their parents are engaged and supportive of them. . Be an askable (approachable) parent.
- Parents have to give their individual affection when children want to talk. Listen calmly and concentrate on hearing and understanding the children's point of view. Speak with children as curiously and pleasantly as possible.
- Avoid humiliating and laughing at what may seem to be foolish questions and statements. Encourage the children to test new ideas in conversation by not judging the ideas and

opinions, but by listening and then offering their own ideas as plainly and honestly as possible.

- Help the children build self confidence by encouraging their participation in activities of their choice. Encourage the children to participate in family decision making and to work out family concern together.
- Adolescents are more independent than children in many aspects of their lives. Nonetheless, they require ongoing parental support in terms of parents remaining open to communication and responsive if help is needed, while, at the same time, fostering adolescent autonomy. Specific parenting skills include warmth, acceptance of individuality, active listening, behaviour monitoring, limit setting and negotiation.
- Parents need to recognize the special role of fathers in supporting the well-being of their children. Fathers' increased psychological support of daughters may be particularly beneficial to them.
- Obviously, adolescent adjustment is also determined by factors outside the family and the parent-child relationship. Even though parents may only indirectly affect how peers, romantic partners and other social influences determine the adjustment of their children, parents' support through the stressful challenges of adolescence remains important.

When family relationships are marked by friction, feelings of insecurity are likely to be prolonged, and adolescents will be deprived of the opportunity to develop poise and more mature patterns of behaviour. This militates against good social adjustments.

What adolescents can do?

1. Avoid looking at your parents as an enemy.
2. Chances are there that they love you and have your best interest in mind even if you do not necessarily agree with their way of showing that.
3. Try to understand that your parents are bearing with their own insecurities, needs and hearing.
4. Share your feelings with your parents, so they can understand you better.
5. Live up to your responsibility at home and school, so that they will be more inclined to grant you the kind of independence you want and need.
6. Bolster your criticism of family, school and government with suggestions for practical improvements.
7. Be as courageous and considerate to your own parents as you would be to parents of your friends.

- **Health:** Adequate health adjustment is an essential component of wholesome personality development for adolescents. An adolescents' home and neighbourhood experiences give them awesome misconceptions about common health habits.

  1. **Eating disorders:** Some adolescents, especially girls put on weight as they enter their teens, leading a life long struggle to get down to levels that are most desirable for both health and beauty. In recent years, two different kinds of eating problems anorexia nervosa and bulimia nervosa are seen.

- **Anorexia Nervosa:** This affects both sexes of varying ages. The typical patient is a bright well balanced, appealing female somewhere between puberty and the early twenties from an apparently stable, well educated well-off family.(The term anorexia is a misnomer because loss of appetite is rare.) An adolescent is pre-occupied with food – with cooking it and talking about it, but she does not eat it herself or gorges herself, and then purges by vomiting or by using laxatives. She has a distorted sense of body image and sees herself beautiful when she is atmost pathetical and skeletal.

- **Bulimia:** Conservative estimates indicate that it affects 5% of general population. A related disorder bulimia, also most common in teenage young women is characterized by eating huge quantities of food followed by vomiting to empty the stomach. The person affected by bulimia is often depressed also.

2. **Drug use and abuse:** People have always relied on drugs to alleviate their unhappiness, as well as their physical ailments and to give a meaning to their lives. Certain drugs may not be harmful in moderation., but adolescents are not known for being moderates. In those years of identity crisis, they often turn to drugs as short cut answers to their problems, and they endanger their physical and psychological health while failing to resolve the problems. Just as adults take barbiturates and stimulants to alleviate unhappiness or depression, a day-to-day pressure, so do youths.
3. **Alcohol:** Use of alcohol and other drugs is one of the major health problems among youth. Young people, usually boys, use alcohol for a variety of reasons such as peer group pressure, low self-esteem and desire for high sensation. Boys are more than twice as likely as girls to drink everyday or to drink a large amount; non-college bound young people drink everyday more than the college going ones. The typical teenage drinker with parents and/or friends who drink is more likely to smoke cigarettes and marijuana. Most teenagers drink moderately and infrequently and have no problems with alcohol, but some youths, like some adults, cannot handle this problem.

   Most teenagers start to drink because it seems for a grown up to do and they continue to do so for the same reason adults do, to put a pleasant grow on social situations, to reduce anxiety and to escape from problems. Teenage drinking is closely linked with delinquent behaviour, but it appears that many young people drink, for the same reasons they also engage in anti social behaviour. The problem drinking does not cause the delinquent behavior, but both grow out of the same needs.
4. **Tobacco:** Smoking a cigarette behind the bar has become a humorous staple of adolescent core. Smoking is related to lung cancer, heart attack and other diseases. Teenagers express personal concerns about the health consequences of smoking. Young people are most likely to smoke when their friends and families do so than if neither parents did. If both parents or one parent smoke, the chances are 4:1 that a youngster will follow it. It is ironic that adolescents who tend to rebel against adult values, see smoking as an adult activity and yet take it up eagerly. Smoking is related to personality. Smokers are likely to be more rebellious, better able to tolerate ambiguity, want to be older, achieve less well in school.

   Other adjustment problems in the area of health are *clumsiness, acne and awkwardness*. A *sex-inappropriate* body-build is far more disturbing to an adolescent than to a child.

- **Social:** The major psychological hazards of adolescents centre around the failure to make the psychological transition to maturity that constitute the important developmental tasks of adolescence. If adolescents are to make good personal and social adjustments, it is important for them to show signs of increasing maturity with each passing year. In the area of social behavior, peer groups show immaturity in a preference for childish patterns of social groupings and social activities with peers of the same sex and in a lack of acceptance, which in turn deprives the adolescent of the opportunity to learn more mature patterns of social behavior. Common obstacles to making transition to maturity are poor foundations, late maturing, prolonged treatment as children, role change and prolonged dependency.

Adolescence and Peer Pressure

As children grow, develop, and move into early adolescence, involvement with one's peers and the attraction of peer identification increases. As pre-adolescents commence with rapid physical, emotional and social changes, they begin to question adult standards and the need for parental guidance. They find it reassuring to turn for advice to friends who understand and sympathize - friends who are in the same position themselves. By "trying on" new values and testing their ideas with their peers, there is less fear of being ridiculed or "shot down".

The fact is, peer pressure can be positive. It keeps youth participating in religious activities, going to 4-H meetings and playing on sports teams, even when they are not leaders. It keeps adults going to religious services, serving on community committees and supporting worthwhile causes. The peer group is a source of affection, sympathy and understanding; a place for experimentation; and a supportive setting for achieving the two primary developmental tasks of adolescence. These are:

(1) identity — finding the answer to the question "Who Am I?" and

(2) autonomy — discovering the self as separate and independent from parents. It is no wonder, then, that adolescents like to spend time with their peers.

Peer relations expand to occupy a particularly central role in young people's lives. New types (e.g., opposite sex, romantic ties) and levels (e.g., "crowds") of peer relationships emerge. Peers typically replace the family as the center of a young person's socializing and leisure activities. Teenagers have multiple peer relationships, and they confront multiple "peer" cultures that have remarkably different norms and value systems.

The adult perception of peers as having one culture or a unified front of dangerous influence, is inaccurate. More often than not, peers reinforce family values, but they have the potential to encourage problem behaviors as well. Although the negative peer influence is overemphasized, more can be done to help teenagers experience the family and the peer group as mutually constructive environments.

Adolescents and the Community

It is critically important that communities provide a safe, supportive, nurturing environment for adolescents as they grow up. At the same time, families must provide limits and expectations for all members to live by. Early marriage among adolescents of specific communities, leads to serious health and social problems. The community an adolescent lives in has a major impact on whether she or he will pay more attention to adults or to other young people. Findings from a study of several hundred teenagers in several communities - a rural area, a poor inner-city neighborhood with many minority residents, and an upper-middle class suburb — tell us that we cannot draw sweeping conclusions about teenagers as if they were all alike.

Effective Strategies for Coping with Peer Pressure

If the negative effect of peer pressure is to be minimized, youth, parents, school and community leaders must come together to establish workable and effective strategies to guide teen behavior and to support their transition from children to mature, responsible adults. Here are several strategies to consider :

- Relinquish the stereotype of peers as a uniformly negative influence on youth

- Nurture teenagers' abilities and self-esteem so that they can forge positive peer relationships.
- Empower parents and educators to help teenagers pursue and maintain positive peer relationships.
- Encourage cross-ethnic and "cross-class" peer interactions and guide teenagers in dealing positively with cultural diversity and individual differences.
- Place sensible restraints on part-time teen employment.
- Support parent education programs for families with teenagers.
- Establish intervention programs for preadolescents with low social skills or aggressive tendencies.

Delinquency

During adolescence the individuals are exposed to new social situations and need more complex skills than those required in earlier stages. The complexities and pressures of modern society, makes the adolescents to behave in ways adults may find uncomfortable and threatening. One such route to show their protest is juvenile delinquency.

Delinquent behavior is closely associated with the less-positive impressions many adults hold of adolescence. Violence and Vandalism (destruction of public and private property) are among the more common types of delinquent behaviors and others run counter to established social-class and legal definitions of acceptable behavior. Delinquency has long been assumed to be a product of lower socio-economic status, twenty or thirty years ago, but today may be more of a middle class phenomenon. Participation in delinquent activities, however, is not the result of any single factor but rather a combination of influences that motivates a teenager to be destructive and perform illegal acts. More delinquents come from homes that are broken by divorce, separation, or desertion, which appears to have experienced deficient socialization and inadequate parenting than non delinquents whose peer relations may have greater influence than parental influence on participation in delinquent activities. Other factors such as involvement with heavy drug use, physical factors such as behavior tendencies associated with a mesomorphic (athletic) physique, lack of adequate parental controls at an early age in life, abuse from parents in childhood and adolescence, and behaviors that occur in association with running away from home, also seem to be identified.

Many delinquent acts involve malicious destruction of property (Vandalism) although delinquency also covers truancy from school as well as petty theft and larceny. Answers on preventing delinquency are lacking. Research, however, indicated that if families strive to help adolescents gain satisfaction from family relationships, minimize feelings of rejection, and provide love along with helping them to understand family dynamics, then participation in problem misbehaviors is reduced.

Type of Offences Committed by Juvenile Delinquents

Delinquency is a symptom of more fundamental problems such as physical, social, psychological, educational, vocational and even psycho social. There are all sorts of crimes – one may be more than one act committed by delinquents and one may commit more than one offence. Boys generally commit crimes involving aggression while girls commit sex related offences. Thefts, burglary, assault, truancy, vandalism, running away from home, murder are the offences most often associated with juvenile delinquents.

Causes of Juvenile Delinquency

1. Home Environment: Lack of love at home, poor parenting, extra marital affairs and strict discipline are some of the common factors at home. Delinquents usually refer their parents to be strict and inconsistent in disciplinary techniques. Poor inter- personal relationship and only parent, broken homes, critical family situations, low social economic status, and large number of children are the other causes leading to Juvenile delinquency.

2. **Peer group:** This plays an important role in the socialisation process of adolescents in supplementing the family with a significant influence on every individual. Rejected adolescents form gangs and indulge in antisocial activities so as to give way to their feeling.
3. **External Environment:** Unhealthy home environment and the area in which adolescents live influence the adolescents' behaviour to some extent. Criminals in the neighbourhood, urban slums where use of drugs and alcohol are more, give poor models for identification, resulting in anti-social behaviour expressions by the adolescents. Studies on stress reveal that the rate of behaviour problems of adolescents tend to be highest in urban areas, where there are many signs of social instability, physical deterioration, overcrowding, poor housing and unemployment.
4. **Personal Problems:** Personality problem like feeling of insecurity, low self-esteem, inadequate feelings due to low academic achievement, parental disciplinary pattern, child abuse experiences during childhood and early adolescence make the adolescents to become impulsive in committing offences.
   - **Emotional:** Adolescence is a hot time of turmoil and distress for most teens. Rates of mental disturbance among teens are very similar to rates of disturbance among adults. An individual is said to be emotionally adjusted if he is able to express his emotions in a proper way at the proper time. The emotional turbulence which are apparent during adolescence get intensified, when the family conditions are disturbed or inadequate. This ambiguity and lack of stable anchorage leads many adolescents to over commit themselves to anti-social acts, getting discouraged, and day dreaming which are some of the emotional problems. There are some universal concomitants of the changes that occur during adolescence. The first is heightened emotionality depending upon the rate at which the physical and psychological changes take place. Secondly, they have a strong feeling of instability which are often intensified by the ambiguous treatment they receive from the parents and teachers. Some psychosocial problems include stress and depression.

"**Stress** is one's physical, emotional, and mental response to change, whether or not the change is positive or negative. Stress is a part of everyone's life, but when it becomes uncontrollable, it can lead to psychological problems as well as physical. The possible **sources of Stress** could be sickness, birth of a brother or sister, school, divorce, death of a parent, poverty, moving to a new home or going to a new school.

The **signs of Stress** are problems in eating or sleeping, increased use of alcohol or other drugs, increased boredom or fatigue, problems in making decisions, becoming anxious or confused over unimportant events, inability to concentrate or pay attention, inability to get organized, weakness, dizziness, and shortness of breath, persistent hostile or angry feelings, nightmares, overpowering urges to cry, run, or hide, frequent headaches and ailments, frequent indigestion, diarrhoea, or urination and frequent colds and infections.

Depression is a physical disturbance created by low self esteem, decreased motivation, sadness, and difficulty finding pleasure in formerly enjoyable activities. Between 10 and 35 percent of girls and 15 and 40 percent of boys in the adolescence age period that did not receive psychotherapy experienced depressed states. Once puberty sets in, girls are twice as likely to become depressed. Some **internal causes** of depression are: blaming yourself for failure, the want of support, particularly from your family, the want to fit in with peers, and the loss of self respect. **External causes** include loss of a boy/girlfriend, divorce, death of a loved one, and schoolwork.

- **Education:** Educational adjustment is the adjustment of the students to the academic environment such as physical teaching, work schedule, authority, discipline, and inter personal relations with the teachers as well as other members of the organizations. Adolescents' educational adjustments depends on the way the school handles academic work, peer relations, parent-adolescents' conflicts, home environment, peer pressure, drug addiction, etc. All these factors influence the adolescents' academic achievement. Low academic achievement and other problems in turn have its effect on the adolescents' self- esteem and self- concept.

Measures to minimize the adjustment problems:

1. Guidance and counseling – is necessary for academic achievement, selection of apt vocational subjects, testing the academic ability, and aptitude, and for psychological problems.
2. Family counseling – is necessary to help the victimized adolescents to rescue in to the normal life.
3. Individual counseling/ Student counseling – is necessary for treating personality problems if there is any, by the student counselor in school/ college.
4. Peer Tutoring – could be organized for an educational problem.
5. Parent's role
6. Teacher's role.

Defining adolescence is a complex task. Biologically, there is a marked increase in the flow of sex-related hormones, as well as a maximum growth spurt and the appearance of secondary sex characteristics. Psychologically, a new sense of self and the formation of the identity take shape, and cognitive changes such as formal operations, the personal fable, and the imaginary audience occur. The social world of the teen undergoes many changes, including the inauguration of new privileges and new responsibilities.

Some youths suffer from a negative self-concept as they may be deviant in the adolescent norm, either due to physical development or physiological changes. The various aspects of puberty can cause the adolescent quite a bit of disappointment. Still it is encouraging to know that, just when they need it, most adolescents develop improved mental abilities that enable them to get a more realistic view of themselves.

QUESTIONS

SECTION "A"

Short Answer Type:

1. What is adolescence? How is it divided into?
2. Why is adolescence considered an important age?
3. Why is adolescence called a dreadful age?
4. What are the external physical changes that occur during adolescence?
5. What are the internal physical changes that occur during adolescence?
6. What are the developmental tasks of adolescence?
7. List out a few factors which affect the physical development of adolescents.
8. Discuss about the various eating disorders during adolescence?

9. What are the various social groupings during adolescence?
10. What is a sociogram ?
11. What is meant by sociometry ?
12. List out the ways by which communication between parents and adolescents can be improved.
13. Discuss about the educational adjustments during adolescence.
14. What are the different types of offences committed by juvenile delinquents?

SECTION "B"

One Page Answer Type:

1. Write about the characteristics of adolescence.
2. Discuss about the social changes during adolescence.
3. What are the common emotional patterns exhibited in adolescence?
4. Discuss about the moral and intellectual development during adolescence.
5. Discuss about the parents- adolescence relationship.
6. What are the health related adjustment problems during adolescence?
7. Discuss about the peer pressure during adolescence.
8. What are the measures to minimize adjustment problems?

SECTION "C"

Essay Answer Type:

1. What are the different adjustment problems during adolescence? Explain in detail.
2. What are the physical changes or development that occur during adolescence?
3. Discuss the various factors affecting the physical development.
4. Discuss about the various developments that occur during adolescence? Explain in detail.
5. Examine the role of peer pressure during adolescence and the effective strategies to cope with it.

UNIT — VII

CHAPTER

11

ADULTHOOD (20-40 YEARS)

OBJECTIVES

To enlighten students about:

- Concept of the period of adulthood - Meaning, stages/subdivisions
- Developmental tasks
- Characteristics
- Growth and development changes in early and middle adulthood – physical, cognitive, emotional, personality, Vocational and psycho-social development
- Stress-Coping with Stress at Family and Work, Mid-life crisis
- Adjustments during Middle adulthood

11.1 INTRODUCTION

No sharp line marks the moment when adolescence ends and the adult years begin. Any definite point that divides these two stages of life is a matter of convenience. There is however, a defined transitional state marking the end of adulthood.

The term "Adult" comes from the same Latin verb as adolescence -"adolescere"-which means to grow to maturity. However, it comes from the past participle of that verb "adultus,"- which means "grown to full size and strength" or "matured". An adult, therefore, is an individual who has completed his growth and is ready for his status in society with other adults.

While the terms "adulthood" and "maturity" are frequently used interchangeably, they have somewhat different meanings. Perkins (1974) points out that adulthood designates a status and a level of development. The term maturity, on the other hand, signifies a progression, quality and direction of development.

With gradual lengthening of the lifespan, adulthood is the longest period of the life cycle, which starts from early twenties and extends to sixties or seventies. Adulthood is legally achieved in our culture today at the age of twenty-one years and extends to the end of life. Specifically, adulthood is attained when an individual achieves a competent level of emotional, social and economic independence, establishes a career or family pattern and maintains a degree of personal, behavioral and conceptual maturity that enables him to live with some measure of satisfaction within a social milieu.

Meaning of Adulthood: Adulthood means different things to different people. To a child, it means special privileges like staying up late or not having to go to school. To a child's parents, being an adult means acting grown up and assuming responsibility. To an adolescent, adulthood means being one's own, establishing an apartment and having freedom from parental control.

Social Dimensions: The primary meaning of adulthood is social. One cannot declare oneself an adult; one is perceived as such. Inevitably, this perception reflects a mature, rational, and responsible person.

Biological Dimensions: Dictionaries define an adult as one who has attained "full size and strength; a fully grown person". This definition implies biological maturity, reaching the limits of physical development and attaining reproductive capacity.

Emotional Dimensions: Being an adult also includes "emotional maturity". It implies a high degree of emotional stability, including good impulse control, a high frustration tolerance, and freedom from violent mood swings. Another requirement of adulthood is to break childish dependency ties with parents and to function autonomously.

Legal Dimensions: Laws attempt to differentiate between who should and who should not be "accorded adult rights and responsibilities". They designate chronological ages at which privileges are granted and duties required to be fulfilled. Thus, our Constitution established the legal voting age as 18.

Stages or Sub-divisions of Adulthood: Adulthood is usually divided into subdivisions or stages. Each subdivision has its own physical and psychological characteristics and also adjustment problems that emanate from these characteristics, cultural pressures and expectancies. Erickson (1950) roughly divides adulthood into the following:

1. **Early Adulthood (20-40 Years) (A span of 20 years):** Though there are marked variations in the ages at which men and women lose their reproductive capacities, forty years is accepted as the traditional age at which the physical and psychological changes that accompany the climacteric in men and the menopause in women begin for the average individual.
2. **Middle Adulthood (40-60 Years) (Another span of 20 years):** The actual loss of reproductive capacities occurs at 60 years. With this, certain changes occur which mark the beginning of physical and psychological decline.
3. **Late Adulthood/Senescence or Old Age (60 years and extends until death):** Whether this will be the shortest or the longest of the subdivision of adulthood, will differ from individual to individual. However, because there is a growing tendency for men and women to live longer than their predecessors in the past, this period may be longer than the early and middle adulthood.

11.2. EARLY ADULTHOOD(20-40 YEARS)

Early Adulthood is unique as a stage of development because it marks a transition from an age-graded to a social-status-graded society. It comprises of the "developing years", when all growth movement is vertical, upward and forward. It is a fast moving period, in which the young adult strives to achieve mastery over the external world, seeking material gains and approval of others.

The period of early adulthood usually brings the beginning of a commitment to a career, the beginning of marriage (or in some instances, an alternate family form), and sometimes, the beginning of parenthood. Adolescence provides the foundation for early adulthood in the form of a relatively stable identity. It is a time when young people strive to gain and maintain their foothold on lower rungs of the ladder that they will climb in their progress toward lifetime goals. Due to variability in the development of adult activities, it is difficult, if not impossible, to pinpoint precisely the stage of adulthood on the basis of age alone.

11.3. DEVELOPMENTAL TASKS OF ADULTHOOD

Becoming an adult also involves the successful completion of a number of developmental tasks. Each society defines what tasks must be accomplished and at what ages. The social and economic roles of early adulthood are so familiar and clearly defined that few early adults have any doubt as to what the expectations of society are. These expectations, indicated as developmental tasks are:

- Achieving a measure of personal autonomy
- Molding an identity
- Developing emotional stability
- Establishing and consolidating a career
- Finding intimacy
- Becoming part of a congenial social group and of a community
- Selecting a mate and adjusting to marriage
- Establishing residence and learning to manage a home
- Becoming a parent and rearing children
- Developing appropriate ways of satisfying one's sex drive

11.4. CHARACTERISTICS OF EARLY ADULTHOOD

During early adulthood, human beings build a foundation for much of their later development. However, the transition from adult to responsibility of adulthood is not necessarily immediate and clear cut. Hurlock (1968) opines that early adulthood is a time when major adjustments must be made; it is a period in the life span of the individual with characteristics that make it distinctive from those that preceded it and from those which follow.

1. **Early Adulthood is the "Settling Down Age":** While childhood and adolescence are the periods of "growing up", adulthood is the time of "settling down". The young early adult exemplifies to play new roles such as that of spouse, parent, and breadwinner, and he develops new attitudes, interests and values to suit these new roles. As he "settles down", the individual develops a pattern of behavior which will be characteristically his own, for the remainder of his life. By the mid-thirties, the average adult has established a life pattern that will remain, with only minor changes, for the rest of his life. Any need to change this pattern, in middle or old age will be difficult and emotionally disturbing for him.
2. **Early Adulthood is the "Reproductive Age":** Parenthood is one of the most important roles in the lives of the majority of the young adults, especially women. However, men of today are taking a more active role in the care of children than was true in the past. The trend today is to marry individuals of approximately the same age, and the reproductive period for men likewise ends around forty in most cases.
3. **Early Adulthood is the "Problem Age":** Young adults, who must make their own decisions about career goals, intimate relationships, social commitments, and moral conduct, usually find these aspects of independence, though exciting, far from easy to deal with. Yet, for most young adults, it is problems faced and usually solved and limitations accepted or overcome, that make the decades from ages 20 to 40 an exhilarating period, when people often feel they are living to the fullest. The early adult years present many new problems, different in their major tasks from the problems experienced in the earlier years of life. Furthermore, the adult is expected to cope with these problems without

supervision, guidance, and help he had from parents and teachers when he was younger. Thus, the adult years are problem years for him.

4. **Early Adulthood is a "Period of Emotional Tension":** While attempting to make several adjustments in the major areas of his/her life, the young adult becomes emotionally upset. In early adulthood, the individual is faced with more adjustment problems than he has ever had to face before, and he is less well equipped to deal with these adjustment problems than he will be later. However, if the adult has high aspirations, and unable to reach them, he may be stressed. Emotional tension is often expressed in worries. What he worries about, however, will depend on what adjustment problems he is facing at the time and how much success or failure he is experiencing in meeting these problems.
5. **Early Adulthood is a Period of Isolation:** Many young adults having become accustomed throughout childhood and adolescence depending on peers for companionship, experience loneliness when responsibilities at home or at work isolate them from groups of their peers. Isolation is intensified by a competitive spirit and a strong desire. To achieve success, they must compete with others, thus replacing the friendliness of adolescence with the competitiveness of the successful adult and they must also devote most of their energies to their work, which leaves them little time for the socialization that leads to close relationships. As a result, they become self-centered, which contributes to loneliness.
6. **Early Adulthood is a Time of Commitment:** As young adults change their role from that of student and dependent characteristic of adolescence, to that of independent adult, they establish new patterns of living, assume new responsibilities and make new commitments, which form the foundation for later living.
7. **Early Adulthood is often a period of Dependency:** In spite of achieving the status of legal adulthood at age eighteen, with the independence this status carries, many young adults are partially or totally dependent on others for varying lengths of time. Many take the financial support of their parents or educational institutions or of the government for granted, but feel no obligation to be dominated in any way by those who have financed their training for their future careers.
8. **Early Adulthood is a Time of Value Change:** Many of the values developed during childhood and adolescence change, as experience and social contact with people of different ages broaden and as values are considered from a more mature stand point. As a result of such changed values, many adults who dropped out of school or college decide to finish their education.
9. **Early Adulthood is the Time of Adjustment to New Lifestyles:** It is always hard to adjust to new patterns of life; the adjustments young adults must make today are especially difficult because what preparation they received in childhood and adolescence was usually unrelated to or unsuited to the new lifestyles.
10. **Early Adulthood is a Creative Age:** What form creativity will take in adulthood will depend upon individual interests and abilities, opportunities to do what they want to do, and activities that give the greatest satisfaction. Some young adults find a creative outlet in hobbies, while others choose vocations in which they can express their creativity.

11.5. PHYSICAL DEVELOPMENT

Physical development includes the growth of the body and its organs during childhood, the appearance of physical signs of aging during adulthood, and the gains and losses in motor abilities that occur over the years. Physical changes during these years may be subtle but they do continue.

In early adulthood-the decades of 20s and 30s, most men and women enjoy a peak of health, strength, energy, vitality, endurance, sensory and motor functioning. The young adult can be expected to have strong and resilient muscles and bones, freedom from degenerative disease, normally functioning endocrine glands, an efficient immune system, and a digestive system that functions smoothly, to enable strenuous work, trouble-free reproduction and peak athletic performance.

Early and middle adulthood are periods of gradual physical decline in many systems of the body. But for the majority of adults, these years are the prime of life. Physical maturities in height and weight have been completed and growth has ceased several years before early adulthood began. Young adulthood is the time when several abilities peak: height, strength, muscle development, coordination, dexterity and sensory acuity. Most of these abilities begin to decline in middle age.

Appearance: During early adulthood, few people notice signs of aging in their appearance. Their skin is smooth and taut, and their hair full and the same color that it has been for years. Many young adults, male and female, worry about their physical appearance as it relates to muscles and body build. Women normally have more fat and less muscle than men. A mirror shows that crow's feet, gray hairs, balding, and slack muscles have started in earnest. The first signs of aging surprise most people

Skeletal development: It is completed as the long bones of the upper legs and arms finish their ossification process (change from cartilage to bone). The long bones of the skeleton grow until we are about 25 years old, and the vertebral column until we are about 30. This may add 1/8 to 1/4 inch to our height. As the bones of females tend to be less dense than the bones of males, they can increase bone mass in young adulthood by increasing their calcium intake and adding exercise. Men tend to grow in stature more than women do, while women's skulls tend to grow more than men's do. Some bones and the skull actually continue to grow throughout our lives.

Muscles and Fat: Muscles continue to gain strength throughout the twenties and reach peak strength at about age thirty, depending on exercise and genetic endowment. Although men have more muscle mass and tend to be stronger than women, physical strength in both sexes peaks during the late 20's and early 30s, declining slowly throughout the rest of life. Co-ordination and dexterity peak around the same time. Until people are about 39 years old, their muscles grow increasingly dense, but thereafter the muscles shrink and their fibers grow fewer in number and smaller in diameter. The "use it or lose it" principle applies to aging muscles. When people do not use their muscles, they weaken- a trend that may set in as early as age 30.

With aging, as the muscle cells atrophy and die, fat cells increase. For this reason, the 60-year-old who weighs the same as she did at age 25 is likely to have more body fat at 60. After the age of 50, healthy men do have fat cells in and between their muscles.

Weight and Height: As young adults, people reach their maximum height. Height remains stable through middle adulthood, declining somewhat in old age. Men can be expected to decrease an average of one-half inch for each decade of age. Between 18 and 24 years of age, males have an average height of 69.7 inches decreasing to about 69 inches by age 35-44 years. Height changes for women follow a similar pattern as for men. At 18-24 years, the average height can be expected to be 64.3 inches, decreasing to 64.1 inches at 25-34 years and remaining constant at 35-44 years.

Weight changes are more noticeable and significant than height changes during this period. The average weight of men between 18 and 74 years is 172 pounds. The average weight of men increases from 165 pounds between 18 and 24 years, to 178 pounds between 35 and 44 years. The average weight of women between 18 and 74 years is 143 pounds. Average weight for adult females show gains from 132 pounds between 18-24 to 149 pounds between 35-44 years.

The Teeth: Most individuals retain all of their permanent teeth during early adulthood. A small percentage has lost all of their upper or lower teeth. The loss of teeth is more likely to occur to women than to men during this period. There is a steady increase in decayed, missing, or filled teeth during the years of early adulthood. The probability of experiencing "periodontal disease" also increases during early adulthood, especially for males.

Wisdom teeth erupt toward the end of adolescence or in the early 20s. Failure of these teeth to erupt may lead to pain and overcrowding and may require surgery. Gum disease or gingivitis, affects many adults and is considered preventable. Proper care includes regular brushing, flossing and avoidance of excessive sweets. Good oral health care includes visits to the dentist every 6 months.

Sensory Systems: Sensory acuity also is at its peak in the early 20s. Maintaining a high level of sensory acuity enables us to participate actively in the life around us. Sustaining the ability to see, hear, taste and smell, keep a sense of balance: touch and feel pain and regulate the body temperature during exposure to heat or cold are important factors in enabling people to maintain contact with the outside world and to adjust to the information that they receive.

Visual acuity: It is the ability to perceive small details. Visual acuity is sharpest in young adults around age 20 years. It reaches a maximum around age 20 and remain relatively constant to 40. It may decline after age 25 owing to decreased elasticity and increased capacity of the lens. By age 40, there is often a decreased ability to see objects at a close distance. This condition known as presbyopia, (Farsightedness) advances with age.

As the lens become less elastic, it begins to lose some power of accommodation (the power to focus so that distinct vision is assured at both near and far distances). Farsighted adults must wear corrective lenses for reading, writing, knitting, or other chores. Nearsightedness, the inability to see distant objects clearly, may begin in childhood or adolescence, and usually does not change much during early adulthood. This happens because as we age, the pupil of the eye gradually gets smaller (allowing less light to reach the retina), and the muscles that cause the pupil to dilate and constrict gradually weaken. Visual acuity remains high until middle age, when people tend to become far-sighted and require glasses for reading. As the years progress, however, depth perception and the ability to adapt to darkness decrease slightly.

Hearing: This usually peaks at about age 13 years. Hearing acuity is best at around age 20, and thereafter gradually declines. The high tones are often lost first, followed by the lower ones a condition known as presbycusis. In most cases, the inaudible sounds have little significance to the activities of daily living. . Many speech sounds are high-pitched s, z, f, g, - for example, may eventually become inaudible. Many factors, such as nutrition, environment, and heredity affect how much and how fast hearing is lost. As is the case with visual deficits, more men than women suffer from hearing impairments. One reason for this is that noise pollution is a major cause of hearing loss, and men traditionally work in noisier occupations.

Taste and Smell: Evidence indicate that the ability to perceive all four taste qualities-sweet, salt, bitter, and sour-declines in later life, although the decrement is small. Throughout adulthood, the taste buds are continually replaced and restored, and the sense of taste generally remains keen throughout most of the adulthood. Sense of smell or olfaction plays a major role in the sensory experiences of food and beverages, and It provides an early warning of fire, dangerous fumes, leaking gas, spoiled foods, and polluted environments. Young adults consistently outperform older adults in odor recognition, odor perception and odor naming.

Touch, Pain and Temperature: Thermoregulation is the maintenance of body temperature during exposure to heat or cold. Body temperature is usually regulated within narrow limits. Sensitivity to touch and pain also remain keen throughout early and middle adulthood. People's ability to smell, taste, feel pain and changes in temperatures and maintenance of balance largely remains unchanged until late life.

Pain is whatever an individual perceives as physical discomfort in response to a stimulus. The phenomenon of pain has four components: (i). reception of the pain stimulus by pain receptors; (ii). conduction of the pain stimulus to the brain by the nerves; (iii). perception of the pain in the higher centers of the brain and, (iv).interpretation and reaction to the pain. An individual's attitude toward the self as well as the origin of pain-producing stimulus affects the intensity of discomfort.

11.6. PHYSIOLOGICAL FUNCTIONING OF OTHER BODILY SYSTEMS

Each system of the body matures at a different rate. By young adulthood, the organs have all achieved maturity, and, consequently, these years are considered to be a period of optimal biographical functioning.

Neurological System: Although the brain reaches physical maturity before 20 years of age, final myelinization and differentiation of the central nervous system occurs at about 25 years of age. The weight of the brain declines about one gram per year beginning at 30 years, but the size or the weight of the brain is no indication of intelligence or wisdom. Both the number of cells in the **nervous system** and the size of the brain decrease after puberty. Changes in **sensation and perception** can be recognized during this stage. However, speed and accuracy of these perceptions are not yet affected. **Reaction time,** the speed at which a person responds to a stimulus, increases noticeably between ages 20 and 30.

Cardiovascular System: At rest, the muscles of the heart may pump 75 gallons of blood an hour; it may pump 750 gallons during strenuous exertion. Cardiac output, which is the measure of the blood volume the heart pumps in one minute, drops by one percent every year after age 20. Maximum cardiac output is reached between ages 20 and 30; after that, cardiac output gradually declines.

By the time a person enters early adulthood, the cardio vascular system has established adult size and rhythm. As people get older, normal changes take place in their cardiovascular systems. The heart becomes more sluggish in its ability to pump blood efficiently. By the 3rd decade of life, selected areas of arteries have begun to thicken. Fat accumulates on these thickened areas and forms soft fatty streaks. These streaks (plaques) are thought to be the precursors of atherosclerosis, an abnormal accumulation of lipids (fats), minerals, and fibrous tissues in blood vessel walls that narrows their lumen (internal diameter) and thus reduces blood flow. The heart and vessels become less elastic with advancing age. This rigidity may contribute to the decreased cardiac output and increased blood pressure commonly seen in later adulthood, leading to "hypertension". Continued untreated, hypertension can lead to heart failure, cerebral hemorrhage (stroke), and other related disorders. Certain practices, including using alcohol and tobacco and eating foods high in cholesterol content, may increase an individual's risk for cardiovascular disease.

Respiratory System: A man's lung function reaches its peak at about 25 years; a woman's peak is at about 20 years. The ability of the **lungs** to move air in and out is known as ***vital capacity***. Vital capacity decreases between ages 20 and 40. This gradually declines owing to loss of elasticity in the lung. The amount of air flowing into the young adult's lungs is 20 to 30 per cent more than it is in older adult. Past the age of 20, the amount of breath that a person can take into his or her lungs in a single breath begins to decline. Between 25 and 85, this vital capacity will drop by 40 percent. The total capacity of the lungs, however, does not drop with age. A gradual loss of alveoli elasticity contributes to a decrease in vital capacity (volume of air that can be expelled following full inspiration). Aerobic exercise augments vital capacity. Vital capacity will diminish at a faster rate if the person is a cigarette smoker.

Integumentary System: During early adulthood, skin is smooth and taut, their hair full and the same color that it has been for years. Some young adults do notice a few grey hairs, but usually physical deterioration is gradual.

The Skin: After adolescence, the skin begins to lose its fine texture and moisture, gradually becoming more dry and wrinkled with age. The skin begins to show some signs of aging in early adulthood. Women begin to notice "smile lines" in their late twenties, and also gain lines at the outer corners of their eyes ("Crow's feet") in their thirties. Because men have more body oil (in the sebaceous glands) than women, their skin is slower to dry and wrinkle. Shaving seems to have rejuvenating effect on the thicker skin of the male by removing dead cells. Many factors-heredity, climate, cigarette smoking, sun exposure, hormonal balance, diet, pollutants in the environment and general health affect the speed of skin aging. Excessive exposure to ultraviolet rays may produce skin cancer, particularly in light-skinned individuals. The types of skin disorders that occur more frequently among young adult males are fungus infections (dermatophytosis), especially of the feet, and malignant or benign tumors.

Hair: Hair, like nails, is composed of dead cells. Each hair is produced by a hair bulb encapsulated in a hair follicle, located under the skin. The hair bulb produces hair cells, pressing them toward the surface to form a single strand of hair. Each bulb remains active for about 4 to 6 years, producing scalp hairs of about three feet in length, although hair length up to 10 feet has been documented. Nutrition, health status and care will affect the health and beauty of the hair.

Graying of hair as a process is irreversible, and no diet or medication can change what has already occurred. Malnutrition can cause changes in the hair, including temporary loss of pigmentation. Stress, as an entity in itself has not been proven as a factor that accelerates graying. Some thinning of the hair of the head in both genders is normal during early adulthood. Although hair grows faster in length between the ages of 16 and 46, there is a gradual decrease in hair density especially at the temples. Baldness can begin in males anytime after puberty.

Gastrointestinal system: Although the production of some digestive juices decreases after 30 years of age, healthy young adults do not experience significant changes in their pattern of digestion or elimination. The rate at which food travels through the gastrointestinal tract is still influenced by factors such as the nature of the food (e.g. high fiber content travels faster than saturated fat) and the state of physical health.

Immunological System: Early adulthood is potentially the healthiest portion of the lifespan. Many young adults have become desensitized to childhood allergies with the exception of asthma and "hay fever". By age 20, people have developed immunity to many of the infectious agents causing illness in children.

Endocrine System: Both the basal metabolic rate (BMR) and secretion of thyroid hormones slowly decrease as a person approaches mid-adulthood. This decrease in the BMR is related to the decrease in muscle mass (which is a large oxygen consuming tissue). The decrease in thyroid hormones (which assist in regulating the BMR) is the result of the slower rate at which they are broken down and removed from the blood. Aging affects the endocrine system by slowing the secretion of hormones, by making cells in various parts of the body less responsive to hormones, by changing the chemical messengers that carry hormonal "messages" into cells, and by changing the levels of enzymes that respond to hormones.

Fluid and Electrolyte Regulation: The regulation of fluids and electrolytes is a good example of how the body strives to maintain equilibrium or homeostasis. The ability to maintain stability of body fluids is greatest during early adulthood, and is least stable at both ends of the human life span.

Reproductive system: *Early and Middle Adulthood*: The body system that is actually functioning at peak capacity is the reproductive system. In women, the menstrual cycle is well established. Women report irregular patterns of menstruation or serious discomfort to their physicians. Generally, men are free of reproductive problem at this stage. The ideal age for a woman to become pregnant for the first time is in her twenties. Her reproductive as well as other systems in her body are mature and more coordinated during early adulthood. In men, testosterone production reaches its maximum daily output during the twenties. Since spermatogenesis continues throughout adulthood, the young man's biophysical ability to father a child should not be affected by any developmental somatic change. The prostate gland, which secretes fluid that mobilizes sperm and carries them out of the penis during ejaculation, starts to age during a man's forties.

Sexuality: Early and middle adulthood may well be the sexual prime of life. True, adolescents have sexual experiences and relationships. But for most people, the social and psychological developments of adulthood greatly enrich sexuality. During the first year that couples live together, their rates of sexual intercourse typically are the highest of their adult lives. After the first four years of marriage, the rate of intercourse declines, even among couples in their twenties.

Health Status: For most people, early adulthood is a time of exceedingly good health. Illnesses are usually acute, and are readily shaken off with minimal disruption to normal routine. Less than one percent of young adults are incapacitated by chronic illnesses. Despite this generally positive picture, many people do begin to develop certain silent diseases that will be problematic later on. The leading causes of death prior to age 35 years are accidents and suicide, followed by cancer and heart disease. After 35 years, however, cancer and heart disease emerge as leading causes of death, followed by accidents, suicide, and liver diseases.

Factors affecting Health Status:

Gender: Throughout adulthood, the death rate for women is lower than for men. This may be partly due to women being more sensitive to early warning signs of illness and more willing to ask for help. In addition, female hormones play a beneficial role in preventing heart disease.

Education: Better health is consistently correlated with better education, which often goes hand in hand with higher socioeconomic status. It is likely that more money enables people to buy better food and health care.

Smoking and Alcohol: Smoking increases a person's risk of many different types of cancer, heart disease, and emphysema, and we now also know about the dangers of passive smoking. Alcohol often is a major factor in car fatalities, suicide, drowning, and family violence.

Exercise: Exercise strengthens muscle-including the heart muscles-lowers blood pressure, increases lung capacity, and even alleviates anxiety and depression. There has been a revolution among young adults in their participation in health-related exercise activities within the past several years.

Nutrition: The number of calories required for normal functioning reaches a plateau in early adulthood. The nutritional status of foods consumed in early adulthood changes to reflect the different needs of individuals at this time of life. Sodium intake and cholesterol levels in the body become areas of health concern during early adulthood. These substances become medically significant at this time because of their implicated role in heart disease and impairment of general well-being in the later stages of adulthood.

The concern about cholesterol level, fat and sodium intake in diet relates to the increasing probability of heart disease, heart attack, arteriosclerosis, and related circulatory disorders. As fats and cholesterol levels increase in the body, there is a great tendency for these substances to collect in the heart muscle and other significant arteries, causing damage. While most of these disorders appear to be noticed in middle age, they are the result of poor eating habits in combination; with the result, aging process begins in early adulthood or even earlier in the life cycle.

11.7. COGNITIVE DEVELOPMENT IN EARLY ADULTHOOD

Cognitive Development: Cognitive development involves changes in the mental processes, which are involved in perception, language uses, learning, attention, and memory, reasoning and creativity. It also includes the "development of intelligence" and "the ability to process information, to learn, to remember, and to utilize this information as needed". Cognitive development also strives to examine the changes that take place in the way people think. It studies "qualities of those thought processes," as individuals seek to comprehend information, solve problems, and engage in the thought that is necessary to survive and to live.

Cognitive advance are closely related to physical and emotion growth. For example, the ability to speak depends on the physical development of the mouth and brain. Some individuals are able to comprehend better than others are, showing much wisdom in the way they control their lives and in the way they go about solving problems and thinking of any alternatives that are presented to them.

Cognitive Development in Early Adulthood: Common sense tells us that adults think differently from children or adolescents. They have different conversations, understand more complicated material, and use their broader experience to solve practical problems. The events of adult life pose new challenges and require that they continually refine their reasoning capabilities and problem-solving techniques. Early adulthood confronts new circumstances, uncertainties and difficulties in the realm of interpersonal relationships, work, parenting, or household management. This calls for decision-making and resourceful thought. Consequently, one must learn to identify problems, analyze them by breaking them down into their relevant components and devise coping strategies. Due to this continued intellectual activity through adulthood, gained through learning, memory, problem solving and many other cognitive processes, older adults have a broader accumulation of knowledge.

Thinking

New ways of thinking in adulthood are "reflective thinking" and "post-formal thought",

Reflective Thinking: is a complex form of cognition defined as "active, persistent and careful consideration of information". Reflective thinkers continually question supposed facts, draw inferences and make connections. The capacity of reflective thinking is thought to emerge between ages 20 and 25s.

Post-formal Thought: Thought in adulthood often appears to be flexible, open, adaptive, and individualistic. It draws on intuition and emotion as well as on logic to help people cope with a seemingly chaotic world. It applies the fruits of experience to ambiguous situations. The higher stage of adult cognition is sometimes called **post formal thought.** Post formal thought is mature type of thinking, which relies on subjective experience and intuition as well as logic. It is characterized by the ability to deal with ambiguity, uncertainty, inconsistency, contradiction, imperfection, and compromise. Post-Formal thought is relativistic. Like reflective thinking, it enables adults to surpass a single logical system and choose among conflicting ideas or demands, each of which form its own perspective, may have a valid claim to truth. It often develops in response to events and interactions.

Formal Operational Thinking: The achievement of formal operational thinking means the individual has developed the ability to engage in four distinct thought processes:

(*a*) Introspection (to think about thought);

(*b*) Abstract thinking (to go beyond the real to what is possible);

(*c*) Logical thinking (to gather facts and ideas to form correct conclusions); and

(*d*) Hypothetical reasoning (to formulate hypotheses and examine the truth of them, and considering numerous variables)

The appearance of formal operations may be delayed until 15 to 20 years of age, and in disadvantaged conditions, it may never take shape. Approximately half of the adult population may never attain the full stage of formal thinking. The years of formal education, intelligence level, and numerous cultural factors also influence the development of formal operational thinking.

Post-Formal Operations: For Jean Piaget, the stage of formal operations constituted the last stage in cognitive development. He depicted adulthood as opening new horizons in thought. During this period, adults not only gain the ability to think about their own mental processes but they achieve the ability to imagine multiple possibilities in a situation and to generate mentally numerous hypothetical outcomes. In brief, adolescence opens to teenagers the prospect of thinking in logical and abstract terms.

Evidence suggests that younger and older adults may merely differ in their cognitive competencies: younger adults seem to place greater reliance on rational and formal modes of thinking; older adults seem to develop a greater measure of subjectivity in their reasoning, and they place greater reliance on intuition and the social context, in which they find themselves. Furthermore, complex cognitive tasks place greater demands on working-memory resources that decline with increased age. Cognitive development is a lifelong process.

Qualitative changes in Adulthood: Most of the research along these lines has centered on the performance of adults of various ages on concrete and formal operational tasks to determine what if any changes occur across the life span.

Operational Task Performance during Adulthood:

Concerning the performance of adults on concrete operational tasks such as conservation, classification and seriation, as well as on a variety of formal operational tasks, some surprising results have arisen out of the studies. Adults do not perform nearly as well as they might and be expected. In a recent review of the literature on cognitive functioning in adulthood, the following major findings were highlighted:

- First, most adults do well on concrete operational tasks – classification, seriation, conservation and so forth. After all, such skills emerge during the later years of childhood, and adults certainly would be expected to possess them
- Second, performance on formal operational tasks is highly variable: some people do well and some very poorly.
- Finally, elderly people do not perform as well as younger adults on either concrete or formal tasks.

In summary, when adults of all ages are tested on Piagetian tasks, many can easily solve formal operational problems, but a surprising number of adults are unable to do so. The only age-related trend in performance is that people over the age of 65 are less successful at formal operational tasks than are younger adults.

Problem Finding: In some ways, adulthood requires a different kind of thinking. Schoolchildren learn to solve teacher-determined problems. Adults need to learn to identify problems that exist and to delineate those that need solving. This involves going beyond formal operational thinking to a fifth stage of development that has been labeled a problem-finding stage.

Practical Problem-Solving Abilities: The ability to solve practical problems presented from real life situations increased during early adulthood and did not peak until the late 40's. Young adults do not appear to be solving the practical problems of everyday living as efficiently as older adults do. This is because there is a tendency on the part of young adults to give less than their optimal performance unless explicitly instructed and motivated to do so. Problem solving abilities may also be improved with training.

Comprehension

(*a*) *Word Familiarity:* A number of studies have been conducted to determine age-related abilities of adults to comprehend linguistic meanings of individual words, sentences, or paragraphs. Tests of word familiarity have shown that adults generally show improvement to ages 50 through 59 (mean age 55), after which scores decline. Educational level was found to be more important than age itself.

(*b*) *Sentence Comprehension:* The ability to comprehend relativized sentences (complex sentences with a number of relative clauses) remains stable until the 60's, after which the ability declines with age. However, comprehension of sentences presented auditorily depends on the complexity of the sentences and partially on the rate of presentation.

(c) *Prose Comprehension:* Bellmore (1981) tested the ability of adults to process and comprehend linguistic meanings of short prose passages that they were asked to read. Older adults (mean age 66.5) were able to comprehend the meanings almost as well as younger adults (mean age 18.3).

Wisdom: One of the advantages of getting older is that people develop pragmatic knowledge that we call wisdom. Wisdom involves the accumulation of a lifetime of expertise in dealing with life tasks, managing situations, and solving problems. Wisdom involves using sound judgments in the conduct of life; it is the developing of understanding through experience and the capacity to apply that understanding to the issues of life. Wisdom may be defined as the expert-level of knowledge in the fundamental pragmatics of life.

Dialectical Thinking: A number of theorists have described an advanced form of adult thought that they call dialectical thinking. According to this view, every idea, truth, or thesis implies an opposing idea or **antithesis**. *Dialectical thinking involves being able to consider both sides of an issue simultaneously and to be able to accept the existence of contradictions* (Rice, 2007).

Klaus Riegel (1975) examines the issue of how we handle competing and contradictory opinions, and proposed that a primary characteristic of adult cognition is what he calls "dialectical thinking". By this, he means that adults readily recognize, accept, and even enjoy conflict and contradictions in values and possible courses of action because sorting out these conflicts forces them to grow intellectually. Dialectical thinking occurs even among concrete operational children as they try to understand concepts like "big", "small", "old" and "young". But adult dialectical thinking often deals with contradictory ideas about morality, religion, ethics and the like, adults do not necessarily feel compelled to resolve the contradictions.

Dialectical thinking sometimes leads to integrating one's beliefs and experiences with the inconsistencies and contradictions that are discovered, so that a continuously new view evolves. The new view recognizes that answers need to be constantly updated to take into account new information The unifying premise of dialectical thinking is that change itself is the universal truth.

Not only are adult dialectical thinkers more sensitive to contradictions-and more appreciative of opposing points of view-but also they have learned to live with them. In marriage, dialectical thinkers can appreciate their spouses' viewpoints that are opposite to their own. They have an ability to evaluate personal, social and political viewpoints, which is not found in all people. Although they can accept contradictions as a basic property of thought, they are sometimes able to synthesize new formulations of ideas that are superior to both opposites. The result is a continuously evolving view of truths about the world.

II. Intelligence: Throughout the lifespan, people draw on their intellectual abilities. Everyday life calls upon people of all ages to learn new facts, faces, figures, and relationships, to recognize and recall all kinds of information, trivial and important, small and large, and to solve problems, difficult and easy. The cognitive changes that characterize mature, adult learning and memory make some older people more adept than younger people at certain kinds of intellectual tasks, although this age advantage is not universal across either individuals or domains.

Any attempt to measure intelligence among adults depends on the type of tests used, their research design, and what the tests intend to measure.

New views of intelligence highlight that intelligence is composed of several different cognitive abilities such as memory, language, reasoning and numerical ability. Each of these mental processes can, in turn, be divided into various sub-processes. Some intellectual functions increase with age; some peak early and are maintained well into old age; others show decline beginning in early adulthood. For example, some skills such as speed-related performances, rote memory and manipulation of matrices do peak in the late teens. Probably these abilities may have a physiological basis or it may be that many teenagers are full-time students, who practice, develop and rely on these skills. Other cognitive abilities, especially judgment and reasoning, continue to develop throughout life. Skills that are used frequently are maintained better than those that are not exercised. There are increasing differences among individuals as they get older.

Fluid and Crystallized Intelligence: Psychologist Robert J. Sternberg believes that intelligence tests are too narrow. Hence, he designed a test that measures three types of intelligence-componential, contextual and experiential. He built on the work of John Horns, Raymond B. Cattell, and Gary Donaldson. These psychologists believe that there are essentially two types of intelligence, which they call "Fluid" (ability to make original adaptations in novel situations) and "Crystallized" intelligence (the ability to reuse earlier adaptations on later occasions).The theory of fluid and crystallized intelligence has provided a useful way of looking at the shifts in adult learning skills.

Fluid intelligence: Fluid Intelligence is a basic cognitive process, which is essential for the identification and comprehension of relationships and the drawing of inferences out of that comprehension. It reflects our innate ability to learn and understand things. Fluid intelligence is the ability to solve novel problems that require little or no previous knowledge, such as discovery, the patterns in a sequence of figures. It involves perceiving relations, forming concepts, to use abstract reasoning and to perceive complex relationships and drawing inferences to form concepts. Fluid intelligence consists of the abilities involved in acquiring new knowledge and skills, including memorizing, reasoning inductively, and perceiving new relationships between objects and events. Also referred to as "cognitive mechanics", these abilities reflect neurological functioning more closely and are more likely to be affected when brain damage occurs. It depends primarily on heredity and on how well our nervous system works, not so much on education or environment.

Presumably, fluid intelligence is "culture-free" and based on the individual's genetic and neurological structures. That is why it is "fluid" or can "flow into" or be applied to a wide range of intellectual activities.

Fluid Intelligence is generally tested by measuring an individual's facility in reasoning, often by means of figures and non-word materials (letter series, matrices, mazes, block designs and picture arrangements), grouping letters and numbers, pairing related words (analogies) or remembering a series of digits (short term memory), abstract thinking, speed of thinking, creativity and problem solving.

Fluid intelligence declines after age 14 and that the sharpest decline came in early adulthood. The decline in fluid intelligence was evidenced by poorer performance on tests requiring abstract thinking, inductive reasoning, relational thinking, and short-term memory, and on tests requiring figural classification, analogy, and the completion of logical series.

Crystallized Intelligence: Crystallized intelligence refers to the acquired knowledge and intellectual skills that come with education and life experiences. Crystallized intelligence corresponds to all of a person's quantitative thinking, judgment, and wisdom. It is the ability to remember and use information acquired over a lifetime. It involves the application of formal reasoning and abstraction and perception of complex relations to tasks that have been learned. Crystallized intelligence shapes the way that people apply their fluid intelligence within specific social and cultural contexts. Crystallized intelligence is also referred to as "cognitive pragmatics", reflecting the notion that what is learned is influenced by culture.

Crystallized and fluid intelligence take different developmental paths during adulthood (Stewart et al, 1988). Formal education, travelling, reading and being around intelligent, stimulating people are all ways of increasing crystallized intelligence. Crystallized intelligence is dependent on education and experience.

It is measured by tests of general information, vocabulary, information, arithmetical reasoning or social situations that presumably assess how much knowledge the individual has derived from her or his experiences, judgment, numerical ability and the ability to understand and use mechanical principles and tools.

Fluid and Crystallized intelligence, taken together, account for the majority of the abilities that adults use in their thinking and problem solving. Many life problems or issues can be resolved by the use of either of the two. Over the life span, an individual probably develops a "cognitive style" so that he or she may solve problems through "brilliance" (or fluid intelligence) or by applying accumulated "wisdom" (or Crystallized intelligence).

Both fluid and Crystallized intelligence increase during childhood and adolescence. Fluid intelligence however, tends to decline gradually during adulthood. On the other hand, Crystallized intelligence continues to increase gradually throughout adulthood. The continued growth of crystallized intelligence, however, depends on continuing process of meaningful cultural involvement including information seeking, reflection, and educational activity. The decline in fluid intelligence is balanced out by the increase in crystallized intelligence.

III. The Information Processing System : At any developmental stage, cognitive skills such as learning, thinking and remembering depend upon the information processing "system." "Processing information" means, "taking information from the environment, manipulating, storing, classifying and retrieving it from memory". Information Processing is an important aspect of cognitive development in broadening the ability to process information. This involves exposure to information, learning, remembering, and utilization of these in helpful ways. Information processing remains relatively stable throughout most of adulthood. In some cases, it may continue to improve in efficiency.

Memory: The ability to remember is basic to all learning and to intellectual and social functioning. It is also basic to making sound judgments. Memory is often divided into two types;

(*i*) **Prospective Memory:** is memory for activities to be performed in the future, for example, remembering to give someone a message or to keep an appointment. Obviously, prospective memory is extremely important in everyday functioning.

(*ii*) **Retrospective Memory:** is memory for past events, for example, remembering the contents of a newspaper article or someone's name.

All studies of memory during adulthood recognize three basic processes: acquisition, storage and retrieval

- The process of acquisition begins with exposure to stimuli so that information can be learned. The process involves making an impression on memory receptors and registering and recording information. Acquisition is the learning or input phase of memory. Unless something is acquired, it cannot be remembered.
- In the process of storage, information is cycled, processed, organized, rehearsed, and stored until needed.
- In the process of retrieval, stored information is obtained by searching, finding, and remembering, either through recall or recognition.

Memory efficiency depends on all three of these processes. Loss of memory represents a decline with advancing age. This is true whether learning is measured in terms of speed or by the amount revealed or recognized.

Human memory apparently operates at several different levels. There are generally three types of memory-sensory, short-term and long-term.

(*i*) **Sensory Memory:** The shallowest level of memory is "Sensory Memory", which records information quite close to the time and form of the perception. Whatever we see, hear, touch, smell or taste something at any time, it registers in our sensory memory. These sights, sounds, odors-tastes, and touches are retained in sensory memories for about one second. The sensory register stores incoming sensory information for a split of second after it is received. The sensory register is revealed in the momentary afterimage, visual or auditory, that remains in the brain after you perceive something. After one or two seconds, the information in this memory disappears unless it is processed into either short- or long-term memory.

(*ii*) **Short-tem Memory:** Short-term memory consists of information that is still "in mind" as it is being used. This is the memory we use between the time we look up a telephone number and the time we dial it. Information remains in the limited storage of short-term memory for up to 15 to 20 seconds, and the information starts to fade unless we rehearse it. While there, information is consciously attended to and processed. For example, a person may repeat a telephone number until he dials it. When he stops holding the number in conscious memory, it is lost. If he wants to remember the phone number permanently, he must encode it for later retrieval. By applying mnemonic strategies such as organizing or imaging information, a person may transfer information to long-tem memory and later recall it (Stewart et al., 1988). We can hold about seven plus or minus two items in short-term memory. In general, adult's short-term memory capacity does not change appreciably during most of adulthood, although there may be a slight decline after the age of 60. Short-term memory also seems to slow down as people age. People may be able to store as much information as they once did, but they are slower at retrieving it.

(*iii*) **Long-term memory:** People's memories of childhood, what they know about the world, and what they understand about people and things comprise information in long-term memory. Information held in short term memory might be transferred into long term memory, a virtually unlimited, permanent storehouse of memories about our past as well as our knowledge about the world. This process of remembering is characterized by the recall of material over a longer period, for example, when an older adult recalls childhood experiences. When they want to retrieve the information from long-term memory, it returns to short-term memory. There it can be consciously manipulated once again. The capacity of long-term memory is assumed to be virtually unlimited. Aging seems not to affect long-term memory adversely. Eighty-year-olds seem to remember information from long-term memory as effectively as 20-year-olds.

Memory Strategies: All people remember better if they use memory strategies. Memory strategies elaborate on information or move it to a deeper level of cognitive processing, making it more likely that the information will be encoded and later retrieved. Encoding strategies that move information to deeper levels of processing increase learning. These strategies include organizing information by category-remembering all the meat-eating plant-eating dinosaurs, for example. Verbal aids to memory, or mnemonic devices, also help-such as remembering the number of days in the month with "Thirty days hath September." Creating a vivid mental image of items to be remembered and systematically rehearsing the information are other memory strategies that increase the depth of processing. Older adult do not use these strategies spontaneously on memory tasks. It has been suggested this failure is responsible for older adult's poorer recall and recognition memory.

Learning: The process of learning results in a relatively permanent change in behavior, which is brought about by a certain environmental experiences or set of experiences.

Learning is not directly observable. That is, we can use the results of learning for the improvement in a child's ability to kick a football, in a student's ability to do well on an examination-but we cannot see the actual process itself. Learning has or has not taken place has to be inferred by observing the learner's changed or unchanged performance, respectively. Performance does not always provide an accurate measure of learning. At all ages, people do learn and remember new things throughout their daily lives. Most people maintain the ability to learn through adulthood.

Such capacity is vitally necessary because each new event in an adult's life requires new knowledge and abilities. Getting married, becoming parents, assuming a new job, moving to another house or community, retiring, and adjusting to a rapidly changing world all require learning.

Factors Influencing Cognitive Development in Early Adulthood: With regard to intelligence and cognitive functioning, young adults reach an individual peak of performance. It is important to note that age is not the only factor that may influence intelligence in young adulthood. Both educational and health backgrounds are just as important as age in determining intelligence in adulthood. Nonetheless, young adulthood is likely to be a time in which the individual has maximum flexibility in forming new concepts and in shifting from one perspective to another. Memory and creativity may also be at a peak.

11.8. EMOTIONAL DEVELOPMENT

Emotions are concerned with the development of feelings and the expression of them in relation to other people. The kinds of feeling that develop, the way that they are expressed, and the extent to which they are controlled are important considerations in a person's life, and especially so in relationships with other people. Thus, to understand the behaviour of an individual requires us to understand the inner emotional life that motivates the individual to act as he or she does. To become a mature adult requires that adults be mature not only physically, cognitively, and socially, but also emotionally. In general, emotional maturity can be classified into three categories, "being emotionally secured"; "being emotionally stable", and "having the capacity to feel for others and to form relationships."

Emotional Maturity

Emotional Security: Being an emotionally secure person means having freedom from excessive negative emotions, and from crippling anxieties, doubts, and fears. All individuals experience some anxiety, doubts and fear, but the extent to which these emotions are expressed determines the relative degree of "emotional maturity" that the individual reaches. Emotionally secure people may have some negative emotions and feelings about themselves, about others and about relationships, but these negative feelings are over powered by feelings that are more positive. Such people have adequate self-concept. They are convinced that others like them, and get along well with others. They think that they perform adequately at work, and they generally do not have unreasoned feelings or fears about the future. Because they have self-confidence, feel adequate and do not have unreasonable fears about what might happen, they are able to be productive and to prove themselves to other people.

An individual who feels a lot of anxiety about many things to the degree that the anxiety is all-pervasive is going to be affected negatively by his or her emotional insecurity. This behaviour becomes undesirable because it affects their overall relationship with others as well as their general contentment and happiness. When carried to extreme, this behaviour is "general anxiety disorder".

Emotional Stability: Emotional stability means, a person has a relative degree of freedom from drastic ups and downs of emotions. Mature people do not usually show positive emotions one day and negative emotions the next. Emotionally stable people are generally free from violent temperamental or emotional outbursts that have little cause. Stable people usually have a high frustration tolerance and can stand a certain degree of denial and frustration without becoming excessively upset. Being emotionally unstable cause many problems in relationships because their behavior causes hard feelings and conflicts. In extreme cases, emotional instability is called "bi-polar disorder" in which individuals go from manic phases to depressive phases with drastic changes of mood, emotions and feelings. In extreme cases, the person who is emotionally cold and loses all capacity to express feelings is classified as a **"psychopath".**

In general, studies indicate that ***"intensity of emotion" declines subjectively as people grow older.*** Emotions become increasingly salient but better controlled with age. Compared with younger adults, older adults typically describe themselves as less emotionally labile and more moderate in their effective responses.

Capacity to Feel: The emotionally mature person has the capacity to feel, whether to feel love or to feel hate. Without the capacity to feel, emotions are dead. People grow up by attachments, giving and receiving affection, relating in warm and understanding way to one another, and developing empathy and the ability to ascertain one another's feelings. Feeling genuine emotions in their relationships with other people, they are able to express these emotions in positive, mature ways. They are able to form emotional relationships based on love, affection, and companionship. Some people who have experienced much abuse, rejection, and the negative relationships with other people sometimes learn to shut off their emotions, so that they reach a non-feeling state in which they will not be hurt. Because of this absence of positive feelings, they miss some of the great pleasure of life.

Subjective Well-being: Another important consideration in emotional development is how people feel about themselves. Subjective well-being is "self-perceived positive feeling or state". It is "an individual's cognitive as well as affective assessments about life as a whole". Most psychologists agree that subjective well-being is an abstract, multidimensional concept that can best be measured by specific indications such as "*life satisfaction, morale, happiness, congruençe and affection*".

Family Relationships: The quality of a marriage has a strong effect on happiness and satisfaction with life. Similarly, marital dissatisfaction in distressed families is highly related to the occurrence of marital tensions. Early experiences with parents had an impact on the well-being of elderly persons. The effect is stronger among those older persons who do not currently have an attachment to an affectionate partner; also, it is stronger for unattached older men than for unattached older women.

11.9. PERSONALITY DEVELOPMENT IN EARLY ADULTHOOD

Personality is the sum total of the physical, mental, emotional, and social characteristics of an individual. It is a global concept that includes all those characteristics that make every person an individual, different from every other person. Personality is not static. It develops over the years and is always in the process of becoming. There is considerable evidence that provides substantial support for stability and continuity of personality in adulthood, although there are indications of change. Individuals exhibit change as well as stability in various personality traits through adulthood.

Five-Factor Model of personality dimensions. This Five Factor Model (FFM) divides the dimensions of personality into the following five categories: extraversion, agreeableness, conscientiousness, neuroticism, and openness/intellect. The big five factors are described as follows (McCrae & John, 1992).

1. **Extraversion (E):** active, assertive, energetic, enthusiastic, outgoing, and talkative
2. **Agreeableness (A):** affectionate, forgiving, generous, kind, sympathetic, and trusting
3. **Conscientiousness (C):** efficient, organized, planful, reliable, responsible, and thorough
4. **Neuroticism (N) :** anxious, self-pitying, tense, touchy, unstable, and worrying
5. **Openness/Intellect (O):** artistic, curious, imaginative, insightful, original, and having wide interests.

Personality has been influenced by both heredity and experiences during childhood, adolescence and early adulthood. During these formative years, traits are more likely to fluctuate than they do later in life. By about age 30, traits usually become quite stable and are likely to remain so throughout the rest of adulthood. Personality shapes people's lives rather than the other way around. Life might somewhat modify the extent of these traits, but the basic structure of personality seems to be there over the life span.

11.10. VOCATIONAL SELECTION, ADJUSTMENT AND DEVELOPMENT DURING EARLY ADULTHOOD:

The Meaning of Work: Studs Terkel, the author of the fascinating work "Working" (1974), writes that work is "a search for daily meaning as well as daily bread, for recognition as well as cash, for astonishment rather than torpor; in short, for a sort of life rather than a Monday through Friday sort of dying". Kahlil Gibran (1923), in his mystical book "The Prophet" put it this way "Work is love made visible".

For some of us, work is a source of prestige, social recognition, and a sense of worth. For others, the excitement of creativity and the opportunity to give something of themselves make work meaningful. But for most, the main purpose of work is to earn a living. This is not to imply, of course, that money is the only reward in a job; friendships, the chance to exercise power, and feeling useful are also important.

Two major psychosocial tasks of early adulthood are to "mold an identity" and to "choose and consolidate a career". These two goals are intertwined because vocational choice is one way to establish identity. Adults are associated with their work; "she is a branch manager of the bank". He is a "superintendent of schools". Among the developmental tasks of early adulthood, those relating to occupation are most important, and most difficult to accomplish. The major adjustments to these new roles must be made in adulthood.

To earn one's bread by the sweat of one's brow has always been the lot of humankind. Work plays an important part in the development of a person's sense of self. For some of us, work is a source of prestige, social recognition, and a sense of worth. For others, the excitement of creativity and the opportunity to give something of them make work meaningful. Nevertheless, for most, the main purpose of work is to earn a living. This is not to imply, of course, that money is the only reward in a job; friendships, the chance to exercise power, and feeling useful are also important.

The meaning most of us derive from working includes both the money that can be exchanged for life's necessities (and may be a few luxuries, too) and the possibility of personal growth. These occupational priorities are what people want from their employment. They reflect the culture and the times in which people live. Research has showed younger workers in upper management are less interested in materialism, power seeking, upward mobility and competition; instead, they emphasize individual freedom, personal growth and co-operation.

Regardless of what occupational priortities, people have, they view their occupation as a key element in their sense of identity. Whether we are a teacher, plumber, corporate executive or stay at home parent, our work defines our daily schedule, social contacts, and opportunities for personal development in important ways. Occupation affects one's life in a host of ways, often influencing where he or she lives, what friends he or she make, and even what clothes he or she wears. In short, the impact of work cuts across all aspects of life. Work, then, is a major social role and influence of adult life. Occupation is an important anchor that complements the other major role of adulthood – love relationships. So important is productive work to people's psychosocial identities that when adult men and women were asked whether they would keep on working even if they did not need the income, the vast majority said yes.

Vocational achievement is important in a society that emphasizes individualism, personal fulfillment, and material success. Success and job satisfaction reaffirm one's identity and provide social recognition. One important task of this period therefore, is to become established in an occupation. In addition, our jobs often define our status, income and prestige, as well as provide us with money to feed, clothe, and shelter ourselves and our families. Some jobs may also encourage personal growth and provide opportunities for creativity, self-development and enhanced self-esteem. In short, our work provides an important context in which self and identity develops.

The central portion of the adult life span for both men and women today is spent at work, and nowadays young adults are working longer than ever. The net result is a decline in their happiness and an erosion of their collective ability to care for children, cook, sleep, visit, and enjoy life. Our young adults are merging work and family life, marked by conflicting career goals and personal needs. A majority of men and women would prefer to work few hours than they do. Some resolve this conflict by adapting to the job requirements, thus delaying having children. Others opt to meet their families' needs by varying work schedules, working from home, working part-time, or by exiting the work force, with ramifications for future employment.

America's work experience has also undergone a significant change over the past 185 years. More than 70 percentage of the U.S labor force worked on the farm in 1820; today less than 5 percentage are engaged in agriculture. Employment in the service industries is about 70 percentage now, the same as for farming over a century and a half ago. For majority of young Americans, the transition to adult occupational roles is postponed by college. Most youth view college education primarily as a mean to a better job rather than as a vehicle for broadening their intellectual horizons.

Most working adults spend more time at their occupations than at any other single activity. The jobs held by parents largely determine the family's social status, place of residence, how often they move, who cares for the children, when family members sleep and eat, and when (and how much) they are together. All these facts made vocations important when most were made decisions. They make vocations even more important now, when over one-half of all women of employable age are also working. In addition, our jobs often define our status, income and prestige, as well as provide us with money to feed, clothe, and shelter ourselves and our families. Some jobs may also encourage personal growth and provide opportunities for creativity, self-development and enhanced self-esteem. In short, our work provides an important context in which self and identity develops.

The Significance of Work for Men and Women: Work provides adults with a number of important opportunities, including earning a living, demonstrating competence, supporting and validating self-esteem, engaging in social interactions, and meeting challenges. People work for a great many reasons. "Self-interest" in its broadest sense, including the interests of one's family and friends, is an underlying motivation of work in all societies. However, self-interest is not simply accumulation of wealth. For instance, a desire for approval, a sense of duty, a wish to conform to custom, a feeling of emulation and a pleasure in craftsmanship also contributes to economic activity. In addition to its economic function, work structures time, provides a context in which to relate to other people, offers an escape from boredom, and sustains a sense of identity and self-worth. Although paid work is becoming an economic necessity for an increasing number of women, a paid job has increasingly come to be seen as the "price for admission" to independence in the greater society and as a symbol of self-worth. For all of us our work is an important socializing experience that influences who and what we are.

Vocation and Life Satisfaction: People are located along a continuum of vocational maturity through their working years; the more congruent their occupational behaviors are with what is expected of them at different ages, the more vocationally mature they are. Discontentment with one's work is strongly associated with unhappiness at home. People who are most troubled about money or who derive little pleasure from their work are most unhappy with their love and sexual relationships.

Vocational Selection: The first major adjustment is the selection of a vocation or occupational selection. Occupational selection is a complex interaction among personal, ethnic, gender, and economic factors. Early decisions about occupations seem to be related to their personalities. People choose occupations to optimize the fit between their individual traits such as personality, intelligence, skills and abilities and their occupational interests. Early occupational choices in adolescence continue to be modified and fine-tuned in adulthood. Many young adults who have had little or no training for a particular line of work go through a period of trying out one job after another, often in different lines of work. This "job-hopping" as it is called often goes on during the twenties or even into the thirties.

It is becoming increasingly common for adults to change careers in midlife, which may be due to changes in the job market for some skills, or due to changes in personal goals. The success of occupational development in young adulthood is reflected by both satisfaction and productivity. Job satisfaction is generally the result of factors associated with both job characteristics and individual characteristics, such as interests and abilities.

Occupational Choices

Early decisions about what people want to do in the world of work are related to their personalities. Holland's (1981) theory highlights that people choose occupations to optimize the fit between their individual traits (such as personality, intelligence, skills and abilities) and their occupational interests. Early occupational choices in adolescence continue to be modified and fine-tuned in adulthood. Occupational selection is a complex interaction among personal, ethnic, gender and economic factors.

Occupational development: Promotion is a measure of how well one is doing in one's carrier. How quickly occupational advancement occurs (or does not), may lead to such labels as "fast –tracker" or "dead-ender" (Kanter, 1976). Bill Clinton became the president at the age of 46, is an example of fast tracker. People who want to advance learn quickly how long to stay at one level and how to seize opportunities as they occur; others soon learn the frustration of remaining in the job, with no chance for promotion. How a person advances in a career seems to depend on professional socialization, which includes several factors besides those that are important in choosing an occupation. Among these are expectations, support from co-workers, priorities and job satisfaction and when friends and members of the social group regard their jobs favorably.

Factors Influencing Vocational Selection

Gender Differences: Boys and girls are socialized differently for work, and their occupational choices are affected as a result. Women choose non-traditional occupations for many reasons, including expectations and personal feelings.

Women and Occupational Development: Women leave well-paid occupations for many reasons, including family obligations and workplace environment. Women who continue to work full-time have adequate childcare and so look for ways to further their occupational development.

Ethnicity and Occupational Development: Vocational identity and vocational goals vary in different ethnic groups.

Bias and Discrimination: Sex discrimination remains the chief barrier to women's occupational development. Pay inequity is also a problem; women are often paid less than men in similar jobs. Sexual harassment is a problem in the workplace. Current criteria for judging harassment are based on the "reasonable woman" standard. Denying employment to anyone over 40 because of age is age discrimination.

Place of Residence: Career choices are influenced by the place of residence. People living in rural areas and small towns tend to choose occupations that are lower in pay and prestige than those living in areas that are more metropolitan areas.

Socio-economic Status: This also influences occupational choices because of differences in life styles and values regarding the importance of education and vocational training.

Tradition of the Family: Father's occupation may significantly influence a male's occupational choice because of a son's identification with the father.

Attraction: The attractiveness of a vocation may influence choice, as jobs are evaluated in terms of prestige, power, income and psychological rewards.

Stability of Vocational Choice: When vocations that follow individual's line of interest are selected, he is more satisfied with the decision he makes and is less anxious to change. Vocational values vary for the two genders. Women are interested in less active, less adventuresome and less dangerous occupations than men are. Women as a whole, tend to be less stable in their vocational choices than men, as married women are often forced to shift their vocational interests and plans to fit into their home responsibilities or to adapt to changes to another community, necessitated by the shift in their husband's jobs. For both men and women, there is a tendency to change vocational values because of experience. As more experience is gained, adults grow older in independence and work in which one is more or less on his own, than on interesting jobs, fame or profit.

Stability of vocational choices throughout adulthood increases with age. Job changes within an occupation are more frequent than occupational changes. Professional workers change least while those in unskilled or the higher white-collar occupations change most. Individuals who are successful in their careers are stable in their vocational choices in adult years.

The next one that influences adjustments to work most is the worker's attitude. Havighurst, from a study of workers' attitudes toward work, has come to the conclusion that they can be divided into two general categories which he has labeled "society-maintaining work attitudes" and "ego-involving work attitudes". The characteristics of these attitudes are explained.

Adjustment to Work: When adults have made a vocational selection, they must adjust to the work itself, to the hours of workday or work week, to their co-workers and superiors, to the environment in which the work is done, and to the restrictions the work imposes on their personal lives. For many young adults, the last factor is often is the most difficult of all vocational adjustments. The next one that influences adjustments to work most is the worker's attitude.

Adjustment by Men: Both the status of the individual and also his family in adult society is determined largely by the occupation of the man; he and his family must adjust to this. There are a number of conditions, important to them that influence men's adjustments to their work. First, if the job allows the adult to play the role he wants to play, he will be satisfied and makes good adjustments to his work. Second, adjustment to work is influenced by how men adjust to authority. Thirdly adjustment to work is influenced by pay rise or lack of them. Sometimes men can advance vocationally only if they are willing to move to other organizations.

Adjustment by Women: There are a number of conditions that influence women's adjustments. Among these, six stand out as important.

- First, when women are unable to find jobs suited to their abilities, training, and expectations, they feel frustrated.
- Second, when women feel they are in dead end jobs, especially as they approach middle age, they talk out their frustrations to their subordinates.
- Third, when women have formed stereotyped occupational aspirations, which mean aspirations below their capacities to avoid rivaling or surpassing male workers, tend to become frustrated, when they discover that their capacities and training justify higher-level occupations.
- Fourth, when women are denied leadership roles in their occupations, they are not only frustrated but resentful when they see these roles going to men, many of whom, they feel, have less ability and training than they have.

- Fifth, many women resent having to carry a double workload one in the work world and one in the home. They may feel guilty because they must neglect many of the homemaking duties other women perform or rely on their children or outside help to assist them.
- Sixth, many women long for the job they gave up when they assumed the roles of housewife and mother.

Vocational Development in Early Adulthood:

Promotion is a measure of how well one is doing in one's career. How quickly occupational advancement occurs (or does not), may lead to such labels as "fast –tracker" or "dead-ender".

During the years of adulthood, primarily the 20's adults can be grouped into five different categories according to the status of their vocational development. They are ***vocational achievers, vocationally frustrated, noncommitted people, vocational opportunists and social dropouts***. The degree of satisfaction derived from jobs has a marked influence on the quality and quantity of young adults' work. Workers who are satisfied with their jobs become dedicated to their work and loyal to the organization. From the personal point of view, job satisfaction contributes to the worker's self satisfaction and this, in turn, contributes to the worker's happiness.

11.11. PSYCHO –SOCIAL DEVELOPMENT OF YOUNG ADULTHOOD

"To love and work"-Sigmund Fraud

"One can live magnificently in this world, if one knows how to work and how to love"

Count Leo Tolstoy 1856

Just like previous developmental stages, an adult continues to experience change- biological, social and psychological development in adulthood. Refinements occur to shape concepts of who one is and what are one's purposes in life. As the individual experiences the passage of time during the early adulthood years, the self continues to unfold in exciting, challenging, and dynamic ways.

Among the developmental tasks of early adulthood, those relating to occupation and family life are the most important, and most difficult to accomplish. A successful journey through adulthood is, for most people, closely tied to a person's involvement with a carrier and romantic partner and family.Our chief developmental task in early adulthood is to form an intimate relationship with another person wherein, they fuse their identities with those of other people. They learn how to commit themselves to relationships, and how to sacrifice and compromise to maintain those relationships. This may occur in the context of intimate friendships, and in the special relationships of spouses or lovers. Young adults who do not successfully resolve the crisis between intimacy and isolation remain psychosocially isolated and their relationships are without spontaneity, warmth, or deep emotional exchanges.

Love and work provide the central themes of adult life. Both place us in a complex web of relationships with others. Our ability to find meaningful work and to establish satisfying intimate relationships socializes us to new roles, usually involving increased personal and financial independence. Finding a satisfying intimate relationship and a career involves role changes. Such adjustments are usually more subtle than in earlier stages of life. Adulthood can be a time of great emotional and personal development, a time of important changes in peoples' roles. For most, early adulthood is a period of adaptation.

Adulthood can be a time of great emotional and personal development, a time of important changes in peoples' roles. Far from being static, adulthood is a time of changes in people's roles and, therefore, in their emotions, motivation, and relations with others. For most, early adulthood is a period of adaptation. They see things differently; they behave differently, and they adjust their beliefs, attitudes, and values in accord with the roles and contents they experience.

Self, Family and Work: Adult development can be described in the context of three separate but interacting systems that focus on various aspects of the self. These involve :

1. The development of the self as an individual
2. The self as a family member (adult child, member of a couple, or parent), and
3. The self as a worker.

Interactions abound. For example, research has shown that the more positive a father's work experience, the higher his self esteem and he is more likely to have an accepting, warm and positive parenting style .

Early years of adulthood are frequently lonely years for both men and women. Their friends of earlier years and their business associates are occupied with family activities, or are preoccupied with courtship. Even the young adult who is married finds himself lonely at times and craves the companionship he enjoyed during the adolescent years. Of the many changes in social interests and activities the young adult must make, major changes are in social participation, friendships, social groupings, popularity and leadership.

Now the young adult relies more on relatives from both sides of the family for companionship than on outsiders, and with them he engages in social activities. The pattern of social participation and the amount will differ for adults who are married as compared with those who are unmarried. The other most important factors that influence social participation are social mobility, social class, environment, gender, and age of sexual maturing.

CHAPTER

12

MIDDLE ADULTHOOD (40-60 YEARS)

OBJECTIVES

To enlighten the students regarding the

- Distinguishing features of middle age-Characteristics, Developmental Task,
- Physical changes and Health and their psychological impact,
- Factors affecting health at midlife
- Stress-Coping with Stress at Family and Work,
- Midlife Crisis, Adjustments during Middle Adulthood
- Cognitive, Vocational and Psycho-Social Development during middle age
- Differences between the thinking of mature adults and younger people
- Factors affecting creating achievement, and how it changes with age
- Changes in work patters and how work contributes to cognitive development
- Role of marriage and divorce at this time of life
- Friendships in middle age
- Parent-child relationships, adjustment with parents and siblings
- Preparation of retirement

12.1. INTRODUCTION

Middle age traditionally extends from age 40 to 60 or 65. However, there are marked individual differences in the ages when the physical changes marking off middle age from early adulthood at one end and old age at the other end occur (103, Hurlock, 1968). The onset is marked by physical and mental changes, as is the end. Popular conceptions of middle adulthood are riddled with clichés like "midlife crisis," "middle-aged spread" and "autumn years" that conjures up a sense of dullness, resignation, and perhaps a touch of despair. Yet the tone of these clichés is far from reflecting the truth of the development. Many adults feel healthier, smarter, and more pleasant with themselves and their lives during these two decades than they ever did. Some middle-aged adults are burdened by health problems, or a decline in intellectual powers, or unexpected responsibilities of aged parents or adult children. Some feel trapped by choices made in early adulthood.

Middle age is a separate and special bracket of the total life experience. Middle-aged adult has reached the peak of development; physically, the middle-aged adult is in good health. However, the beginning signs of physical aging begin to emerge. On the other hand, the individual has accumulated a broad range of social, personal and work skills. For this reason, middle age has sometimes been viewed as "prime of life". Roles that have occupied so much of adult life come to a close during this period such as reproductive, parenting and work roles. Individuals are challenged to adjust to these and other changes in making new adaptations to the demands of life at middle age. One of the most challenging adjustments focuses on the unique characteristics of family life at this point in the life style (Bigner. J., 1983).

The middle years of adulthood represent a transitional period in the life span. During this time, individuals experience both continuity and change in many aspects of their lives as adults. Middle adulthood is a period when adults try to make sense of the continually changing demands of parenting, the shifting roles in intimate relationships, the changing world of work, and the issues in the larger world. Altogether, it is a period of multiple concerns. However, the beginning signs of physical aging begin to emerge. On the other hand, the individual has accumulated a broad range of social, personal and work skills. For this reason, middle age has sometimes been viewed as "prime of life".

Middle adulthood is a period when adults try to make sense of the continually changing demands of parenting, the shifting roles in intimate relationships, the changing world of work, and the issues in the larger world. Altogether, it is period of bewildering array of concerns. The middle adulthood years are a period of stability and continuity in personality and outlook. It is in the context of continuity and change during the middle years that reflection and reassessment occur which, take place within the context of three inter-connecting world-self, family and work (Craig,).

Middle age is an especially difficult time in the life span. How well individuals adjust to it will depend on the foundations laid during earlier stages in the life span but especially on the adjustments they made to the roles and social expectations of adult society. Good mental health, acquired in adulthood, will go a long way toward easing the adjustments to the new roles and new social expectations of middle age.

12.2. DEVELOPMENTAL TASKS OF MIDDLE ADULTHOOD

Understanding adulthood is closely tied to considering how the major life events, such as moving away from the parents' home , marrying, sending the oldest child into the world, retirement, and so forth, affect the continuity of individuals' lives. Havighurst,(1972) suggested that the developmental tasks of middle adulthood are to:

- Accept and adjust to physiological changes of middle age.
- Attain and maintain a satisfactory occupational performance
- Establish and maintain an economic standard of living
- Assist teenage children to become responsible and happy adults
- Relate to one's spouse as a person
- Adjust to aging parents
- Achieve adult social and civic responsibility and develop an interest in adult-oriented activities, which prevailed during early adulthood.
- Develop adult leisure-time activities

Not all these tasks are mastered simultaneously or in the same way by all people. Individual differences in the rate of development may result in some tasks being accomplished earlier or later than others are. Thus the mastery of most of the developmental tasks of middle age prepare the individual for successful adjustment in old age.

12.3. CHARACTERISTICS OF MIDDLE AGE

Ten of the most important characteristics, which make middle age distinctive are listed below and briefly explained.

1. **Middle age is a Dreaded Period:** Middle age is the most dreaded period in entire life span, next to old age. For example, to a woman middle age means loss of her sexual, reproductive ability, and loss of her job-that of mother and, to some extent that of wife. As the family "nest" empties, the woman becomes more and more lonely and depressed. Hence, she dreads this period. To the man, middle age means diminished physical as well as sexual vitality, signs of aging, which make employment precarious, and the suspicion that he is losing his ability to attract women.
2. **Middle Age is a Time of Transition:** Middle age is the time when men and women leave behind the physical and behavioral characteristics of early adulthood and enter a period of life where new physical and behavioral characteristics will prevail. Transition requires learning new behaviour patterns and playing new roles. Role change is likely to result in a crisis of major or minor severity.
3. **Middle Age is a Time of Stress:** The common sources of stress leading to disequilibrium during middle age, could be divided into four major categories.
   (*i*) Somatic stress, which is due to physical evidence of aging
   (*ii*) Cultural stress, stemming from the high value placed on youth, vigor and success by the cultural group
   (*iii*) Economic stress, resulting from the financial burden of children's education and providing status symbols for all family members
   (*iv*) Psychological stress, which may be the result of the death of a spouse, the departure of children from the home, boredom with marriage, or a sense of lost youth and approaching death
4. **Middle Age is a "Dangerous Age":** The usual way of interpreting "dangerous age" is in terms of the male who wants to have a first fling in life, especially in his sex life, before old age catches up to him. In doing so, he often becomes unfaithful to his wife or divorces her to marry someone young enough to be his daughter. It is a time when individuals break down physically from overwork, over-worry, or careless living. It is also a peak age for suicide, especially among men.
5. **Middle age is an "Awkward Age":** The middle-aged person is no longer "young" nor is he yet "old". As a result, he, like the adolescent, suffers from the discomforts and embarrassments of both. Feeling that he has no recognized place in society, the middle-aged person tries to be as inconspicuous as possible. The desire to be inconspicuous is reflected in the clothing preferred by middle-aged people. The more inconspicuous they are, the less out of place they will feel in a society that worships youth.
6. **Middle age is Time of Achievement:** Middle age is mainly a time of self-evaluation. During middle age, both men and women normally reach their peaks of achievement and reap the benefits of the years of preparation and hard work that preceded it. Normally, the peak is reached between forty and fifty years, after which the individual rests on his laurels and enjoys the benefits of his hard-won success until he reaches the early sixties. Middle age is the period when leadership in business, industry, and community organizations is the reward for achievement.
7. **Middle age is evaluated by a Standard:** Double standards of evaluating men and women are used during this period. In spite of growing trend toward egalitarian roles for men and women in the home, in business, industry, the professions, and in social life,

there still exists a double standard regarding aging. The first common double standard relates to physical changes-when men's hair becomes gray, when they develop lines and wrinkles on their faces and a middle-aged paunch in place of a once slender waistline, they are usually regarded as "distinguished", whereas similar physical changes are judged as "unattractive" in women. The second area in which the double standard is apparent is in the approved way for members of the two gender to age.

8. **Middle Age Is a Time of Readjustment:** Every adult must adjust to the physical changes that come with middle age. Adjustments to changed roles are even more difficult than adjustment to changed physical conditions. Men must adjust to the changes that approach to retirement and their changed physical condition necessitated in their work, while women must adjust to changing the role of housewife or that of worker in business or industry to being an "isolate" when formerly being the center of home activity.

12.4. PHYSICAL CHANGES AND HEALTH

As people move into middle age, they begin experiencing some of the physical changes associated with aging. Of course, middle age is when people typically get wrinkles, grey hairs and a bulging waistline. However, middle age adults also achieve new heights in cognitive development, change their behavior if they choose, develop adult relationships with their children and ease into grandparenthood. Along the way, they must deal with stress, changes in the way they learn, and the challenges of dealing with their aging parents. How well the middle aged body functions is directly correlated with genetic constitution, nutrition, exercise, rest, cognitive awareness, emotional outlook, stress, and concomitant disease or disabilities.

Physical Changes :

Appearance: There is rather little change in an individual's physical appearance during early adulthood. But, middle adulthood is marked by dramatic changes in physical appearance.

There is a tendency to gain weight, especially, in the area of the waistline, known as the "middle-age spread." This gain is partly due to the accumulation of excess fat and partly to changes in body composition. By middle adulthood, fat is about 20 percent of body weight.

- **There is a redistribution of body fat:** The abdomen and hips become larger and the bust and chest become smaller (compared with the stomach and hips)
- **Changes in hair.** Among men, baldness increases, as does graying of the hair and there is a gradual growth of stiff hair in the nose, ears, and eyelashes during middle age and among women, there is an increase in the growth of hair on the upper lip and chin.
- **The skin becomes less elastic:** The skin on the face, neck, arms, and hands becomes coarser and begins to show wrinkles. Bags under the eyes are common accompaniments of aging. Dark circles under the eyes, bluish-red discolorations, often in the shape of spider web, around the ankles or on the mid-calf are prominent.
- General posture and movements become less smooth

Weight and Height: The trends of aging that first appeared in early adulthood continue to occur in middle age. Gender differences are evident in both weight and height during this period; however, men show an average decrease while women show an average increase in body weight in middle age. In addition, over-eating and under-exercising results in more people being noticeably overweight during middle age than during any earlier period. The declining weight trend begins in the fifties for humans and primarily involves the skeletal muscles, liver, kidneys, and adrenal glands. As back muscles, connecting tissues, and the bones lose strength, the vertebrae collapses somewhat, causing some individuals to lose nearly an inch in height by age 60, occurring more rapidly among women than among men.

Muscular Ability: Variations in peak muscular ability depend very much on the type of activity. If the man or woman has done hard manual work for the major part of his life, his muscles will be strong at middle age, though they will have fewer resiliencies than previously. Most men and women, however, look and act as if their muscles were soft and flabby. This is especially apparent in the areas of the chin, upper arms, and abdomen. Aerobic activities may be reversing this trend in middle age weight gain and muscle loss.

Bones: The bones become gradually more brittle with a consequent tendency to break more easily and to require a longer time to heal after they are broken. Some middle-aged people develop difficulties with their joints and limbs, thus causing them to walk with difficulty with a degree of awkwardness rarely found in younger people.

The Teeth: The primary change affecting the teeth in middle age is a condition called osteoporosis. As a result, teeth become loosened in the socket and eventually are lost. The condition occurs throughout the skeletal system and is not restricted to the mouth area. The cause of osteoporosis is not known but may be related to low calcium intake in the diet.

Changes in Sensory Abilities

Vision: The degenerative and functional changes in the eye result in decrease in pupil size, acuity, and glare resistance, and a tendency toward glaucoma, cataracts, and tumors. Common symptoms of aging in the eyes includes a gradual loss of accommodation (focusing ability), de-pigmentation of the iris, loss of retinal reflexes and changes in the lens and cornea. The ability to focus on nearby objects decreases for most people in their forties, leading to a diagnosis for far-sightedness and possibly a prescription for bifocals. Adaptation to darkness and recovery from glare also take longer time, making night driving somewhat more taxing.

Hearing: Hearing also seems to be susceptible to decline at 40, with the result that the individual must listen more attentively than he formerly did. We begin to lose the ability to detect certain tones. Typically, the ability to hear high-pitched notes declines, but the magnitude for the change varies appreciably among individuals. At age 50, about one in every three men and one in every four women have difficulty understanding a whisper. Our ability to understand human speech also appears to decrease, as we grow older. Due to the loss in the ability to hear, many middle-aged people start to talk very loudly, and often in a monotone.

Other Senses: There are other gradual changes in sensory functioning during middle adulthood. Changes in taste occur after age fifty. The taste buds begin to atrophy inside the cheeks at first and then progressively toward the back of the tongue.

After age forty, **sensitivity to smell** also declines significantly. The sense of smell grows weaker in men, because of the increase in the hairy network of the nose, and this affects the sense of taste. **Sensitivity to pain** increases at about forty-five years of age and continues to increase beyond sixty years.

Tactile Sensitivity: Touch, Temperature, and Pain: Research reveals some decrease in **tactile acuity** with increasing age, and the loss is small, though, and a number of individuals over 60 retain high sensitivity. Temperature and pain sensitivity are impaired in only a small percentage of the elderly.

Thermoregulation: Thermoregulation is the maintenance of body temperature during exposure to heat or cold. Elderly people may require a more intense thermal stimulus to elicit the appropriate behavior responses in the home. Such stimuli may result in greater heat flow and elevated risk of dysthermia in the aged. The elderly are at high risk of mortality from excessive heat and excessive cold.

Sense of Balance: Hair-like projections in the inner ear, which are activated by the flow of fluids as the body changes positions, act as sensory preceptors that pick up and pass on information to the brain about body positions and orientations that constitute our sense of balance. A maximum sense of balance is achieved between 40 and 50, followed by decline, and an increase in postural sway. One consequence is that older people tend to fall more often. The fact that women lose their balance more than men do, explain their greater frequency of falling as they grow older.

12.5. CHANGES IN PHYSIOLOGICAL FUNCTIONING

Changes in the exterior of the body do not occur without a parallel change in the internal organs and their functioning. There is increasing sluggishness in the functioning of the most glands of the body. The pores and skin glands are slower than they formerly were in ridding the skin of the waste materials, with the result that there is an increased tendency to body odors. The different glands connected with the digestive processes likewise function more slowly with a consequent increase in number and severity of digestive disorders. Many middle-aged men and women must deal with dental plates that increase the difficulty of chewing. Constipation is very common in middle age.

The Circulatory System: The circulatory system shows signs of aging in the years of middle age. Three basic changes may be observed:

(1) a decline in the elasticity of the arteries (Arteriosclerosis commonly called as "hardening of the arteries"). The walls of the arteries become brittle as middle age progresses and this leads to circulatory difficulties(Atherosclerosis).

(2) An increasing accumulation of fatty deposits in the arterial tissue and

(3) a general decline in the pumping ability of the heart muscle. Two conditions appear with increasing frequency in middle age, that is, major abnormalities of the heart and circulatory systems.

Hypertension and coronary heart disease account for the two leading causes of visits to physicians among middle age individuals. The role of diet and lack of regular exercise and the contribution of fats, cholesterol, and sodium in the diet are considered to be the prime culprits of atherosclerosis among middle aged individuals. However, as middle age progresses, change in heart size may be noted in some individuals, with hypertrophy (enlargement) occurring primarily in the left ventricle. The heart rate at rest and the maximum heart rate during the strenuous exercise also decrease. As a result, cardiac output normally decreases about 1% per year.

The Skeletal System: Individuals can expect to experience the first indication of arthritis and rheumatism in middle age. Arthritis is an inflammation of a joint, accompanied by pain and changes in the structure of the joint. Rheumatism is the term given to a variety of conditions that are characterized by stiffness and soreness of muscles and pain in joints. Both these conditions become chronic in nature as individuals experience middle and late adulthood. Osteoporosis (loss of bone mass), also characteristic of aging, is accompanied by degeneration of joint tissue limiting movement as aging occurs. There is a widely recognized decline in movement skills during the adult years. But there is no evidence that this decline causes a decline in job performance.

Strength and Endurance: Strength and endurance gradually decline during middle adulthood, although exercise can certainly slow the rate of decline. Even if people decline a bit physically, they usually can find ways to compensate.

Menopause and Female Mid-Life Change: Fertility declines gradually once a woman is past her twenties, but it declines more quickly during her forties, as menstrual periods get shorter and more irregular. Now her ovaries slowly stop functioning and, when she is about 50 years old, menstrual cycles grow longer and more erratic. Finally menstruation stops altogether, and a woman has reached ***"menopause"*** the most readily identifiable signs of the climacteric. The muscular walls of the vagina grow thin and less elastic. The walls also produce fewer normal secretions, so the vagina feels dryer. The average age at which there is a complete cessation of menses is around

47 to 52 years. Younger women also undergo an early menopause should they have their ovaries surgically removed.

Symptoms that have been commonly attributed to menopause include hot flashes (feeling of extreme heat), the hot flushes (the flushing of the skin), and episodes of profuse sweating, fatigue, dizziness, headaches, insomnia, nervousness and depression. Women who take estrogen tend to live longer than other postmenopausal women do. It seems that estrogen reduces mortality primarily by cutting a woman's risk of heart disease, and osteoporosis. Women, who remain sexually active and regularly masturbate or have intercourse, have less atrophy of their vagina and higher levels of estrogen.

Women are relieved that they no longer have to worry about becoming pregnant and some report an improvement in their sex lives. Women are more likely to feel upset if they view menopause as signaling end of their attractiveness, usefulness and sexuality. Women with pre-existing or long-standing difficulties may be more susceptible to problems and react more adversely in the climacteric than less vulnerable women.

Male Mid-Life Change: In middle age they are likely to experience enlargement of prostate gland. As the prostrate enlarges, it may impinge on the urethra, which may contribute to a decreased force in the urinary stream, a difficulty in beginning urination, and an increased urge to urinate, particularly at night.

Testosterone levels may slump gradually with age. Although aging can contribute to declining male virility in many cases, impotence (may be temporary) results from drugs, medical conditions (diabetes, cardiovascular disorder and cancer) and social habits including smoking, alcohol consumption and lack of exercise, stress, depression, grieving, illness and accidents. The middle year calls for readjustments and reassessments, some of which may be unpleasant, and most commonly, the troubling events are spread over one or two decades. When they coincidentally cluster, they create conditions for some men that can be devastating.

Sexuality: The old are considered as a sexual or sexless and a display of erotic interest by old people is regarded as unnatural and undignified. If men have maintained elevated levels of sexual activities from their early years, and if acute or chronic ill health does not intervene, they are able to continue some form of active sexual expression into advanced age. However, if aging males are not stimulated over long periods of time, their responsiveness may be permanently lost. Social habits and styles of life affects our health in many ways, thereby affecting the middle aged person's sexuality.

Health: Nutrition, smoking, alcohol and drug use, physical activity and other influences continue to affect health in middle age, and beyond. People who do not smoke, are not overweight, and exercise regularly at midlife, not only live longer but have shorter periods of disability at the end of life.

Middle aged adults are less susceptible to cold and allergies, and their incidence of accidents decrease. However, the "silent diseases" such as arthritis, diabetes, and peptic ulcer, hypertension, and health problems brought on by excessive alcohol consumption, smoking which causes chronic bronchitis, emphysema, lung and oral cancers and coronary-artery disease increase. The death rate for people 45 to 54 years of age is twice that of 35 to 44 year-old people. For people aged 55 to 64 years, the rate is more than twice that of those aged 45 to 50 years.

Variations in Changes: Generally, men in our culture show signs of aging sooner than women, may be due to the fact that women see to it that signs of middle age are quickly covered up. There is also a tendency for the rate of aging to differ in different socioeconomic groups. In general, those from higher socioeconomic groups appear younger than their years, while those of the lower socioeconomic groups look older than they actually are.

Besides socio economic status, other indirect influences such as race, or ethnicity and gender, continue to affect health. One important influence is stress, whose cumulative effects on both physical and mental health often begin to appear in middle age. In addition, individual differences in personality and emotionality may affect how people physically endure the challenges of midlife.

12.6. STRESS - COPING WITH STRESS AT FAMILY AND WORK PLACE

By middle age, people may tend to be more realistic in coping with stress. They have a better sense of what they can do to change stressful circumstances, and may be better able to accept what cannot be changed. They also have learned more effective strategies for avoiding or minimizing stress.

Stress at Work Place

Stress that is work-related-has become a worldwide epidemic. When people feel they are in the wrong job, or when efforts to meet job demands are out of proportion to job satisfaction and other rewards, stress can result. Stress, which is intense, frequent and prolonged can play havoc with physical and mental health and can increase the risk of high blood pressure and heart disease. Over worked employees, will be likely to make mistakes, to be angry at their employers, to have problems with health and family life, to neglect themselves, to lose sleep, to have difficulty coping with everyday events and eventually to look for new jobs.

Stress at family

One of the most difficult challenges facing adults is trying to balance the demands of occupation with the demands of family. In the majority of two-parent households today, both adults work outside the home, largely because families need the dual income in order to pay the bills and maintain a moderate standard of living. Many women, in addition to juggling work and family, are under special pressures in the workplace, especially in corporations, where their superiors often are men. Another frequent source of stress is "sexual harassment" leading to psychological pressure, which creates a hostile or abusive environment.

12.7. ADJUSTMENTS DURING MIDDLE ADULTHOOD

The Midlife Crisis: Middle adulthood is the time when many individuals deal with the meaning and direction of their lives. The most noticeable changes in midlife are physical ones. Perhaps for the first time, adults are confronted with their own morality and realize that they have limitations, weaknesses, and lack control over certain inevitabilities in life such as aging and death. Most of them had a crucial struggle both within themselves and with their environment when they began to examine their lives up to this time. The main stressors for men are economic and work related. Middle-aged women typically feel stressed about lack of companionship with their husbands, possibilities of their young adult children's making bad marriages, and concern about their work. The individual, however, considers his experience as threatening and may behave in a way that is often labeled as irrational. This refers to the extreme nature of the decisions taken such as divorcing after many years of marriage, making radical changes in jobs, participating in extramarital affairs, dressing flamboyantly or inappropriately for one's age, and others.

Marital adjustments: Marital satisfaction tends to be at its lowest ebb when the children are of school age as in their teenage years. If the husband and wife have been busy working and raising children, as well as being active in community affairs, they may have drifted apart, spending less time communicating, playing, and being together. It is easy to get so absorbed with other activities, that the marriage suffers from lack of attention. Parents who stayed together until their children were grown now feel freer to dissolve their relationships. Some do get divorced. For others, however, middle age can become a time for revitalizing a tired marriage, for rethinking their relationship, and for deciding that they want to share many things in life together.

The Post-parental Years: The term "post-parental" years usually refers to the ages after the last child leaves home or/and until the husband's retirement. Some writers prefer the term "empty-nest years" for them, after children are born, one is always a parent. The biggest adjustment for the wife (if her whole life has been spent in childrearing, is, in filling the gap after the children leave. However, many women breathe a sigh of relief after the last child leaves. At last, these women are now free to live their own lives. Many husbands do not feel too great a loss when the children leave, especially if they have reasons to be proud of them and their accomplishments. While there are adjustments to be made during the empty-nest years, there are increased opportunities to enjoy life as a couple. Middle-aged parents have been called the "sandwich generation" because they are caught between care-giving responsibilities for their children and their elderly parents.

Work versus Early Retirement in Middle-age: About 80% of 40-59-year-olds tend to work primarily for financial reasons, whereas at 60, intrinsic values such as enjoyment of work, wanting to remain productive, and feeling valued and respected become more important determinants of whether a person will continue to work. However, many of today's middle aged and older persons-caught between inadequate savings or pensions and a strained social security system, or simply unwilling to give up the stimulation of work-are choosing "not" to retire or to try a new line of work. Thus, retirement is increasingly a transition within, rather than from midlife.

The main predictors of retirement age are circumstances. Marital status also can make a difference, as decisions about timing of each spouse's retirement have to be negotiated by the couple. Married men from lower socioeconomic status, those with traditional career plans, those who are dissatisfied with their jobs, and those who have planned for retirement are most likely to retire early.

12.8. COGNITIVE DEVELOPMENT DURING MIDDLE AGE

Adult functioning-especially, intelligence has received lot of attention from researchers. Most of the debate has been over whether intelligence declines with age, and if so how much and in what ways. Because of this considerable research, investigators have reached considerable agreement as to how cognition develops during adulthood. The leading theory is that of J.L Horn who argued, that intelligence does decline in some ways, but in other ways it does not (Dacey J.S & Travers J.F, 2006).

Speaking, middle-aged people are in their prime. Seattle Longitudinal Study of Adult Intelligence, conducted by K. Warner and his colleagues found no uniform pattern of age-related changes for all intellectual abilities.

During middle adulthood, the straightforward cognitive growth of earlier years begins to wave and intellectual development becomes more multidirectional, multifaceted and individualized. Rather than mastering skills that are suited to a wide variety of situations, the adult acquires knowledge that is more specialized and expertise that reflect professional, personal and relational needs. Life circumstances related to health, marriage, occupation and other events also influence the courage of cognitive development. As a result, intellectual growth moves in more idiosyncratic directions during the middle adulthood years (Craig).

During middle adulthood, the straightforward cognitive growth of earlier years begins to wave and intellectual development becomes more multidirectional, multifaceted and individualized. Rather than mastering skills that are suited to a wide variety of situations, the adult acquires knowledge that is more specialized and expertise that reflect professional, personal and relational needs. Life circumstances related to health. marriage, occupation and other events also influence the courage of cognitive development. As a result, intellectual growth moves in more idiosyncratic directions during the middle adulthood years (Craig).

Despite some classic studies (e.g, Knowles, 1989; Taub,1975), considerable disagreement is there regarding whether there is a serious drop from early adulthood to late adulthood in the ability to learn, considerable disagreement over this matter still exists. For example, many studies have shown a marked decline in paired associate learning (the ability to remember associations between two lists of words) (Kimmel, 1974). Obviously, memorizing pairs of words is itself of no great importance but much essential learning is based on this skill. In most of these studies, however, the measure of how well the association have been learned is speed of response (Dacey & Travers. 2006).

There are myths about the cognitive functioning and learning skills of the middle-aged adults (Schiamberg, 1985).

Intelligence declines in adulthood: Despite wide individual differences, most participants in the Seattle study showed no significant reduction in most abilities until after the age 60, and then not in all or even most areas. Virtually no one declined on all fronts, and many people improved in some areas (Schaie, 1994). Consistent with previous research, successive generations score progressively higher at the same ages on reasoning, spatial orientation, and verbal abilities (Papalia et al.,2007).

Intelligence and cognitive skills tend to remain rather stable in adulthood. In fact, reasoning and verbal skills may actually improve (Birren, 1976). The middle-aged individuals' ability to think is, overall, likely to be as good as in early adulthood (Schiamberg, 1985).

Adults can't effectively learn new things: Middle-aged adults are supposed to be "set in their ways"– so set, in fact, that they cannot or will not learn new way of thinking or doing things (Schiamberg, 1985). Almost any adult can learn almost any formal and informal subject and skill, provided she or he is given sufficient time and attention. Although, there is a trend toward an increasing range of individual differences in adulthood, adults can still learn new things if their self-confidence has not been. Self-confidence is particularly important because some adults tend to underestimate their learning ability by overemphasizing their limited formal school experiences. They also tend to underestimate the large gains made in practical and specific knowledge and experience (crystallized intelligence) (Knox, 1977) (Schiarnberg, 1985).

Adults continue to learn informally throughout their lifetime in the worlds of work. family, and community or neighborhood. Many adults engage in self-directed activities as well as in formal part-time educational programs. In most cases, when adults engage in sustained and systematic learning activities, the intent is to improve their performance. In other words, adults typically want to use what they learn, Knox (1977) has identified the following *factors that have a primary influence on learning in adulthood* (Schiamberg, 1985):

Condition: Physiological condition and physical health can affect learning and cognition in various ways. Sensory impairment. such as poor vision or hearing can restrict sensory input. III health can restrict attention given to external event.

Adjustment: The effective assessment or facilitation of learning is less likely when there is substantial personal or social maladjustment in the learning situation. Social maladjustment is usually associated with learner's defensiveness and anxiety and should not be confused with moderate levels of arousal and motivation. If a person believes that he or she can deal with a situation, it may be a challenge, if not, it may be perceived as a threat. People deal best with failure when they have experienced many successes. Support and assistance is especially important for adults with few recent educational experiences.

Relevance: The adult's motivation and cooperation in the learning activity is more likely when the tasks are meaningful and of interest to the learner. Active interest and participation are more likely when the learner helps identify objectives, selects learning tasks, and understands procedures.

Speed: Especially for older adults, time limits and pressure tend to reduce learning performance. Optimal learning performance is more likely when learners can proceed at their own pace.

Status: Socioeconomic circumstances are associated with values, demands, constraints, and resources that can affect learning ability. Level of formal education tends to be the status index most highly associated with adult learning. The influence of status on learning depends on the type of learning activity. For example, for learning the metric system, oral communications might be more effective for blue-collar adults, and white-collar adults might learn abstract concepts through written communication more effectively.

Outlook: Personal outlook and personality characteristics, such as open mindedness or defensiveness, can affect the way in which an adult deals with specific types of learning situations (Knox, 1977) (Schiamberg, 1985).

The results of K. Warner Schaie and Christopher Hetzog's 21 year cross-sectional study of intelligence indicated some decrements that begin to appear during middle age. For example, their study highlighted decrease in scores for verbal meaning, spatial ability, inductive reasoning, numerical abilities, and word fluency. Although the overall trend in middle age is one of gradual decline, any decline before age 60 years is likely to be so slight that it will have little practical importance (Schaie and Hetzog, 1983). Many people think that what is really important in adult cognitive development is not the kind of intelligence measured by Schaie and Hertzog's test. We should look at how people identify important problems in their lives and how people use both reason and intuition to solve these problems (D & D). A general finding is that elderly people need more time for responding than typically is provided; they are at a disadvantage when this time is not available. When sufficient time for response is available, the performance of elderly people is only slightly inferior, or not inferior at all to that of young people. Another factor in learning ability that has been studied is motivation to learn. It has been suggested that persons in middle and late adulthood are less motivated to learn than younger people (Dacey & Travers, 2006).

It also had been found in laboratory experiences that older adults are more likely than younger adults, to make the "omission error." That is, when they suspect they may be wrong, they are more likely to refrain from responding at all and therefore, are scored as having not learned the task. However, when asked what they think the answer is, they are often right. In addition, the meaningfulness of the task affects motivation. It is clear that the motivation for middle-aged and elderly adults is different from that of younger adults, and many experiments have not considered this in studying learning ability. Not all new learning by middle-aged adults takes place in a formal school setting. Employees in many different types of work settings are asked to keep abreast of innovations. Other social experiences, such as practicing a religion, going to a library, watching television, and serving as a volunteer, involve new learning. Learning is now more than ever a lifelong task (Dacey & Travers, 2006).

It also had been found in laboratory experiences that older adults are more likely than younger adults to make the "omission error." That is, when they suspect they may be wrong, they are more likely to refrain from responding at all and therefore, are scored as having not learned the task. However, when asked what they think the answer is, they are often right. In addition, the meaningfulness of the task affects motivation. It is clear that the motivation for middle-aged and elderly adults is different from that of younger adults, and many experiments have not considered this in studying learning ability (Dacey & Travers, 2006).

Decline in cognitive ability due to aging can often be offset through motivation and new learning experiences. Not all new learning by middle-aged adults takes place in a formal school setting. Employees in many different types of work settings are asked to keep abreast of innovations. Other social experiences, such as practicing a religion, going to a library, watching television, and serving as a volunteer, involve new learning. Learning is now more than ever a lifelong task (Dacey & Travers, 2006) .

Intelligence: New views of intelligence highlight that intelligence is composed of several different cognitive abilities such as memory, language. reasoning and numerical ability. Each of these mental processes can, in turn, be divided into various sub-processes. The term "general intelligence" is being abandoned as a scientific concept and subject of study. More and more, researchers are proposing several quite distinct cognitive abilities. Horn has now added supporting abilities to the concepts of fluid and crystallized intelligence. These include short-term memory, long-term memory, visual processing and auditory processing. Howard Gardner (1983), contended that there are eight different cognitive abilities. His list includes linguistic. musical, logical-mathematical, spatial, bodily-kinesthetic, interpersonal, intra-personal, and naturalistic intelligence.

In Robert Sternberg's (2002) view, successful intelligence consists of analytical components (solving problems) creative components (deciding what problems to solve), and practical components (devising effective solutions). He suggests that intelligence is not so much a matter of quantity but rather, a matter of balance, of knowing when and how to use the analytic, creative, and practical intelligence components. This ability peaks in the middle adult years. Because most people in these years have a better understanding of themselves they can capitalize on their strength and compensate for their weaknesses (Dacey J.S & Travers J.F, 2006).

Finally, intelligent mental operations may be broken down into subcategories, most of which appear to peak at the beginning of middle age. These categories are case-based reasoning (including analogical, precedent-based, and legal reasoning); law-based reasoning (including logical, rule-based, principal and scientific reasoning; and dialectical reasoning (including dialectical reflection and argument reasoning). A key factor in the ability to continue to be productive well into the later years is memory (Dacey J.S & Travers J.F, 2006).

No aspect of adult functioning has received more research than intelligence. It was debated over whether intelligence declines with age, and if so how much and in what ways. Because of this considerable research, investigators have reached considerable agreement as to how cognition develops during adulthood. The leading theory is that of John L Horn who argued, that intelligence ***does*** decline in some ways, but in other ways it does not. He believes that some abilities increase throughout the life span, whereas others steadily decline from middle adulthood on.

Horn has distinguished between two aspects of intelligence, ***fluid and crystallized*** (Cattell, 1965; Horn,1982; Horn & Hofer,1992) The two can be distinguished as follows:

Fluid intelligence: *is the ability to solve novel problems that require little or no previous knowledge, such as discovery, the patterns in a sequence of figures*. Fluid intelligence consists of the abilities involved in acquiring new knowledge and skills, including memorizing, reasoning inductively and perceiving new relationships between objects and events. It involves *perceiving relations, forming concepts, and drawing inferences*. It is measured by tasks that show age-related declines (speed tasks, tests of reaction time) Also referred to as "cognitive mechanics", these abilities reflect neurological functioning more closely and are more likely to be affected when brain damage occurs. These abilities. which are largely determined by proper functioning of the nervous system, tend to decline with age (Papalia et al.,2007; Dacey J.S & Travers J.F. 2006).

Crystallized Intelligence: Crystallized intelligence refers to the accumulated knowledge and skills that come with education and life experiences. It is the ability to remember and use information acquired over a lifetime. Crystallized intelligence is also referred to as "cognitive pragmatics", reflecting the notion that is learned and therefore influenced by culture. It demonstrates the cumulative effect of cultures and learning of task performance and is measured by tests of verbal ability (vocabulary, general information), responses to social situations and dilemmas and cultural knowledge. These abilities, which depend largely on education and cultural experiences, remain stable or even improve with age. It is measured by tests of vocabulary, general information, and responses to social situations and dilemmas (Papalia et al., 2007).

Fluid and Crystallized Intelligence together constitute what Horn calls "Omnibus intelligence". Typically, fluid intelligence has been found to peak during young adulthood, whereas crystallized intelligence improves through middle age and often until near the end of life. (Papalia et al.,2007).

Horn (1982) argues that crystallized intelligence, an individual's accumulated information and verbal skills, continues to increase throughout the life span. However, he believes that fluid intelligence, the ability to reason abstractly, begins to decline in middle adulthood. This decline in fluid intelligence may average to 3-7 IQ points per decade for the three decades, spanning the period from 30 to 60 years of age (Santrock, 2007) (Dacey J.S & Travers J .F, 2006) .

Middle-aged adults may make up for losses in this basic neurological ability by gains in areas affected by learning and experience-higher-order abilities necessary for independent, productive living. Improvements in these crystallized abilities may be related to career development and the exercise of family responsibilities. Advances in verbal memory during middle age are especially notable, since memory loss is a major worry of many people at midlife. Given the strong performance of most middle-agers in this area, objective evidence of substantial memory deficits in persons younger than 60 may indicate a neurological problem.

K. Warner Schaic (1983; 2000) conducted an extensive study of intellectual abilities in the adulthood years. Following main mental abilities were tested among 500 adults in 1956.

- Vocabulary (ability to understand ideas expressed in words)
- Verbal memory (ability to encode and recall meaningful language units, such as a test of words)
- Number (ability to perform simple mathematical computations such as addition, subtraction and multiplication)
- Spatial orientation (ability to visualize and mentally rotate stimuli in two and three dimensional space)
- Inductive reasoning (ability to recognize and understand patterns and relationships in a problem and use this understanding to solve other instances of the problem) (Santrock, 2007)

The results indicated that the highest level of functioning for four of the six intellectual abilities occurred in the middle adulthood years. For both women and men, performance on vocabulary, verbal memory, inductive reasoning and spatial orientation peaked in middle age. Only two of the six abilities - numerical ability and perceptual speed- declined in middle age. Perceptual showed the earliest decline, with this beginning in early adulthood.

Seattle Longitudinal study highlighted that middle age was a time of peak performance for both some aspects of crystallized intelligence (vocabulary) and fluid intelligence (spatial orientation and inductive reasoning) (Santrock, 2007)

Wisdom: Wisdom can be defined as "expert knowledge about the practical aspects of life that permits excellent judgment about important matters (Baltes and his Colleagues, 1993;2006). This practical knowledge involves exceptional insights about human development and life matters, good judgment and understanding of how to cope with difficult life problems. Thus wisdom, more than standard conceptions of intelligence, focuses on life's pragmatic concerns and human conditions.

The Varied Courses of Cognitive Abilities: Cognition & Dialectical Thinking: Dialectical thinking is an organized approach to analyzing and making sense of the world one experiences that differs fundamentally from formal analysis. The latter involves the effort to find fundamental fixed realities-basic elements and immutable laws; the former attempts to describe the fundamental process of change and the dynamic relationship through which the change occurs (Basseches, 1980). An example of post-formal thought would be the understanding that a family quarrel might be nobody's "fault" and that the solution does not involve one of the parties "giving" in or changing their view of the situation. Instead, the dialectical approach consists of understanding the merits of different or opposing points of view and looks at the possibility of integrating them into a workable solution. This dialectical approach to problem solving is apparent when you think of situations where you have been on both sides of the same issue-for example being a child arguing with you parents, and then being a parent arguing with your child. One reason why post-formal operations are attributed to older individuals is that life experience is probably necessary to see the "bigger" picture. Schaie has proposed a four-stage model of cognitive development that is quite different from Piaget's in that it covers the entire life span and is not confined to pre-adulthood (Vander Zanden, Crandell & Crandell, 2007).

Schaie's (1994) four stages are as follows:

1. Acquisition stage: What should I know? (childhood-adolescence)
2. Achieving stage: How should I use what I know in career and love? (Young adult).
3. Responsible/executive stage: How should I use my knowledge in social and family responsibilities (middle adulthood)
4. Reintegrative stage: What should I know? (old age)

Even though the question in stage 1 and 4 are worded the same, in stage 4, the acquisition of information is guided by one's interest, attitudes, and values. An older adult is willing to expend effort on a problem she or he faces in everyday life.

This interest in problem solving might shed light on another aspect of cognition-creativity. J.P. Guilford (1967) distinguished two sorts of thinking-convergent and divergent.

Convergent thinking is very much like formal operations-the application of logic and reasoning to arrive at a single correct answer to a problem.

Divergent thinking is more open-ended, and multiple solutions are sought, examined, and probed thereby leading to what are deemed creative responses on measures of creativity. Creativity goes beyond problem solving and penetrates into problem generation. A creative person not only solves problems but also sees problems of which others are not yet even aware. Creativity seems to demand imagination, motivation, and a supportive environment-characteristics, that probably do not gel for the individual until middle adulthood. This might explain why it is during middle adulthood that the peak period of creative productivity occurs.

The Role of Expertise: Mature adults show increasing competence in solving problems in their chosen field because of specialized knowledge or expertise-a form of crystallized intelligence. Advances in expertise continue at least through middle adulthood and are relatively independent of general intelligence and of any declines in the brain's information- processing machinery. It was suggested that with experience, information processing and fluid abilities become "encapsulated" or dedicated to specific kinds of knowledge, making that knowledge easier to access, add to and use. In other words, "encapsulation" "captures" fluid abilities for expert problem solving. Thus, although middle-aged people may take somewhat longer than younger people to process new information, but in solving problems in their own fields they are able to do so with judgment developed from experience (Papalia et al.,2007).

Expert thinking often seems automatic and intuitive. Experts generally are not fully aware of the thought processing that lie behind their decisions. They cannot readily explain how they arrive at a conclusion or where a non-expert has gone wrong. Such intuitive, experience-based thinking is characteristic of what has been called post formal thought (Papalia et al.,2007).

Integrative thought: Although not limited to any particular period of adulthood, post-formal thought seems well-suited to the complex tasks, multiple roles and perplexing choices and challenges of midlife. An important feature of post-formal thought is its "integrative nature". Mature adults integrate logic with intuition and emotion; they integrate conflicting facts and ideas; and they integrate new information with what they already know. They interpret what they read, see, or hear in terms of its meaning for them. Instead of accepting something at face value, they filter it through their life experiences and previous learning. Society benefits from this integrative feature of advanced thought. Generally it is mature adults who like Gandhi, becomes moral and spiritual leaders and who translate their knowledge about the human condition into inspirational stories to which younger generations can turn for guidance. Post-formal thought also may help in solving practical problems (Papalia *et al.*, 2007).

Practical problem solving: It is often believed that the ability to solve practical problems is affected by age. Much research on practical problem solving has not found the declines sometimes seen in measures of fluid intelligence, and some research has found marked improvement at least through middle age (Papalia *et al.*, 2007).The best practical problem solvers were people in their forties and fifties, who based their answers on everyday experience.

Some studies focus on "instrumental" problems, or activities of daily living, such as reading a map. These abilities are highly related to fluid intelligence and show age-related decline. Declines may occur sooner in people with especially slow perceptual speed.

By contrast, studies that deals mainly with "social" problems. These studies suggest that people of different ages interpret problems differently and see different kinds of solutions as effective. When problems are relevant to older adults' lives and feelings, the participants show thought that is more complex. On this type of problem, both middle-aged and older adults tend to do better than younger ones; they have more extensive and varied repertoire of strategies to apply to different situations. One thing seems clear; middle-aged people tend to be effective practical problem solvers. If the functions of intelligence is to deal with real life problem, the strength of mature thought in midlife are plain (Papalia *et al.*, 2007).

Overall, the results of various research studies have led to three general conclusions about intellectual changes during adulthood.

I. In general. most intellectual abilities increase or remain stable throughout early and middle adulthood until the 60's at which time selective decrements in certain skills can be noted. However, there is little evidence for comprehensive declines in intelligence, even in very old adults.

II. Biological differences have a powerful influence on intellectual differences in adulthood but the effects vary with different intellectual abilities and the age of the sample.

III. Intellectual functioning is also affected by education background, current health status and mental well-being. Adults who experience major illness or depression for example, also show concurrent declines in intellectual performance, Conversely, intellectual functioning is enhanced by good health, involvement with others and intellectual stimulation in adulthood. In these respects, intelligence becomes more individualized and specialized with increasing age.

Memory in Middle Adulthood

A key factor in the ability to continue to be productive well into the later years is memory. Certainly, intelligence cannot be separated from memory. Human mind can process information like lightening, but if he/she cannot recall the proper information, processing abilities are useless. A number of studies have found deterioration in some types of memory function as people age. For example, prospective memory is the memory "required to carry out planned actions at the appropriate time, such as meeting a friend for lunch or taking a medication. Prospective memory, involves retrieval of an intention to act that has been stored in long-term memory". This type of memory may decline with age. Researchers have found that middle adults have more difficulty than younger adults with prospective memory, particularly when it involves monitoring of time.

On the other hand, some researchers have produced differential results. Whiting and Smith (1997) found that middle adults have more difficulty than younger adults do, in memory tasks requiring more cognitive effort, such as recall. More automatic processes, such as recognition, do not decline as much with age. In addition, middle adults have more difficulty than younger adults do in spatial learning. Advances in verbal memory during middle age are especially notable, since memory loss is a major worry or many people at midlife. Middle aged adults have more difficulty than younger adults do, in memory tasks requiring more cognitive effort, such as recall. More automatic processes, such as recognition, do not decline as much with age. In addition, middle adults have more difficulty than younger adults do in spatial learning. In a study of how adults learn a route from one location to another, middle adults had greater difficulty in remembering the route than younger adults but were as good at recognition of landmarks along the route.

Practical Intelligence: Many developmentalists who study adult intelligence, believe that traditional intelligence tests asses little-used knowledge and skills. Decline in these abilities with age reflects their disappearance due to lack of use, as most adults do not use their entire time in these intellectual tasks. On the contrary, most adults try to solve the real world challenges of managing a home, advancing a career, balancing family finances, analyzing information from the newspaper or television and understanding the needs of family members, neighbors and colleagues. Some of the other measures of practical intelligence concerns career decisions, consumer behavior, conflict resolution, finding one's way in complex physical spaces, and managing an office. Problems in areas like these not only concern real life situations but also involve the kinds of intellectual abilities and knowledge that adults consider to be increasingly important as one matures. Hence, assessment of adult intelligence should encompass the skilled knowledge that is relevant to practical functioning. Current interest in practical intelligence underscores that adult intelligence is truly multidimensional and multidirectional in nature and that inter-individual variability is related to differences in life experiences of individuals. In reaction to the shortcoming of traditional approaches to testing adults' intelligence, different views of intelligence have emerged (Cavanaugh, 1991; Dixon,)

- First, adults are often more intrinsically motivated to master them because these challenges entail every day, real world reasoning, than they are with abstract intelligence measures.
- Secondly, practical intelligence draws more heavily upon an adult's personal experiences and back ground. They are more likely than traditions intelligence tests to involve skills that are strengthened and improved through regular use.
- Third, unlike conventional intelligence measures, which allow for a single correct answers, solutions to these practical problems can be evaluated in a number of different ways.

Practical intelligence increases throughout most adult years, with some decline in late adulthood. Because real-world intelligence depends partly on experience, it is not surprising that middle-aged adults perform better on these measures than do young adults. However, there are limits to the benefits of additional experience, and by the late adult years, the skills of practical intelligence may become more narrowed to those capacities that are especially pertinent to one's personal life.

In closing, it should be noted that measures of practical intelligence are not unrelated to traditional adult intelligence measures. Practiced intelligence draws upon the skills of both fluid and crystallized intelligence (depending on which kind of measures is used) because real-worked dilemmas require not only flexible problem solving but cultural knowledge and experience. In other words, knowing what to do when the refrigerator does not work requires a capacity for insightful inferences and some knowledge of how refrigerator operates. Moreover, it be due to their reliance on fluid intelligence that some form of practical intelligence show later life declines, while other kinds of practical measures of fluid intelligence that rely more on crystallized intelligence to grow.

Current interest in practical intelligence underscores that adult intelligence is truly multidimensional and multidirectional in nature and that inter individual variability is related to differences in life experiences of individuals.

The Development of Creativity: The role of creativity has become an even more important aspect of cognitive functioning. "Creativity" shows no apparent decline during middle adulthood Studies of the total productivity of creative people suggest that the peak of creative performance may be reached in middle age, or in some cases, in later adulthood. For scientists, the period from forty through about sixty years of age was marked by a fairly constant stream of production, with a relative decline from sixty through seventy. Creativity in the humanities appeared to be sustained from about thirty through seventy years of age. Even when "peaks" are reached in middle age, people can continue some creative activities well into later adulthood

12.9. COGNITIVE DEVELOPMENT DURING MIDDLE ADULTHOOD

Although perceptual speed declines steadily beginning at age 25 and numerical ability begins to decline around 40, peak performance in 4 of the 6 abilities, inductive reasoning, spatial orientation, vocabulary and verbal memory-occurs about halfway through middle adulthood. During middle adulthood, the straightforward cognitive growth of earlier years begins to wane and intellectual development becomes more multidirectional, multifaceted and individualized. Rather than mastering skills that are suited to a wide variety of situations, the adult acquires knowledge that is more specialized and expertise that reflect professional, personal and relational needs.

Decline in cognitive ability due to aging can often be offset through motivation and new learning experiences. Various social experiences, such as practicing a religion, going to a library, watching television, and serving as a volunteer, involves new learning.

Intelligence: Successful intelligence consists of analytical components (solving problems) creative components (deciding what problems to solve), and practical components (devising effective solutions). It is found that intelligence is not so much a matter of quantity but rather, a matter of balance, of knowing when and how to use the analytic, creative, and practical intelligence components. This ability peaks in the middle adult years. Because most people in these years have a better understanding of themselves they can capitalize on their strength and compensate for their weaknesses.

Practical Problem Solving Abilities: The best practical problem solvers were people in their forties and fifties, who based their answers on everyday experience. These abilities are highly related to fluid intelligence and show age-related decline. Declines may occur sooner in people with especially slow perceptual speed. When problems are relevant to older adults' lives and feelings, the participants show thought that is more complex.

Practical Intelligence: Decline in these abilities with age reflects their disappearance due to lack of use, as most adults do not use their entire time in these intellectual tasks. Some of the other measures of practical intelligence concerns career decisions, consumer behavior, conflict, resolution, finding one's way in complex physical spaces, and managing an office. Problems in areas like these not only concern real life situations but also involve the kinds of intellectual abilities and knowledge that most adults consider to be increasingly important as one matures. Hence, assessment of adult intelligence should encompass the skilled knowledge that are relevant to practical functioning.

Current interest in practical intelligence underscores that adult intelligence is truly multidimensional and multidirectional in nature and that inter-individual variability is related to differences in life experiences of individuals.

Integrative Thought: Although not limited to any particular period of adulthood, post formal thought seems well-suited to the complex tasks, multiples roles and perplexing choices and challenges of midlife. An important feature of post formal thought is its "integrative nature". Mature adults integrate logic with intuition and emotion; conflicting facts and ideas; and new information with what they already know. They interpret what they read, see, or hear in terms of its meaning for them. Instead of accepting something at face value, they filter it through their life experiences and previous learning.

Memory in Middle Adulthood: A key factor in the ability to continue to be productive well into the later years is memory. Certainly, intelligence cannot be separated from memory. Advances in verbal memory during middle age are especially notable, since memory loss is a major worry of many people at midlife. Middle aged adults have more difficulty than younger adults do, in memory tasks requiring more cognitive effort, such as recall. More automatic processes, such as recognition, do not decline as much with age. In addition, middle adults have more difficulty than younger adults do in spatial learning.

Development of Creativity: An older adult's interest in problem solving might shed light on another aspect of cognition-creativity . The role of creativity has become an important aspect of cognitive functioning. "Creativity" shows no apparent decline during middle adulthood. Creativity in the humanities appeared to be sustained from about thirty through seventy years of age. It is during middle adulthood that the peak period of creative productivity occurs. Even when "peaks" are reached in middle age, people can continue some creative activities well into later adulthood.

12.10. VOCATIONAL DEVELOPMENT

Career and Work in Middle Adulthood:

Most people reach the peak of their expertise, power, and prestige in middle age. Exactly what constitutes the top for anyone varies according to his different aspirations. Many skilled teachers, doctors, and therapists who do not exactly get promoted, but also enjoy their jobs so much that they feel they are already at the top, and resist efforts to move themselves into administrative positions. Similarly, creative people such as musicians, artists, and writers may gain in prestige and respect as their skills increase, but, unlike that of a sales person who gets promoted to marketing manager, their job continues to be essentially the same through the years. For people who realize in midlife that their career dreams are not going to come true may precipitate a midlife crisis. However, crises also may occur for those people who reach the top, only to find that success does not guarantee happiness.

Midlife Career Changes: Career decisions are often open-ended in a society undergoing dramatic changes. People with "stable" career patterns stay with a single vocation and, by midlife, often reach positions of power and responsibility. Middle-aged men with stable careers tend to be either "workaholics" or "mellowed". It is not uncommon for career changes to occur at midlife. Some midlife career changes are consequence of losing one's job; others are self-motivated. For many people, midlife is a time of evaluation, assessment and reflection in the terms of the work they do and want to do in the future. Any work issue that some people face in midlife are recognizing limitations in career progress, deciding whether to change jobs or careers, whether to rebalance family and work, and planning for retirement.

Factors Influencing Career Change at Midlife:

Environmental Factors:

- Family events such as divorce, death of a spouse, change from full- to part-time employment, departure of the last child from home.
- Job Situation changes such as mandatory retirement, job loss owing to technology advancements, demands from employers to upgrade training.
- Social trends, such as new jobs coming from advancement in technology, high inflation rates lowering value of money, women's liberation movement encouraging alternatives for women.

Internal Factors:

- Midlife crisis initiates questioning of job satisfaction.
- Desire to pursue neglected interests.
- Desire for more personally rewarding or challenging work.
- Desire to upgrade social status and income.

Job satisfaction in midlife: Older workers report that intrinsic factors, such as getting a feeling of accomplishment, exercising skills, making decisions, and turning out a quality product, are more important than are extrinsic factors, such as pay and work environment. Interestingly, older workers may become dissatisfied with supervisors, pay, and promotions, but enjoy the work itself so much that they still have high levels of overall job satisfaction. About five years before the compulsory retirement age (whether it is 60, 62, 65or 70), or by the end of the fifties and early sixties, there is usually a sharp drop in vocational satisfaction among men.

Job satisfaction may also wane as middle age progresses because men begin to feel the pressure of work due to their general slowing down and increased tendency toward fatigue, both of which are natural accompaniments of aging. In addition they resent the attitudes of some younger workers who not only can do the work more easily than they but who often seem to be counting the days until the older men retire and they can take their places. None of these factors contributed to job satisfaction.

Middle-aged women, even more than men, fail to derive the satisfaction they should from their work. And like men, their dissatisfaction increases with each passing year until they welcome the compulsory retirement age.

Vocational Adjustment:

Middle-aged adults may reach their peak in position and earnings, but also be saddled with financial burdens from rent or mortgage, child care, medical bills, home repairs, college tuitions or bills from nursing homes for care of an elderly parent. Middle-aged adults' adjustments to their social expectations, vocation and family are comparatively more difficult than young adults. Establishing and maintaining an economic standard of living grow increasingly difficult with the rapid changes in the economy that have been taking place in recent years and with increased use of automation, that often throws middle-aged persons out of work. They find that the jobs for which their training and experience have fitted them no longer exist.

The various conditions that influence the vocational adjustment of middle aged men and women are as follows:

1. **Satisfaction with Work:** Middle-aged men and women who like their work will make far better vocational adjustments than those who have stayed on jobs they disliked because of earlier family responsibilities and who now feel "trapped".
2. **Opportunities for Promotion:** For workers who approach the age of compulsory retirement, their chances for promotion grow slighter and they are likely to be pushed aside to make way for younger workers. This has an adverse effect on vocational adjustments.
3. **Vocational Expectations:** With compulsory retirement now coming in the mid to late sixties, the chances of promotion after fifty are slim, and the chances of getting a new job are even slimmer, except at a lower level and with lower pay. As retirement becomes imminent, middle-aged workers assess their achievements in light of earlier aspirations. This assessment, whether favorable or unfavorable, has a profound effect on vocational adjustments.
4. **Increased Use of Automation:** Certain aspects of automation may negatively affect vocational adjustment, such as boredom and lack of pride in their work, the possibility of losing their jobs to young workers, increased speed required on the job, which makes many older workers nervous, and unwillingness to retain because of the proximity of retirement.
5. **Role of the Wife:** If a wife is dissatisfied with her husband's status at work, his pay, or the fact that his work takes him away from home and she is lonely now that the children are grown, the husband too may become dissatisfied. Women whose husbands object to their working and constantly complain about their being out of the home may also experience job dissatisfaction.
6. **Dominance of Big Business:** Middle-aged workers whose companies merge with others may find that there is no place for them in the new organizations or that their jobs are on lower levels than before. This is especially true of jobs in the managerial levels.
7. **Attitude toward "Big Business":** Workers who take pride in being associated with big, prestigious companies will make better adjustments to their work than those who regard themselves merely as little device in big machines.
8. **Attitude toward Co-workers:** Middle-aged workers who resent the treatment they receive from their superiors or their subordinates and who regard younger workers as shiftless and careless will have less favorable attitudes toward their work than those who are on friendlier terms with their co workers.
9. **Relocation:** With the consolidation of small businesses into big corporations, many workers are forced to relocate as factories and offices are moved near the parent company. Middle-aged workers who must move in order to keep their jobs or be

promoted to better ones often have more difficulty in adjusting to the new location than younger workers have.

12.11. PSYCHOSOCIAL DEVELOPMENT IN MIDDLE ADULTHOOD

Four important aspects of middle aged life today are: ***relationships in marriage, relationships with aging parents, relationships with siblings, friendship and divorce.***

Marriage at Middle Age

Middle age is often a time when husbands and wives reappraise their marriage. The ***midlife transition*** (a period during which people seriously re-evaluate their lives up to that time) often causes a person to simultaneously examine current relationships and consider change for the future. Often, whatever tension exists in a marriage is suppressed while the children still live at home. As they leave to go off to college or to start families of their own, these tensions are openly expressed. When the children leave, they are forced to recognize how far apart they have drifted. In effect, they engaged in "***emotional divorce.***"

After the initial period of negative emotions that follows this disruption of the family often called the ***empty nest syndrome***, married couples can evaluate the job they have done with their children. They realize that they have more freedom and privacy and fewer worries. This period after the children leave home is now much longer than it used to be. Husbands and wives now can look forward to spending 20 or 30 years together as a couple rather than as a large family.

The Happy Marriage: The most common reasons for happy marriage were friendship, love and similar interests and backgrounds. There are many factors to consider, including the role of culture and gender on marriage and conflicts within a marriage. Another factor related to marital satisfaction is how well married couples can balance the different roles that they have within the family. Husbands and wives may need to balance the demands of their relationships with each other, their roles as a parent and their work and leisure time. In addition, marital satisfaction can be affected when the wife earns more than the husbands do. It is found that high marital satisfaction in couples was associated with significantly higher rates of parenting satisfaction and also religion.

The Unmarried Individual: In general, a person who has never married by middle age will not get married. Such people tend to have either very low or very high education level. A number of possible explanations could account for this. These women may choose higher education and a career over marriage. They may believe marriage will hold them back.

Relationship with Aging Parents

Middle age is also a time when most people develop improved relationships with parents. Most of the parents themselves, gain a new perspective on parenthood and so re-evaluate the actions taken by their own parents. Also grand children can strengthen bonds that may have weakened when their parents left home when they were young adults. As elderly parents grow older, they sometimes become dependent on their middle aged children. Most people fail to anticipate the costs and emotional strains that the aging of their parents can precipitate.

Relationships with Siblings

The importance of sibling relationships for a child's cognitive and social growth is recognized now. Sibling relationships have the potential to be the most enduring that a person can have because most siblings are born within a few years of each other, and such a relationship can last 60, 80 or even 100 years. One would hope that a growing maturity would lessen rivalry. Certainly adult siblings are faced with more serious and important tasks than are childhood siblings. For example, most middle aged siblings must make mutual decisions concerning the care of their elderly parents and eventually deal with the aftermath of their death. Couples now are having fewer or even no children. Children will therefore, be less available to parents for companionship and psychological support. On the other hand, parents and their siblings will be living longer with more active lives.

The Middle Aged Divorced Person

Midlife is a time when divorce is less likely to occur- most divorces take place during the first five years of marriage and the number tapers off rapidly after that; nevertheless, the proportion of divorced persons in midlife is relatively high, because many who divorced earlier have never remarried. Men and women over 40 years, experience significantly more turmoil and unhappiness than younger people do at the same stage of divorce. The reasons are clear: length of time of marriage, complex economic and property linkages, a web of social relationships, and a generally higher standard of living.

Divorced women experience significant declines in income, increased rates of poverty, and dramatic life style changes upon divorce; generally, they cannot improve their economic situation unless they remarry. Furthermore, because most women who divorce at midlife are already working, they have little room to manoeuvre for more income after divorce.

Friendships

Middle age is a time when friendships become fewer and more precious. Actually it is found that individuals begin to narrow their range of social partners long before middle age. The most dramatic decline occurs between the ages of 18 to 30. Emotional closeness, however, increases throughout adulthood in relationships with relatives and close friends. These relationships with a select few then become increasingly close and satisfying during the middle adult years.

Adulthood means different things to different people. While early adulthood is a stage of development, middle adulthood is a period of making sense of continually changing demands of parenting, workplace etc. Early adulthood focuses on settling down, rearing kids, and commitments. Men and women enjoy a peak of health, strength, energy, and vitality. But, middle adulthood focuses on transition, mid life crisis and readjustment. Men and women begin showing the signs of onset of aging, both physically and mentally, during this period.

QUESTIONS

SECTION "A"

Short Answer Type:

1. Spell out the developmental tasks of early adulthood?
2. What are the subdivisions of adulthood?
3. Specify the characteristics of middle aged adults.
4. Distinguish between fluid intelligence and crystalline intelligence.
5. What is mid-life crisis?
6. Give a key note on memory of adults.

SECTION "B"

One Page Answer Type:

1. Discuss the developmental tasks of young adults.
2. Middle age is the age of empty nest- Discuss.
3. Briefly explain the characteristics of young adults.
4. Describe the developmental tasks during middle adulthood
5. Describe the vocational adjustment in middle age.
6. Explain the various characteristics of middle age.
7. Discuss about the adjustments to changed life patterns.
8. Write about the problem solving abilities of young adults.
9. Give an account of the psycho-social development of young adulthood.
10. Write a note on mid-life changes in females.

SECTION "C"

Essay Answer Type:

1. Explain the factors contributing to marital adjustment.
2. Explain the conditions influencing vocational adjustments in middle age.
3. Discuss in detail about the physical and physiological changes in early adulthood.
4. Briefly describe the vocational development and adjustments of adulthood stage.
5. Examine the cognitive changes taking place in adults.

UNIT — VIII

CHAPTER

13

OLD AGE (60 YEARS & ABOVE)

OBJECTIVES

To enlighten students about:

- Concept of the period of adulthood - Meaning, stages/subdivisions
- Developmental tasks
- Characteristics and needs
- Changes in Old Age- physical, physiological and cognitive
- Family and Personal Relationships in Late Adulthood
- Problems of the Aged , Adjustments in Old Age
- Status of the Aged in Our Recent Society; Welfare Services for the Aged.

13.1 INTRODUCTION

All people, animals, plants as well as non-living matter are never static, instead, they constantly change, become older and undergo changes with the passage of time. Ageing is a natural and universal process, and should be regarded as a normal phenomenon. It should not be confused with disease or disintegrative force. It is a continuous process of progressive **change** in all the structures and functions of the body and all aspects of the organism. Such changes as decline in body efficiency, a maladaptive change in structure and a stoppage of reversal of growth may be observed in this age. Old age is the closing period in the life span. It is a "period of moving away from some previous and more desirable period" 'the prime of life' or 'the years of usefulness'.

The older years are the last stage of life, which includes many more years than any previous life stages. Even though all stages of life encompass a process of growing older, or "aging", this is the only time when people are labeled thus. It affects the individuals and social groups in different ways, depending on whether they have a strong constitution, or whether, conversely, they are weak and have already lost much of the strength they ever had. Another decisive factor is the type of working conditions encountered during a person's career, which vary from one job to another.

Just as adolescence is a process not only of growth but also of widespread change, so is aging, from its start, is far from mere process of decline. Moreover aging does not destroy the continuity of what we have been, what we are and what we will be. Extending from the age of sixty-five until death, old age or late adulthood is a dynamic period of life that has its own challenges. It is the time when individuals must come to terms with declining capacities, and eventual death, although the age at which this occurs varies widely.

What is aging?

Neither biology nor medicine can give an answer to this question. We can describe the signs of aging which begin to appear in human as soon as full maturity has been achieved. The year of late **adulthood** marks the period of life in which people are known as **elderly**. The period is characterized in many ways with the decline that occur in almost all aspects of development .Like the process of maturing, aging does not take place at the same rate in every individual or in the same sequence or with the same intensity. The onset is gradual under normal conditions, more drastic and more rigid under stress.

Concepts Explained

In 1914, the term "geriatric" has come from the Greek word ***geron*** which means "to age, to become, to awaken" and the fields of **geriatrics** and **gerontology** were born.

Gerontology: The word gerontology is derived from the Greek 'geron' meaning "old man" and 'ology', meaning "the study of". It refers to the biological science that studies the aging process of life from physiological, pathological, psychological, sociological and economic points of view. It concerns the social, economic and human aspects of the lives of the aged. As a science, gerontology is concerned with all facets of aging, with all forms of life, not human alone, and even with inanimate objects.

Geriatrics: Geriatrics is the branch of medical science that deals with the physiology and diseases of the elderly. It deals with the health, treatment and research of illnesses usually occurring in old age and with the aging process.

The term **"senescence"** refers to the process of growing old with accompanying decrease in functional abilities. "Senescence" is the gradual weakening of our bodies that usually begins sometime during early adulthood and continues until we die. This does not imply marked deterioration of organic systems, cognitive power or of acquired skills, since many adult qualities and traits are often preserved; but, there is usually lessened activity and poorer self application. It is sometimes confused with senility.

Senility, on the other hand, although closely allied with senescence implies a substantial loss of organic and functional integration. It refers to some degenerative condition of the brain with problems of confusion and disorientation. It does not occur in all old persons as senescence does. An accelerated rate of deterioration is a more definite criterion of **Senility**. The retention of earlier adult powers and characteristics is low. A regression to satisfaction of merely biological and emotional needs is frequent. Senility is fairly common in old age.

13.2 LAUNCHING OF OLD AGE

The time at which old age begins is ill defined. It varies according to period, place and social rank. Sixty years is taken as the arbitrary dividing line between middle and old age. However, it is recognized that chronological age is a poor criterion to use in marking off the beginning of old age because there are such marked differences between individuals in the age at which aging actually begins. Most men and women today, because of better living conditions and better health care, do not show the mental and physical characteristics of aging until the mid-sixties or even early seventies.

Whether old age will be a short or long period will be determined by how long the individual lives. While old age is just a state of mind to many people, there are several cultural events tied to chronology that are landmarks of the beginning of late adulthood. Age sixty-five is usually considered a milestone and as the beginning of late adulthood. Events that coincide with attaining sixty-five and the beginning of old age include retirement from major work roles, Beginning of Social Security Benefits and Medicare Coverage, Income-tax Advantages, Reductions in Transit Fares and admission prices and special-purchase privileges.

Though ageing is a multidimensional process and it is not easy to determine when it starts, yet for the purpose of understanding, it can be discussed at four levels — ***biological, psychological, sociological or situational and socio-psychological or behavioral.***

Biological aging refers to anatomical and physiological changes that occur with age. For example, the capability to reproduce offspring is a phenomenon associated with biological aging. Changes in sensory-motor performance, muscle strength, brittleness of the skeletal structure, visual acuity reaction time, and balance are other examples of biological aging which may influence attitudes and behavior.

Psychological aging consists of a general decline in the mental abilities that accompany old age.

Sociological aging refers to changes in social roles- loss of spouse, vulnerability to disease, compulsory or voluntary retirement, loss of income, loss of status, loss of authority and birth of a grandchild.

Psycho-Social aging refers to systematic changes in personality needs, expectations and behavior as well as changes in roles and changes in relation to others. Disengagement from active social and economic life may result in feeling of meaninglessness and loneliness.

Increasingly chronological age does not mean much. Gerontologists are more likely to consider a person's "functional age". The concept of functional age combines the physical, psychological and social factors that influence people's roles or attitudes.

13.3 AGE DIVISIONS OF LATE ADULTHOOD

The Young Old: (60 to 69 Years): This is a transition period marked by many adjustments such as retirement and declining strength, sharp reduction in expectations of behaviors.

Middle-Aged Old: (70 To 79 Years): Increasing deaths of friends and spouses, reduced participation in home and community activities; increasing health problems, contracting social world.

Old-Old: (80 to 89 Years): Assistance needed in maintenance of social contacts, occurrence of many health problems and may become institutionalized or may lead a very sheltered life.

Very Old-Old: (90 to 99 Years): Health problems are more severe and serious, very limited activity .

Much of the recent interest in maturity and old age grows out of the increasing "proportion" of older persons in our society which results from the longer life span as well as from the lower birth rate. Longer life spans result from economic growth, better nutrition, healthier life styles, improved control of infectious disease, safer water and sanitation facilities and advances in science technology and medicine.

Health and longevity are closely linked to education and other aspects of socio-economic status. Certain predictors of health and length of life were beyond the individuals' control: the parent's social class, cohesion of the childhood family, ancestral longevity and childhood temperament. Other predictors, besides higher education, were at least partly controllable: alcohol abuse, smoking, body mass index, exercise, marital stability , and coping techniques.

The economic impact of a graying population depends on the proportion of that population which is healthy and able-bodied. In this regard, the trend is encouraging. Many problems that used to be considered as unavoidable part of old age are now understood to be due, not to aging itself, but to life style factors or diseases. Some physical decline with age is inevitable. However, personal life style seems to play a crucial role in the extent and pace of such changes.

The "aging" process whereby the proportion of children in the population decrease and those of older persons increase is known as "aging" of the population. Proportion of older adults in the population of industrialized countries has increased tremendously in this century, due mainly to better health care and to lowering women's mortality rate during childbirth. As we move in to the 22nd century, older adults will be a major marketing target and they will yield considerable political and economic power. The sheer number of older adults will place enormous pressure on pension systems (especially social security), health care (including long-term care) and other human services.

12.4. DEVELOPMENTAL TASKS OF LATE ADULTHOOD

Similar to other periods of life span, old age has special adaptations that need to be made, and special tasks to be achieved if the individual wishes to live efficiently, happily and confidently on that age level. The only difference is that the developmental tasks of old age are the final or ultimate ones in life and resolve about the conditions of life in that time period. Bigner (1983) points out that the developmental tasks of the aged differ from those of earlier stages in two fundamental ways:

1. There is a focus on maintenance of life rather than discovering more about it and,
2. The tasks center on happening in the person's own life rather than on the lives of others.

Developmental tasks of the late adulthood are as follows:

- Adjusting to Decreasing Physical Health and Strength
- Adjusting to Retirement and Reduced Income
- Adjusting to Death of a Spouse
- Establishing an Explicit Affiliation with One's Age Group
- Meeting Social and Civic Obligations
- Validate Value, Meaning and Responsibilities of Life Lived
- Preparing for Own Death
- Maintaining Maximal Independence in Activities of Daily Living

13.5. CHARACTERISTICS OF LATE ADULTHOOD:

1. **Aging is a Phase of Life and Biological Process:** Every organism that is born must age with time and decay.
2. **Old Age is a Period of Change:** Aging, from its start, is far from mere process of decline. It is a continuous process of progressive change, which in turn alters the aging person's conduct, emotions, self-control, personality and relations with others. While in the early part of the lifespan, the changes are evolutional that lead to maturity of structure and functioning, the changes in old age are mainly involutional, showing a regression to earlier stages. Its consequences range from altered structures and functions of the component tissues of the body to an altered relationship of the organism to its physical and social environment.
3. **Old Age is a Period of Decline:** Olga Knoff (1975) defines aging "as the decline in functional capacity, lessened resilience and increased vulnerability to disease." Every one of these manifestations is progressive and irreversible. With increasing age comes a decline, a regression or return to an earlier pattern of behavior and a simpler level of functioning. Decline comes partly from physical and partly from psychological factors. The physical cause of decline is a change in the body cells due not to a specific disease but to the aging process. Psychological causes consist of unfavorable attitudes toward oneself, other people, work and life in general which can lead to senility.
4. **Individual Differences Occur in the Effects of Aging:** Individual differences due to aging have been recognized for many centuries. Like the process of maturing, aging, does not take place at the same rate in every individual or in the same sequence or

with the same intensity. Ageing affects different people differently, due to variations in gender, heredity endowments, socio-economic and educational backgrounds and patterns of living.

5. **Old Age is Judged by Different Criteria:** Young children tend to judge age in terms of physical appearance and activities. To them, old people have white hair and no longer go to work every day. By the time, children become adolescents, they judge old age in much the same way as adults do, in terms of the person's appearance and what the person can and cannot do.
6. **Social Attitudes towards Old Age:** People who hail from countries where respect for the elderly is customary, treat them usually with more consideration and respect. Members of the upper classes, on knowing that the elderly hold the purse strings to family fortunes, tend to treat elderly members of their social group with more respect than do those of the middle and lower class , and sometimes those who are financially responsible for their own elderly family members, may resent them also.
7. **Poor Adjustment is Characteristic of Old Age:** Elderly people tend to be more subjective to maladjustments than those who are younger; it may be that they are disproportionately subject to emotional and mental problems. The incidence of psychopathology rises with age. Functional disorders-notably depressions, paranoid states- increase steadily with each decade as do organic brain disease after 60 years.
8. **Aging Requires Role Changes:** Just as middle aged, old people must learn to play new roles. Because of unfavorable social attitudes, few rewards are associated with old age roles, no matter how successfully they are carried out. Feeling useless and unwanted, elderly people develop feelings of inferiority and resentment- feelings that are not conducive to good personal or social adjustments.
9. **The Desire for Rejuvenation is Widespread in Old Age:** The minority group status accorded to most elderly persons has naturally given rise to a desire to remain young as long as possible and to be rejuvenated when the signs of aging appear. Today, many people are still looking for ways to slow down by resorting to food fads or the extravagant use of age-defying cosmetics and have undergone face-lifts to remove the telltale signs of aging.

13.6 NEEDS OF THE AGED

At every period of life, man has specific psychic needs that must be satisfied in one way or another if he is to preserve his psychic balance. The specific needs of the aging may be classified as:

1. **Physical Need:** Being old and infirm, the aged are unable to exert themselves very much and to climb stairs. They require support wherever the floor level is not uniform. Proper light and ventilation are required in the rooms. The arrangement of furniture and fixtures should permit free movement in the house. In using a kitchen, bathroom and toilet, the old often need special arrangements.
2. **Economic Need:** With age, the activity of man shrinks and comes to a near halt at a certain stage. In general, this has a direct relation to earnings. Need for security is most important. The primary consideration here is, of course, his anxiety concerning his material welfare. The older a man becomes, the more he is forced to realize that as his productive powers decline, so his income will decline.
3. **Socio-Psychological Need:** An old person's need for security is not restricted to financial and economic considerations alone. He wants continuity in his personal relationships and in his physical environment. When people come to the end of their days and a

feeling of helplessness descends upon them, they also need to be supported, with love and kindness. Men depend on women to a very considerable extent.

Aged people often suffer from a feeling of loneliness and consequently they badly need companionship and greater involvement in community life. Their housing should be so located and designed that they can make good use of their spare time and develop a sense of involvement with the community. They should be able to lead a secure life and interact with others.

4. **Recreational Need:** A considerable amount of leisure time is available in old age. In the designing of neighborhoods, the recreational needs of the aging should be kept in view while allocating space for parks, community centers and recreation centers.

13.7 PHYSICAL CHANGES IN OLD AGE

Aging is a dynamic process. Human body consists of billions of cells for which, life and death are continuous events. However, the body is a self- renewing machine only up to a point. The body continues to grow as long as new cells are produced, faster than the death of old ones. On the contrary, if more cells die than the production of new cells, the ravages of old age set in. In addition, death can occur when any one system fails even though all other systems are still intact.

Aging during the later years of the life cycle is characterized by the general, gradual decline or deterioration in functioning. This is especially noticeable in physical functioning as organs experience the degenerative process of aging. Furthermore, within the same person there are also variations in the rate of aging of different parts of the body. For example, the reproductive organs age sooner than the other organs. Different part of the body resist aging more than others, and the various abilities fade at different rates.

This process of aging generally begins soon after the individual has reached the age of 30. Generally, aging contributes to make the body organs work less efficiently. For the most part, the decline in functional capacity of organ system is very dramatic. For example, almost every test of physical strength and quickness are high among people who are in their twenties. These measures of physical capacity indicate a slow decline after that time. For many, with increasing age (late forties) a number of physiological changes become apparent.

Organ Reserve and Homeostasis

In our daily lives, our hearts, lungs, kidneys and other organs are rarely required to function at their maximum capacity. Under stress, however, each organ in a healthy young adult today can put forth four to ten times its usual effort. This extra capacity that we can call on when we need it, is known as **organ reserve. Organ reserve** enables our bodies to maintain **homeostasis,** or a relatively stable internal environment. With age, as organ reserve gradually diminishes, it becomes harder to maintain **homeostasis**; if a person is unable to do so, disease and death follows. It is probably the depletion of organ reserve and the consequent inability to maintain homeostasis that causes older people to die from relatively minor illnesses such as pneumonia or flu, which are rarely life threatening in young people.

There is some evidence that homeostasis is less efficient in older people. Wounds heal more slowly. It takes longer for the breathing and heart rate to return to normal. Heat losses are less quickly restored. Sleep habits may undergo a change. The thyroid gland is smaller, resulting in a lower rate of basal metabolism. The pancreas loses some of its ability to produce the enzymes that are used in sugar and protein metabolism. Most glands function at close to normal rates all through life.

Physical Appearance

Aging also revamps the physical appearance. One of the most obvious of these changes occurs in the skin, which becomes dryer, thinner, and less elastic, producing marked wrinkling and making blood vessels and pockets of fat much more visible. In addition, dark patches of skin known as "age spots" are visible. Often hairlines may recede, hair may continue to become thinner and grayer, and in many people, eventually become white. In women, one of the most dramatic physical changes is **menopause,** the cessation of menstruation. This usually occurs between the ages of 45 and 55; it signals the **climacteric**-the end of ovulation and the termination of reproductive capacity. There is no parallel event for men; men can produce viable sperm at all ages, but their reproductive capacity does decline gradually over their adult years.

Weight Changes

Body weight is often lower in late adulthood, partly because muscle tissue becomes reduced. For both genders, the reduction in muscle strength is especially apparent in the legs, necessitating slower walking and sometimes use of a cane or walker. Another reason for lower body weight is **osteoporosis,** loss of bone calcium that causes bones to become more porous and fragile. Bone loss usually occurs at a rate of 1 to 2 percent a year after menopause in women. The progression of weight loss continues for men but begins for women during late adulthood. The average weight of an elderly woman is 146 pounds as compared to an average weight of 164 pounds for an elderly man. These continued losses in weight, can be attributed to continuing decline in physical activity, less food being consumed, poorer health, and other related factors, resulting in a reduction of muscle and tissue mass as people grow older through these years. Lean body mass decreases slightly because of a gradual decrease of bone, muscle, cartilage and connective tissue mass. Because of the loss of lean body mass, there is a relative increase in the body's fat content.

Height Changes

Reduction in **height** also continues in late adulthood for men and women. The average height of elderly men is 67.3inches, while that of elderly women is 62.3 inches. Most older people are more than an inch shorter than they were in early adulthood, because their vertebrae (the small bones that make up the spine) have settled closer together resulting in compression of the spinal column. Further, the muscles that hold the vertebrae have become less flexible, making it harder to stand as straight as in earlier years. Older people characteristically have a stooped posture with the head held forward and down from the body.

Shape Changes

Body shape is affected by redistribution of fat, which collects less in arms and upper face and more in the torso (especially the abdomen) and the lower face (especially the jowls and chin). Although many old persons have problems with obesity, appetites usually are less keen. Stamina and strength are greatly diminished regardless of calorie intake. The basal metabolic rate (BMR), a measure of the body's update of oxygen for metabolism decreases .

Changes in Balance

Changes in **balance** make older people increasingly likely to fall. They seem to fall often, appear to be clumsy as though their bodies are not quite coordinated. These are at least in part linked to changes in *Somatic* (*or kinesthetic*) *sensitivity*. Over time, the integration of somatic sensation mediated by vestibular cues for maintaining balance seem to deteriorate. For various reasons (some of which can be traced to sensory impairments and some to a breakdown of the brain's integrative capacities), the dizziness or vertigo reported by many elderly is attributed to dysfunction in these two areas. A loss of vestibular function in the inner ears may give old people difficulty with balance.

They may sway slightly when standing or experience dizziness when rising, when viewing heights, or when trying to climb hills. They may lose their balance and fall quite frequently.

Causes for Physical Changes

Explanation of why senescence occurs, differ among biologists who study this phenomenon. Some feel that **hormones** become less effective in promoting regeneration of their target cells. Others feel that every individual may have a genetically preprogrammed "clock of aging" within his or her cells that dictates how and when the cells progressively slow down their metabolic activities. Research suggests that aging occurs partially because the pituitary gland controlled by the hypothalamus of the brain stimulates the production of smaller quantities of thyroid hormones by the thyroid gland.

Physical changes that accompany aging appear at different times and in different ways in all individuals. Persons who have escaped chronic or debilitating diseases into their later years and who exercise regularly and watch their diets carefully stand a much better chance of retaining a vigorous appearance than persons who have experienced debilitating illness, chronic disease, obesity or muscular atrophy. Chronological age cannot be used as a predictor of physical declines. The reasons for physical decline, or lack of it, are poorly understood.

13.8 PHYSIOLOGICAL CHANGES IN OLD AGE

Growing older brings with it several physiological changes. One of the most obvious is a decline in the individual's capacity for physical work and exercise. Physiologists have found that the maximum oxygen intake declines by 60% and the maximum ventilatory volume declines by 57% during exercise between 30 & 70 years of age. Some of the most important physiological changes that occur in the neurons, the cardiovascular and respiratory systems and the sensory systems can be considered.

Nervous System:

The most important normal changes involve structural changes in the neurons, the basic cells in the brain, and in communication among neurons. Two structures in neurons, namely, the dendrites and the axon, are most vital in normal aging. Because neurons do not physically touch each other, they must communicate via **chemicals called neurotransmitters**. With age, the levels of these neurotransmitters decline, but do not result in Alzheimer's or related diseases.

There are some structural changes in the nervous system and brain that occur as the person ages. Several changes occur in the central nervous system that are related to aging:

- First, the speed of nerve cell function slows as age increases. Speed of message along nerves drops to 10% between age 40 and 80.
- Second, the numbers of cells diminish, and only the axons, not the cell bodies are replaced as aging occurs.

These two factors in addition to decreased oxygen to the brain may combine to produce a reduction or slowing in reaction time that is common among the elderly. Reduced oxygen levels available to the brain can contribute to other conditions that are troublesome to the elderly individuals. Change in sleep patterns, difficulties with memory, and general irritability can be related to both decreased cerebral blood flow and to changes in the biochemical functioning of the brain in old age.

Cardiovascular System

Of all the organs in man's body, the heart and the blood vessels are the ones in which aging produces the most detrimental change. Most of the other organs, such as the lungs, kidneys and brain would probably last 150 years if they were assured an adequate blood supply. The heart and arteries are the weakest link in the chain of life. Certain changes that occur in the heart, as age increases in late adulthood are:

1. ***Continued accumulation of fatty tissue in the heart muscles*:** Fat deposits are found in the heart and in the arteries. Eventually, the amount of blood that the heart can pump per minute will decline to roughly 30%. The muscles in the heart tend to become stringy and dried out with the passage of time. The heart shrinks in size during the normal course of aging and the fat in the heart increases. The amount of muscle tissue in the heart also declines, due to its replacement by connective tissue.
2. ***Thickening of the valves*:** The valves of the heart lose their elasticity and deposits of the calcium and cholesterol may further decrease their efficiency. The heart of an older person pumps 70% as much blood as that of a young man. Increase in hardening, and loss of elasticity of the arteries, narrowing of the diameter of vessels, stiffening of the arterial walls increase in systolic blood pressure by 20-25%. Arterial walls become harder and more resistant to blood flow as their collagen content increase, and calcified fatty deposits accumulate within the arteries. The condition is known as "atherosclerosis", and it results in a decrease of the supply of oxygenated blood that gets through to vital organs . These changes appear irrespective of life styles, but they occur more slowly in people who exercise, eat low fat diets and manage to lower stress effectively. In later life, many heart diseases involve the coronary artery, which has a tendency to harden and narrow and may become partially blocked. Poor circulation of blood, whatever the cause may be, result in trouble or breakdown of the kidneys and other organs. Poor circulation to the brain causes many personality deviations in older persons.

Coronary heart disease increases steadily in adulthood. This disorder stems from a diminished blood supply to the heart muscles itself caused by Hypertension, Atherosclerosis and/ or Coronary aneurism (ruptured blood vessel in the heart muscle). The reduced level of oxygen supply to the heart muscle over a long period can lead to heart attack, heart failure, or death. When the heart muscles do not get enough oxygen, severe chest pain known as **angina pectoris** develops. If the blood supply is completely cut off or is too low or too long, the heart muscle is damaged; this is called as **"myocardial infarction"** (heart attack). Heart attacks can be fatal. Cardiovascular diseases such as heart attack, irregular heartbeat, stroke and hypertension increase dramatically with age. As people grow older, their chances of having a stroke or cerebral vascular accidents increase.

Respiratory system

It is hard to distinguish age-related changes in the lungs from those caused by air pollution, smoking and respiratory infection. Aging results in the reduction of respiratory efficiency. The lungs have a lowered capacity for inhaling and exhaling air in late adulthood. This decrease in efficiency is caused by various factors:

1. The collagen composition of the lungs decreases with age, causing them to become less elastic and reduces their capacity to inhale, hold and exhale air. Nevertheless, at 85 years of age, a person can still inhale in a single breath about 60% of what he could at age 25 years. This decline is the main cause of shortness of breath after physical exertion in later life. Maximum lung capacity in old age is 56 % and breathing capacity is 43%. Moderate exercise is ideal for keeping oxygen intake and blood flow at their level of highest potential, thus slowing down the aging and deterioration process.
2. A weakened diaphragm and chest muscles that help expand and contract the chest, and

3. Related conditions such as scoliosis that reduce chest capacity. Some functioning air sac membrane are replaced by fibrous tissues, interfering with the exchange of gases within the lungs. There is a decrease of oxygen utilization due to a decrease in the size of the lungs in senescence.

With aging, respiratory problems are mostly due to stiffening of the rib cage and air passages and destruction of the air sacs in the lungs from pollution and smoking. Several respiratory conditions affect the health and well-being of elderly persons, including cancer of the lungs, emphysema, and pneumonia. These are aggravated by smoking, air pollution and random gas in homes. Asthma is a common type of "Chronic Obstructive Pulmonary Disease (COPD)", usually seen in older adults as an incapacitating respiratory disease.

The Musculoskeletal System

The ability to move about freely and comfortably is highly valued among the elderly. As aging occurs, this ability becomes more restricted due to changes in muscle and bone functioning. After about the age of 50 years, the number of active muscle fibers steadily decreases, and eventually the typical diminished appearance of the older person occurs. The involuntary smooth muscles that operate under the autonomic nervous system are affected only slightly, as compared to the other structures. They appear to function without difficulty even until late senescence. The ligaments, however, do tend to contract and harden, causing the familiar hunched-over body position.

Several age-related changes can be observed in the functioning of the muscles and skeletal system in late adulthood:

- muscles atrophy (becomes reduced in size), restricting movement and lessening strength;
- a loss of elasticity in muscle tissue permitting less flexibility with increased stiffness and reduced mobility;
- Osteoporosis (softening of bone tissue) leading to easier bone breakage and alteration of back alignment resulting in a "hump back" posture called "kyphosis" and an S-curved spinal column called "scoliosis";
- back pain increasing in frequency and intensity reflecting changes in the disks of the vertebrae.

Digestive system

Digestive system also seems to alter with age. In fact, complaints about the digestive system are among the most common of all the complaints of the aged. There is a reduction in the amount of saliva, gastric juices and enzyme action, thus upsetting the digestive process. Because the digestive system is highly sensitive to emotional disturbances, anxieties and worries that accompany old age will play an important part in bringing about stomach deterioration. In old age, the most commonly reported disorders include frequent constipation, hernia, gall bladder conditions (stomach inflammation) and diverticulitis. Constipation is a frequent complaint of the elderly. Of greater concern for the elderly are the high rate of hemorrhoids and the use of laxatives to produce bowel movements.

In Hiatus hernia, commonly found among overweight women, a portion of the stomach slides up next to the esophagus. Digestive disorders of this condition include indigestion, gastritis (stomach inflammation), chest pain and difficulty in swallowing. It is usually treated with therapeutic methods rather than with surgery.

Diverticulitis is an inflammation of a portion of an intestine and is a condition similar to appendicitis. Individuals experience pain, nausea and change in bowel habits. It can usually be treated without surgery unless the affected area of the intestine perforates or ruptures.

Gall bladder problems in old age involve gallstones and inflammation of the gall bladder. The gall bladder contributes bile to the digestive process. Gallstones arising from insoluble substances in the bile-can form material produced by this organ. They cause little trouble, unless they block the duct leading from the gall bladder to the intestine. Gall bladder "attacks" are usually very painful and are accompanied by nausea and vomiting .

The Genitourinary System

Elderly individuals can experience a variety of disorders and changes relating to the reproductive organs and those of the urinary system (kidneys, bladder, and urethra). In late adulthood, individuals experience a decrease in the blood flow through the kidneys as well as a gradual decrease in the efficiency of the kidneys in removing waste from the blood. Among people of advanced age, urinary incontinence or the inability to retain urine in the bladder until voluntarily released is a very real and embarrassing problem.

Because of these changes, certain conditions can be expected that affect the structures of the urinary system. Bladder infections such as cystitis occur frequently. Men commonly experience enlargement of the prostate gland, which can cause blockage of the urine flow, leading to bladder infections and other complications. Women experience more problems with the functioning of the organs of the urinary system than men.

Age-related disorders that affect women's reproductive system include problems of the vaginal area, possible prolapsed uterus, and various malignancies. Cancer usually involves the cervix and vulva and the breast. Cancer of the breast is the leading cause of death among elderly women.

The Immunological System

The immunological system works by recognizing, isolating, and destroying viruses and other disease-causing microorganisms. Two key components of the immune system are white blood cells known as β-cells and T-cells. The former creates antibodies that attack foreign bacteria and viruses. T-cells are called "helper cells" because they release substances that help β-cells to divide and to produce antibodies more efficiently. One reason the immunological system becomes less efficient as people age is that there is a reduction in these cells.

Sometimes, the system mistakes one of its own body's organs for a foreign invader, and attacks that organ, resulting in "auto-immune" disorders such as rheumatoid arthritis, a chronic disease characterized by stiff, swollen painful joints. Aging together with chronic stress, can depress immune functions, making older people more susceptible to respiratory infections and less likely to ward them off.

Vocal Changes

Vocal changes are partly caused by the hardening and decreased elasticity of the laryngeal cartilages. The voice becomes more highly pitched and in advanced old age, it becomes less powerful and is restricted in range. Singing and public speaking show deterioration earlier than do normal speaking voices in younger individuals. Speech becomes slower, and pauses become longer and more frequent; slurring often occurs due to pathological changes in the brain.

Sensory and Psychomotor Functioning

During the period of senescence, the sensory functions seem to be one of the first areas of the body to deteriorate. Due to declining deficiency of the sense organs to function properly, many older people experience sensory deprivation as aging occurs. This deprivation has marked influence for the elderly person in maintaining an adequate degree of mental alertness and contact with reality.

Sensory processes have received considerable attention in the investigation of the effects of age on mental capacities. New technologies, such as corrective surgery for cataracts and improved hearing aids or cochlear implants to corrective hearing loss, help many older adults avoid sensory limitations. Inventors are redesigning the physical environment to meet the needs of an aging population.

Vision: Many older people have trouble perceiving depth or color or doing such daily activities as reading, sewing, shopping, and cooking. Losses in visual contrast sensitivity can cause difficulty in reading very small or very light print. Vision problems can cause accidents and falls. Older drivers' higher collision risk may be related not so much to loss of visual acuity (sharpness of vision) as to impaired visual attentiveness, slowed reaction time, less efficient coordination, and slowed visual processing. Declines in cognitive and motor skills may be contributing factors. Moderate visual problems often can be helped by corrective lenses, medical or surgical treatment, or changes in the environment.

Most visual impairments (including blindness) are caused by cataracts, age-related macular degeneration (center of the retina gradually loses the ability to sharply distinguish fine details), glaucoma (damage to the optic nerve caused by increased pressure in the eyes), or diabetic retinopathy (a complication of diabetes not related to age). More than half of people over 65 years develop **cataracts.**

Sensitivity to Temperature Changes: Older people tend not to adjust to changes in temperature as well as do younger people, and therefore are more susceptible to both hypothermia (too cold) and hyperpyrexia (too hot). Sensitivity to temperature changes decreases among the elderly. Elderly individuals may fail to notice a drop of up to 9 degrees Fahrenheit. Consequently, older people tend to be susceptible to "hypothermia"- a condition in which body temperature falls more than 4 degrees Fahrenheit and persists for a number of hours. It can be life threatening, especially because the aging body becomes less able to maintain an even temperature in winter weather. Early symptoms of hypothermia include drowsiness and mental confusion. A loss of consciousness follows. Similarly, sensitivity to touch and pressure also decrease with age.

Taste and Smell: Both **taste and smell** show age-related decrements that frequently result in an inability among the very old to distinguish among various foods or odors. Changes can be expected in both taste and smell perceptions in old age.

In the case of taste, the tongue loses "papillae" with age, and the number and sensitivity of taste buds decrease with age. There are fewer taste buds and hormonal changes reduce their functioning. Young adults average 245 taste per papilla, but persons 70 to 85 years-old average only 88. The best evidence indicates that until age sixty, the ability to perceive sweet, sour, bitter and salt-the four basic tastes- do not changes at all. During the sixties, some gradual erosion is noticed most particularly with salty flavors, but even these are minor.

The inability to distinguish various tastes or flavors that is sometimes noted is often caused by other things; among these, smell appears to play a large role. As a result of these decreases, food does not taste as good as it once did. If these changes are combined with poorly fitting dentures, people may lose interest in food and their nutrition will suffer. Simply seasoning food a bit more may perk up an appetite.

Sustained age declines in **smell** occur after age 70 in many people. For most people, the sense of smell is fairly keen until about age 60 years and it drops off sharply after 80. People do not smell odors as well in old age because of a decrease in the number of nerve fibers found in the nose as age increases.

Effective sensory processes are apt to be directly related to psychological well being. An individual's potential for interaction with the environment is grounded in his or her receipt of and responses to sensory inputs. Fortunately, most people have sensory acuities far in excess of what is normally required for simple awareness. After a certain point, however, any further depreciation of sensory processes is likely to manifest itself in behavioral or psychological aberrations.

In late twentieth century cultures, persons of considerably different ages have probably had sharply contrasting life experiences. For example, the diets they ate earlier in life, the medical care they received, their educational background, and many other things about them may be different. It is possible, then, that many persons born in recent decades may show smaller declines in sensory capacities as they age, than persons born in earlier decades.

13.9 COGNITIVE DEVELOPMENT IN LATE ADULTHOOD:

Adult cognitive development is best described as **multidirectional,** because some abilities increase, others wane, and some remain stable, over the course of adulthood. In early adulthood, cognitive progress is most apparent in the growth of post-formal thought and the changes that arise from higher education. Intellectual changes are more diverse during **middle adulthood,** with some competencies (such as crystallized intelligence) showing sustained growth while others (related to fluid intelligence) begin to decline. Adults achieve mastery and expertise in areas of reasoning that is most meaningful and useful to them throughout middle adulthood. By late adulthood, the forces of biological decline and accrued experience exert different pulls on intellectual development, and they push cognitive development in opposite directions.

Formal Operations in Late Adulthood

The most mature level of cognition, formal operations, begins during adolescence and continues to develop throughout adulthood. It is heavily influenced by formal education and cultural factors as well. However, the use of formal operations appears to depend heavily on the particular problem and the individual's past experience.

Reasoning and Problem Solving

Older people do far better at solving everyday problems than results of laboratory procedures might lead one to expect. Retirement and widowhood, for example, require new forms of social learning from older adults. They must adapt to new social roles and learn new social skills. Adults in their sixties learn just as much as younger adults about pension's benefits, financial, legal, and recreational planning, medical benefits and health care, nutrition, and exercise. Retired adults who later switch careers again draw heavily on new learning and memory. Many older people, especially those with years of formal education, read regularly. Many also use television and radio as sources of information.

Intelligence and Processing Abilities

Early theorists and researchers maintained that universal decline in intelligence during adulthood is evident as a function of intrinsic, biologically-based aging processes. Does intelligence diminish in late adulthood? The answer depends on what abilities are being measured, and how.

Learning, thinking and remembering are basic information processing skills that probably become less efficient in late adulthood. A general slowdown in central nervous system functioning, as measured by reaction time, is widely believed to be a major contributor to changes in cognitive abilities and efficiency of information processing. Some abilities, such as speed of mental processes and abstract reasoning, may decline in later years, but aspects of practical and integrative thinking tend to improve throughout most of adult life. Older adults tend to decline in abilities used for learning and acquiring new skills. Certain abilities, such as reasoning, spatial abilities, and memory, do not seem to decline as rapidly as processing speed. Although changes in processing abilities may reflect neurological deterioration, there is much individual variation, suggesting that declines in functioning are not inevitable and may be preventable.

Older adults, like younger ones, test best when they are physically fit and well rested. Neurophysiological problems, high blood pressure, or other cardiovascular disorders, which can affect blood flow to the brain, can interfere with cognitive performance. The purpose of intelligence, of course, is not to take test but to deal with challenges of daily life. As people get older, an important test of cognitive competence is the ability to live independently, as measured by seven **Instrumental Activities of Daily Living** (IADLs): managing finances, shopping for necessities, using the telephone, obtaining transportation, preparing meals, taking medication, and housekeeping.

Learning and Aging

Psychologists are finding that the distinctions they once made between learning and memory are becoming blurred. Learning parallels the encoding process whereby individuals put into memory the material presented to them. Older human beings can and do learn. They would be incapable of adapting to their environment and coping with new circumstances if they did not. Some older adults have been successfully taught certain cognitive skills. They can also form new concepts, if more slowly than younger people. They can also be trained in perspective taking and describing things for others-referential communication.

Age differences in learning may be influenced by the pacing of the learning task and by the motivation, caution, and distractibility of the subject. For these reasons plus others, it has been difficult for researchers to determine whether and to what extent the observed decline in learning is a result of aging.

Memory: "Memory is power". Learning and memory are very much related to one another; it is virtually impossible to separate one from the other, and changes in age that affect one will affect the other. Memory is important as it enables us to remember tasks, faces, lists, instructions, and our personal past and identity. Perhaps that is why people put such a premium on maintaining a good memory in old age. Many older adults use it to judge whether their mind is intact. As people age, they tend to worry most about their memory because they know that memory loss may be an early sign of serious mental problems.

Short-term memory: This memory usually is efficient in older people unless the person has to manipulate the information in some way. For example, if asked to repeat a string of digits, older people perform as well as younger people; if asked to repeat the digits backwards, however, they do not do as well. Short-term memory seems to decline with age in some people.

Long-term memory: Aging seems not to affect long-term memory adversely. Eighty-year-olds seem to remember information from long-term memory as effectively as 20-year-old. Memory for pictures seems stronger in both older and young adults than memory for words. All age groups are better at recalling a list of words that have been accompanied by line drawings than simply the list of words.

Creativity and Wisdom

Two aspects of cognition that have been examined for age-related differences are creativity and wisdom. Each has been the focus of stereotypes; creativity is assumed to be a function of young people, whereas wisdom is assumed to be the province of older adults.

Wisdom: *One of the advantages of getting older is that people develop pragmatic knowledge that we call wisdom.* Wisdom involves the accumulation of a lifetime of expertise in dealing with life tasks, managing situations, and solving problems. Wisdom involves using sound judgments in the conduct of life; it is the developing of understanding through experience and the capacity to apply that understanding to the issues of life. Wisdom may be defined as the expert-level of knowledge in the fundamental pragmatics of life.

Years of experience confer uniquely valuable insights on important life issues that are complex and often involve uncertainty. Wise perspectives are thought not only to be well-informed but to also accept the contradiction and ambiguities of life experience in offering constructive, and often novel, approaches to practical problems. Wisdom is reached through learning from one's parents, formal schooling, or divine gift. Most people seem to agree that wisdom entails understanding life's purpose, that it takes time and study for wisdom to develop and that wisdom is reflected in behavior. Wisdom is difficult to define precisely, and even more difficult to study.

Creativity: Researchers define creativity in adults as the ability to produce work that is novel, high in demand, and task- appropriate. Creativity is an aspect of intelligence, the novel combining of elements, a divergent leap of thought. Although creativity requires a certain level of intelligence, intelligence alone does not guarantee its presence. They may also focus on the creative process and use tests to reveal the originality, fluency, flexibility, and unusual responses of people across the lifespan.

Spiritual Values

Closely related to the idea that the old are more wise and philosophical than the young is the idea that the old are more spiritual. In many cultures over many centuries, the very old have been the spiritual leaders. They are the elders of the church. More Popes for instance, have been elected in their 80s than in any other decade of life. Obviously, it is hard to measure spirituality just as it is hard to measure wisdom. We do have data, however, on the importance of religion in people's lives.

Psychomotor Speed

Psychomotor speed is the speed with which a person can make a specific response. Psychomotor speed (also called reaction time) is one of the most studied phenomena of aging, and hundreds of studies all point to the same conclusion. People slow down as they get older. In fact, the slowing-with-age finding is so well documented that many researchers accept it as the only universal behavioral change in aging yet discovered. The most important reason for the reaction time to slow down is that older adults take longer to decide that they need to respond, especially when the situation involves ambiguous information. Although response slowing is inevitable, the amount of decline can be reduced if older adults are allowed to practice making quick responses or if they are experienced in the task.

Attention: Researchers view attention as having three major components: selection, vigilance, and control. Taken together, these components comprise the processes that enable people to perform a variety of functions. For example, when we are talking with someone at a party, we have to focus on what that person is saying and filter out all other noises.

Selective attention involves the selection of relevant information and inhibition of irrelevant information. Older adults tend to perform poorer than younger adults on most selective attention tasks.

Vigilance, also called sustained attention, involves the maintenance of attention over time. Listening for one's name to be called at a take-out restaurant, watching for the traffic light to change, and monitoring a screen connected to security cameras are all examples of vigilance tasks.

People's abilities to focus, switch, and divide attention are referred to as *attentional control.* If older adults are told where to focus their attention, if a cue is provided to help them shift attention or if the task is simple, then they perform about as well as younger adults. But if the rate at which attention must be shifted is fast or if the task is complex, older adults do less well.

13.10 FAMILY AND PERSONAL RELATIONSHIPS IN LATE ADULTHOOD

The most important thing in life is relationship. Whether it is friendship or family ties, having relationships with others is what keeps us connected. Our lives are shaped and shared by the company of others- both consensual and non-consensual. Throughout our lives, a group of people journey with us (such as our family members, friends etc), providing support in good and bad times and a protective, secure cushion under ideal conditions. The term social convoy is used to refer to this group. A functioning network of social ties is necessary in times of stress, illness, and aging – and includes both emotional support and practical assistance as needed. This enables the person to explore and learn about the world. The personal relationships special to late adulthood are: marital relationships, widowhood, children and grandchildren, siblings, and friends.

Consensual/ Marriage and Family Relationships of the Aged

Unlike other family relationships, marriage -at least in contemporary western cultures- is generally formed by mutual consent. It has characteristics of both friendship and kinship ties. It can provide both the highest positive and negative emotional feelings a person experiences. Marriage relations take on a special nature in late adulthood unlike that in previous stages of the life cycle. The time perspective of the elderly together with the shift in roles away from parenting and work give marriage a different focus at this time in life.

Older adults live in a family unit consisting of an aged husband and wife. Relatively few older adults live in multigenerational households. They tend to remain independent and self-reliant; simply stated, older adults prefer to maintain their own households if at all possible. Nevertheless, contact between family members is surprisingly frequent. Women usually marry older men and outlive them. Today, about one marriage in five, last for fifty or more years. With the couples living longer, married couples are finding that they have more years together after their children leave home, and are having longer relationships with generations of their kin.

Relaitonship with the Spouse

The first important adjustment centering on family relationships of the elderly people is that they must establish good relationship with their spouses. Being in love is still important for successful marriage in late adulthood. Older spouses also value companionship and open expression of feelings, as well as respect and common interests. But problems may arise from difference in values, interests, and philosophies. With the role change from the worker to retired, most men spend much more of their time at home than they ever did before. How well they will adjust to each other in the old age when the retirement forces them to be together depends on how many interests they have in common. Mutual supportiveness reflects three important benefits of marriage: intimacy (both sexual and emotional), interdependence (sharing of tasks and resources), and the partners' sense of belonging to each other. The success of a marriage in late life may depend on the couple's ability to adjust to the personality changes of middle age, which often lead women and men in opposite directions.

Strengths and Strains in Late Life Marriage:

Marital Happiness: Indication of good adjustment in family relationships is necessary not only during old age but throughout the period of marriage. Those who are unhappily married in old age by contract are generally those who are unhappy almost from the start of their marriage but whose marriages were never dissolved because of moral or religious reasons or because of feelings of obligation to remain together for the sake of the children. The ten rights of the old person are entitled to be:-

- The right to be treated as a person
- The right to be treated as an adult
- The right to a fair chance on our own merits
- The right to say about our own fate
- The right to a future

- The right to have fun and companionship
- The right to be romantic
- The right to your help in becoming interesting to you
- The right to professional help whenever necessary
- The right to be old

However, if the elderly are to be happy it is not enough that society meet their physical and economic needs. They will still have the need to be needed, the need to have a function in society-to have a respected place in the eyes of others and to be doing something which is interesting and significant in one's own eyes...the need for good support.

Marital Satisfaction: Both marital satisfaction and adjustment begin declining during the early adulthood, a leveling off during the middle adulthood, and an increase in satisfaction during the late adulthood. Marriages tend to be happier and more companionable in older persons. Older married couples with grown children and without children, report the same feelings of satisfaction, harmony, and absence of stress and many say it has improved.

Reasons for High Levels of Marital Satisfaction:

- One probable reason is that spouses who are still together late in life, have chosen to be together. Couples, who stay together despite differences, eventually arrive at a mutually satisfying relationship.
- Second reason is that most old people are more satisfied with life in general. Their satisfaction may stem from factors outside the marriage, the end of child rearing or more money in the bank. Children are launched. Younger couples may experience increased conflict over child-rearing and domestic responsibilities, and financial costs associated with educating and raising children.

It may be speculated that individuals reporting such high levels of satisfaction may represent people who are in relatively good health, have adequate incomes, and have worked out interactional differences earlier in their married life. They are likely to have active sexual relationships, engaging in sex more than once a week. Sex is no longer for reproduction. It includes real intimacies and mutuality, with a great deal of more caressing and tender lovingness. The partners are likely to have similar levels of intelligence, and the husband is likely to be older than the wife. How couples resolve conflicts is a key to marital satisfaction throughout adulthood. Patterns of conflict resolution tend to remain fairly constant throughout a marriage, but older couples' greater ability to regulate their emotions may make their conflicts less severe.

Not all old age marriages are happy. Some elderly persons become increasingly hostile toward each other. They separate or file for divorce. Extramarital affairs are not unknown among the elderly, nor are late-life marriages or remarriages. Wives, over time may become more assertive with or more dominant over their husbands, especially if the husband's health is failing. Some aging husbands and wives perceive that they have lost their power to accomplish change by giving vent to their emotions. Consequently, they may practice silence or make noncommittal comments.

Kinds of Problems Aged Couples Experience

Late life marriage can be severely affected by advancing age and physical illness. Ill health may make one partner so dependent on the other that his or her self-esteem suffers and the caregiver is overburdened. Spouses who have to care for disabled spouses, may feel isolated, angry, and frustrated, especially when they are in poor health themselves. Such couples may be caught in a "vicious cycle". Care giving spouses who are optimistic and well- adjusted to begin with, and who stay in touch with friends, usually cope best.

The reduced income that usually follows retirement may cause financial strain. Furthermore, relationships with grown children, and perhaps even with the couple's own aged parent, may be additional sources of stress. However, couples who have a history of working together and supporting each other usually are able to weather the storms, and perhaps even to strengthen their own relationships because of them Men experience adjustment difficulty in assuming household roles in later life. When men do take on household roles, certain tasks are likely to be sex-typed in nature.

Divorce: Divorce in late life is rare; couples who take this step usually do it much earlier. Most couples apparently figure they have made it this far, so they will stay together, no matter what. Older divorced men and women are markedly less happy and more pessimistic about life than are their married or widowed counterparts. Divorced and separated people express much less satisfaction with family life than married people do. Divorced men also are extremely isolated, much more so than divorced women. For both sexes, mental illness and death rates are higher; perhaps because social support networks for older divorced people are inadequate.

Remarriage and the Elderly: Remarriage in later life is another recent trend, and research findings suggests that this has profound consequences on a family, especially if it follows, a divorce in midlife or later. Some older people are reluctant to remarry, however, because they fear having to take care of a new spouse, a role that many of them have only recently relinquished with their prior spouse. Although the number of people over 65 who remarry is relatively small, at least two studies have found that these marriages tend to be very happy indeed.

Elderly Singles: "Never Married": The proportion of older men and women who have never married has declined dramatically in recent years. In more than half of the world, only five percent or less of elderly men has never married. These people may constitute a "distinct type of social personality" that does not need or want intimacy. Recent studies have found that many elderly singles have rich social networks. In general, elderly singles tend to be independent, and to express considerable satisfaction with their lives. The elderly who remain single tend to have more emotional and physical pathology than the married elderly does.

Widows and Widowers: One of the painful inevitabilities of intimate relationships in old age is that one partner will lose the other and face the pain of bereavement. Sometimes, widowhood comes unexpectedly. Sometimes it is anticipated, such as when it comes after an increasingly debilitating illness that may have dominated the couple's life for many years. The possibility of death may have been considered, but when it actually occurs, it is still quite a shock. Reactions to the loss of a spouse vary greatly depending on the nature of the marital relationship, the circumstances leading up to the death, and the coping resources of the survivor.

Adjusting to the death of a Spouse: Men and women react differently to widowhood. For most people, the death of a spouse follows a period of care giving and is one of the most traumatic, stressful and life-altering event. A person's reactions to losing a spouse vary according to how companionable the marriage was, how much warning the person had of the approaching death, how independent the person is, how supportive family and friends are, and how many financial burdens are left to the widow or widower. A good marriage leaves a gaping emotional void: the loss of a lover, a confidant, a good friend, and a steady companion. Even in a bad marriage, the loss is felt.

- Firstly, the survivor no longer has the role of spouse. This may be especially hard for women who have structured their lives around caring for a husband and enjoying his company.
- Widowhood also affects working people of both genders who no longer have a spouse to come home to, and retired men and women who have no one to talk to or argue with.

Social life also changes. Both friends and family usually rally to the mourner's side immediately after the death, but when they go back to their own lives, the survivor has to carve out an entirely new life structure. Married friends, uncomfortable with the thought that this could happen to them, too, may avoid the widowed person when they are most needed. Widowed people do see friends more often than married ones do, after a little time has passed.

Non-marital Kinship Ties

Some of the most lasting and important relationships in late life are the ones that come, not from mutual choice (as marriages, homosexual partnerships, and friendships do), but from kinship bonds. They are:

Relationships with Grown Children: Aging adults seek to spend more of their time with the people who mean the most to them, such as their children. Contrary to popular belief, older people generally do not want to live with their children. The elderly value their privacy and independence. Those with adult children prefer to live near but not with them, what psychologists term "intimate distance."Ill health often makes older people more dependent and thereby increases contact with family members. When older people have to live with one of their children because of the parent's failing health, they are likely to feel grateful for having someone to care for them, sad and angry about needing the care, and distressed about leaving their own homes. Most of all, parents usually worry about being a burden, and want to contribute whatever they can to the household. While most prefer to live in their own homes, this is not always possible due to financial and health conditions. About one third of the elderly share households with their children. Elderly individuals who live alone usually have a high frequency of social contact with at least one of their children

The balance of mutual aid that flows between parents and their adult children tends to shift as parents age, with children providing a greater share of support. Role reversal between elderly parents and their adult children are typical. Older parents continue to show strong concern about their children, think about them often, and help them when needed. Elderly parents tend to be distressed or become depressed if their children have serious problems. Many elderly people whose adult children are mentally ill, retarded, physically disabled, or stricken with serious illnesses serve as primary caregivers for as long as both parent and child live.

In sum, most elderly are not so isolated from kin and friendship network as is commonly believed.

Relationships with Siblings: Many of the older people have at least one living sibling, and this relationship is likely to be the longest-lasting one of their lives. Brothers and sisters play important roles in the support networks of older people. Siblings, more than other family members, provide companionship, as friends do; but siblings more than friends also provide emotional support. Conflict and overt rivalry generally decrease by old age, and some siblings try to resolve earlier conflicts. However, underlying feelings of rivalry may remain, especially between brothers. Among older adults, relationships with brothers and sisters may deepen, and feelings of closeness may intensify-even though overt communication such as visits, letters, and phone calls may become less frequent. Older siblings usually visit each other several times a year, although the frequency tends to decrease as they age. Maintaining connections with a sibling is important for most adults. Sisters are especially vital in maintaining family relationships and well-being, perhaps because of women's emotional expressiveness and traditional role as nurturers. Older people who are close to their sisters feel better about life and worry less about aging than those without sisters, or without close ties to them.

The death of a sibling in old age may be understood as a normative part of that stage of life, but still, survivors may grieve intensely and become lonely or depressed. The loss of a sibling represents not only a loss of someone to lean on and a shift in the family constellation, but perhaps even a partial loss of identity.

Friendships

Happiness and well-being in old age are not guaranteed by having children and grandchildren. However, satisfaction and happiness in later life are consistently associated with having friends. Friendship is unique relationship involving mutual give-and-take-changes. By late life, a person's social network consists of friends for several decades. Among older adults, friendships typically are no longer linked to work and parenting. Instead, they focus on companionship and support. Friends serve as confidants and sources of support in ways that children, nieces, and nephews, for example, typically do not. Friends are a powerful source of immediate enjoyment; the family provides greater emotional security and support. Friends are a buffer against the impact of stress on physical and mental health.

Friends provide us with acceptance, support, and companionship, which are as vital to our sense of self-worth in late adulthood as they are when we are younger. Friendship is a unique relationship because people choose their friends. The element of choice in friendship may be especially important to older people, who may feel their control over their lives slipping away. Overall, in terms of companionship, friends are more important and satisfying to older people than are their offsprings. Well into old age, past 85, women continue to see their friends about as much or more often, and feel the same way about them. Older men see friends less, see them more in group activities rather than on an intimate one to one basis, and consider friendships less important.

13.11. PROBLEMS OF THE AGED

The inevitable physical, psychological and social changes and the ability of the old person to adjust to these changes determine his or her mental health to a very large extent. But the characteristics of old age, often lead to poor adjustment and unhappiness.

Health Problems

Normally, old age is a period of increasing poor health. The most common illnesses are constipation, hemorrhoids, and digestive disturbances of all kinds, cancer and different forms of heart disorders, circulatory and metabolic disorders, mental disorders, etc. Old people also suffer from physical disorders making them semi or complete invalids before they die, malnutrition too is a common problem, especially in India. This comes from both psychological as well as economic reasons, may be due to lack of appetite, due to depressions, loneliness etc, inability to eat because of dental problems, or inadequate absorption of nutrients from the food due to malnutrition. The old often suffer from dizziness, giddiness, weakness and defective vision, which can lead to accidents. These may often make them disabled for life. In addition, many old people suffer from imaginary illness and concentrate on any ache or pain they may have, thus increasing it out of proportion. It serves to attract attention to themselves as well as winning sympathy from others.

Relationships and Problems with Family

Not only inability is a problem for the retired but his whole family also suffers. The increased hours spent at home by an unhappy and dissatisfied retired man, lack of opportunities for social contacts with other men which he had daily during his work, and the feeling of uselessness which many retired men experience, all contribute to the creation of problems for the entire family. The retired man is likely to make undue demands on their family members especially on his wife thus creating stress or friction. He may have difficulties in his relationships with his children and grand children. Sometimes, the retired person knows or senses that his family feels unwanted of him; such unfavorable attitudes on the part of the retired worker and his family cause many clashes, which disrupt family harmony.

Parental Dependency

One role reversal, which is especially difficult, is from having their children depend on them, to being dependent on their children. Many elderly people, even when they are dependent upon their grown up children for financial support and companionship are unable and unwilling to reverse the role of authority they formerly had over their children. They continue to treat them as children causing their grown up children to resent, especially when they are the ones who are supporting and taking care of the physical and social needs of their parents. Financial dependency on their children is a bitter pill for most parents to swallow.

Vocational and Retirement Problems

Because of financial necessity, being physically and mentally able to work, or for the status giving satisfaction work brings, many older people want to continue working, if they could get employment. Unfortunately, they have fewer opportunities available. The jobs available may be monotonous jobs, far below the level of their ability or the status. It is frustrating and humiliating experience, if his boss is a younger and often less experienced person than him.

The individual who prepares ahead for retirement will make better adjustments. On the contrary, the individual who resists retirement, as a result refuses to prepare himself psychologically for it, by creating new interest and activities to replace the old work, will make poorer adjustments. Unfavorable attitudes towards retirement affect the individuals' health often causing a physical decline, and pre-death. As Harwitz (1965) has pointed out, "Retirement shock" is a new sickness of the aged that will cause negative influence on their health, emotional stability, social consciousness and self. Men than women feel the problem of retirement greatly

Emotional Problems

Emotional instability during old age leads to problems in adjustment. There is a tendency for the old to be pathetic and to show decreased emotional responsiveness. They are less responsive, show less enthusiasm than they did when they were younger. Their emotional responses are less varied and less appropriate to the occasion. This is especially true in institutionalized elderly people who make poorer adjustment to old age. The elderly person often shows signs of regression in emotional behavior such as negativism, or temper tantrum. They have little capacity to express warm and spontaneous feelings towards others, because they feel that such feelings are unlikely to be reciprocated by others. The old person is likely to be irritable, quarrelsome, fearful, worried, and disappointed. Disillusions and feelings of persecutions are more common.

Personality Problems

It is a common belief that old people are quarrelsome, demanding, selfish, self-centered and generally impossible to live with. There are many personality changes in aging persons, that give rise to many problems in adjustments. One of the main changes is the change in self- concept. There is an undue concern and preoccupation about an individual's physical and mental handicaps, from being 'independent' to dependency, from aspiring to decline. All these predispose the aged to exaggerate their loneliness, fear of losing their place in the community and to worry over their financial status. Milder forms of personality problems cause disturbances of memory, faulty attention, hallucinations, hysterical disorders, neurotic depression etc. With advancing age, there are a number of personality breakdowns requiring admission to mental institutions.

Economic Problems

With retirement come economic problems too. This has serious efforts on the individuals' concepts of self, the status he holds in the family, and the prestige he has in the eyes of the community.

This leads to many emotional problems with their damaging effects. Much of the resistance against retirement is from fear of the future in which there will not be adequate money to provide for the remaining years of life. This problem affects the wife's attitude toward her husband's retirement and intensifies the adjustment problems for both.

Leisure and Recreational Problems

Leisure is even more dangerous for the old than for the young as too much inactivity is a catalyst for sensitivity and death. One of the major problems the old face is how to occupy their leisure time. Because of their decreased ability and decline in income, many activities they indulged in their younger days are not possible now. If the elderly is living in an institution, there are great opportunities for recreation with the older people, while at home there are fewer opportunities especially if the economic status is poor.

13.12. ADJUSTMENTS IN OLD AGE

"Every man desires to live long, but no man wants to be old". This maxim from Jonathan Swift may help to explain why, even today, old age can take us by surprise. People often avoid thinking about their upcoming transition to "senior citizen" and "retiree" for so long, that they fail to prepare for it. Inadequate financial planning can leave older people "newly poor" shortly after retirement and thus poor for the rest of their lives. Like other age groups, the elderly like to have friends of their own age and recreation to enjoy with those friends. However, retirement communities that offer these attractions are mostly for the financially secure. Other elderly people may live in houses with dreary loneliness, eking out an existence in substandard housing and on substandard diets. From the biological and psychological points of view, aging is characterized by a reduction in the adaptation to environmental changes and to the stresses of living. Responses to stress are slower and the elderly need much time for adjusting to physiological changes.

Health Adjustment

One of the most ominous threats to the elderly is prolonged illness. The aging body is highly vulnerable to the ravages of disease and injury. Among the most frightening threats are disease that attack brain-Alzheimer's disease and Pick's disease, for example, both of which cause disorientation, poor judgment and death within 5 years; there is no known cure for either. In addition to these physiologically based disorders, the psychological stressors of old age can provoke various psychological disorders. One that deserves special attention here is depression. Rates of depression are high among the elderly, and suicide rates are considerable higher than among younger adults. Most people who deteriorate and die shortly after retirement do so from the worsening of an illness that predated retirement and served as a major determinant of their retirement decision.

Adjustment to Retirement

Retirement is a relatively new idea. It did not exist in pre-industrial society, nor does it exist in some societies today. The move from an agrarian society to a predominantly industrialized society brought in its wake the phenomenon of "retirement." Retirement took hold in many industrialized countries during the late 19th and early 20th centuries as life expectancy increased. Eventually, mandatory retirement at age 65 became almost universal.

Retirement means vastly different things to different people. It may signify the abrupt and unsought termination of one's livelihood; a welcomed relief from the tedium of a boring job, or the natural conclusion of a successful career and job well done. It may provide more time to pursue already established and pleasurable activities, enough time to engage in activities that were previously "out of the question" or release unlimited amounts of unoccupied time. Retirement may be associated with a broadening or expansion of one's life style or signal the beginning of severe "cutbacks." Whatever the specific, subjective and objective meanings of retirement, it involves "separation from a sphere of activity that has provided social order, economic remuneration, and some degree of personal identity and prestige for the greater part of the adult years." In fact, most worl ing people today think of retirement as just reward and a deserved rest.

Retirement is one of the major social problems. Havighurst and Altrach (1953) point out that retirement is the greatest man-made problems in the lives of most of the people. Relinquishing lifetime patterns and suddenly changing habits of a lifetime give rise to an experience, which is often very traumatic for the elderly people. It is emotionally disturbing to the individual, if he is forced into retirement by dismissal, serious illness or discontinuance of the employing organization. It seriously affects the type of adjustment he makes to retirement.

Until fairly recently, retirement was believed to cause a major identity crisis replete with personal disorganization and distress, familial disruption, and failing health. Research makes it clear that the crisis view of retirement is overly pessimistic and exaggerated. Nevertheless, retirement does bring into play several concomitant variables, any one of which may turn out to be problematic. However, most retirees make quite adequate adjustments to these additional variables.

Although adjusting to retirement has many faces, an individual rarely experiences a devastatingly sudden loss, drop, or decline in any one aspect on retirement. The preretirement lifestyles reflect the financial, marital, residential, and leisure-time adjustments. The point is that adjustments necessitated by retirement are numerous, but not of overwhelming magnitude; rather, they tend to reflect the individual's preretirement status. Thus, adjustment as outcome is partially predicated on one's preretirement status.

Financial Adjustments

Generally speaking, the average retired individual can be expected to have an income that is reduced by one-third to one-half of its preretirement value. The types of day-to-day adjustments made necessary by declining income in retirement vary as a primary function of the amount of discretionary money available. For some individuals and families it requires finding less expensive forms of recreation, travel, or vacations and perhaps eating out less often. For those with few, if any, discretionary money, it entails living a "no frills" life of simply trying to meet one's essential financial obligations and hoping that no unforeseen and costly crises arise. For those who must live on inadequate retirement incomes, the adjustment may include delaying prophylactic, or even needed health care, postponing household repairs, finding cheaper (and often less nutritional) foods, or doing without other conveniences and necessities, such as telephone, heat and clothing.

Marital adjustments

Most people are married and living with their spouses when retirement occurs. On retirement, women are likely to return to full-time status as homemakers. In contrast, most retired husbands do not have a readily available role to fall back on, that provides for structured use of the increased leisure time. Many husbands apparently react or adjust by taking on a more active role (and often managerial attitudes) in the running of the household. Others simply make more wok for their wives.

In the upper and middle classes, a more androgynous approach to sex roles allows and encourages sharing of household activities before retirement. The increased involvement of retired husbands in home-based activities is therefore, seen as desirable by both spouses. Regardless of socioeconomic background, the most troublesome adjustment occurs when the husband simply spends his increased leisure time "lazying around the home," expecting his wife to cater to his every need, in addition to her other chores. Under these circumstances, the wife is more apt to resent and complain about her husband's intrusion into her domain.

Simply stated, part of the adjustment of both spouses to retirement requires the renegotiation and reallocation of household responsibilities and activities. Although this aspect of retirement can further strain marriages, it can also serve as the impetus for achieving new heights of marital satisfaction. When both share the responsibilities, more time is available for leisure activities.

Leisure-Time Adjustments: When defined simply as "free or unrestricted time," the amount of leisure increases considerably on retirement. Although virtually any activity used to occupy this free time is considered a legitimate leisure-time activity, most activities tend to fall into four basic but sometimes overlapping categories:

(1) **Physical activities** that include but are not limited to camping, fishing, golfing, hunting, aerobics, swimming, gardening, and chores around the home;

(2) **Social activities** including visits with family, friends and neighbors, playing cards, and volunteer work;

(3) **Cultural activities** such as concerts, sporting events, club or church meetings, or community improvement; and

(4) **Solitary activities** which include all avenues of reading (books, magazines), watching (television), and listening (radio, music), pursuing college courses, sewing, or other hobbies.

Since one's choice of leisure-time activities at any age is affected by many variables, including the amount of leisure time available, income level, health status, talents and abilities, interests, and personal needs, adults of any given age can be expected to vary widely in terms of their preferred leisure activities. Elderly adults tend to engage in activities that are more passive, solitary, and home based.

Many retirees find more time to engage in activities that benefit the welfare of others, thus extending Erikson's task of generativity into the late adult years. Such personal investments are unlikely to develop "out of the blue" in the retirement years; the truly rewarding leisure activities of retirement are most likely to be rooted in interests and identities developed earlier in life.

Factors Influencing Adjustment

How successfully or unsuccessfully the individual will adjust to the problems arising from changed physical and mental conditions and changes in status which come from aging, will be influenced by many factors, some of which are beyond the individuals' control.

(*a*) *Social Attitudes:* A culture where the role of the elderly is clearly defined, adjustment is easier than where roles are ambiguously defined. There is however, a general agreement on a pattern of limited "age-appropriate activities" for the elderly than the pattern approved for middle aged. For e.g., retirement age.

(*b*) *Personal Attitude:* Good adjustment in old age is greatly affected by the individual's attitude towards aging and the effects it has on him as an individual. When his attitude is resistant, it will be a serious obstacle to successful adjustment. Unfavorable concepts of self, based on the belief that his days of variety have ended, lead to poor adjustment and unhappiness in old age.

The individual who is financially stable, whose family status is favorable and whose health enables him to continue to engage in activities that are enjoyable to him will have fewer emotional disturbances and will make a better adjustment to old age than the individual whose status is less secure and less satisfactory. To be happy the individuals must feel that he is useful to society and that his services are of value to his family and the community.

13.13. STATUS OF THE AGED IN OUR RECENT SOCIETY

The familial ideal for an Indian is the traditional Hindu joint family. The main features of the traditional joint family are that it is three-dimensional in depth, its members live under the same roof, and all share the property of whatever kind. It is a self-sufficient unit, socially and economically, the center of the universe for the whole family, the arbiter of life's important decisions, the supplier of daily and life time needs, the reservoir of deep loyalties and a bond of affection. It is within this family circle that all-important decisions are taken with respect to education, career and marriage and all-important events take place-worship, weddings and other celebrations, births and deaths and their appropriate ceremonies.

In India, the elderly have been traditionally assigned a place of honor and respect, as exemplified by religious and social values. The aged also participated in the management of affairs of the family and the community to a large extent. Their advice was sought in emergencies and in critical situations. Thus, Indian society was "Aged Integrated"- socially, psychologically, economically and culturally.

The forces of modernization and technology changes have resulted in changes in life styles and values. Nowadays, the traditional joint family system has given way to the modern nuclear family system where the aged finds less and less place. The breakup of the joint family because of urbanization and industrialization and their attendant socio-economic factors pose a serious problem for these aged people and the society, if their presence and problems are not correctly understood. They are increasingly isolated and left out. They are unable to cope up with the speed of the modern world. Young men are increasingly hesitant to take up the burden of their parents in those hard days of inflation.

In many ways, older persons are accorded less prestige and less deference than they previously were accorded in earlier historical periods. For the most part, they possess less economic and political power than the middle aged. Studies raise doubts about the generalization that the aged lose status as a direct consequence of urbanization and industrialization. Nevertheless, it is true that our society has come to be characterized as one where the primary value has been placed upon youth and where the aged are often disparaged.

The later adult years are frequently characterized by changes in the structure of the family, children are usually well into their own careers and families, and are independent. The older adult may have to depend on children, especially financially, rather than the other way around. A particularly devastating change may be the death or serious illness of a spouse. when the individual loses her or his partner and must face this loss and learn to cope with widowhood.

The position and status of the old however, are seriously undermined by factors such as:

- Changing values, growing individualism and rising aspirations for consumer goods as a result of the impact of education and urbanization.
- Westernization and industrialization, which prompt the younger generation to give supremacy to themselves.
- Less number of children due to acceptance of the small family norm and hence greater vulnerability in the matter of dependence.
- Participation of women in employment in cities in white collar jobs, leaving the old unattended during day time and creating stress situations or prompting them to press for separate residence so that they will not be burdened with such problems.
- Migration of the younger members to cities for alternative sources of livelihood, acute paucity of accommodation in urban area and the exorbitant rents which act as a strong disincentive to bring old parents to live with their children.

- Complexities of modern life and living which discount the value of traditional systems and practices and place a premium on lateral transmission of knowledge in contrast to vertical transmission from the older generation, thereby devaluing the knowledge and experience of the old.
- Fast pace of social change which accentuates the inter- generation differences in values and life styles; the Indian practice of total involvement of parents in their children and not developing or cultivating other interests including leisure- time pursuits which could sustain their interest and keep them occupied in their old age.
- Large investments than in the past on the education and upbringing of children which result in less resources being available for the care of the aged and, which together with the inflationary pressures cause disproportionately greater hardship to the old.
- The total economic dependency status of most old people in the absence of old age social security benefits.

13.14. WELFARE SERVICES FOR THE AGED

Change may be taking place in attitude about aging and the aged individual. Older people themselves are fighting back against ageism. Many associations of retired persons keep the needs of the elderly in front of legislators, and every legislator knows that a higher percentage of people from 65 to 74 years of age vote than do people in any other age group. Our culture promotes and values youthfulness over age and many of its ideas about old age are stereotypes that are largely negative in nature. Aging has a negative connotation in our culture along with the individuals who are the elderly. The rise in the number of aged in India and the rapidly changing society and its impact on the aged indicates that the aged persons must be taken care of. The major needs of aged ones are in sectors like environmental, occupational, economical, leisure and health. They need groups of friends with whom they can share common interests and spend their time. Developed countries have started non-institutional services for older people. They are known as Golden Age centers, Day care centers, and Recreation centers or hobby clubs for senior citizens. In India there are 525 units existing in the country to look after the elderly. Of them 306 consists of homes, while 20 are day centers.

Old age Concessions available in our country includes:

1. 10 kgs of food grains per beneficiary per month are provided free of cost to senior citizens.
2. Indian Airlines is providing 50% concession for senior citizens on normal economy class fare for all domestic flights with certain conditions.
3. Indian railways provide 30% fare concession in all mail expresses including Rajdhani/ Shatabdhi trains to senior citizens. Further a provision has been made to allot lower births to senior citizens
4. In railway, special counters have been provided for senior citizens
5. Special seniors are allowed to register telephone connection under N-OYT special category
6. Separate queues for older persons in hospitals for registration and clinical examination.
7. Higher rates of interest on special schemes for senior citizens in all nationalized banks.
8. Government is giving assistance to voluntary organizations under the Grant- in- aid scheme in the field of social welfare of the aged.
9. Under the National Social Assistance Programme (NSAP) 1995, beneficiaries above 60 years would get a pension of ₹ 75 per month.

Old age is a continuous period whereby decline in progressive changes like body efficiency, or maladaptive change in structure take place. It is the closing period of human lifespan. Poor adjustment is the characteristic feature of these aged. Assistance or support in physical, economical, recreational, and social need increases.

The Elderly are generally considered wise and they are revered in the society for their wisdom and experience. But, major adjustment problem in this phase of life arises during the death of a spouse and/or retirement. Hence, their emotional, physical and economical problems pile up. Therefore, it is the phase where they require utmost care from the family, friends and society at large.

QUESTIONS

SECTION "A"

Short Answer Type:

1. List out the physical changes taking place in old age.
2. Spell out the physiological changes of an aged person.
3. Explain old age, geriatrics and gerontology.
4. Write a note on age divisions of late adulthood.
5. Mention the developmental tasks of the aged.
6. Specify the role of retirement in old age.

SECTION "B"

One Page Answer Type:

1. Explain the characteristics /Nature of aging of an old person.
2. Discuss the role of society and family in caring for the aged.
3. Elaborate on the socio-psychological needs of the aged in India.
4. Describe the common changes seen in sensory functioning in old age.
5. Describe briefly the physical changes occurring in old age.
6. Give an account of the physical and economic problems of the aged.

SECTION "C"

Essay Answer Type:

1. Discuss the problems and attitudes of families towards the aged in the past and present.
2. Discuss the problems during old age and remedial measures for it.
3. What are the problems and services available for aged in India?
4. What facilities are available for the aged in Indian society?
5. Bring out the available welfare programes for the aged.
6. Explain the status of the aged in India.
7. Examine the characteristics and problems of the aged in detail.
8. Give an account of the cognitive changes in the elderly.

BIBLIOGRAPHY

Bibliography

1. Ablex. Dunn, J.(1983), Sibling Relationships in Early Childhood. Child Development,54,7876-811.N.J.Prentice Hall.
2. Anderson John. E. (1957) Human Development and Personal Adjustment. Henry Holt and Company, Inc.,U.S.A . pp 511-541.
3. Ardy Friedberg (1982) Get Strong: A teenagers guide to body building and Weight lifting. Publisher: Scholastic Paperback)
4. Bandura , A., and Walters, R.H.(1963). "Social Learning and Personality Development" .:New York:Holt ,Rinehart, Winston.
5. Bandura,A. (1973) "Aggression: A Social Learning analysis".Englewood Cliffs. N.J.Prentice Hall.
6. Bankart, C.P. and Anderson , C.C.(1979) Short term Effects of Prosocial Television Viewing and Play on preschool boys and girls . ***"Psychological Reports"***, 44, 935-941.
7. Barbara Newman, Philip Newman (2008) **Development Through Life: A Psychosocial Approach.** Wadsworth/ Cengage Learning, California, U.S.A.
8. Baumrind , D.(1966)." Child development" . The effects of authoritative parental control on child behavior.
9. Birren J.E (1964)- Handbook of Psychology of Aging , Englewood Cliffs , N.J Prentice-Hall Inc pp 169; pp 334 – 351.
10. Birren J.E (1975). History of Gerontology in Aging, Scientific Perspectives and Social Issues, Eds N.Y.D Vannostrand Co.
11. Bigner Jerry.J- (1983). Human Development – A Life Span Approach(1983), Macmillan Publishing Co Inc , New York .
12. Burnside, I.M., Ebersole, P., Miones, H.E. (1979) .(Ed) Psychosocial Caring Throughout The Life Cycle. Mc Graw-Hill. NewYork .
13. Carol.K.Sigelman and David.R.Shaffer (1995). "Life Span Human Development (2nd edition)", Brooks/ Cole publishing Co-operate, Pacific Grove., California.
14. Clara Shaw Schuster, Shirley Smith Ashburn (1992). **The process of human development:** a holistic life-span approach. Lippincott
15. Corsaro, W.A. (1985). Friendship and Culture in the Early Years. Norwood, NJ:

16. David F. Hultsch (1983)- Human Development - A Life Span perspective , Mc Graw Hill Book Co , New York .

17. David Reed Shaffer, Katherine Kipp-(2009) Developmental Psychology: Childhood and Adolescence, Cengage Learning, California, U.S.A.

18. Diane.E.Papalia, Sally Wendkos Olds, Ruth Duskin Feld man (2004). " Human development" 9th ed..Tata Mc Graw.Hill, New Delhi

19. Don C. Dinkmeyer, Sr., R. Dreikurs (1963) Encouraging Children to Learn. Brunner-routledge

20. Dworetzky and Daves, 1989). "Human Development – A Life Span Approach". Late Adulthood – Physical , Cognitive and Personality Development. pp. 459-89

21. Elaine U.Polan, Daphne R.Taylor (2007). Journey Across the LifeSpan (4th edition):Human development and Health Promotion; F.A.Daves Company. United States.

22. Elizabeth.B.Hurlock (1981),"Developmental psychology- A Life Span Approach". Tata McGraw Hill Publishing Co. Ltd., New Delhi.

23. Elizabeth.B.Hurlock (2005).6th ed. Child Development. Tata McGraw Hill Publishing Co. Ltd., New Delhi.

24. Elizabeth.B.Hurlock (1978) –Child Growth and Development, Kessinger Publishing, United States

25. Elton B. McNeil (1969) – Human Socialization , Brooke/ Cole Publishing Co , California Federal council on Aging (1961) : White House Conference on Aging chart book Washington , D.C Government printing office p 60.

26. Erik Homberger Erikson (1980) **Identity and the life cycle** W W Norton & Company Incorporated

27. Feldman, Robert. S (2010). "Development Across The Life Span ,Pearson Education India

28. Fergas P. Hughes and Lloyd D. Noppe (1990) Human Development - Across the Life Span. pp. 235-237.Prentice Hall.

29. George Kaluger and Merien Fair Kaluger (1974)-Human Development, The C.V.Mosby Co. St.Louis

30. Grace J. Craig, Wendy L. Dunn (2009) Understanding Human Development Prentice Hall

31. Harry Bakwin, Ruth Mae Morris Bakwin (1972) Behavior disorders in children. W.B.Saunders Co, Philadelphia, London.

32. Hartup, .W.(1983). Peer Relations. In E.M. Hetherington(Ed.) Review of Child Development Research, University of Chicago Press, U.S.A.

33. Havighurst R.J. (1972) Developmental tasks and Education, 3rd Ed. David McKay Co., New York. pp84.

34. Hendricks, John and Hendricks C Davis (1986) – Aging in Mass Society – Myths and Realities " 3rd Ed , Little Brown Co . Boston

35. Higgins, E.T.Ruble..D.N. & Hartup.W.W.(Eds). (1983). Social Cognition and Social

Development: A Sociocultural Perspective. New York: Cambridge University Press.

36. James O.Lugo & Gerald L.Hershey (1979) Human Development-A psychological,, biological and sociological approach to the lifespan-2nd Ed. MacMillan Publishing Co. Inc Newyork. pp656-693.

37. **John Dworetzky, Nancy J. Davis** (1988) Human Development: A Lifestyle Approach. West Publishing Company

38. John.S.Dacey (Boston college) and John.F.Travers (Boston college) (2006) ."Human development- Across the Life span"(6th ed.).Mc Graw Hill, New York.

39. John Peter Zubek, Patricia Anne Solberg(1954) Human development McGraw-Hill,

40. John.W.Santrock (2007). "A Topical Approach to Life Span Development"(3rd ed.) 2nd reprint. Tata McGraw-Hill Education

41. Karen Freiberg-(2011) **Annual Editions: Human Development 11/12** McGraw-Hill Education

42. Kathleen Stassen Berger (2005), The Developing Person Through the Life Span; 3rd Edition Part VI .Worth Publishers, Macmillan,India. pp.441-481.

43. Laura.E.Berk (2007), Child Development. 7th edition, Prentice Hall of India Private Limited, New Delhi.,

44. Lawrence Joseph Stone, Joseph Church(1979) Childhood &Adolescence: A Psychology of the Growing Person ,Random House.

45. Lawrence J. Friedman (2000) **Identity's Architect: A Biography of Erik H. Erikson** Harvard University Press,

46. Marian.E.Breckenridge, M.S, Margret Nesbitt Murphy, (1958)- "Growth and Development of the Young Child", sixth edition, W.B.Saunders Co, Philadelphia, London.

47. Mavis.E.Hetherington and Ross.D.Parke (1986). Child Psychology – A Contemporary View Point. 3rd edition. Mc Graw Hill Book Co. New York.

48. McNeil Elton B (1969) – Human Socialization, Brooks/Cole Publishing Co. California.

49. Mussen P.H, Conger J.J & Kagan (1974).Child Development & Personality, Harper & Row Publishers, New york..

50. Mussen P.H. (1973, series Ed.), Hand book of Child Psychology: vol ,4, Socialisation, personality and social development (pp.103-196), New York: John Wiley.

51. Overton, W.F.(Ed).(1983). The relationship between social and cognitive development. Hillsdale, NJ. Erlbaum.

52. Parpal, M. & Maccoby, E.E.(1985). Maternal responsiveness and subsequent child compliance. "Child Development", 56, 1326-1334.

53. Pati R.N, Jena S. B (1989, 2000)- Aged in India : Socio-Demographic Dimensions. Sarup Book Publishers. New Delhi

54. Paul Henry Mussen, John Janeway Conger, Jerome Kagan (1970 -) **Readings in child development and personality** Harper & Row

55. Paul Boris Baltes, Hayne Waring Reese, John R. Nesselroade (1988) **Life-Span Developmental Psychology:** Introduction to Research Methods Lawrence

56. Perkins Hugh V (1974) – Human Development and Learning 2nd Ed, Wadsworth Publishing.Co.Inc. PP 415 – 449.
57. Perlmutter, M. (Ed). (1986). Cognitive perspectiveson children's social and behavioraldevelopment: The Minnesota symposia on child psychology, vol 18. Hillsdale, NJ : Erlbaum.
58. Philip F. Rice. (1992,2007) Human development: a life-span approach. Macmillan Pub. Co.
59. Pikunas, Justin(1976) Developmental psychology; Adult; Child Development. New York, McGraw-Hill
60. Pryor, J.B. & Day, J.D. (1985) , The development of social cognition. New York: Springer – Verlag.
61. Raffini, J.P. (1993). ***Winners without losers: Structures and strategies for increasing student motivation to learn.*** Upper Saddle River, NJ: Prentice Hall.
62. Rajammal.P.Devadas and Jaya.N.(1991)" A Text Book On Child Department", MacMillan India Limited.
63. Reyner, Erick (1971) – Human Development – "An Introduction to the Psychodynamics of Growth, Maturity and Aging" – National Institute for Social Work Training Series No.22, George Allen and Unwin Ltd, Lond, pp.158 – 170.
64. Rice, K.G, and Myer, A.L (1994),"Preventing Depression Among Adolescents: Preliminary Process Results Of A Psycho- Educational Intervention Program, Journal of Consultant Psychology,73,147-152.
65. Richard M. Lerner and David F. Hultsch (1983)- Human Development - A Life Span perspective , Mc graw Hill Book Co , New York .
66. Richard M. Lerner, Graham B. Spanier, (1980) Adolescent Development: A Life-Span Perspective. McGraw-Hill
67. Robert.I.Watson, Henry Clay Lindgren.(1973) "Psychology of the child" 3rd ed..John Wiley & Sons. Inc.,. New York .
68. Robert J. Hoffnung and Kelvin L. Seifert(1999) Child & Adolescent Development. Houghton Miffin Co. Boston/ Cengage Learning, Connecticut, U.S.A.
69. Robert Stephen Feldman (2005) **Development across the life span** Pearson/Prentice Hall,
70. Robert V. Kail, John C. Cavanaugh (2010). Human Development: A Life-span View. 5th ed Cengage Learning, Connecticut, U.S.A.
71. Rosalind Charlesworth,(1987) "Understanding Child Development"- For Adults Who Work With Young Children,2nd edition. Louisiana State University Delmar Publishers inc.,
72. Rubin, K.H. & Ross, H.S. (Ed). (1982). Peer relationships and social skills in childhood. New York: Springer – Verlag.
73. Saxon,S. V., Etten,M.J. (1978,2002) -Physical Change and Aging. New York Springer Publishing Co .
74. Schiamberg L.B. (1985,1992). Human Development. 2nd Edition. Macmillan Publishing Company, New York.

75. Smith E.D (1972) – Handbook of Aging, Barnes and Noble Books,

76. Specht, Riva and Craig, Grace J . (1982) – Human Development , Prentice Hall Inc , Englewood Cliffs , New Jersey.

77. Stewart, Alison Clarke, Susan Friedman ,Joanne Koch. (1985). " Child Development: A. Topical Approach", John Wiley and Sons, New York.

78. Stewart, Alison Clarke, Perlmutter, Marion and Friedman Susan (1988) – Lifelong Human Development – John Wiley and Sons, New York.

79. Suriakanti.A.(1997), " Child Development- An Introduction" 3rd edition, Kavitha Publications.

80. Vander Zander J. W .(1989) Human Development , Mc graw Hill Book Co , New York pp 519-48

81. Wadsworth, B.J. (1984) . Piaget's theory of cognitive and affective development, 3rd ed. Longman,.New York.

82. Zeece, P.D. (1999). Things of nature and the nature of things: Natural science-based literature for young children. ***Early Childhood Education Journal***, 26(3), 161-166.

83. www.earlymoments.com. Promoting Literacy and a Love of Reading

84. www.best books for kids.com / benefits of reading.html

85. Early Childhood News. Promoting the development (2008) of Scientific Thinking Ruth Wilson, Ph.D (biweekly newsletter)

86. Facility Requirements for Daycare centers www.ehow.com

87. Preschool Program_ Early childhood education www.kindergarten/preschool.com